UNIVERSITY EXPANSION IN A CHANGING GLOBAL ECONOMY

UNIVERSITY EXPANSION IN A CHANGING GLOBAL ECONOMY

Triumph of the BRICs?

Martin Carnoy, Prashant Loyalka,
Maria Dobryakova, Rafiq Dossani,
Isak Froumin, Katherine Kuhns,
Jandhyala B. G. Tilak, and Rong Wang

Stanford University Press
Stanford, California

Stanford University Press
Stanford, California

Printed in the United States of America on acid-free, archival-quality paper

Library of Congress Cataloging-in-Publication Data

Carnoy, Martin, author.
    University expansion in a changing global economy: triumph of the BRICs? / Martin Carnoy, Prashant Loyalka, Maria Dobryakova, Rafiq Dossani, Isak Froumin, Katherine Kuhns, Jandhyala B. G. Tilak, and Rong Wang.
        pages cm
    Includes bibliographical references and index.
    ISBN 978-0-8047-8601-0 (cloth : alk. paper)
    ISBN 978-0-8047-8641-6 (epub)
    1. Education, Higher—BRIC countries.   2. Higher education and state—BRIC countries.   3. Comparative education.   I. Loyalka, Prashant, author.
II. Dobriakova, M. S., author.   III. Dossani, Rafiq, 1954– author.   IV. Froumin, Isak D., author.   V. Kuhns, Katherine, author.   VI. Tilak, Jandhyala B. G., author.
VII. Wang, Rong, 1969– author. VIII. Title.
    LC2610.C37 2013
    378—dc23
                                                                                2012045129

Typeset by Newgen in 10/14 Minion

Contents

Figures

Tables

Preface and Acknowledgments

THIS STUDY BEGAN ON A RELATIVELY SMALL SCALE AT Stanford University in 2007 as a comparison between university reforms in India and China, with a focus on engineering education, and as a part of the International Initiative at Stanford. The International Initiative was a major effort by Stanford to promote interdisciplinary international research, bringing people together in the university from different departments who might otherwise not address important research problems. With Stanford's strong interest in information technology and engineering education and the rapidly growing numbers of engineering graduates in India and China, this seemed an ideal subject for interdisciplinary research. Several committees headed by Coit Blacker, director of the Freeman Spogli Institute, administered the Initiative. One of these committees was charged with making annual research awards on a competitive basis to a few projects from many proposed, and ours was fortunate enough to be one of those chosen.

With the help of Min Weifang, a Stanford graduate and vice president of Peking University, we immediately partnered with the relatively new China Institute for Educational Finance Research (CIEFR) at Peking University, directed by Wang Rong. In India we partnered with Jandhyala B. G. Tilak, at the National University of Educational Planning and Administration (NUEPA) in New Delhi. Because of its broader interest in studying higher educational change in China, CIEFR devoted significant resources to the project. NUEPA also met part of the project costs from its own resources. A major contribution was that CIEFR hired Prashant Loyalka from Stanford as a full-time researcher, and he ended up conducting the study in China. Loyalka also participated in the student surveys and administrator interviews that we organized in association with NUEPA in Indian universities and played a key role in writing this book.

In the next year, with the support of the Fund for the Improvement of Post-Secondary Education (FIPSE's international programs are currently managed by the International Foreign Language and Education Service of the Department of Education) and the Russian Ministry of Education, Stanford's School of Education and Department of Economics initiated an educational partnership with the National Research University Higher School of Economics (HSE) in Moscow to improve the teaching of economics in Russia and the teaching of the economics of Russia and research on Russia at Stanford. That partnership is still under way in 2012. Among its many other achievements, the cooperation between Stanford and HSE brought Russian researchers—Isak Froumin, the vice rector at HSE, and Maria Dobryakova, a sociologist at HSE—into our comparative project on university expansion and change, and allowed us to include Russia's university system in the study. Others at HSE, such as Gregory Androushchak, also participated. Katherine Kuhns, a Stanford School of Education doctoral student with long experience in Russia, helped manage the joint research project with HSE, wrote her dissertation on the politics of higher educational change in the Russian Federation, and made major contributions to the Russian sections of the book.

The final country in the study, Brazil, came into the project by a less direct route. Brazil has a considerable history of research on higher education and a number of existing surveys of students and institutions. With the intellectual leadership of Jacques and Simon Schwartzman, and with the financial help of the Centro de Estudos de Políticas Públicas e Educação Superior at the Federal University of Minas Gerais (UFMG) and Stanford's Center of Latin American Studies, we were able to organize a two-day meeting on higher education research at UFMG in Belo Horizonte in early August 2009, bringing together a large number of higher education experts covering a series of important issues from finance to affirmative action to engineering education. That was followed by a small cooperation with Simon Schwartzman at the Instituto de Estudos do Trabalho e Sociedade in Rio de Janeiro. However, almost all the work done on the Brazilian data was carried out at Stanford based on the available research, the large databases at the Instituto Nacional de Estudos e Pesquisas Educacionais (INEP), and support on various questions from the experts who came together in Belo Horizonte. Thus, the blame for any Brazilian inaccuracies must fall on the Stanford team.

Unlike many international research studies, which are collections of papers from authors in different countries writing separately on a similar subject, our research was truly a unified collaborative. All the authors were involved in fieldwork in each of their countries, all reflected on the results from all four countries, and all commented extensively and repeatedly on the final product. We also met three times during the course of the study to discuss interim results. The first meeting was at NUEPA in New Delhi in 2008, the second was at HSE in Moscow in 2009, and the third was in 2010, organized by CIEFR in Beijing. As mentioned, an independent meeting was organized in Brazil in 2009. Some of us also met regularly at international professional gatherings and presented the interim results of the project. This took place, for example, at the World Congress on Comparative Education in Istanbul in 2010, the 55th Annual Conference of the Comparative and International Education Society meeting in Montreal in 2011, and the American Society for Higher Education meeting in Charlotte in 2011. We came together again to present a draft of this book in a one-day seminar/webinar at Stanford in April 2012.

As we learned, international interdisciplinary cooperation on this scale is a long process. The fieldwork in India, China, and Russia took more than two years, and just bringing together the data we collected and writing the book required almost two years. Besides the book, the project has resulted in three dissertations (Loyalka and Kuhns at Stanford, and Pradeep Chowdhury at NUEPA in India) and a number of journal articles—more will come in the future. At Stanford, the project achieved its goal of bringing people across campus to focus on a problem of common interest—it involved economists, political scientists, and engineers. Perhaps the most important result is that many people from many countries and different disciplines worked for more than four years as a team, learned from one another, and gained such a much greater understanding of one another's societies.

• • •

The authors would like to thank Stanford University's International Initiative at the Freeman Spogli Institute, Stanford's Center for Latin American Studies, the U.S. Department of Education's FIPSE program, Peking University's China Institute for Educational Finance Research, the National Research

University Higher School of Economics (Russia), the National University for Educational Planning and Administration (India), and the Federal University of Minas Gerais for their contributions to the funding of this project. We would also like to thank Stanford professors Anthony Antonio, Krishna Saraswat, and Philip Wong for their advice at various stages of the project, as well as participants in the Seminar on Higher Education at Stanford's School of Education and Philip Altbach, Eric Bettinger, Gustavo Fischman, Nick Hope, Francisco Ramirez, Simon Schwartzman, Sheri Sheppard, and Robert Verhine, who participated in the conference/webinar on the book in April 2012 and who so conscientiously read and critiqued various chapters of the manuscript. The Stanford Center for Latin American Studies and the Leman Foundation funded the webinar, and we are also grateful for that support.

UNIVERSITY EXPANSION
IN A CHANGING
GLOBAL ECONOMY

1   The State and Higher Educational Change

THIS IS A STUDY OF HIGHER EDUCATION EXPANSION AND quality in the world's four largest developing economies—Brazil, Russia, India, and China—known as the BRIC countries. These four economies are already important players globally, but by mid-century, they are likely to be economic powerhouses (O'Neill, 2001). Whether they reach that level of development will depend partly on how successfully they create quality higher education that puts their labor forces at the cutting edge of the information society. It is difficult to imagine large economies reaching advanced stages of development in the twenty-first century without high levels of innovative, well-trained, socially oriented professionals.

How effectively the BRICs improve and expand universities also affects the developed countries. This is especially true of university education in technology fields of study, such as various types of electronic/communications engineering and computer science. Skilled engineers and scientists are essential to high-technology industries, and these industries are, in turn, important to economic development in the information age. If the BRICs can train large numbers of highly qualified engineers and scientists, the poles of technological innovation could shift away from the United States, Europe, and Japan or—at the least—become increasingly shared between these old centers and the new (Freeman, 2010).

For this reason, we place special focus in this study on the increase in enrollment of engineers and computer scientists. Further, the perceived and actual growth in demand for graduates with technical/professional skills has been an important force in at least three of the BRICs in shaping the nature of the higher education expansion, and in several of the BRICs a new emphasis on university research and development in technical fields has been a dominant theme of the past decade.

Evaluating the potential success of the BRIC countries in developing highly skilled technical professionals is not the only reason to study their higher education systems. We want to learn how these governments go about organizing higher education because this can tell us a lot about their implicit economic, social, and political goals, and their capacity to reach them. Although the BRICs are acutely aware of their new role in the global economy, their governments must negotiate complex political demands at home, including ensuring domestic economic growth, social mobility, and political participation. Because more and better higher education is perceived by the public to be positively associated with all these elements of a developed society, BRIC governments' focus on their university systems has become an important part of their domestic economic and social policy.

Thus, the state—that is, the political system and the way it is reflected in government organization and policies—is key to our analysis of higher education development in the BRICs. Many studies of higher education focus on the development of individual institutions or particular groups of institutions (for example, Clark, 1983; Altbach, 1998; Kirp, 2004). Others stress the important role played by economic market forces in higher education expansion (for example, World Bank, 2000). Still others argue that global institutional environments are the most important cause of what happens to higher education at the local and national level (Meyer et al., 2005). There is much to be said for each of these theories of change. Yet, although all recognize that the national state is a player in the change process, all downplay its powerful role in shaping the national higher educational system in response to institutional inertia, international institutional environments, and global and national economic contexts.

In this study we take a different approach. We ask how each national state actively develops its higher education system, including achieving mass expansion and aiming for greater "quality," in the context of the many forces, global and local, that impinge on its society. Further, we ask why each national state takes the particular approach it does to higher educational expansion and improvement.

Our focus on how national states develop their higher educational systems means that we necessarily situate our discussion of university expansion and quality in the context of governments' educational policies. These, in turn, reflect much broader struggles over social goals and the distribution of national resources. While there is widespread recognition of the importance of an efficient state to promote economic development (see, for example, World Bank, 2004), there is a distinct paucity of research on *how* states in developing countries try to reorganize access to and the delivery of university education to create new knowledge. Little is known about how effectively countries are developing the scientific and managerial cadres that will lead the economy into science-based development. Further, much of what happens in higher education today is heavily influenced by what happened in an earlier period. For the countries we are interested in, the political system (the state) in earlier periods had rather different political and social goals than today's state. However, the way the state functioned and higher education was developed in the past carry over into the present and profoundly affect the shape and possibilities for making change (Meyer et al., 2005; Altbach, 1998).

Given the constraints imposed by historical conditions, it is not surprising that state higher education strategies in the BRICs for both expansion and improvement vary. Indeed, one important piece of evidence supporting our state-centered analysis is the great variation we observe among countries in the mechanisms that the state uses to shape higher education. If market forces dominated the shape of higher education, we would tend to find much greater similarities. Similarly, if global institutional environments dominated national strategies, we would also observe much greater convergence.

The variety of approaches suggests that *national* political environments— including each society's previous sets of state political-financial strategies that formed the current system—heavily influence current approaches to financing higher education.

Various levels of bureaucratic expertise (or the lack of it) and the inertia of the state's institutions—inertia that takes different forms in different countries—also play an important role in the politics of expanding and financing higher education.

Nevertheless, given the current globalized environment, it is not surprising that there are a number of commonalities in the strategies that BRIC states have used to respond to the demands of changing economies and expanding enrollment in the past two decades. For example, all four states have, for better or worse, turned increasingly to making students and their families share in the costs of expanding higher education, either through tuition in public institutions or promoting the expansion of full-tuition private universities and colleges. Some of the BRICs are also putting increasing resources into a few elite institutions, while "mass" institutions absorb most new students at relatively low cost to the institutions but relatively high cost to the students.

We make the case that the effectiveness of such strategies and others to help the university system "overcome" inherited trends and to "re-create" higher education in the current historical context is a good indicator of whether BRICs will become economic powerhouses by the mid-twenty-first century.

Besides its focus on the state, our study is unusual for two other reasons. First, it is empirical. Analyses of higher educational systems are typically descriptive and, if empirical, concentrate on particular aspects of the system, such as financial aid, the degree of equity, or the relationship between student outcomes (graduation rates, posteducational economic performance) and inputs (such as student characteristics, student family background, and higher education institutional characteristics). We take a more comprehensive view of the system and therefore have gathered data or use existing data on students, institutions, and socioeconomic-political contexts (including higher education finance and payoffs to educated labor) to develop a broad picture of the higher education system in each country at this particular moment in time. We also situate that picture in a historical pattern of change.

Second, the study is comparative. By measuring similar variables in each country, we draw insights into how differing socioeconomic, historical patterns of change, and especially political contexts, are related to *national* and *subnational* differences in how higher education develops. Using a comparative approach allows us to draw generalizations about shared patterns of change in these large countries' systems and why such shared patterns may exist.

We find that all of the BRIC states have greatly increased the numbers of university graduates in their labor forces, as well as the number of technical graduates and even the number of *well-trained* technical graduates. But they are not equally effective in their strategies to improve the overall quality of their higher education systems. Nor are they equally effective in providing access to higher education for disadvantaged students and distributing government funds fairly to different social class groups in their societies. Despite this, we find that students in their final year of university in the BRICs appear to be generally satisfied with their engineering and computer science education even when they have attended second-tier, often not high-quality, institutions. This is the case even for the high fraction who have paid tuition to attend those institutions. Although we focused on engineering and science students, we believe that student satisfaction extends to those studying in many other fields. Thus, some BRIC states may be doing only a fair job of building high-quality university systems that are broadly accessible and fairly financed across social groups, but they all seem to be achieving sufficient short-term political legitimacy through the satisfaction of those who do get access. Whether this is enough to build the innovative super-economies that Brazil, Russia, India, and China hope to be is a question we will try to answer in the pages that follow.

Background of the Study

Is There a Higher Education "Revolution" in BRIC Countries?

There has been a spate of new writing on the "revolution" in higher education globally (most prominently, Altbach et al., 2009; World Bank, 2000). This literature focuses on a number of important issues. The *first* of these is that there has been an enormous expansion of higher education worldwide in the past thirty years, and much of this expansion has been in the developing countries. Many reasons are cited for the rapid growth of enrollment in higher education. Population growth and the rapid expansion of primary and secondary schooling have in and of themselves increased demand for higher education places. Yet there is also a sense around the world that more higher education graduates are needed in economies that want to shift from traditional manufacturing to high-tech production and more human-capital-intensive services.

The objective signal that this may be so is the increasing private return to those who complete their university degrees (Murphy and Welch, 1989, 1995; Psacharopoulos and Patrinos, 2004). The dominant thinking, even in the 1990s, was that the highest yield investment in education was in primary schooling (Psacharopoulos, 1985; World Bank, 2000). Whether that assessment was correct or not (see Bennell, 1996, for a strong critique of Psacharopoulos's methodology and empirical results), it is now apparent that as primary and secondary education became universalized in more highly industrialized and postindustrial countries, the payoff of higher education rose in absolute terms, especially compared to the rate of return to investment in lower levels of schooling (for the reasons why this may have occurred, see Carnoy, 1972, 1995). Higher returns from university education have increased the demand for places in universities and in other postsecondary education institutions.

The *second* issue the literature emphasizes is the fundamental change in the traditional view of higher education as a public good, entirely subsidized by government funding. Altbach and colleagues (2009), along with others, claim that in contrast to this earlier view, governments today are more likely to consider higher education a private good, whose benefits accrue mainly to those who receive it. This implies that much of its cost should be borne by students and their families, not the broader taxpaying public.

The *third* "revolution" in higher education touted in the literature is the internationalization and globalization of university systems. Millions of students now study outside their own country and often stay in their host economy to work after completing their studies. English has become the dominant language of higher education, particularly in sciences and other technical fields. The U.S. research university has become the model for the notion of the "world-class" university. Research—both published and unpublished—becomes rapidly available through the Internet, and researchers worldwide communicate in real time through e-mail, blogging, and texting. University curricula are available through open courseware, so university instructors anywhere in the world can employ the latest ideas in how to teach courses. Further, a number of universities in the developed countries are opening branches in developing countries, essentially using developed country "brands" and often faculty to attract paying students in the developing countries. Finally, the European Union has initiated the Bologna process, which attempts to make the Union's university systems more uniform. The purpose of that form of "internationalization" is to make it easier for students to study outside their own country's postsecondary institutions and still obtain a common degree. The Bologna process illustrates the concept of the universal credential, in which students can study in different countries, obtaining a credential recognized in all participating economies (Clotfelter, 2010).

The *fourth* "revolutionary" trend claimed for the new higher education is the increasing use of information technology in reaching a broader clientele. This clientele is mainly working adults who want to hold jobs and study at the same time, but it also includes a new generation of young people more amenable to online, flextime learning. The potential of the Open University or correspondence school has been around a long time (Nelson Mandela got his degrees through UNISA, South Africa's correspondence university, and the University of London's external program), but with the advent of the Internet, the possibilities of watching streaming video lectures and engaging in intensive interaction with tutors and peers through e-mails and site blogs have opened up a whole new range of distance teaching methods. Professors in some elite U.S. universities are beginning to offer mass open access to full participation in their courses through the Internet. A recent report from the U.S. Department of Education (Institute of Educational Sciences, 2009) suggests that students learn the course material as well in virtual higher education courses as in traditional universities. Despite this promise, and despite the great expansion of distance education, no virtual university nor a virtual course has attained the status of a first-rank institution, even though some, such as the Open University of Catalonia, also stress research (Carnoy, 2005), and it is possible that in the future, first-rank institutions will give course credit in some form to those students who successfully complete the institution's mass open courses on line.

There is little doubt that all four of these major trends in higher education exist and that they are important. As we show in this study, however, they may misrepresent themselves as true breaks with the past and, aside from the rapid expansion of enrollment, may not be the most important trends to focus on, at least in terms of defining how the large developing countries are moving to reform their university systems in the new global environment.

In our view, a key change taking place in higher education in the BRIC countries (and in many other countries) is the *increasing differentiation* between the "mass" universities and colleges, which absorb the vast majority of students in the BRIC countries, and the "elite" universities, which, particularly in China and Russia, are being pushed to become "world-class" research-type universities and serve a relatively limited group of students. Although in all four countries, there is concern in the state bureaucracy about quality in the mass universities, and even signs in some, such as China, of trying to reverse differentiation, the academic distance between the two types of higher education institutions is growing, not only in terms of the amount of public and private resources per student, but possibly in the quality of the courses, the expectations of students, and the labor market opportunities for students graduating from the increasingly differentiated institutions.

This is not just an artifact of the process of expanding enrollment in higher education. Nor is it just the result of the "natural differentiation" among tertiary-level (and, usually, also among secondary-level) institutions that characterizes most countries' educational systems (OECD, 2008). We argue that this new trend is the result of government policies in BRIC countries of trying to strengthen research and the training of elite cadres in a limited group of institutions while satisfying broader goals of absorbing demand for higher education at a much lower cost. These policies may change in the future, no doubt. However, at this historical juncture they represent the various BRIC countries' approaches to growing and changing their higher education systems.

The governments of developed countries generally expanded their higher education systems in the second half of the twentieth century more uniformly. Their systems were differentiated, but they devoted increasing resources per student to each level in those differentiated systems. Burton Clark (1983) even argued that the mission of differentiation among U.S. institutions, from open-access community colleges to more selective universities, has been the key to achieving both expansion and excellence in the national system. True, an increasing proportion of the resources to finance higher education eventually came in the form of fees (even for public universities) levied directly on students and their families. But there is no evidence that the resource distance between the higher and lower ends of the systems increased. For much of the period, the growing availability of highly trained young professors and the growth in the economy needed to provide jobs for them in Europe, the United States, Japan, and the former Soviet Union almost certainly kept the quality gap more or less constant among different tiers of the system.

And once cost sharing did occur, students attending elite public universities were asked to contribute a much larger absolute amount—tuition that was about the same relative to the total cost of their schooling as the tuition paid by students who attended lower-tier institutions. So, if anything, the shift from university as a "public" to a "private" good was carried out fairly equitably by charging students more in elite than in mass higher education institutions.

In contrast, the BRIC countries—three of them (Brazil, China, India) latecomers to "massifying" postsecondary enrollment—appear to be financing higher education expansion in ways that are regressive. A small percentage of students, who come mostly from higher social class backgrounds, attend elite universities and are highly subsidized to do so. The mass of students are incorporated into low-cost second-tier universities and are less subsidized to do so. We show that even in Russia, where a high percentage of college-age youths attend universities, public spending on higher education is distributed disproportionately to students from the very-highest-income families. The distribution of benefits is a complex calculation because many, if not most, of the students who get into the nonelite universities in Brazil, India, and China are also from higher social class backgrounds and end up with lower subsidies or pay higher fees. Even with broad affirmative action policies as in India, many of the students from disadvantaged castes are from the more advantaged of those groups. In Russia, which has had a mass higher education system since the Soviet era, there is some evidence that students who do not qualify by national examination for state-paid places and have to pay tuition come, on average, from lower social class backgrounds than those who are fully subsidized by the state.

In any case, the alleged "traditional" role of a rising average level of education contributing to greater social mobility may be a truncated process in the BRIC countries. By financing higher educational expansion inequitably and by increasing the gap in quality between lower- and higher-tier institutions, the BRICs may effectively be offsetting the social mobility impact observed in developed countries during their earlier higher education expansion (Shavit et al., 2007).[1]

We propose further that the rapid development of higher education enrollment in the industrializing countries—a notable feature of how the world picture of higher education has changed in the past twenty years—is less a revolution and mainly a logical "catch-up" in the long history of higher education enrollment growth worldwide. As income per capita and education systems in developing economies grew since the late 1980s, so did their university enrollment. The absolute growth has seemed more rapid than in similar development periods of the now postindustrial economies in Europe, the United States, Japan, and the former Soviet Union for three main reasons: the combined population of the BRIC countries is immense; China, India, and Brazil had a very low fraction of their university-age populations enrolled in higher education in 1990; and China did indeed engineer an unusually rapid university gross enrollment rate increase between 1996 and 2010. Yet there is nothing unexpected about the way in which higher education enrollment has increased in the developing countries.

The Changing Role of Direct State Financing

The other key feature of higher education in these countries is the powerful role of the state in shaping what happens more generally. In all the BRICs, an important part of higher education enrollment expansion is in public institutions. Yet state financing has shifted into three main models of cost sharing: tuition for all students in public and private universities, creating a fee-based track at public universities, and private provision of higher education services. The explanation of *why* states allow for the expansion of private provision is less clear. Some analysts consider that states do this because they recognize their own inefficiency in the provision of social services and that privatizing higher education (deregulating higher education so that more private providers can enter the higher education "market") is allocatively and technically more efficient than sticking to publicly run universities (World Bank, 2000). Carrying this analysis to its logical conclusion, if privatization of higher education were a good indicator of greater economic and social efficiency, nations with higher education systems run mainly by private providers could have better prospects for future economic growth in the knowledge and information age.

There are two reasons to reconsider this perspective. On the one hand, rapidly expanding private provision of higher education may indeed result from *low* state capacity to deliver quality education (and other social services) at any level, not just in higher education (James, 1993). A "weak" state is also likely to have greater difficulty getting its wealthier citizens to pay taxes to generate the revenue needed to provide higher education with government funds. Because low state capacity is probably a major negative factor in a nation's economic development, this could suggest that nation-states with a growing fraction of students in privately run higher education institutions have poorer, not better, prospects for future economic development. Some private education may be more efficient than public education, but generally in countries with either low- or high-quality public education, private education is at best only slightly better (see, for example, Somers, McEwan, and Willms, 2004). This is logical because private and public schools draw from the same pool of teachers and other resources (school administrators, for example). So low-capacity states could make some efficiency gains from privatizing higher (and other levels of) education, health care, and so on but not enough to overcome the larger impact on economic growth and social progress of an inefficient, low-capacity state.

On the other hand, increased private provision of higher education may not reflect the inadequate capacity of the state to provide public services, but rather a strategic choice by the state with particular equity and efficiency goals in mind, allowing the state to devote more resources to elite public universities. One major reason for the state's choice to expand private education or to implement cost sharing through charging fees in public universities is high or increasing private economic returns to university degrees in most countries. The increase in payoff has been especially large for investing in some fields of study, such as business/economics, law, medicine, engineering, and computer science. We argue that governments have been able to lower their direct public funding of university expansion because the payoff has become high enough to induce many more students and their families to contribute, especially for study in the high-return fields.[2]

Charging tuition in public universities in theory also allows the state to have more influence over which professions to promote through direct subsidies and student grants (those with high externalities) and which to let "clear" (those with high private rates of return and low externalities) through allowing market prices to prevail and (in some countries) providing loans to students to invest at market price. None of the countries we study have necessarily done this, but it would be much easier to implement such strategies with the existence of tuition fees against which loans and grants could be used to provide incentives to students to pursue certain careers and not others (Johnstone, 2003).

Furthermore, admissions rules, tuition fees (in India, Russia, China, and much less in Brazil), curriculum (in India, Russia, Brazil, and less in China), and even examinations in private colleges and universities (in India and Brazil) or for fee-paying students in public universities (in Russia) are tightly controlled by the state. Granted, major aspects of organizational behavior are considerably different in privately run colleges and universities than in the public higher education system. Even so, highly regulated private institutions or the highly regulated environment of fee-paying students in public universities could just as easily be considered as reflecting the state's emphasis on the highly public (regulated) nature of college education even when financing increasingly comes from students and their families.

Even when the state charges little or no tuition (fees) for public higher education and when the vast majority of students attend public universities, as is the case in many developed countries, the state may not consider higher education a public good—in the strict economic definition of a public good as one that largely has collective benefits. Rather, the state may, on political grounds, be providing a general subsidy for middle- or upper-middle-class families (or a particular group, such as the Malays, in Malaysia) to invest in the university education of their children.

Yes, there is an "externalities" argument to providing such subsidies (in the case of education, the value to society of having a highly educated labor force and citizenry). But there are also blatant political reasons—especially the powerful political role of the middle class or a particular ethnic group aspiring to maintain or improve their children's social position through access to low-cost higher education. The state may be using spending on public education to reward certain groups for supporting the political agenda of a particular political/economic class. In addition, the state can rationalize low or no fees by insisting that this policy is a benefit to low socioeconomic groups because the policy reduces barriers to entry for those whose families have little income. Meanwhile, highly selective university entrance examinations and highly differentiated elementary and secondary schools prevent all but a few low-income youths from entering these high-cost subsidized institutions.

In that sense, the state is using general public funds mainly to increase the private returns of its favored political support groups—this can hardly be considered a "public" good. Rather, the state enables its favored political base to *reprivatize* public revenues in the form of private returns to investment in its human and social capital. "Externalities" arguments can be used as political cover for such reprivatization, but states distinguish little among various programs of study in providing free public higher education to the middle class, whereas externalities surely vary greatly among different professions.

For all these reasons, focusing on the private/public good dichotomy and, indeed, the public/private management discussion is probably not the most helpful way to delve into the process of change in higher education systems. That discussion may be important, but we think it is more useful to view the state as the locus of change in a country's higher education system and the public/private issue as part of a broader analysis of the state's political-financial strategy to meet its economic growth, income distribution, and political legitimacy goals. If increased cost sharing in public higher education or allowing the relative number of private university places to increase under government-regulated or unregulated conditions is a politically viable tactic that meets these goals, the state is likely to pursue such a political-financial strategy. The important issues are much less the private/public good dichotomy, and more the resulting effectiveness (quality of output) and distributional consequences of the strategy, both of which are linked to the state's political legitimacy.

The National Nature of Higher Education Systems in the Age of Globalization

That said, isn't the national state's importance fading out as the global economy gathers steam? (Castells, 1997). Shouldn't that translate into higher education systems being more influenced by global factors than by national political and financial conditions? The case for economic and institutional cultural globalization is a strong one, and some believe that "globalization" is a euphemism for the spreading hegemony of U.S. economic and cultural power. Thus, for the analysts who hold this view, leading national universities in developing countries should be a primary space for national cultural production, but they are constrained from doing so in a global economy dominated by U.S. definitions of culture, science, and research, and the way that leading U.S. universities prepare students (Marginson and Ordorika, 2008; Cantwell and Maldonado-Maldonado, 2009; Li, Shankar, and Tang, 2011).[3]

The United States, through the vast amount it has been spending on basic research *in universities* for the past sixty years, has indeed come to dominate scholarship in a variety of fields, particularly technical fields, in which research is expensive. This includes physical, natural, and social sciences; medicine; and even other less expensive research fields, such as education. The U.S. model of the state investing heavily in basic research in universities has not been typical of other countries until recent years, and then only in Europe, but it has been a primary force in defining the post-1945 U.S. elite research university—the "hegemonic" institutional form emphasized by those who push this type of analysis.

By centering its basic research in universities, the United States has been able to attract students from all over the world—again, especially in technical fields—to work on research projects and get advanced degrees. Because of the availability of research funding in universities and generally better financial support for faculty than elsewhere, the United States has also been able to hire foreign university personnel who want to focus on research and to work with doctoral students in a research university environment. The interesting side effect of this process is that many of the foreign students—research-trained Ph.D.s formed in the large, prestigious U.S. universities and shaped by the culture there—ended up teaching in the United States.

Much of this concentration of academic strength in the United States began well before the current phase of globalization, and it was largely the product of policies by a U.S. state focused on military power and competition with the Soviet Union, which was accompanied by a demand for basic military-oriented research, as well as an emphasis on a specific policy of greatly expanding university-trained talent to foster economic development. Fascism and World War II did much to contribute to U.S. academic dominance by driving hundreds of world-class scholars and artists out of Europe into the waiting arms of U.S. universities.

In other words, if there is global hegemony of U.S. higher education, it is because the U.S. state developed a research-intensive higher education system that served a series of purposes, including establishing U.S. military dominance and creating the basic research foundation for new technology and new products that would increase the return to U.S. capital, thereby increasing domestic economic growth and producing the highly skilled talent that would maintain and expand U.S. global hegemony. That said, once globalization became increasingly prevalent, the movement of highly skilled graduate students from developing countries to the United States (and other developed economies) began to grow rapidly, and the current situation described by such analysts as Marginson and Ordorika (2008) took shape.

If one believes, as all the university-ranking organizations apparently do, that research and publications are key indicators of being "world class," the relative research and development (R&D) spending per student in universities is potentially a good measure of the quality of university education. As we show in Chapter 7, although all the BRICs are expanding the amount and proportion of R&D spending in universities, the spending per student, especially in India and Russia, is very low.[4]

On the one hand, this trend could be misleading because research money should be related to the number of advanced graduate students, but, on the other hand, the low figures for India, Russia, and even China and Brazil (relative to the developed countries) are a good indicator of how little universities are involved in research compared to the number of students being taught in the higher education system. This suggests that an average professor in a BRIC university is much less likely to be involved in research than in the developed countries. China would have to increase its R&D spending per student in universities by six times to equal the U.S. figure and by ten times to equal Japan's university research spending per tertiary student (NSF, 2010). Russia and India are in a much less advantageous situation. Nevertheless, these comparisons are not the only indicators of higher educational quality, so they should be interpreted cautiously. They suggest only that the BRIC countries will likely have to make some major investments in order to bring their higher education systems in line with the U.S./European models of research universities.

Other countries may want to copy this model because they may want to counter U.S. economic hegemony. They hope that the model will produce for them the same kind of innovative and highly skilled labor and, they hope, the same high-yield innovations that have driven U.S. (and, to some extent, world) economic growth over the past thirty years (see Li, Shankar, and Tang, 2011). So when BRIC states want to develop U.S./European style world-class universities, a key logic underlying that strategy is to help make their economies more competitive with highly developed ones. Economic growth is itself an important source of political legitimation for BRIC governments. But, in addition, "world-class" universities are symbols of modernization and development, lending credence to state claims that its nation is a global player, competing with the United States, Europe, Japan, and other developed countries.

The effort to establish "world-class" universities, particularly in China and Russia (Moscow State University is listed in the top 100 of the Academic Ranking of World Universities [ARWU] or the "Shanghai List," while Tsinghua and Peking Universities are ranked 49 and 71 in the *Times* Higher Education [THE] 2011–2012 rankings), but also in India and Latin America (the University of São Paulo is already in the top 200 universities of all three lists, although India has no universities in the top 300 in any list), and in some small countries (Saudi Arabia, Qatar, Singapore) is partly driven by national states wanting to emulate the United States' innovation and technology-led growth and partly by the ideological value in their own countries of having such universities.

The apparent thinking is that a few more excellent universities based on the U.S. model will help each of these nations produce the skilled talent to develop their own new technology. This new technology, in turn, they argue, would contribute to rapid economic growth nationally (elevating China's, Russia's, India's and Brazil's competitive position regarding developed countries). And, to the extent that having U.S.-style prestigious research universities dotting the BRICs' landscape makes those countries look more like world powers, this would also legitimize BRIC states' hegemony at home and, eventually, globally. In less ambitious terms, the same argument holds in the other large developing countries and even in the small countries. After all, Israel is a center of high-tech innovation based on local production and on the importation of very highly skilled engineers and scientists.

Even as this drive to improve a limited number of universities gains momentum, the vast majority of universities and colleges in the BRIC countries are being called upon to continue to absorb growing numbers of students, with limited public resources for achieving that expansion. Expanding mass university access may be as fundamental to the state's economic growth goals through human capital improvement as developing U.S.-style, well-funded elite institutions. Also, mass access may be even more important for state legitimacy. The question is whether simply supplying relatively low-cost and possibly declining-cost-per-student higher education, increasingly financed by families themselves, will fulfill these economic growth and legitimacy goals. We try to answer these puzzles by studying, among other things, the quality and trajectory of mass higher education in the BRIC countries.

The Centrality of the State

In all four countries, the state has considerable power to provide incentives or disincentives in the economy. This is much more the case in China and Russia than in Brazil or India, for long-standing historical reasons. China and Russia's states emerged from orthodox Communism in the late 1970s and early 1990s, respectively, to develop into forms that could be best characterized as state capitalist rather than capitalist states. This form of the state tightly controls both the political and economic spheres, although free markets exist alongside state and state-tied private enterprise (firms run by individuals with close ties to individuals in high state positions and dependent on their support). India and Brazil were at one time colonized by European imperial powers, with India gaining its independence only in 1947. The postcolonial states in both Brazil and India have been essentially capitalist but in the second half of the twentieth century took quite different forms, with India maintaining a democracy and Brazil's democracy moving in and out of military dictatorship. After 1990, the Indian and Brazilian states can best be characterized as free-market, free-trade capitalist with mildly social democratic redistributive tendencies (for example, on India see Chibber, 2010).

Today, in all four countries the state depends heavily on rapid economic growth and increasing consumer well-being for its legitimacy, replacing coercion as a main option for maintaining regimes in power. Although that growth is still closely tied to international capital and international markets, in recent years all four states have shown increasing independence from dominant developed-country states. Thus, it is fair to argue that within the constraints imposed on these states by the power of global markets to limit their ability to develop economic policies that work independently of international capital and commodity markets, all the BRIC states strive to provide their populations with increased employment/higher wages but still give priority to capital accumulation. Capital accumulation may be controlled by domestic and foreign private capital (India and Brazil), domestic and foreign private capital and state capital (China), or domestic private capital and state-tied private capital (Russia).

In this context, all the BRIC states face domestic pressure to greatly expand the higher education system, in part because economic globalization (and in China and Russia, the transition to a market economy) has helped increase the payoff to higher educated labor (Carnoy, 1995). A high return to university-educated labor identifies that level of education with social mobility and better employment, thus increasingly tying state legitimacy to state policies providing access to higher education. As we discussed above, however, high economic payoffs to higher education give the state the option of making families share in the costs of investing in their children's university studies. The higher the perceived payoff, the more willing families are to pay a "user tax" on education.

Besides its impact on economic payoffs to higher education, globalization also increases competition among states for global "legitimacy" (Meyer, Ramirez, and Soysal, 1992; Meyer et al., 2005). In the case of higher education, this has emerged in the form of both competing to expand the systems (what proportion of college-age youths graduate college) and to improve their quality—hence the "world-class" university phenomenon.

The state also faces direct pressure on its higher education policies from institutional actors, who represent the large and growing higher education "industry" in all four BRIC countries. Institutional actors, as we show in later chapters, are hardly monolithic. They represent different kinds of institutions.

We conceptualize these forces influencing the development of higher education in Figure 1.1. The model puts the national state at the center of four key factors influencing the way that it develops its higher education system and seeks political legitimation through its higher education policies:

- The level of economic returns to individuals who invest in higher education
- Demands from a population that perceives higher education as key to social mobility and economic success
- Pressure from political/economic elites to improve the quality of higher education in the context of a globalized (ideological) conception of "quality"—a form of domestic legitimation-seeking through international validation
- Pressures from a heterogeneous group of higher education institutional actors for policies that benefit those actors, whose interests are shaped, in turn, by previous constructions of the higher education system

Before turning to discussing theories of how BRIC states respond to these four key factors, we need to describe the factors in somewhat more detail.

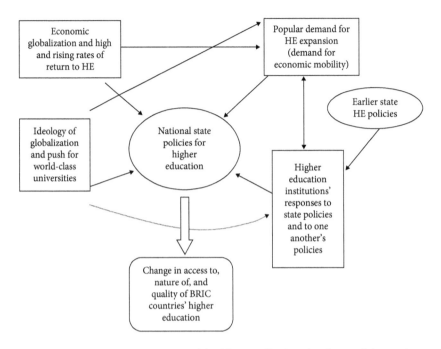

FIGURE 1.1 BRIC countries: A model of forces affecting the shape of change in higher education

Globalization and Changing Economic Payoffs to Higher Education

Two of the main bases of globalization are information and innovation, and they, in turn, are highly knowledge intensive. Internationalized and fast-growing information industries produce knowledge goods and services. Today's massive movements of capital depend on information, communication, and *knowledge* in global markets. And because knowledge can be highly portable in the forms of increasingly mobile workforces and new technologies, it lends itself easily to globalization.

Governments in a global economy need to attract foreign and generate local capital, and this capital needs to be increasingly knowledge intensive. This translates into pressure to increase the average level of education in the labor force. The payoff for higher levels of education is rising worldwide as a result of the shifts of economic production to knowledge-intensive products and processes, as well as because governments implement policies that increase income inequality. Rising relative incomes for higher-educated labor increase the demand for university education, pushing governments to expand their higher education and, correspondingly, to increase the number of secondary-school graduates ready to attend postsecondary institutions. In countries that were previously resistant to providing equal access to education for young women, the need for more highly educated low-cost labor tends to expand women's educational opportunities. By increasing the demand for university graduates more rapidly than universities can expand their supply, globalization puts continuous pressure on the educational system to expand.[5]

Not all programs of study are equally affected by the increased demand being generated in the globalized information economy. In most countries the payoff from business/economics education has risen considerably since the 1980s because of the rapid growth of the market economy (including small and medium enterprises, financial services, etc). In many countries, such as Brazil, China, and India, the earnings of engineers, computer scientists, and physical scientists have also been positively affected by the new structure of economic growth. As a result, in Brazil and India the demand for university places to study these subjects has increased even more rapidly than for university places more generally, and many of the brightest students in these countries choose to study in those programs. In China, whereas the absolute number (but not the proportion, which is declining somewhat) of engineering students has increased rapidly over time, the college entrance exam scores of students entering engineering are similar to those of students entering other majors. In Russia the supply of engineering education is larger than the demand, but even there, the payoff to engineering graduates (not necessarily to those practicing engineering) remains higher than to all but business graduates because of the "good in math, therefore good for a career" signal associated with engineering graduates.

Higher rates of return (both private and social)[6] for higher education have important effects on the rest of the educational system and on income inequality. Rising rates for higher levels of schooling mean that those who get that education are benefited relatively more for their investment than if they had invested only in lower levels of schooling. Those who get to higher levels of schooling are also generally those from higher social class backgrounds. This is acutely so in such societies as Brazil, China, and India, which are already highly unequal and in which 35 percent in Brazil, approximately 15 percent in China, and 18 percent in India of the age cohort attends higher education institutions.[7]

If rates of return for university are pushed up by globalization, intensifying the competition for access to higher education, higher-educated, higher-income parents tend to step up the amount they spend on primary and secondary school and tutors and special programs to ensure their children's university enrollment. Even in the public system, wherever possible, parents with more motivation and resources will seek "selective" public schools that serve higher social class clientele. These same parents, willing to spend on the "best" (often private) primary and secondary schools for their children, end up fighting for high-quality, highly subsidized (or essentially free) public universities, and many of them do everything they can to get their children into the most highly subsidized part of the system, but also because it is usually the highest-quality part of the system.[8]

Thus, the state's higher education strategies should be (and are) influenced by relative economic payoffs to education and by the relative payoffs to different professions. Furthermore, the state needs to be concerned with the distribution of access to higher education by different socioeconomic groups for both efficiency and equity reasons. Whom the state chooses to represent politically (explicitly or implicitly) and how it assesses the trade-offs between "efficiency" and equity affect the higher educational financing system and who gets the major benefits from state spending. Thus, in India the state has chosen to emphasize greater equity for designated disadvantaged castes and through affirmative action provides subsidies to these groups as well as the highest-scoring students from higher social class backgrounds. Brazil has also recently instituted affirmative action in federal universities but simultaneously has long heavily subsidized high social class students in these very same universities. In China and Russia, there are few if any affirmative action programs left after earlier Communist regimes had used them as part of their equalization policies.

Popular Demand for Higher Education Expansion

Pressures on the higher education system generated by a combination of increasing payoffs to investment in university, population growth, rising incomes, and higher completion rates of secondary education have important political implications for the state. The central government and, to varying extents, local governments, in the BRIC countries are closely identified with providing access to higher education places and controlling who gets access through examination systems, tuition setting, public subsidies, scholarships, and loan programs. Various groups in society, from those who have relatively high levels of family resources and fight for higher educational subsidies so that their children get an even better "deal," to those lower-income families whose children are excluded from higher education and therefore feel frustrated, have a vested political interest in the state's expansion strategies. How the state handles expansion, access, and the "quality" of higher education can influence the national state's political legitimacy and, often, local government legitimacy as well. In all four BRIC countries, the local authorities have at least some responsibility for higher education, greater in India (where the states have long fought for more power over higher education because of the patronage possibilities involved), Brazil, and China than in Russia, where almost all funding for higher education is controlled by the central state.

As we shall discuss below, the close connection that the population perceives between state higher education policy and access to a high-value investment good creates a direct relation between the state's higher education policies and the state's political legitimacy. State higher education strategies can also affect political legitimacy indirectly. State legitimacy is closely related to families' material well-being and employment and to better prospects for their children, which, in turn, depend on economic growth. If the effectiveness of educational policies is related to the rate of economic growth, the state's political legitimacy may be considerably raised or diminished by the quality of its educational strategies. This applies even to such nondemocratic states as China and quasi-democratic states such as Russia.

The Ideology of Globalization and the Push for "World-Class" Universities

There is also an important ideological component to globalization. That ideological component is rooted in the notion that the quality of national culture (and by implication, the prestige of the national state in the eyes of other nations) is measured in terms of the quality of its educational system, particularly its universities. The notion itself is rooted in the ideology of Western conceptions of progress, but the more important characteristic of this ideology of globalization is that the arbiters of such educational quality, and hence of the national culture, are international organizations, such as the Organization of Economic Cooperation and Development (OECD), the World Bank, UNESCO, the International Education Association (IEA), and, because of the "quality" of their universities (measured in these terms), the United States and Europe.

This ideology has been characterized in the recent globalization literature as a "world-wide field of power in which research-intensive universities in the United States exercise a global hegemony" (Marginson and Ordorika, 2008: 1). It is symbolized by the Academic Ranking of World Universities

(ARWU) (otherwise known as the "Shanghai List"), the *Times* Higher Education World University Rankings (THE), and the QS World University Rankings of the world's top universities and the effect of these world rankings' existence on national state decisions regarding higher education. Universities in the English-speaking nations constitute 71 percent of the top 100 research universities.[9] To the extent that nations are concerned with getting their universities into that top 100, the implication is that they need to copy the U.S.-U.K. model of the university. That model is the standard of quality, and indeed, the model is being strongly promoted by the international organizations.

Accepting this notion suggests that university programs and organization should be rethought around training students for much higher "global knowledge" standards. The movement to emulate U.S. and European universities is evident in a number of policy pronouncements across the developing countries. In part, this probably reflects an accurate measure of educational quality, but in part, it also reflects an ideological component of globalization—of accepting a certain conception of quality that has been defined by the dominant countries themselves.

The more direct impacts of globalization on knowledge production can also be considered as having an ideological component, strongly related to the ideology of educational quality discussed above. As we have argued, globalization and information technology are driving profound changes worldwide in the way we work, use our leisure time, and think about our place in the world. We have suggested that much of the effect is transmitted from the global economy to universities through the generally rising economic payoffs for university graduates and particularly to certain fields of postsecondary study. It is also transmitted through other manifestations of globalization: highly skilled professional labor is increasingly mobile, and its mobility is helped by the needs of research universities, research institutes, and multinational firms in the developed countries for postgraduate student labor, especially in technical fields (Carnoy, 1998), and, increasingly, many fields of research are becoming transnational because many of the world's problems are global—environment, health, education, security, and even culture.

These are "objective" phenomena, in the sense that as they are manifested nationally, and they produce real material incentives. Yet how they are interpreted and how states respond to them are shaped by ideology, and a powerful element of that ideology comes from outside the BRIC nation-states. For example, the conception of "valuable" knowledge to which university (and, more generally, formal) education adheres is rooted almost entirely in U.S. and European standards of knowledge. Many have challenged this standard as ideological, serving to maintain unequal power relations between developed and less-developed nations and between higher and lower social class groups within countries (Marginson and Ordorika, 2008; Poulantzas, 1980). Further, many of the changes in labor markets associated with changes in the global economy may be and are tilted in particular directions by national political ideologies—for example, the Canadian government has promoted policies that have kept income distribution from becoming more unequal, and the U.S. government has generally done the opposite (Freeman, 1994).

Thanks to the Internet, international cooperation in research is also made easier, so it is likely that dominant elite research universities in the United States and Europe will increasingly shape research agendas in developing countries. Universities in developed countries are also pushing into developing countries with programs and even campuses to exploit developed-country university brands.

Our analysis argues that this external ideology primarily influences universities through the state. This differs substantially from the mainstream literature on higher education and globalization. For example, Altbach and colleagues (2009) explicitly assume that the response to globalization—the international research networks, internationalizing student bodies, university extensions into other countries, and the quest for world-class quality—is situated in higher education institutions themselves. In other words, it is higher education institutions that initiate the response to globalization and shape the dynamic of the new internationalization: "globalization is something that happens to universities and internationalization is how universities respond" (Cantwell and Maldonado-Maldonado, 2009: 30).

This approach has some empirical validity. Seen from on high, it is universities (faculty members) in developed countries that seek out faculty in universities abroad and seek to install branch campuses in developing countries. It is universities that develop exchange programs and developing-country students who seek to study in the United States, Europe, and Japan, looking for the best opportunities to advance their careers. Developed-country universities try to attract such students because, as graduate students, they serve as valuable assistants on large-scale research projects, especially in engineering and science (Carnoy, 1998), and, as undergraduates coming from much higher socioeconomic backgrounds than most local students, they pay much higher fees than locals.

However, this analysis has serious limitations. We recognize the relative autonomy of higher education institutions and understand that many of them do initiate responses to the ideological components of globalization. Yet most institutions depend on the state for funding and are often propelled by state-sanctioned initiatives to pursue internationalization. Professors may be able to establish international research networks but cannot engage in international research on even a moderate scale without state funding. The major movements of students internationally take place because of state funding, often with developing-country-channeled incentives.

There is little doubt that the movement to develop "world-class" universities is state led and depends on active state support. The state needs the active involvement of universities willing and able over time to become more like U.S. and European research universities. But without explicit support of the state, state research funding, and state funding to hire new faculty, no university in the BRIC countries can begin to look like a U.S. or European research university. Assuming that universities in developing countries are the main responders to globalization ideology is therefore a misreading of the process of change—whatever change takes place first and foremost involves the state, with universities playing active but subordinate roles.

BRIC states vary in their responses to the "world-class" university phenomenon. China and Russia tend to be much more interested in creating "world-class" universities in a direct way, systematically increasing resources to a chosen few universities, while focusing other higher education institutions' attention on enrollment expansion. Brazil and India, to the contrary, have their elite institutions but are not systematically "picking winners." Thus, in those latter two (more politically democratic) countries, the ideological component regarding university quality in relation to the external world is weak. Of far greater ideological salience in Brazil and India is whether expansion is equitable and whether it sacrifices quality to achieve greater equity.

Higher Education Institutions' Pressures on the State

Universities in all the BRIC countries do have a good deal of autonomy, and a significant proportion have some funding and support from provincial authorities or are private and are funded by tuition revenues. Many universities have more active and entrepreneurial leadership. Many others do not. This is why it is not far-fetched to accept the analysis of those who put the university itself at the center of change. Indeed, some economics-based analyses see competition among universities, similar to competition among private firms, as the driving force behind innovation and improvement (World Bank, 2000).

Our model of change would be remiss if we did not study differences in the responses of universities to the national and global contexts, given state higher education policies. Universities are at once places of innovation, fostering new ideas, and internally conservative, attempting to preserve academic traditions and cultures rooted in the past. Our study suggests that universities may appear conservative because they are the product of earlier state reforms that have "trained" university administrators and faculty to behave effectively within that earlier context. Such institutions and particularly their faculty try to preserve the conditions under which they know how to be effective. Many of the older faculty are also just trying to preserve their jobs.

Further, universities may appear to be conservative because the state has implicitly assigned them (or allowed them to assign themselves) a fundamentally conservative role—to absorb increasing numbers of secondary-school graduates and train them into bachelor and professional degree graduates according to relatively strict and inflexible standards. This role does not require innovative techniques or quality improvements; to the contrary, doing research and being at the cutting edge of the field could help faculty become more knowledgeable in their subject but could also interfere with teaching increasing numbers of students as universities expand.

In Chapter 5 we examine closely how university actors respond to state efforts to change national university systems through financial policies, legislation, and other direct state strategies. These strategies vary considerably among the four countries we study, and so do the reactions by universities—not surprising given the different political contexts in the BRICs. Higher education institutions' faculties and administrators have learned how to operate to preserve their interests in well-established structures, and it is in those actors' interest to preserve institutions that they know and understand. At the same time, new actors, such as government reformers and social entrepreneurs, come on the scene and establish new institutions or work to reform existing institutions (such as trying to transform them into "world-class" universities)—usually promoted by state policies. It is in those new actors' interests to pursue a different set of goals. We observe this tension between the old and the new institutions (and the actors promoting them)—usually instigated by tensions within the state power structure. This is more true in Russia, India, and Brazil than in China—and it is more important to shaping the direction of the university system in Russia and India than either Brazil (where the rapidly growing private sector is hardly subject to pressures from public institutions) or China. Yet such tensions exist in all four countries and play some role in the change process even in China, where higher education administrators and faculty in all universities are generally more likely to go along with change initiated from above whether it benefits their institutions or not.

Theories of BRIC States and Higher Education

Our analysis of higher education systems differs substantially from those that underlie previous studies. Past research has made universities and their behavior or global economic forces or global institutional culture the driving force of change. We center on the national state in the BRIC countries and how it crystallizes various pressures on higher education expansion, equity, and quality improvement into reform policies.

We break considerably in other ways with traditional analyses of higher education in the context of recent globalization. Our analysis deemphasizes the internationalization of teaching and learning, and the public/private and learning technology issues, focusing instead on a more comprehensive conceptual framework that puts politics, economics, and ideology as the main forces of change.

Institutions also play a role in the model. They vary in response to the pressures coming from national state policies and the context of globalization. Yet the source of this variation is not necessarily the result of individual players. There are a number of reasons for institutional variation, among them varying roles assigned to institutions by previous state reforms and, related to those previous roles, the financial incentives, signals (including regulations), and direct controls (in China, the government appoints university presidents; in Russia, the government has direct influence on selecting the candidates for the rector's position) coming from the state under present-day policies.

Although we center our analysis on the state, it is not feasible to formulate a single theory of BRIC state behavior to explain the way that BRIC states respond to the pressures for expansion and quality improvement. All states need to reproduce political power to survive, and various theories of the state present different views of how political power is reproduced—whether the mass of voters is in control of that reproduction; whether it is powerful interest groups lobbying the electorate; whether political power resides in those who control capital, and through capital, the economy; or whether power resides directly in the structures of power, including knowledge, the means of communication, ideology, and the state's control of the means to repress dissent (see Carnoy, 1984, for a summary). However, these theories are situated in the particular historical contexts of their societies, and the four BRIC countries have very different political, economic, and social histories. This makes it difficult to come up with a single, unified theory of state behavior for the BRICs.

Nevertheless, for all their different histories, in today's globalized economy, BRIC states do have in common that they reproduce political power largely by seeking political legitimacy, that they seek this legitimacy at both a domestic and international level, and that they consider their higher education policies as playing a potentially important role in achieving legitimacy.

The main argument is that these states use the expansion of education, including university education, to promote capital accumulation in the hands of the powerful (either private owners of capital or the state itself) with political legitimation in the eyes of workers and employees (Offe, 1973). In this theory, education helps realize the self-interest of the state actors (including the intellectual elites in public universities) to increase state revenue and reproduce state power (Weiler, 1983). Different groups in the state bureaucracy may have different views on how best to reproduce state power—that is, to keep control of the state's revenue and how it is to be used—but ultimately competing bureaucratic groups are situated in a state that must legitimate itself or collapse. Expanding education and reforming it serve the state because more and better education—in the state's collectivity of competing bureaucrats' view—increases the probability that workers find jobs, gives workers the hope that they and their children can move up the social and economic ladder, and simultaneously increases the profitability of capital through higher worker productivity, which in turn, increases state revenues and bureaucrats' power and legitimacy.

The BRIC states vary greatly in their political and economic organization. China and Russia, although market economies, have strong elements of state capitalism. In Russia a significant fraction of capital is controlled by a relatively small group of individuals associated with the state. In China the Communist Party hierarchy still controls the use of capital but does not "own" it in the same way as the state oligarchy does in Russia. That said, the Chinese Party–controlled state has much more direct control over the economic and political system than does the Russian state. Nevertheless, both of these regimes, which control the media and other ideological apparatuses as well as have considerable influence over capital, still seek legitimacy internationally and domestically because that legitimacy is apparently important to their continued control of the economy and the structures of power.

Legitimacy includes developing higher education policies that respond to domestic demand by both families and enterprises for more higher education and to international ideology that places high value on elite research universities. The Russian and Chinese states do not need to be as responsive to a capitalist class independent of the state that might question spending public monies on mass education rather than subsidizing capital directly. Yet, like some capitalist elites in traditional capitalist countries, state capitalists in Russia and China are concerned with universities teaching ideas that threaten the current control of capital and economic development policies. In both countries these ideas about the control of capital can conflict with the state's political hierarchy's control over the political and economic process.

Brazil and India are more democratic capitalist states with strong colonial legacies. Again, there are many competing theoretical frameworks to understand why they develop their educational systems the way they do. There is considerable evidence that the Brazilian and Indian states generally have pursued strategies to shape and control their higher education systems, have expanded them at different rates during different periods, and have tried to improve their quality with relatively little success. Again, a persuasive case can be made that these patterns reflect state responses in Brazil and India to the vision that private (and state) owners of capital have of economic development, to the needs for educated labor and professional elites associated with that vision, and to pressures from the working classes to improve their employability and to give them hope for social mobility.

In both India and Brazil, the division of power between the national and state governments is a key determinant of state behavior. But it is telling that until less than a generation ago, Brazil and India expanded education quite slowly, even when compared to other developing countries. It is also telling that their opening up to the global economy, which reflected a change in their elites' economic development vision (and in Brazil the result of enormous financial pressure from U.S. and international Brazilian debt holders), is associated with the beginning of a rapid expansion of educational access. In India's case, this is also associated with a shift in political power to the provinces and increasing power of the regional parties in national government and policy making, at the same time as the economy globalized (around 1990) and changed the political imperative toward expanding the system.

In the chapters that follow, we use secondary data on national labor markets and higher education financing; interviews at thirty to forty technical higher education institutions in each country regarding their financing, expansion strategies, and perceived position in the overall national higher education structure; questionnaire data from several thousand graduating-year students in each country; administrative data on college entrance exam scores; information from employers; data on courses, syllabi, and classroom instruction; government statistics; and data from other domestic and international studies to develop a sense of how the BRIC country higher education systems are changing, using the conceptual framework outlined above.

We show that BRIC states are, indeed, at the core of higher educational change in their countries. Chapter 2 documents how all BRIC governments have expanded enrollment in higher education rapidly in the past fifteen years, China particularly rapidly from a very low base and Russia from a very high base. Chapter 4 discusses how all the BRIC countries achieved this expansion using different financial strategies, with Brazil and India relying heavily on tuition-based private college enrollment growth and China and Russia relying on public university enrollment growth but with cost sharing through tuition charges. As shown in Chapter 3, a main reason that expansion could take place with such a high proportion of direct private contributions in this period was the high (and rising) private rates of return to students attending higher education, particularly to students in certain programs of study, such as engineering, computer science, business, and economics.

Our study also demonstrates that BRIC states have focused their attempts to raise quality in higher education mainly by putting more resources in a limited number of elite research institutions, along the lines of the "world-class" university movement, and counting on second- and third-tier institutions to educate the mass of new students at much lower costs and, in Brazil, China, and Russia, at *increasingly* lower costs per student compared to elite institutions (Chapters 4 and 7). We argue that, overall, these mass institutions have been given greater autonomy but less incentive to improve quality and greater incentive to keep costs low (Chapter 5). BRIC government efforts to increase overall standards and quality accountability for mass higher education institutions appear to be a much lower priority than developing a small set of elite universities that can "compete" on the world stage.

In Chapter 7 we assess the quality of higher education in the BRIC countries, especially for engineering and computer science students, and analyze the probable differences in quality between elite and nonelite institutions.

Quality in higher education is difficult to define and even more difficult to evaluate, but we present a large number of indicators that take us a long way toward understanding how effective higher education systems in the four countries are. We find that the quality of graduates varies among the four countries and diverges greatly between elite and mass institutions. The increasing divergence between the elites and nonelites raises serious issues about the longer-term quality of the vast majority of university graduates in the BRIC countries.

Despite this increasing divergence, we found that the engineering and computer science students we interviewed in China, India, and Russia in both first- and lower-tier institutions were generally satisfied with the education they were getting and with their job prospects (Chapter 6). In other words, by the act of expanding access to higher education, even if the quality of that education is not objectively high, BRIC states have been able to keep most students satisfied. Russia has done so in part by making higher education accessible to almost the entire college-age group. Current demographics in China will also allow a high fraction of the college-age group to access some kind of postsecondary education by 2020. Brazil and particularly India—where a smaller proportion of college-age students get access to a postsecondary education—have pursued affirmative action programs that have succeeded in bringing many disadvantaged students into colleges and universities who would not have had access without those programs. Although the reason that students are "satisfied" may be because they have little information on which to compare their institution with others, and because completing any higher education seems to have at least some labor market value, their satisfaction (and their parents' satisfaction) has real meaning in political legitimacy terms.

This analysis also suggests (in Chapter 8) that perhaps because they are democracies, have relatively restricted higher education systems, and have a high proportion of low-income voters, Brazil and India pay more attention to equity in their highly unequal access higher education and put less emphasis on raising quality. In contrast, Russia and China, as more authoritarian states and world military powers that are very conscious of their global standing and with decades of a political system that stressed equity, put more emphasis on building quality elite institutions than on access for low-income groups. This is logical in Russia, which already has a very high percentage of its young people (including those from disadvantaged groups) attending university, but the lack of attention to equity in China could have negative consequences for Chinese development, both politically and economically.

A Few Explanatory Notes on
BRIC Higher Education Systems

Higher education in the BRICs is a complex collection of institutions that varies from country to country. Throughout this study, we try to compare apples to apples. For example, we focus mainly on the expansion of undergraduate (first-degree) programs, which may differ in length but have a particular economic and social standing in these four societies. Yet countries such as China have a high percentage of their enrollment in shorter (two- and three-year) higher education programs, comparable to community colleges in the United States. In engineering, India also has a considerable fraction of student enrollment in three-year "diploma" courses, designed to prepare technicians rather than full-fledged engineers. The BRICs also have varying percentages of students who continue on for graduate degrees and varying emphasis on postgraduate training. All these constitute parts of a nation's higher education system, and it is important to distinguish each piece in estimating how many students are in the system and what the system purports to be doing.

Even the parameters of undergraduate degree education vary, so we need to spend a few paragraphs explaining those differences among the BRIC systems.

In Brazil higher education is composed of universities, faculties, university centers, and a small number of other types of institutions offering four-, five-, and, in medicine, six-year programs. Some institutions are run by the federal government, others by state governments, a relatively few by municipalities, and a higher percentage by private providers, some confessional (mostly Catholic) and many, if not most, for profit. Shorter-degree vocational tertiary education represents a small (11 percent) proportion of enrollment in postsecondary education.

Somewhat more than half of China's about 30 percent of youths enrolled in higher education institutions are enrolled in four-year bachelor's degree programs in universities run by the central government and (mostly) by provincial governments. The other (somewhat less than) half is in three-year professional tertiary-education programs. An increasing proportion (about 20 percent) now attends privately run institutions that are regulated by the central and state governments. Although we focus on the approximately 15 percent of students attending four-year university programs, the shorter-course higher education institutions are an important part of China's overall design for higher education. However, the restricting of access to the more prestigious four-year institutions is also important in understanding China's higher education system.

India's system is complex for those not familiar with the organization of British higher education. Most students attend public and private colleges, which must all be affiliated with universities (now mostly attended by graduate students), which are largely public and are responsible for regulating the educational processes at the colleges. Most students overall in India are in three- and four-year "degree" programs leading to the equivalent of a B.A. or B.S. degree. All engineering degree programs are four-year programs. However, about 10 percent of students in colleges are enrolled in "diploma" programs, equivalent to China's three-year professional tertiary education. Many of India's diploma students are enrolled in engineering colleges, and they represent a much higher fraction of all engineering students than the 10 percent diploma students in India's total higher education system. Recent data suggest that about 55–60 percent of total college enrollment is in private unaided (no government funding) institutions (Planning Commission, 2012), but enrollment in private engineering colleges is closer to 85–90 percent of total engineering enrollment, as we detail in Chapter 2.

Higher education in Russia is largely (about 84 percent of enrollment) in public institutions, all of which are controlled by the central government, and a very high percentage of students in the higher education system (about 82 percent) attend universities. The other 18 percent attend postsecondary vocational institutions. The vocational student percentage is declining quite rapidly (in 2003 it was more than 25 percent of tertiary students). Those attending universities until recently were in five-year "specialist" degree programs, but over the past few years, Russia has gradually shifted to the Bologna structure, with a four-year bachelor's degree.

One of the great difficulties that researchers face in using secondary data on enrollment and graduates is to separate out students who are undergraduates completing the equivalent of a first degree from students in short-course programs. Some countries, such as China, include vocational shorter-degree students in many of their enrollment reports, but statistics are easily available to separate out shorter-degree students. Russia does not include short-degree students, and Indian statistics sometimes separate out diploma students from those in the "degree" programs and sometimes not.

There is another (related) difficulty in determining the percentage of university-age youths enrolled in higher education institutions. In addition to worrying about how many students are in university-level programs, it is difficult to ascertain the relevant age group to use as reference. We use eighteen to twenty-two as our reference group. This is probably accurate for China, where almost 100 percent of students finish in four years, but is probably quite inaccurate for Brazil, where a high percentage do not finish with their cohort. It also may be somewhat inaccurate for Russia, where first-degree programs until recently were all five-year "specialist" programs. We analyze these issues in Chapter 2 when we estimate enrollment rates.

2   The Great Higher Education Expansion

FORTY MILLION: THAT IS THE NUMBER OF YOUNG PEOPLE who have graduated from universities and other four- or five-year higher education institutions in the BRICs from 2005 to 2010, equal to the population of California, yet only a fraction of the number who will graduate in the decade of the 2010s. This impressive figure is the result of the huge leap in college enrollment in the past twenty years outside the developed countries and particularly in the BRICs. An expansion of such magnitude changes the world's higher education landscape. Notably, the BRICs' enrollment leap has included great numbers of students studying engineering, computer science, and other technical subjects so important to the worldwide boom in new technology and the knowledge economy. The tens of millions of new graduates and especially the millions of new graduates in technical fields have the potential to radically change where the production of high-value products takes place in world markets. They also have the potential to affect developed countries' high-skilled labor markets and could greatly increase the level of global basic and applied scientific innovation (Freeman, 2010).

In this chapter we discuss in broad terms the historical foundations of BRIC university systems, how the BRICs' higher education systems are being transformed by their enrollment growth, the strategies that BRIC states are using to achieve that growth, and the varying role that the growth of technical higher education—specifically, engineering and computer science—plays in that transformation. It is crucial to understand these changes if we are to assess their meaning and the future impact they could have on global society.

We argue that (1) the higher education enrollment growth in the BRICs beginning in the mid-1990s is just the latest round of educational expansion worldwide in the twentieth century and that (2) it was shaped, as elsewhere, by the history of earlier periods of expansion in these higher education systems.

Yet, at the same time, enrollment growth in the BRICs generally differs significantly from earlier expansions in the developed countries. A main argument of our study is that the differences have the following characteristics:

- In all four BRICs, as their university systems began to incorporate many more students, they became *increasingly differentiated,* with an emphasis (although this, too, varied from country to country) on strengthening a limited number of elite institutions and incorporating the mass of new students into lower-cost universities and colleges, increasingly diverse, with the expansion of nonuniversity tertiary programs and nonselective private institutions.

- The expansions have been—to a significant degree—*financed by tuition fees paid to public or private universities by students and their families,* in part made possible by the increasing economic value of higher education (especially certain fields of study) in an increasingly globalized economy.

- They also became *increasingly vocationalized* (less general university education and more professional education). Again, we contend that this is partly the result of the increasing value of professional education in globalizing markets.

- Except for China, which reinstated its "historical" university entrance examination at the end of the Cultural Revolution, they became more so than in the past, *increasingly "legitimated and regulated" by entrance tests* at the state and national level and, in the case of Brazil, even requiring a national specific subject exit test for students graduating from each university department.

- This latest expansion was marked, at least in India and Brazil, by increasing concern for access to higher education by traditionally excluded students.

In the chapters that follow, we develop the details of this argument—the economic context, the financial strategies, the institutional features of the systems and how universities are reacting to these rapid changes, the changing composition of the student bodies, and the implications of state strategies and structural changes for higher education quality and equity.

A Brief Look Back

To grasp how quickly BRICs' traditional university systems are changing, consider that in 1990, Brazil, India, and China together had about 8.5 million students studying in postsecondary institutions, whereas the United States, with about one-eighth their combined population, had 13 million higher education students. Put another way, in 1990, Brazil's higher education enrollment as a percentage of its total population was the same as the United States had in 1935. India had the same level of college student enrollment in the population as the United States in 1920, and China's postsecondary enrollment in the population was about one-third of India's—similar to Europe's highly elite system in the 1930s (Table 2.1). Only 3–4 percent of China's college-age population attended universities and higher vocational institutions in the early 1990s.

Putting this "revolutionary" expansion in perspective, it is reminiscent of a higher education "revolution" we have seen before—in the developed countries. Except for China's fifteen-year leap from a very low level of (four-year) university enrollment to approximately 15 percent of the age group, even with the huge absolute increases in enrollment in the BRICs, the changes in enrollment *rates* are similar to those that took place in continental Europe, the United Kingdom, and Japan twenty years earlier, from 1965 to 1990, and in the United States from 1950 to 1970 (see Table 2.1). Further, Russia's higher education expansion in the 1990s was different from the other BRICs—it came from a much higher initial enrollment rate (comparable to Europe's) but was similar to the other BRICs because of relatively slow growth in the 1970s and 1980s and the large increase in enrollment beginning in the mid-1990s.[1] That said, the changes in enrollment in these emerging economies are important because of the *very large absolute numbers* involved and because they signal a possible long-term shift of intellectual power away from the developed economies.

At the beginning of the last decade of the twentieth century, three of the BRICs had universities that served only an elite few (as did Europe's and Japan's universities in 1965 and the United States' in the 1940s). Their higher education systems had expanded over the previous decades (although negligibly in China, including a shutdown during the decade-long 1966–1976 Cultural

TABLE 2.1 Higher education enrollment per 100,000 population: Europe, Japan, United States, and BRIC countries, 1920–2010 (total tertiary-level[a] students enrolled/100,000 population)

Country	1920	1925	1930	1935	1940	1945	1950	1955	1960	1965	1970	1975	1980	1985	1990	1995	2000	2005	2010
France	125	145	197.5	185	190	308	334	446	595	1,049	1,581	1,970	1,998	2,318	2,995	3,696	3,444	3,562	3,525
Germany	198	144	196	113	72		256	350	499	632	830	1,684	1,987	2,540	2,810	2,627	2,499	2,749	3,179
Italy	136	112	112	144	259	418	310	288	356	583	1,283	1,749	1,981	2,075	2,519	3,125	3,111	3,439	3,372
Sweden	155	151	165	194	174	209	241	312	500	885	1,756	1,985	2,062	2,200	2,248	2,966	3,899	4,744	4,910
United Kingdom[b]	134	124	135	136	92	137	242	239	382	579	1,084	1,308	1,468	1,824	2,170	3,316	3,442	3,813	3,969
Japan	140	221	283	273	338	546	471	617	762	1,110	1,764	2,017	2,065	1,944	2,328	3,124	3,138	3,160	3,058
United States	564	742	895	1,020	1,132	1,495	1,508	1,606	1,983	2,840	4,148	5,238	5,311	5,118	5,591	5,362	5,449	5,908	6,673
Brazil	39	39	47	68	43	58	98	119	135	189	452	993	1,162	1,040	1,074	1,197	1,638	2,490	3,421
USSR/Russia[c]					430		770		1,240		2,040		2,190		1,900	1,880	3,240	4,800	6,599
India[d,e]	19	26	26	31	40	54	73	113	150	217	692	746	515	581	585	608	916	1,074	1,731
China	na	na	na	na	na	29	25	48	138	89	6	54	117	168	186	256	596	1,173	2,344

SOURCES: Derived from population statistics and the following sources: B. R. Mitchell (1978). *International Historical Statistics: Europe.* New York: Palgrave. B. R. Mitchell (2003). *International Historical Statistics: Africa, Asia, and Oceania, 1750–2000.* New York: Palgrave, Table I2. B. R. Mitchell (2003). *International Historical Statistics: The Americas, 1750–2000.* New York: Palgrave, Table I2. NCES (2007). *Digest of Educational Statistics.* Washington, DC: NCES. USSR/Russia data are from *Federal Service for Government Statistics: Russian Statistical Yearbook 2009* (www.gks.ru/free_doc/2008/b08_13/07-44.htm). 2010 data are from UNESCO, Institute for Statistics, Data Centre (http://stats.uis.unesco.org/unesco/tableviewer/document.aspx?ReportId=143).

[a]Total tertiary level includes university undergraduate and graduate students and nonuniversity postsecondary students.

[b]UK data are for university only until 1950, then for total tertiary education (for example, in 1985, UK had only 429,000 university students, 34% of total tertiary students).

[c]Stanislav Mercuriev (1991), "'Soviet' Higher Education in a Changing Political, Social and Economic Context," *Prospects* 21(3): 413–420, estimates much higher numbers for the pre 1960 period.

[d]Until 1980, British India (including Burma).

[e]India only beginning in 1985.

Revolution). But as of the early 1980s, Brazil, China, and India still retained their long tradition of serving children of professional and political elites to prepare them for government service, the liberal professions, and some for working in universities and research institutions. Greater access to primary and secondary school in China made universities more open to lower social strata youth than in Brazil or India. However, India did begin affirmative action for lower castes beginning in the 1980s. Even so, in 2004–2005 the Indian higher education gross enrollment ratio (GER) for those eighteen- to twenty-three-year-olds from the lowest 40 percent of income families was only 2.4 percent, compared to a 27.5 percent GER for those in the highest income quintile (UGC, 2011, Table 5.06). In Brazil and India, universities were also places of political activity, traditionally tolerated because of the higher social class of the students participating in such activity.[2]

Russia

The Soviet Union was the one exception to this educational elitism among the BRICs. The USSR greatly expanded its universities and particularly its post-secondary polytechnics in the 1920s and 1930s so that by 1940, it had one of the highest proportions of youth attending postsecondary institutions, second only to the United States. This level continued after World War II, but enrollment growth slowed in the 1970s and 1980s. However, the most important feature of the USSR's expansion was that it became, after the United States and the often-touted German nineteenth-century Humboldt University model, the first higher education system to shift from a mission of European-style elite formation (also the focus in Russia before 1917) to one of universities serving economic development goals and focusing on training cadres for the military-industrial complex. It also separated research from teaching, with research taking place almost entirely in academies of sciences, not universities.

China

The Soviets passed this new mission and model to the Chinese in the 1950s, and these Soviet-styled institutions grew quickly. By 1960, enrollments had increased nearly sixfold, to almost one million students (H. Li, 2010). Growth in enrollments persisted until the Cultural Revolution began in 1966, at which point many higher education institutions were closed and academics stagnated for the next ten years (Chang, 1974). China's market-oriented reforms of the late 1970s resurrected not only the economy but also awakened policy makers to the importance of higher education. Policy makers at that time recognized that a strong higher education system would produce much needed human capital for the economy, advance science and technology, and enable the country to compete in the global marketplace (Ngok, 2006). The earliest reforms included restoring the merit-based national college entrance examination that had existed before the Cultural Revolution, reestablishing academic course offerings, and gradually expanding enrollments.

The precursor of favoring an elite group of universities was also put into place at this time: of 715 higher education institutions, 98 were "designated as keypoint (*zhongdian*) colleges, a 1950s policy resurrected by Deng Xiao-Ping, whose role was to lead the way in raising the quality of higher education (Bastid, 1984: 193). Further, the government implemented a policy of reducing the number of academic secondary schools and rapidly increasing the number of vocational schools. This was a conscious effort to reduce pressure on university expansion and to prepare a skilled workforce for manufacturing expansion (Bastid, 1984; Rosen, 1985). Even as primary education was being universalized, a system of elite keypoint primary and secondary schools was also put in place to prepare an academic elite group of students (some for higher education). This step favored children of professional and political elites because these schools were in urban county seats only (Bastid, 1984: 194).

India

India and Brazil did not have communist revolutions that overturned traditional elite higher education systems. Quite the opposite: they maintained their elite social class student bodies by restricting access to university systems until two decades ago. India's higher learning institutions go back around two thousand years, but modern universities were established in the nineteenth century during the British occupation. The British introduced limited primary and secondary education and a small number of colleges to train Indian civil servants, engineers, and other professionals needed to provide services in the colony. This British colonial legacy of restricting even primary and secondary education to a relatively few played out after independence in the highly elite university system (which also included affirmative action by the 1980s) and its tight link to the civil service (Carnoy, 1974). The colonial government created the federal university system, in which the lead institution— the university—was owned and operated by the provincial governments. It affiliated the institutions (colleges) that actually provided education, which were in private hands. Their goal was to provide a high-quality education to elites for careers in the colonial administration. The state government prescribed policies that the universities implemented through setting standards, with no further involvement through strategy setting, funding, or operational control.

Indian elites became the driving force in the later colonial period as the system evolved from a set of private colleges to the federal university system. It corresponds to the earliest typology in the literature of an elite system consisting of "elite institutions . . . dominated by relatively small elite groups" (Trow, 1973: 6).

During colonial times the provincial governments began to invest in relatively high-quality higher education for a limited, elite student body. This was in support of national policy—that is, there was a congruence of objectives between the national and provincial governments. After independence the provincial governments prioritized access over quality. They achieved this by promoting new public colleges, whose governance and the governance of the affiliating university were tightly controlled by the provincial governments. The rapid growth and the politicization of governance negatively affected quality.

The national government under Prime Minister Nehru, partly in response to the declining quality and partly for ideological reasons, established a few centers of excellence with generous funding support and foreign collaborations, particularly with the Soviet Union. The Indian government established a network of elite universities—the Indian Institutes of Technology and Indian Institutes of Management, for example—characterized by a highly competitive, meritocratic selection process. These institutions were closely linked with India's space and nuclear programs, and reflected the Soviet and the Chinese experience in developing engineering education. The quality of higher education, by the end of the Nehruvian era, was bimodal: a small clutch of well-funded, high-quality professional institutions at the top managed by the Education Ministry in New Delhi and catering to the highest achieving high school graduates, and a mass of largely nontechnical, poorer-quality universities, run by the states, catering to a second tier of socioeconomically elite students with lower levels of academic achievement.

Indira Gandhi attempted to improve quality by halting the expansion of the provincial universities. The rate of growth of higher education institutions fell from the 26 percent rate under Nehru to 10 percent under Gandhi. The states refocused their mission on equity through what the central government believed were more relevant fields of instruction, such as agricultural programs, vocational training, and adult education. These changes, introduced within the existing central university governance model, failed to improve equity and quality. One reason for this failure was that the national government did not attempt to change the university's governance model, which continued to be led by provincial politicians, though with less power than before. A second reason was that even though the expansion of numbers of provincial universities slowed down, the number of colleges continued to grow and student enrollment increased. In effect, the central government had little control over what happened at the state level, except to insist on the expansion of more agricultural, engineering, and technology colleges. Yet, given the governance structure in the hands of local politicians, the main incentive at the state level was for continued expansion, with little regard for either equity or quality.

A new set of governance reforms began in 1984 in response to these failures. The goal of equity was redefined: it changed from defining what could be taught—e.g., more agriculture-oriented programs—to improving the access of underprivileged groups through affirmative action in access to all programs, and this shift occurred because of the increasing political power of "disadvantaged" castes and classes in the national and provincial governments. To control rising public costs, the establishment of independent private colleges was allowed.

Brazil

Brazil was also a colony until the early nineteenth century, and its colonizer, Portugal, was even less interested than the British in promoting local education, although a few Brazilians did study at universities in Portugal. Higher education institutions existed in Brazil at the end of the eighteenth century, but Brazil's first university was formed in the middle of the nineteenth century, late by Latin American standards.

It was only with the Republic and the new constitution, in 1889, that higher education could expand, and it did so in a decentralized fashion. The expanding system included Catholic, local-state-level public, and private institutions. During this First Republic, a large number of new institutions came into being, all organized to train students for the liberal professions and none as universities (Durham, 2005). When the Vargas regime ended the Republic in 1930, the church dominated the small (33,000 students) higher education sector, with 44 percent of total enrollment in Catholic institutions. As Daniel Levy writes, "Brazil's first private wave had arisen for much the same major reason operating elsewhere in Latin America—State toleration of a Catholic reaction to public secularism. . . . In the Brazilian context, a certain demand-absorbing function might also be noted, given restricted public sector admissions" (1986: 178).

The 1931 University Law and legislation promulgated by Vargas were compromises between the conservative forces of the church and progressive secular intellectuals. They established the university as the preferred form of higher education institution but did not eliminate the autonomous professional schools and allowed for the continued role of private higher education. It also gave the state total control over regulating the system, including the private sector (Durham, 2005). It "reinforced the belief that the main role of higher education was to provide training and certification for the established professions" and the "principle that in granting degrees, higher education institutions acted on behalf of the state, extending legally binding professional credentials" (Balbachevsky and Schwartzman, 2011: 36).

This situation continued under the Second Republic (1945–1964) and the military takeover of 1964. The 1968 reform by the military government was driven by an idealistic goal of a "unitary higher education system, exclusively constituted by public, tuition-free, research oriented universities" that came to dominate public policy thinking on higher education in Brazil (Balbachevsky and Schwartzman, 2011: 37). The 1968 reform reorganized the public system along the U.S. model, replacing the old chair system with faculties organized by departments and full-time contracts for faculty, and instituted a credit system for courses. There was considerable resistance to these reforms (in part because of resistance to the military government), but most of its elements were implemented by the early 1970s. Graduate programs improved as well, and the federal government's budget for universities grew enormously in the next decade, by more than 500 percent in 1972–1986.

The 1931 and 1968 university legislation established the bases for the relation between universities and the state until the late 1990s. Federal universities were controlled and regulated by a strong bureaucracy under the Ministry of Education and the National Council of Education, appointed by the Minister, which was responsible for supervising national educational policies and all higher education institutions: "The most relevant regulatory bodies are still in place and have been enlarged by many other federal initiatives. The combined activities of all these bodies created a labyrinth of laws, decrees, and regulations" (Balbachevsky and Schwartzman, 2011: 37).

One of the most interesting features of the state's close control of the higher education system is the role it designated for public institutions and their subsequently moderate growth in the face of explosive demand for increased university places from the 1960s onward. For example, from 1970 to 2000, there were only 39 new public universities formed (16 of them in the decade of the 1990s) and no net growth in other types of public higher education institutions. In the same period, there were 70 new private universities created and an almost doubling of other types of private institutions, from 430 to 870. In addition, public universities were slow to set up evening courses, which lower the cost of attending in terms of income foregone (Durham, 2005). As Levy shows, in 1960, 44 percent of students were in private universities, in 1970, 50 percent, and by 1962, 60 percent (1986: 180).

For different reasons, then, China, India, and Brazil had delayed expansion of their higher education systems until very late in the twentieth century and had maintained restricted access largely to an elite few—even though in China and India, that elite few did include some youths from socially disadvantaged groups. In India and Brazil, the best explanation for the continued elitism of universities was the dual colonial legacies of relatively little education for the local population and the privileged position of elites well after independence. University education remained a "right" for those who had been able to take the most advantage of colonization or, in the case of Brazil, immigrants who had already been relatively well off in Europe. This "right" to free higher education was increasingly legitimized by entrance examinations in which mainly the privileged were likely to succeed because they were able to attend elite public and private secondary schools.

Differentiation, Rationalization, and Vocationalization

Despite these legacies, all three countries greatly expanded their postsecondary enrollment after 1990 and began the transformation of their higher education systems. To varying degrees, the relative number of universities catering to youths from elite families is declining, and the relative number catering to students from middle- and some working-class families is rapidly increasing. Higher education systems geared to elite formation are gradually turning into mass systems like those in today's United States, Japan, many European countries, and Russia.

Burton Clark (1983) named this strategy "differentiation" and celebrated it as a way to open the university system to many more high school graduates. Rather than just increasing enrollment at elite universities and therefore depreciating the value of higher education for those who attend such institutions, differentiation expands second- and third-tier institutions to absorb the mass of new entrants. Clark's reference point was the state of California's massive and diverse higher education complex: a number of private universities (some elite) and its three tiers of public institutions, including the University of California (in 2009, about 220,000 students in 10 universities, some relatively elite); the widely accessible state college system, now the state university system, of 23 campuses and 430,000 students; and the "open" community college system of two-year institutions enrolling about 1.5 million students. Clark rightly viewed California's system as highly democratized and serving a broad spectrum of youths seeking postsecondary education.

As we show in Chapter 8, even the widening of opportunities through higher education expansion can potentially result in greater inequality if students from advantaged backgrounds disproportionately enjoy new or better-quality educational opportunities in higher-tier (more selective institutions) as the system expands to absorb more students from lower social class groups (Shavit et al., 2007; Ayalon and Shavit, 2004; Hannum and Buchmann, 2003). Raftery and Hout (1993) claim that inequality between different social strata continues until advantaged groups are saturated in a particular level of education, and after which time disadvantaged groups begin to gain more access to that level. Lucas (2001) further claims that advantaged groups constantly find or create new educational opportunities through which to maintain their higher status, thus preventing disadvantaged groups from being on an equal footing.

Given the probability that higher educational expansion does not result in "equal access" because of educational differentiation, in order for it to "work" in democratic (and even in most nondemocratic) societies, the allocation mechanism of students to each level in the differentiated structure cannot be *overtly* based on social class, wealth, political position, or other forms of parents' elite status. The state's stake in organizing mass differentiated higher education systems is political legitimacy, and for the past seventy years, legitimacy has increasingly hinged on the appearance of objectivity in judging access to higher education institutions.

In *The Big Test* (1999), Nicholas Lemann showed how the Scholastic Aptitude Test was the brainchild of Henry Chauncey, Harvard's assistant dean of students in the 1930s, who wanted to broaden Harvard's recruitment beyond the exclusively elite, preparatory school educated student body of the time. The test was intended as an "objective" criterion (acceptable even to the privileged Harvard alumni) to select the brightest student regardless of birth status. Supported by Harvard's president, James Conant, Chauncey was a product of his time, influenced by the class-conflict politics of the Depression era. He and Conant believed that in a democratic society the best and the brightest minds should be the "new elite," replenishing the previous generations' best and brightest without regard to their families' social or economic status. Elite universities would still be elite, but the meaning of the term would change. Such institutions would be developers of highly skilled professionals who would lead from their intelligence rather than their social class. Scientific thought, not internalized ideologies or sociopolitical tradition, would be the basis of elite formation. From its beginnings as a recruitment tool at Harvard, the SAT became ingrained in American academic culture as a sorter for different levels of the higher education system. And as university systems expanded elsewhere, testing specifically for the purpose of differentiating the types of universities that students could enter eventually spread to the rest of the world.[3]

As Lemann makes clear, testing as an antidote to social class reproduction worked only marginally. Even with testing, U.S. elite universities ended up with largely high-social-class-based student bodies. Today, they are more diverse than in the 1930s, but universities such as Harvard and Princeton still get an inordinately high fraction of their students from private preparatory schools, essentially recruiting new students from the same privileged groups that attended Harvard and Princeton in the past. Further, as should have been obvious to the reformers, those with more family resources would end up with higher test scores, either by attending high schools that prepared them for the test or by paying for test training. This is precisely what happens in other countries as well.

The more interesting legacy of the "best and brightest" movement of the 1930s is the reconceptualization of "elite formation" and the impact that it has had on the definition of university excellence. Testing students was part of a broader effort to extend the scientific basis of scholarly work to the way universities defined themselves and, ultimately, to converting all university education to the formation of different levels of professionals and to the scientific rationalization of the division of labor. The differentiation of higher education not only fits into this rationalization at the highest levels of the labor market; it also somewhat democratized elite universities and incorporated them into an overall hierarchy of educating a professional workforce. They were at least partly transformed from a set of separate institutions specifically developing intellectual, political, and business leaders into part of a larger system of sorting students "scientifically" to optimize productivity for economic, social, and political efficiency.

The Soviet Union found this the perfect model for its growing university system even before Chauncey and Conant tried to remake Harvard.

Universities in the USSR were considered vocational/professional training institutions already in the 1920s, preparing higher-level labor for an emerging military/industrial power. The way to political power was through the Communist Party, not elite higher education. But the way to economic efficiency in a command economy was through human capital planning. Young people were allocated to certain levels and types of differentiated higher education based on their revealed academic performance, and then allocated to jobs in the growing industrial economy. The focus on investing in higher-level human capital as a source of economic growth was an important feature of the Soviet system in the 1920s and 1930s (Carnoy and Samoff, 1989). This was consistent with Marxist ideology, which considered labor power the locus of creating economic value, and it differed with contemporary policies in the rest of Europe, which had expanded primary education in the late nineteenth century but in the 1930s still considered secondary and higher education as more "academic"—the reserve of the socially privileged rather than a key to economic and social development.

In that regard, the new communist government shared this developmentalist vision of secondary and postsecondary education with the capitalist, but less socially class bound United States. The American government had explicitly viewed secondary and higher education as a driver of economic development well before other countries. Thomas Jefferson introduced the notion of a regional public university as a driver of local development when he founded the University of Virginia at Charlottesville, in 1820. Later, land grant colleges were established in states under the Morrill Act beginning in 1862. The Universities of Iowa and Kansas were the first, although Michigan had already issued its own land grant prior to the federal act.

The Soviets added affirmative action (extra points on the test given for Communist Party involvement, or working class or peasant parents) to provide a modicum of greater equality, consistent with communist ideals. However, as in the United States, the children of the higher educated in the USSR had such a vast academic advantage that, aside from the premium awarded for party activity, class-based affirmative action had a relatively small impact on access to preferred jobs. The communist government also implemented spatial diversification away from the traditional intellectual centers (similar to the U.S. model of land grant colleges) so that youths in the far-flung reaches of the USSR could attend universities and that those areas could develop economically. This was probably much more of a force for social equalization than affirmative action.

The other "new" feature of the Soviet higher educational system was the direct product of Leninist-Stalinist repression of critical thought and of the extreme vocationalization of education in the drive toward industrialization and developing military technology. This was the emphasis on technical education, with university-level engineering, mathematics, and the physical sciences as the top of the technical education pyramid. Even today, long after the demise of the Soviet system, Russian higher education produces more undergraduate degree (mostly five-year degrees in the case of Russia) engineers than European countries or the United States and about one-third as many as India produces bachelor's (four-year) degrees (see Chapter 7). This is notable, given that India has ten times the population as the Russian Federation.

Western universities never reached the degree of vocationalization achieved in the Soviet system—in the West, universities have always retained some of their intellectual and critical thinking traditions, including those higher education institutions in the second and third tiers, such as the California state college and community college systems. This was not the case in the USSR and the People's Republic of China.

These country particulars are important because they shape the way higher education is expanding in the BRICs today. Further, the evolution of higher education in the United States and the USSR affected how higher education expanded in all countries in the second half of the twentieth century. The huge growth of higher education in these dominant political powers became closely identified with differentiation, and differentiation was identified with entrance testing and vocationalization, all the way up to the elite universities. This was the case in capitalist *and* communist economies. Thus, even elite formation became increasingly influenced by scientific rationalization and a focus on producing professional labor.[4]

This is precisely what occurred in Brazil, China, and India in the 1990s as their university systems emerged from educating a narrow group of youths to "professionalizing" a much broader proportion of their young population. Universities became increasingly depoliticized—in the sense that their mission became much less the development of a political and scientific elite—and increasingly focused on teaching marketable skills more generally for higher-level jobs.

As time goes on, this mission redefinition through testing and vocationalizing the university curriculum (even in elite universities), is morphing into measuring university effectiveness based on achievement outcomes. As we discuss in the chapters that follow, Brazil has led the way in measuring how much students know at the end of their programs of university study by test-ing final-year students in hundreds of university departments. The test, called the *Provão*, was introduced in the late 1990s during the Cardoso government in response to fears that many of the private universities were producing sub-standard graduates. A number of German states use a series of outcome cri-teria, not including tests, to allocate funding among universities, and Russia is considering doing the same. Most recently, the OECD board of governors has approved the development of final-year tests for various fields of study in universities to be applied across countries in a form corresponding to the PISA test of secondary school students. This would be one measure of student outcomes in higher education and would implicitly compare how well uni-versities in each country are fulfilling their scientific, economic development mission.

The details of the BRIC countries' expansions after the mid-1990s reflect many of the particularities of their communist (Russia and China) and colo-nial (India and Brazil) legacies, as well as the financial imperatives of rapidly increasing enrollments in relatively low-income countries. We now turn to establishing the framework for the discussion in later chapters by describing—in broad strokes—the nature of the expansion of higher education in each country.

China's Higher Education Boom

Chinese higher education has been transformed since the late 1990s. Only 4 percent of the eighteen- to twenty-two-year-old cohort or about 3 million (three- and four-year degree) students attended postsecondary institutions in 1996, but this rose to 24 percent of the age cohort, or about 27 million students, by 2009 (Figure 2.1).[5] As Figure 2.1 also shows, somewhat less than one-half of these students attend two- or three-year vocational higher education institu-tions. Thus, about 14 million students were in four-year institutions in 2009.

Rapid economic growth since China implemented market reforms in the late 1970s has supported the expansion in enrollments by enabling greater government investments in higher education. Large increases in per capita income also enabled the Chinese state to "tax" families wanting to invest in their children's higher education through the introduction of college tuition fees in the late 1990s. An increasing number of families were both able and willing to pay these fees as economic reforms gradually increased the demand for higher educated labor and the returns to college (see Chapter 3).

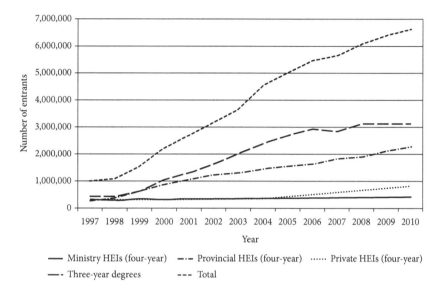

FIGURE 2.1 China: Number of entrants into higher education institutions by type of institution, 1997–2010

SOURCE: National Bureau of Statistics. 1998–2010. *China Educational Statistics Yearbook.* Beijing.
NOTES: "Ministry HEIs" refers to four-year public universities under the central government. "Provincial HEIs" refers to four-year public universities under the jurisdiction of provincial governments. "Private HEIs" refers to four-year private institutions, including "independent schools" (*duli xueyuan*). The 1997–2003 data for private HEIs are not available and are also not included in "Total."

Besides introducing general policies such as tuition or "cost sharing," the Chinese government has also carefully managed the nature of the growth of the higher education system. The Ministry of Education, in consultation with provincial governments and higher education institutions, fixes a "student enrollment plan" at the start of each year to determine the number of high school graduates from each province who can be admitted into each major of each university. Through the annual enrollment plans, policy makers have chosen to expand student quotas in various types of universities at different rates.

In the 1990s, many of the top 100 universities underwent mergers with institutions previously under the jurisdiction of various specialized central ministries. These were designated aspiring world-class institutions and have received special funding.[6] As we explain in greater detail in Chapter 4, the state invested many more resources into these "elite" universities but kept enrollment growth rates relatively low. Figure 2.1 shows how the enrollments in the elite universities were kept fairly constant over the decade of higher education expansion.

In contrast, the state allowed almost all the massive increase in enrollment to take place in universities under the jurisdiction of provincial education bureaus, which expanded the number of students by about six times from 1997 to 2009. This was a deliberate move on the part of the state to "separate" the function of developing a mass of university-educated professional workers from the function of producing research-oriented and "elite" graduates in "leading-edge" or "world-class" universities. Even so, there are provincial universities that are also research oriented, produce many Ph.D.s, and blur the distinctions, even though they do get less funding per student than the elite central universities.

High-tuition private four-year universities expanded at a notably slower pace, from 1.01 million (total) students in 2004 to 2.19 million students in 2009 (NBS, 2005, 2010); this reflects the government's decision (thus far) to keep the proportion of private to public university enrollments rather low (about 20 percent). Three-year public and private vocational colleges also multiplied enrollments by about six times from 1997 to 2009. Thus, much of the increase in college attendance has been caused by the expansion of postsecondary vocational institutions that now constitute about 45 percent of total higher education enrollments (NBS, 2010).

The rapid, controlled, and differentiated expansion has enabled many more students to have the opportunity to go to college, but expanding nonelite institutions so quickly has also raised the potential for large inequalities within the higher education system itself (Shavit et al., 2007). Loyalka (2009) discusses how rigid education policies at different pre-tertiary schooling stages in China (including the college applications and admissions process) likely exacerbate unequal student sorting by socioeconomic status across four-year institutions. For example, the annual enrollment plan mentioned above is set so that provinces with higher per capita incomes are allocated more spots in college and more selective colleges proportional to the size of their eighteen-year-old age group (Loyalka, 2009). For example, Beijing, Shanghai, and Zhejiang (some of the most developed regions of China) send roughly 20–25 percent of their eighteen-year-olds to four-year universities, while Henan, Yunnan, and Guizhou (some of the least developed regions of China) send roughly 8 percent.[7]

The underlying principles surrounding the allocation of college places to different provinces (including the criteria and formula used by policy makers) are not made publicly available. It is not clear, for instance, to what degree the allocation is determined by financial considerations (i.e., provincial governments provide funding to institutions within their borders and thus demand higher college quotas for their own populations). It could also be that central policy makers feel pressured by local demand or believe in a social efficiency argument in which more developed provinces should be given greater access because they have proportionally more (well-trained) high school graduates. Even if these types of rationale exist, the basic inequality between provinces in attending colleges and more selective institutions has not escaped public notice. How policy makers will deal with interprovincial college quota allocations will be a challenge as China continues to expand its university system over the next decade.

However, perhaps the most visible instrument for sorting students into and across the mass, differentiated higher education system in China is the college entrance exam. The exam, or *gaokao,* pronounced "gow-kow," has even gained international notoriety for influencing the entire education system in terms of what students learn before they get to college (LaFraniere, 2009). The exam has been criticized more for placing too much pressure on students and their parents and for promoting rote memorization to prepare for the test rather than more creative, dynamic skills and abilities.[8] Some elite universities are quietly urging the government to consider providing them greater room to use their own admissions criteria. However, it is not clear whether the government's recent experiment to give some universities limited autonomy to select a small proportion of students through their own application and admissions policies would increase or exacerbate equity across universities. Furthermore, for the time being, decreasing inequality in higher education likely relies much more heavily on interventions at pre-tertiary education stages (see Chapter 8).

Another major feature of China's higher education enrollments is the high percentage of students studying various fields of engineering. While the percentage of engineers in four-year institutions has declined somewhat from the 1990s, it still remained at 32 percent in 2009 (NBS, 2010). Researchers have rightly noted that in order to compare trends with developed countries such as the United States, we should count the total number of engineers graduating from four-year institutions as well as comparable definitions of engineering majors (Gereffi et al., 2008). Yet the more than one million students entering engineering majors (albeit engineering with an unadjusted, broader definition) in four-year institutions in 2009 is about nine times that of the

United States (NBS, 2010; National Science Board, 2010). Moreover, the vast majority of freshman engineering students in China will not be able to change majors and will graduate with a degree after four years. In the United States, undergraduate engineering students often change majors, drop out, or fail to graduate on time.

The high proportion of technical graduates also characterizes the graduate level, where, despite a gradual decline over the past ten years, engineering M.A. students make up more than 30 percent of total M.A. students and engineering Ph.D. students make up more than 40 percent of total Ph.D. students. The number of Ph.D.s awarded in engineering in China is about 15,000 annually (NBS, 2010), more than in any other country worldwide, although Russia produces a higher number of engineering Ph.D.s relative to its population. In 2009, India awarded only about 1,140 Ph.D.s in engineering fields, Russia about 7,500, and Brazil only 1,300. In Chapter 7 we explore the implications of this output of Ph.D.s for the quality of BRIC engineering education.

The differentiation between elite and mass universities was bound to have an impact at the organizational level of the two types of institutions, with administrators at many of the lower-tier institutions mainly concerned with effectively mounting undergraduate programs for increasing numbers of students and keeping costs low, whereas in the elite institutions, we observe administrators as being more concerned about improving quality, including hiring better-qualified professors more likely to produce high-quality research (see Chapter 5).

The future for expanding and improving higher education is laid out in China's "National Medium and Long-term Plan for Educational Reform and Development (2010–2020)" (hereafter known as "the 2020 Plan"). The 2020 Plan calls for increasing total college enrollments to 33 million by 2020 (about 45 percent are planned to be three-year vocational college enrollments), modestly increasing the private provision of higher education, and, overall, placing much greater emphasis on improving quality. Chinese policy makers are restricting access to universities through a secondary school policy that places almost half of secondary students in vocational high schools that mainly prepare students for the workplace. Furthermore, China's population is rapidly aging (in contrast to India's and Brazil's), and the number of college-age youths is declining rapidly, making it almost certain that the county's gross enrollment rate will reach the target of 40 percent of the age cohort (about 55 percent of those in four-year universities) by 2020. The great drop in college-age population will relieve some of the pressure on the government in the coming years to continue expanding higher education and, in principle, will allow it to focus more on quality. Yet this assumes that the mass of students channeled into vocational high schools will not demand access to higher education.

India's Provincial-Led Private Higher Education Expansion

More rapid economic growth, beginning in the 1990s, has contributed to India's higher education expansion, both in the number of institutions and the number of students enrolled (Tilak, 2008; Bhushan, Malhotra, and Gopalakrishnan, 2009). In 1985 there were fewer than 6 thousand colleges with about 4.5 million students; by 2009–2010 there were more than 32 thousand colleges with 17 million students (of which about 14 million were undergraduates). The number of universities (including institutions deemed to be universities and institutions of national importance) tripled, from about 200 to 600 (MHRD, 2011). In 2009–2010 higher education in India employed approximately 700,000 teachers (MHRD, 2011). Although all this represents massive growth in India's higher education system, the proportion of the age cohort attending higher education increased but remained relatively low, reaching about 15 percent in 2009–2010.[9] Even so, this gross enrollment rate varies greatly among states, from above 45 percent in Delhi and 35 percent in Uttarakhand to below 10 percent in Assam, Jharkhand, and Rajasthan (MHRD, 2011). This is partly related to the proportion of the population living in rural areas because estimates in 2005–2006 place the gross higher education enrollment ratio at about 7 percent in rural areas and 20 percent in urban areas (MHRD, 2010; Thorat, 2006).[10]

In 2010–2011 almost three-fifths of total students, including undergraduates, postgraduates, and diploma-level (short-degree) students were enrolled in arts and sciences, about another 17 percent in business (commerce/management) courses, about 17 percent in engineering and technical education, and 4 percent in medicine (Table 2.2). If we restrict our measures to those enrolled in undergraduate degree programs, the proportion of engineering and technical students was closer to 14–15 percent, higher than in Russia and Brazil, and, among the BRICs, only lower than in China.[11] As Table 2.2 shows, engineering/technology enrollment is rising far more rapidly than any other specialty—much more so than business—and the sheer number of those enrolled in and graduating from engineering institutions is also increasing at a high rate. In 2010–2011 there were probably about two million undergraduate

TABLE 2.2 India: Enrollment[a] by field of study, 1990–2010

Faculty	Total enrollment 1990–1991	%	Total enrollment 2001–2002	%	Total enrollment 2010–2011	%
Arts	1,789,480	40.4	4,069,632	46.1	6,177,730	36.4
Science	869,119	19.6	1,754,110	19.9	3,127,042	18.4
Commerce/management	969,882	21.9	1,575,940	17.9	2,904,752	17.1
Education	99,613	2.3	114,678	1.3	569,961	3.4
Engineering/technology	216,837	4.9	605,597	6.9	2,862,439	16.9
Medicine	150,458	3.4	275,943	3.1	652,533	3.9
Agriculture	46,908	1.1	52,833	0.6	93,166	0.6
Veterinary science	11,063	0.3	14,270	0.2	27,423	0.2
Law	234,538	5.3	280,449	3.2	327,146	1.9
Other	37,349	0.8	77,643	0.9	232,691	1.4
Total	4,425,247	100	8,821,095	100	16,974,883	100

SOURCE: University Grants Commission. Various years. *Annual Reports*, appendix tables.
[a]Enrollment includes "graduate" (undergraduate), postgraduate, and diploma level (short degrees).

students enrolled in engineering institutions, about four times the number a decade earlier. In the mid-1990s, Indian engineering colleges were producing about 50,000 four-year degree graduates annually. By 2006, this figure had risen to almost 250,000, and, based on enrollment figures from 2005, we have projected this number to be more than 400,000 graduates by 2010. Correspondingly, in fifteen years, from 1990 to 2005, the stock of first-degree graduate engineers in India more than doubled, from 500 thousand to 1.2 million. At current graduation rates, the figure today should be approaching more than 1.5 million. The number of engineering graduates per one million population is as high or higher than in many developed countries, but because only a fraction of these work as engineers, other measures of the number of engineers per million population in the mid-2000s shows India (214) as lower than China (340) and considerably lower than many countries, particularly Japan (765) and South Korea (1435) (Banerjee and Muley, 2007).

One of the most important features of the enrollment growth pattern in recent years is the rapidly increasing number of new private colleges that rely almost exclusively on tuition. They are commonly known as unaided (no financial aid from the government) or self-financing colleges, offering accredited courses in engineering, management, and medicine, as well as vocational courses preparing young people for work in the IT sector. According to the latest report of the Planning Commission (2012; Tilak 2011b), private higher education accounts for about four-fifths of enrollment in professional higher education and 60 percent overall. Banarjee and Muley estimate that 76 percent of annual student intake in engineering colleges was in private unaided institutions in 2006–2007 (2007: 69).

It is difficult to get precise information on more recent enrollment breakdowns, but we have estimated that the percentage of private institutions, student approved intake in those institutions, and actual admission increased rapidly since 2006–2007, despite the recent doubling by the central government of the number of IITs (from seven to sixteen) and the opening of many more NITs. Based on a search of individual state technical education websites, we were able to get sufficient information for nine states[12] to make a reasonable estimate of the percentage of approved student intake in 2010–2011/2011–2012.[13] We found that taking into account the expansion of intake into IITs and NITs, about 90 percent of intake was in private unaided institutions. Data for Karnataka also suggest that private unaided engineering college admissions are only about 75 percent of their approved intake places. Assuming that the admissions percentage in private unaided colleges is similar in other states, and that available places are all filled in government colleges and the IITs/NITs, we calculated that about 87 percent of engineering undergraduate enrollment in 2010–2011/2011–2012 was in private unaided institutions. These figures are all approximate, but they suggest strongly that private engineering colleges are absorbing a high proportion of the increased enrollment in engineering.

Nevertheless, the meaning of *private* in India needs to be interpreted carefully (Tilak, 1999, 2011a). For one, all private colleges must be affiliated with a public university to be accredited, and they are subject to public university controls over curriculum and the examinations that students must pass to get credit for the courses. In the Indian system, universities are distinguished from colleges in that universities as educational institutions mostly provide only graduate (generally known as postgraduate) education (some also provide limited undergraduate education), university faculty teach and do research, and universities have autonomy to organize their own curriculum for each course of study and to set their own course examinations. The more important university function is to be the affiliating body for independent member colleges. Colleges are mostly undergraduate institutions, although many also offer postgraduate degrees. In the case of engineering studies, the public universities obtain considerable oversight from national public bodies such as the All India Council of Technical Education (AICTE) in technical education, the Medical Council of Education in medical education, and the UGC in general education, all of which regulate the curricula in each field of study.

Private affiliated (aided and unaided) institutions and public colleges and universities are also subject to *central/state* government controls over their admissions and tuition policies. They must admit certain percentages of disadvantaged students by category of student. As we describe in more detail in Chapter 4, when we discuss India's higher education financing, Indian states regulate tuition for a high fraction of the students admitted by private unaided colleges, including affirmative action students and those scoring high on state government administered college entrance tests.

This complex public-private relation that governs more than 50 percent of enrollment in the higher education sector and close to 90 percent of enrollment in engineering makes it extremely difficult to define the meaning of *private* in Indian higher education. *Private* includes a high formal degree of government control over the content of the curriculum and the standards used to measure learning, hence what should take place in higher education classrooms (but not necessarily does), yet also includes the freedom for private unaided colleges to accumulate surplus and expand operations.

The rapid expansion of unaided colleges affiliated with universities is gradually transforming not only the landscape of where students choose to go to postsecondary education, particularly in certain fields, but also seems to be gradually transforming the role of public universities into regulating, degree-granting institutions and away from teaching or research (Kapur, 2010). They are also acting as a strong pressure group against giving autonomy (deemed university status) to private colleges. At the same time, it is difficult to imagine that universities and state and federal agencies (AICTE) are able to keep track of this mass of self-sustaining institutions and their academic operations.

In the words of one analyst, "These private institutions are helping to meet the growing demand that the public sector cannot. Private institutions are less subject to political instabilities and day-to-day political pressures that often bedevil public institutions in developing countries. They are also more nimble and able to respond to changes in demands from employers and labor markets. Yet despite these positives, these institutions are of highly variable—and often dubious—quality" (Kapur, 2010: 6). They are also subject to pressures from their management bodies, which may be governed more by economic or political considerations than educational ones.

Factors that make it possible for fee-based colleges to be the main vehicle of enrollment growth in India are the limited supply of undergraduate places in public and private aided colleges, the low fraction of college-age youths in higher education, and the relatively high social class of students currently in the market for college places. These students' parents are willing and able to pay tuition fees, in some cases very high tuition fees, for their children to get a college education. In our survey of final-year students in four-year engineering colleges, we found that 80 percent of students' fathers and 60 percent of students' mothers in the sample had college education. In India, this is an extremely high socioeconomic group. A second condition is that the government fixes tuition for students from disadvantaged castes at a relatively low level. We show later in the study that another condition favorable to the growth of private education is a high rate of earnings payoff for a college education, and it is especially high for graduates in technical fields.

How robust these conditions are as the higher education system expands to incorporate increasing numbers of Indian youths is a major question. The answer will clearly affect the strategy for expansion. As we show for Brazil, which has a larger fraction of college-age youths in college, the private higher education sector faces increasing excess capacity as it fails to incorporate lower socioeconomic background students. Similarly to India, the private sector is of lower quality than the public system and of particularly low quality for students who do not qualify for low-tuition places and cannot afford to pay high fees.

Brazil's Dual Higher Educational System

We noted that Brazil's higher education system is the product of a postcolonial history deeply rooted in primary-good export production and the generally limited expansion of the education system. In the 1970s and 1980s, for example, gross enrollment in higher education was a low 5–12 percent of the age cohort.

This limited access to higher education in Brazil meant that the average social class of students enrolled was very high. By the 1980s, with the gradual decline of elite public higher secondary schools, three of every five public university students had attended private secondary schools. Their families could afford the high tuition fees in private secondary education to increase the chances of gaining access to free public higher education.

As in China and India, then, Brazil's major higher educational expansion came late, in the 1990s. The proportion of Brazilian students attending private higher education has been high for many decades (it reached 60 percent in the 1970s), but the expansion after 1997, unlike enrollment growth in 1980–1995, was almost entirely absorbed by private institutions. Enrollment in the higher education system as a whole increased from 1.8 million students in 1995, of whom 1.1 million were in private institutions, to 2.7 million students in 2000, of whom 1.8 million were in private institutions, to 5.4 million students in 2010, of whom 4.0 million were in private institutions. Between 1997 and 2010, the proportion of higher education students in public universities, centers, and other types of institutions declined from more than 39 percent to 28 percent. Among institutions designated as universities, attended in the past thirty years by somewhat more than one-half of higher education students, the increase in private enrollment has been steadier, rising from 38 percent to 58 percent in 1980–2010. Yet even in this category, the increase accelerated in the years after 1996. Figure 2.2 shows this pattern of enrollment expansion.

Thus, Brazil's higher education system is very different from the other BRICs in three important features: first, public universities have traditionally been essentially free (similarly to the other BRICs in the 1980s) and continue to be free of tuition (among the other BRICs, this is true only in the declining proportion of "free" places in Russian universities). Second, a high fraction

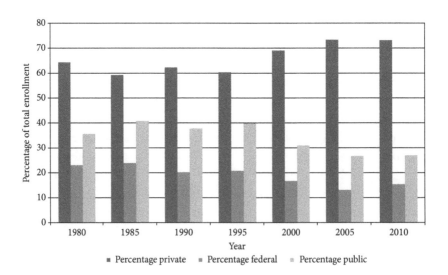

FIGURE 2.2 Brazil: Proportion of higher education enrollment in public, private, and public federal institutions, 1980–2010 (percentage)

SOURCE: INEP. Various years. *Sinopse Estadistico da Educacão Superior.* Brasilia: INEP.

of university and other postsecondary students attend private institutions, where they pay tuition to cover much, if not all, of the costs of running those institutions. Third, a number of those private institutions are religious-based, almost all Catholic. These are partly subsidized by religious organizations and have nonprofit status, but they still charge tuition—many of them relatively high tuition.

This presents an interesting paradox. Because the (public) federal universities and many of the state universities are among the most prestigious in the country and students who are admitted pay no tuition, most of the "best" students (as in the other BRIC countries) try to enter programs of study at public universities, particularly federal universities. There are also prestigious private universities, so students who score high on the end of secondary school examination may also attend such private institutions. As everywhere, those who score high on the secondary school test are also likely to come from higher social class families and, in addition, from private secondary schools. Moreover, as we will show in Chapter 4, public, particularly federal, universities spend much more per student, on average, than most private universities. Therefore, the public sector invests far more, on average, in the higher education of children of wealthier families than of the poor.

And like India and Russia, Brazil uses entrance examinations for secondary school graduates to allocate free (or in India, lower tuition) places in the best public universities. In Brazil these exams are not universal, although this is changing, with the federal government pushing for the use of a single federal entrance examination, called the ENEM. Almost all federal and most state universities have their own examinations, as do many private institutions (some have shifted to the ENEM). These individual university entrance examinations are all classified under the generic name *vestibular*, or entrance test. As in the other three BRICs, there is wide variation in the number of applicants per available place by type of university and program of study. The most demanded programs of study in Brazil are medicine, health/pharmacy, and applied social sciences. In 2001 there were almost 40 applicants per place in federal and state institutions in medicine, 19 in health/pharmacy, and 15 in applied social sciences (Schwartzman, 2004, Table II). Engineering and computer science was fourth, with about 12 applicants per place in public universities. Even in private institutions, the demand for medicine was high, with 12 applicants per available place. However, this was not true of other programs of study in private institutions, where in 2001, only 1.8 students applied for every place, compared to almost 10 applicants for every place in public institutions (Schwartzman, 2004, Table II; also Table 2.3 here).

With the enormous expansion of private higher education and the moderate expansion of public institutions after 1997, we would expect that the ratio of applicants to places would fall in the private sector and less so in the public. That is indeed the case. Table 2.3 shows that the ratio of applicants to available places fell sharply in private institutions and less in public universities. However, that is only part of the story. Whereas in public institutions, very few places go unfilled, private higher education has a growing overcapacity. By 2004, about one-half the available places went unfilled, up from 22 percent in 1997, although this proportion has not increased since 2004 (Table 2.3). Therefore, students appear to apply in large numbers to private institutions, most as a hedge against not being admitted to a public university, but a significant fraction of those admitted to private universities (essentially everyone who applies) do not attend even if they are not admitted to a federal or state university. Certainly, tuition costs act as a barrier for many. On the other hand, almost everyone who is admitted to a federal or state university apparently accepts admission. That said, the number of new entrants to private universities increases every year. The interesting question is why the private sector has created so many new higher education places when they are not being filled.

Engineering and computer science students are an increasing percentage of Brazilian undergraduates. Engineering enrollment increased in the past ten years from 180,000 students in 1999 to 546,000 in 2010, rising from 7.5 percent of the total in 1999 to 10 percent in 2010. If we add in computer science majors, the percentage has increased from 9.4 percent to 11.9 percent (INEP, *Sinopse,* various years). Engineering students are also more likely to be enrolled in public universities than the entirety of the Brazilian student body, although this is gradually changing. The percentage of engineering students in private institutions is increasing more rapidly than the overall percentage. In 1999 less than 49 percent of engineering students enrolled were in private institutions, but by 2010 this figure had risen to 62 percent. In the same period, the percentage of all higher education students enrolled in private institutions increased from 65 percent to 73 percent.

Table 2.4 shows the evolution of engineering and computer science *graduates* over this same period of time. Whereas engineering enrollment represented 6.5 percent of total enrollment in 2004, engineering graduates represented only 6.1 percent of total graduates from Brazilian higher education institutions in 2010, six years later. This suggests that engineering students graduate at a somewhat lower rate than students studying in other programs.

TABLE 2.3 Brazil: Ratios of applications and unfilled places to available places, by type of institution, 1994–2010

Year/type of institution	Number of applicants (thousands)	Available places (thousands)	Applicants/ available place	Enrolled (thousands)	Unfilled places (thousands)	Unfilled/ available places (percentage)
1994						
Federal	683	85	8.0	76.3	8.7	10.2
State	523.8	58.5	9.0	55	3.5	6.0
Municipal	85.6	33.9	2.5	28.7	5.2	15.3
Private	944.6	396.9	2.4	303.4	93.5	23.6
1997						
Federal	752.4	88.7	8.5	86.4	2.3	2.6
State	577.7	64.3	9.0	60.5	3.8	5.9
Municipal	95.7	40.8	2.3	34.9	5.9	14.5
Private	1,290	505.4	2.6	392	113.4	22.4
2001						
Federal	1,198.2	123.5	9.7	121.2	2.3	1.9
State	962.6	101.8	9.5	97.1	4.7	4.6
Municipal	63.3	31.2	2.0	26.3	4.9	15.7
Private	2,036.1	1,152	1.8	792.1	359.9	31.2
2004						
Federal	1,287.6	124.0	10.4	122.9	1.1	0.9
State	1,058.9	131.7	8.0	125.4	6.3	4.8
Municipal	84.9	52.8	1.6	38.9	13.9	26.3
Private	2,622.6	2,011.9	1.3	1,015.9	996	49.5
2010[a]						
Federal	2,252.5	248.5	9.1	269.2	−20.7	—
State	1,041.4	138.3	7.5	134.9	3.4	2.4
Municipal	70.9	58.5	1.2	31.6	26.9	46.0
Private	3,334.1	2,674.9	1.2	1,366.2	1,308.7	48.9

SOURCES: Ministerio da Educação, INEP, Diretoria de Estatísticas e Avaliação da Educação Superior (2005). *Censo da Educação Superior 2004, Resumo Técnico.* Brasilia: author, Tabelas 28, 41, 54. Ministerio da Educação, INEP, Diretoria de Estatísticas e Avaliação da Educação Superior (2010). *Sinopse Educação Superior, 2010.* Brasilia: author, Tables 4.1 and 4.3.

[a]The 2010 data for number of applicants and available places refer to those subject to selection process through the *vestibular* or other examination; enrollment data refer to total enrollment, whether by selection or other processes.

TABLE 2.4 Brazil: Higher education engineering and computer science graduates, 1999–2010

	Number of graduates (thousands)			Percentage in private institutions		
Year	Total higher education	Engineering programs	Computer science	Total higher education	Engineering programs	Computer science
1999	324.7	18.7	6.3	65.4	44.9	68.3
2003	528.2	24.8	10.7	68.0	47.6	73.8
2005	717.9	30.5	15.6	72.7	58.4	78.8
2007	756.8	40.3	14.0	74.4	56.6	77.1
2010	829.3	50.7	14.3	78.5	62.3	81.1

SOURCE: INEP, *Sinopse Educacão Superior,* 1999, 2003, 2005, 2007, 2010, Table 6.2.

The data also show that Brazil graduated only 51,000 engineers in 2010 and another 14,000 computer scientists. As a proportion of the population, this is less than India (assuming India graduated more than 300,000 engineers in 2009) and much less than China or Russia, but as much proportionately as the United States.

Another important issue is who attends public and private higher education institutions. As Schwartzman (2004) noted, the assumption was that the much more selective federal and state universities would enroll a much higher social class student able to take advantage of cultural capital and investing in better secondary schools. Meanwhile, private institutions would enroll those lower social class students who could not gain access to free public higher education. This assumption turns out not to be correct, in part because the proportion of youths eighteen to twenty-four years old who attend higher education in Brazil was still very low in the first decade of the 2000s.[14] According to Schwartzman, in 2002, 48 percent of students in private institutions came from families whose earnings were in the top 10 percent of household incomes, whereas only 35 percent of students attending public institutions came from such rich families. Less than 4 percent of students in private institutions came from families in the bottom 40 percent of income earners, whereas almost 8 percent of students in public institutions (still not a high percentage) came from that low-income segment. Eckert Baeta Neves (2009) made similar estimates for 2007 and found that 34 percent of the students enrolled in private institutions came from families in the top decile of income earned compared to 30 percent of those enrolled in public institutions. About 8 percent of students in private institutions came from families in the bottom 40 percent of income earners, and about 13 percent of students in public institutions came from families in that socioeconomic group. Thus, the proportion of students attending university from the lowest-income families has increased somewhat with the great expansion, approximately from 3 percent to 8 percent in private institutions from the bottom 40 percent of income earners and an increase from 7 percent to 13 percent in public institutions from that group. Yet the main point still holds true: students attending private higher education institutions are somewhat more likely to come from families with high income than students attending public institutions. This is the opposite of what we would have expected, given the higher academic requirements for getting into public institutions.

Two efforts are under way to increase access by lower-income students to university. The first, conducted by individual universities, each in its own way, is affirmative action for students of color of low income who, in some university programs, attended public secondary school. The second is a recent program to subsidize low-income students' tuition in private universities that agree to participate in the program. Given the high excess capacity in many private institutions, this is a profitable way to fill seats and do good at the same time, provided that the federal government, under whose purview private institutions fall, can effectively monitor them so that they provide good academic training for the subsidized affirmative action students. We discuss these programs in more detail later in the study.

In the early 1990s, Castells and Carnoy identified the shift from the "political" and elite formation roles of Latin American universities to a more "scientific-technical" objective as a key reform for future success (Castells, 1991; Carnoy, 1993). This was the result of the expansion and differentiation of Latin American higher education. Brazil was just beginning its major enrollment expansion by significantly increasing private higher education. The system had moved to a more "meritocratic" selection process, relying more on examinations, and was about to increase greatly the number of places available, albeit in private, tuition-based institutions. Competition was already fierce to get into the better institutions and into the more "desirable" and "technical-scientific" programs, such as medicine, pharmacy, business (applied social science), and engineering, and it was increasingly possible to do those programs in private institutions. The transformation of the Brazilian system from the highly politicized universities of the 1950s and 1960s was fairly complete, even though, as we have seen, they remain mainly accessible to youths from families that earn high incomes. The probability of an eighteen-year-old from a family in the bottom 40 percent of the income distribution to have attended a university in 2007 was less than 3 percent.

In addition to the *vestibular,* Brazil introduced testing in the final year of university programs in the late 1990s. The Cardoso government feared that many private universities absorbing the vast majority of new students coming into the system were of low quality. Of the 30 universities with the largest enrollment in 2008, 19 were private—the 5 biggest, with a total of almost 500,000 students, were private (Ministry of Education, INEP, 2009, Table 1.2). Government regulation of Brazilian private universities is minimal, so the concern that secondary students refused entrance to public universities may be paying for poor-quality higher education is real. The *Provão,* as the test was called, was replaced in the early 2000s by the ENADE in response to criticism that universities took students of greatly varying initial scores, so they were unfairly gauged by a final test. The ENADE tested students at the end of the first year of their course work and in the penultimate year. Not all programs are tested every year, but it is possible to have a good idea from the ENADE of program quality, and the federal and state universities are much more likely to be at the top of the ratings even when value added is the measure. We discuss such measures of program quality later in the study, but it is worth mentioning here that, for example, in 2008, of the top-scoring 300 computer science departments on the ENADE test (of 653 that took the second specific competencies test), 215 were private programs, 48 were federal, 30 were state, and 7 were municipal. Of the bottom scoring 353 programs, 321 were private, 20, municipal, 8, state, and only 3 federal. Although this is not a value-added evaluation, it does suggest the hierarchy of programs, and a large number of otherwise unregulated private programs are characterized by low end-of-course scores.

One interesting aspect of the Brazilian government effort to monitor programs through testing is that it is a continuation of the rationalization and differentiation of the higher education system. Another is that its purpose is mainly to inform the public of program ranking based on aggregate student final scores rather than direct monitoring of programs, quality of teachers, dropout rates, or other criteria that might be much more relevant to overall quality than a final score on a test, which could be largely a function of incoming scores. Peer effects are important to students, and probably the most important to most Brazilians in choosing among programs (other than tuition cost), but just knowing the *vestibular* score of entering students would serve to know what academic level of students attend each program.

The ENADE data could be used to approximate value added in each program, taking into account dropouts and other factors, but this has not been done to date. Thus, its main impact, if any, is to send a signal to private institutions that they are being monitored.

In Chapter 4 we go into more detail about how the financing of the education system in Brazil is even more unequal than the enrollment data suggest. We also discuss attempts by public universities and the Brazilian government to promote increased access to higher education for youths from lower-income groups.

Russia's Post-Soviet Move Toward Universal Higher Education

Because Leninism and Stalinism controlled intellectual discussion through the Communist Party apparatus, universities became largely centers of high-level technical training, where specific technical knowledge was privileged. In the industrial model of the time—"Fordism," in Antonio Gramsci's terminology (1971)—the Soviets considered that the educational system should produce young people for particular, technically well-defined jobs in state-run and state-prioritized industries, even to the extent of linking technical universities directly to those industries (many of these technical universities still exist, even though the industries themselves are in severe decline or barely exist).

As the command economy went into economic and political crisis in the late 1980s and early 1990s, funding for higher education declined by about 40 percent, and so did enrollment, by about 10 percent. Beginning in 1995, however, funding and enrollment recovered, and Russia witnessed an enormous increase over the next twelve years in the number of students seeking degrees. In public institutions, enrollment more than doubled, and combined public and private institutions increased by 2.8 times. By 2008, Russia had one of the world's highest percentages of young people enrolled in higher education (see Table 2.1, showing the number per hundred thousand population).

With its already high proportion of the age group attending postsecondary institutions, there was no radical transformation of public higher education itself. The Russian government continued to allocate government-paid places to universities for different fields of study, by university and by field, based largely on historical numbers. This practice has maintained demand for "traditional" fields of study because students apply for free places by field. As in the past, these places were allocated to the highest-scoring students on entrance exams (as India allocates low-tuition places). Until recently, each university administered its own entrance examination, so students applying to multiple universities had to take multiple examinations. This was part of the attempt to maintain the "meritocratic" allocation of students to various universities, but it promoted considerable corruption, with teachers from each university ready and willing to prepare students for that university department's exam. In 2001 the federal government initiated, and in 2009 fully implemented, a national examination in each subject that all applicants would take, but certain universities could also supplement the national exam with a university test. This national examination has yielded interesting results in terms of the average entering test scores by department and university (see Chapter 6).

The Yeltsin government did make an important change financially that opened the door to the great expansion in the early 1990s by introducing private cost sharing (tuition) for "excess demand" over and above the free places. Tuition-based financing had a particularly large effect on highly demanded fields of study such as economics and business, and, as Figure 2.3 shows, by 2006, almost one in two students in Russian government institutions was paying tuition. This has continued to increase, and the figure stood at 55 percent in 2010. Most universities moved to expand enrollment in fields that would draw tuition-paying students because that was money the universities controlled. Many public universities established branches in different regions and even in small towns. Often, up to 90 percent of student places in these branches were tuition-based.

Along with the introduction of a large number of small private institutions (as in China) to handle the "overflow of the overflow" of tuition-paying students in public universities, cost sharing and private education helped to finance the rapid increase in enrollment after 1990, especially after 1998, when economic growth recovered. Of the 7.5 million students in Russian higher education in 2007 (including a small percentage in distance education), more than 60 percent were either paying tuition in public institutions (44 percent) or were attending a private institution (17 percent). If we assume that enrollment in private institutions increased somewhat to 1.3 million by 2010, the proportion rose to 63 percent paying tuition.

In 1990 Russia already had considerable enrollment in engineering education at the undergraduate level. Although this has declined in percentage

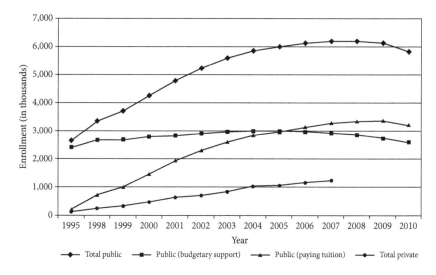

FIGURE 2.3 Russia: Higher education enrollment in public institutions, fully subsidized places and fee paying, 1995–2010 (in thousands)

SOURCE: Federal Service for Government Statistics. 2011. *Russian Statistical Yearbook.* www.gks.ru/bgd/regl/b11_13/IssWWW.exe/Stg/d2/07-56.htm (accessed Aug. 3, 2012).

terms, in the 2000s about 13–14 percent of higher education students (including polytechnic education) graduated in the field of engineering and engineering-related technical specialties. This means that probably about 150,000 young Russians graduate annually with some kind of specialist engineering or computer science degree (see Figure 2.4). This is less than India and China, but relative to its population, Russia produces more engineering graduates than either of those BRICs and far more than Brazil. In 2010 Russia graduated 37,000 "specialists" (five-year degree) in electronics and informatics, far less than India or China, but almost as many as the total of all engineering graduates in Brazil.

Not only is Russia unique among the BRICs in its early expansion of higher education; it is unusual among all the world's countries in another way: it has reached such a high level of incorporating youths into postsecondary institutions that for the next ten years or so a more general slowdown of population growth (common to many European countries) is resulting in an absolute decline in youths seeking to enter higher education. This, combined with the economic recession of 2008–2009, has major implications for higher educational reform, which we discuss in Chapters 4 and 5.

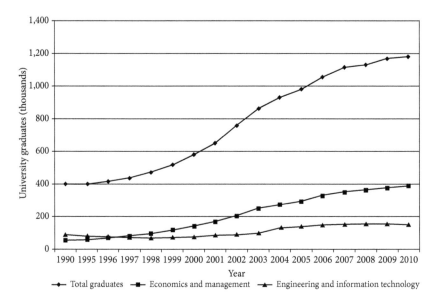

FIGURE 2.4 Russia: Specialist graduates from public Russian higher education universities, economics & management and technical fields, 1990–2010 (in thousands)

SOURCE: Federal Service for Government Statistics. 2011. *Russian Statistical Yearbook.* www.gks.ru/bgd/regl/b11_13/IssWWW.exe/Stg/d2/07-56.htm (accessed Aug. 3, 2012).

Summing Up the Great Expansion

In the last decade of the twentieth century, four of the world's most populous countries began to expand their higher education systems significantly. Three of these countries—China, Brazil, and India—had small proportions of their college-age youths in university as late as in the mid-1990s. However, this situation changed rapidly in Brazil and China, and, even with relatively smaller proportional change (although this seems to be speeding up in the past few years), the very size of India's population made its higher education expansion huge in terms of absolute numbers of students and graduates. The fourth country, Russia, already had large numbers of students attending universities, thanks to fifty years of communist ideology emphasizing high-level technical education to support Soviet industrial and military development.

The characteristics of these new expansions were different from the way university systems increased enrollment in the past. Unlike the United States, Europe, and even Russia earlier in the twentieth century, *all four BRIC countries relied heavily on direct tuition payments by families to bring in large numbers of new students into higher education institutions.* Russia and China emphasized cost sharing in public institutions as well as allowing private institutions to handle "overflow," whereas India and Brazil promoted the expansion of private universities and colleges charging students tuition to cover costs—in Brazil, this has been carried to the point were only about one-fourth of students attend public institutions. In effect, the fully subsidized public universities that still dominate European education and, until the 1970s were the norm in the United States, still exist in Russia and Brazil, but they serve only a minority of students.

Another feature of the new expansions is the *highly competitive allocation of students to higher-cost institutions through state- and public university-run examination systems*—a continuation and amplification of the "meritocracy" movement of the 1940s in the United States, with all its defects. At the same time, all these systems provide for the possibility that practically all students who complete secondary school can go on to some form of higher education if they are able and willing to pay. Thus, in the three countries (Brazil, China, and India) where there is still relatively limited access to "good" public universities, the social class background of students who attend private universities and colleges is higher than for students who attend public universities and colleges despite the greater difficulty of gaining access to much lower tuition public institutions. Although the social class background of students in the good public universities is also very high in these countries, increased numbers of lower social class students are entering higher education, and this is particularly true in public higher education institutions.

As we shall show in Chapter 4, this results in an interesting pattern of subsidies to more academically talented, higher social class students, at the same time as less academically able higher social class students have to pay rather high fees to attend generally less good private institutions. In any case, access to universities for lower social class students to higher education is limited except in Russia, with its extremely high proportion of students in the postsecondary system and in India, where lower-caste students are afforded entrance to colleges under a broad affirmative action program. Brazil's affirmative action programs in public universities and government incentive programs to admit more low-income and black students to private universities are also beginning to have an effect on student social class composition.

Another major difference between China and Russia/India/Brazil is the relative enrollment in technical education. Engineering students represent about 32 percent of all undergraduate students in China, and the percentage is higher in elite versus nonelite universities. More than 40 percent of Chinese Ph.D. students study in some engineering field. Given the huge numbers of university students in China, the number of engineering and computer science graduates that the system produces is also very large—in 2009, more than 700,000 graduates annually and more than 15,000 engineering Ph.D.s annually (NBS, 2010; NSF, 2010). In Russia, enrollment in technical higher education has been growing less rapidly than overall enrollment (economics/business administration is the fastest-growing field of study), but students in technical fields still represent about one in seven higher education students. This enrollment is disproportionately (compared to total enrollment) filled under the Russian government's quota of tuition-free places. Thus, unlike China (and India and Brazil), engineering is not a field that is increasingly sought by incoming students. As we will show, this is somewhat paradoxical because, in addition to economics/business, the payoff for engineering education remains high in the Russian labor market.

China has a high percentage of students enrolled in engineering courses, but the figure is not increasing; in contrast, the growing demand for engineers in India and Brazil's labor markets is having a major effect on enrollment rates in engineering, particularly in India, where in 2010, about 17 percent of undergraduates entered engineering/technical education, more than double the proportion ten years earlier, and Brazil, where the percentage is increasing more slowly, is still the lowest among the BRICs, but up to 11 percent in 2010, likely to surpass Russia in the next five years.

Although Chinese universities charge students tuition to become engineers and Russia mainly does not, in both countries engineering students are heavily subsidized in their studies. This is much less true in Brazil, where more than 60 percent of engineering students are in private institutions paying full tuition (still, this is less than the more than 73 percent of all undergraduate students who attend private institutions) and 35+ percent are fully subsidized in public universities. India is the extreme case: more than 90 percent of engineering students enroll in private institutions. Although many of them are subsidized by government controls on the amount of tuition they pay, the subsidies are far lower than in Russia and China.

The variety of strategies represented in the BRICs both to meet the large and growing demand by young people for more education and to train a twenty-first-century workforce provides us with a rich source of understanding states' approaches to high-value public services in the current economic and political environment. We now turn to analyzing the details of how these emerging economies finance higher education, why they pursue the strategies they do, and who ends up paying and benefiting from expanding access to the system. This will tell us a lot about the nature of these societies and even more about how each state views its role in economic and social development.

3 Economic Returns to Investing in Higher Education and Their Impact in the BRIC Countries

A MAIN REASON THAT INDIVIDUALS AND GOVERNMENTS invest in education is that they believe it has an economic payoff. This is not the only reason for investing, but it is an important one. Families take economic costs and benefits seriously in deciding how much and what kind of education to buy for their children. Because education is expensive, if it has economic value, that helps justify the resources families and societies spend on it. When higher education is publicly funded, so the cost to families is less of a barrier to entry, more students choose to attend school. When the payoff is low for education—especially for higher education—there is less interest in attending university and less urgency to complete university studies. In some economically advanced countries such as Italy, even though higher education is essentially tuition free, the proportion of young people graduating from universities is surprisingly low. One explanation is that the average payoff for a degree is also low (Boarini and Strauss, 2010). Italian university graduates earn more than those with secondary schooling, but apparently not enough to draw a high fraction of youths into further study and to complete their studies. As we shall show, because of conscious wage compression by communist states, relatively lower demand for higher education also characterized Russia in the two decades before the collapse of communism.[1]

In this chapter we make the case that in the first decade of the 2000s, the private and social payoffs for higher education in the BRICs were relatively high and rising relative to payoffs for investing in secondary education, particularly for study in technical fields, and that these relatively high payoffs help explain both why BRIC governments expanded enrollment so rapidly and why they have been able to shift the cost of higher education to families through "user taxes" (tuition fees).

We also show that where rates of return are highest or rising most rapidly—in Brazil, in China, in India's technical fields of study, and in Russia's business and economic degrees—the greatest pressure exists for expanding higher education, and the greatest fraction of higher education costs is paid by "taxing" families directly with tuition payments. Since, as we argued earlier, we are particularly interested in the expansion of engineering and computer science education because of the role that these graduates play in the high-value high-tech economy, we estimate the relative payoff for engineering as a profession compared to the average of all university graduates. Again, it turns out that in all four countries, engineering graduates do very well compared to almost everybody else. In India there seems to be more pressure on the higher education system to maintain or expand engineering (and computer science) education than many other programs of study except business and economics (where perceived returns may be even higher). This is not evident in Brazil, China, and Russia despite high returns. We will attempt to explain this apparent contradiction. Doing so helps us gain insights into how societies and their labor markets differ and how these differences affect how much and how the state finances the higher education system.

Are States Driven to Invest in Higher Education Because of High Returns?

The case that governments invest in educational expansion because they are responding to economic payoffs is rather circuitous. For many decades now, based on only somewhat convincing data (for example, Psacharopoulos and Patrinos, 2004), international agencies and the media have inundated us with arguments that because education contributes to economic growth, it is important for governments to expand access to education. More recently, with the flood of international test score data, the same agencies and media that argued for greater access have begun pushing for improving the *quality* of *each year* of education to increase economic growth (UNESCO, 2005).

Whether or not there is a direct relation between a more educated labor force and higher economic growth, do governments actually respond to such arguments, as our model in Chapter 1 (Figure 1.1) suggests? Have BRIC states expanded their higher educational systems in the past twenty years because they thought the economic payoffs for higher education were high? We try to make the case in this chapter that the answer to this question is probably yes, but in an indirect fashion. If the payoff for individuals investing in education is high—an indicator that a more educated labor force does have higher productivity—there will be political pressure on governments to provide greater access to educational services, and at ever higher levels of schooling.

Democratically elected governments, such as Brazil's and India's, can avoid giving in to such pressures, but at the peril of their political legitimacy. One of the problems for democratic governments regarding educational investments is that the payoff in the form of added growth is long term, much longer than particular regimes stay in power. Even so, political pressures from populations seeking to improve their children's economic opportunities are probably a main mechanism through which capitalist democratic governments decide to expand access to education.

Two of the BRIC countries we study—China and Russia—have had communist governments that emphasized educating their populations as part and parcel of their economic development goals. Those governments believed they would promote economic growth through more educated labor and that they would stay in power long enough to get the political benefits of this higher growth (Carnoy and Samoff, 1989).

Before the 1990s in China and Russia, it was top-down government policy that drove investment in education, and government investment in education was driven directly by the government's political development goals. Ultimately, however, as economic growth became important to the legitimacy of the authoritarian state, it smoothly adjusted its strategies (China) or went through a major transition (Russia). By the 1990s, policy makers in both countries felt pressure to deliver on longer-term economic goals through expanding higher education. Because such authoritarian states have longer-term political horizons, they can seek legitimacy through longer-gestation investments in growth such as education. This is the case even when they have (highly state influenced) market economies.

Thus, in modeling why the state expands access to university and may want to improve university "quality," an important factor is the payoff for higher education. A high *private* payoff—higher earnings compared to private costs—to higher education motivates individuals to invest in higher education and puts political pressure on the state to provide more access to higher education in order to maintain its political legitimacy, and a high *social* payoff—higher earnings of individuals plus any "externalities" accruing to society as a whole compared to private plus public costs—to higher education motivates the state to invest more public resources in higher education to increase economic growth—the longer the political horizon of the state, the more motivated it is to invest in higher education on these grounds.

High Payoffs and Higher Educational Finance

The case for why high private payoffs enable governments to shift the costs of higher education to students and their families is more straightforward. When the private payoff for higher education is high and possibly high and rising, it is relatively easy to convince much of the population to pay at least part of the cost of college or university. In contrast to the relatively low private payoff for university in many European countries (see Boarini and Strauss, 2010), we show below that the payoff overall for higher education in Brazil and China is very high, and in India and Russia it is high for those who study in certain programs—say, business, economics, and engineering. In Brazil, almost 75 percent of all higher education students pay tuition to private institutions, and in China, 100 percent of students pay tuition either in public or private universities. It would be hard for either the Brazilian or Chinese governments to make families finance so much of the expansion of the higher education system unless the payoffs were high enough to make families feel that they were getting a reasonable return on their investment. In India and Russia, it is precisely for those programs of study with high payoffs that demand for tuition places is greatest and where tuition-paying enrollment has been greatest. Again, if the private economic returns for those tuition payments were not relatively high, the Indian and Russian governments would have had difficulty financing higher education expansion with user taxes.

Rates of Return to Education

Before analyzing the changing economic payoffs for higher education in the BRICs, we should explain how these payoffs are defined and some of the pitfalls inherent in estimating how much economic value higher education really has for individuals and for the larger society.

From the individual's standpoint, the payoff for taking additional education is measured by the higher income (net of income taxes) the individual earns because he or she has completed that extra schooling, plus the consumption benefits that more education provides over a person's life, such as greater enjoyment of cultural activities or higher social status, plus the direct consumption benefits that come from just being in an educational setting and enjoying the learning process itself. Sometimes, being in school or university is not very pleasurable, particularly for those who are not very academically successful, so the direct consumption effects can be negative. This can be an important reason that people drop out of school.

Private costs of education include the income forgone by students while they attend school or other educational activities; the additional expenditures associated with taking education, such as uniforms, books, transportation, and fees; and possibly the negative consumption effect of sitting in classes, as we mentioned above. Because costs occur early in the stream of costs and benefits, costs have a much greater weight in the educational investment decision process. The problem is that private costs, such as income foregone and the extra spending by students and their families to attend school or university—which play such an important role in the educational investment decision process—can be more difficult to measure than private benefits.

From society's point of view, the benefits of additional education are the private benefits plus the "externalities" of having a more educated labor force and population. "Externalities" are those benefits that accrue to the entire population and are not captured by those who take additional education. These can be more civilized collective behavior, a more productive work environment, scientific innovation with widespread general benefits, a wiser choice of political leadership, a better use of natural resources, and a healthier population. In some models of economic growth, more-educated workers increase the productivity of all workers. The social costs of additional education are estimated by adding public spending on education to private costs.

Because all these costs and benefits are spread over a long period of time, we need a measure that takes into account the preference that we have for the present over the future. The most common measure used by economists of the value of education that includes the time factor is the rate of return. The rate of return is equivalent to the interest paid on savings or the rate of return from investing in a stock, real estate, or any other form of investment that has a payoff over an extended period.

Estimating rates of return to education is not easy. The differences in earnings we observe for workers with, say, college degrees compared to earnings of workers who have completed secondary schooling are not just the result of more education. Those who finish college or a more selective university might be more productive even if they had not taken more education or had gone to the less selective university because they might be more adept at learning the skills necessary for higher-productivity jobs with or without additional (or more prestigious) education (Dale and Krueger, 2002). Attributing all the higher earnings only to the skills that students picked up in college would overestimate the value of going to college for anyone who is not as quick a learner as those we observe who have already completed college. Similarly, if students' social advantages (for example, higher family income or wealth) are important in college completion, higher social class students who are not so academically able may end up with degrees while academically able lower social class students may not. In that case, the additional income associated with a college degree might reflect the value of social background more than ability, but the rate of return for college education itself would still be overestimated. Families may know this because less academically able and lower social class students are less likely to invest in a college education than are the more able and higher social class students. Even so, if the private rates of return for investing in higher education as measured by income differences are high, more young people will want to attend university than if the rates are low.

We also need to make separate estimates of the rate of return to higher education for women and minority groups if we think that they face different labor market conditions from majority-group males. Women and minority groups may be discriminated against, so their earnings may not represent their "true" economic productivity. We can learn a great deal about, say, men and women's behavior in taking more education by understanding how the payoffs for their educational investments differ.

Usually, because externalities are difficult to measure, the social rate of return is estimated by using the same average earnings streams as in the private rate estimates but then adding income taxes back in. Such approximations of social benefits are problematic. Earnings differences do not necessarily equal productivity differences, especially when a high percentage of those with certain levels of education, such as university, work in the public sector or in oligopolized sectors of private industry and services. From a private individual's standpoint, it makes little difference what the additional earnings represent because private investment decisions are based on expected returns. Yet for society, the reason behind higher incomes makes a difference in assessing whether to invest in more education or not.

Economists have wrestled with these issues for the past fifty years, and they have made much progress. Their general conclusion is that despite the mix of the effects of schooling, student ability, and student social class in earnings differentials associated with more schooling, schooling itself does affect earnings (Ashenfelter and Krueger, 1994; Ashenfelter and Rouse, 1998; Card, 2000; Angrist and Krueger, 2001). Further, rates of return to education as measured by earnings differences appear to be consistent with the contribution that a more educated labor force makes to economic growth—that is, earnings differences represent, to some degree, productivity differences (Krueger and Lindahl, 2001).

Factors Influencing Changes in the Rates of Return

In the pages that follow, we review how the rates of return for higher education in the BRIC countries have behaved in the recent past, what those estimated rates imply for the economic value of higher education, and how the expansion of higher education in each country may be related to the rate of return. All this will help us understand how families and governments are viewing investment in universities.

We show that in the past thirty years in the BRIC countries, the rates of return for higher education have risen. This has occurred in part because of rapid economic changes in all four countries, including their incorporation into the global economy, and, in Russia and China, the transformation from command to increasingly market economies.

Economic growth from the mid-1990s to 2010—the period in which the BRICs' higher education made its great leap—was rapid. China and India's growth rates were the most rapid, Brazil's were the lowest in per capita terms, and Russia recovered from a major decline in the early 1990s as the country shifted radically to a market economy. We argue below that these features of economic growth, as well as the past pattern of educational expansion, had an important influence on the payoffs for higher education graduates and therefore on the rapidity with which BRIC university enrollment increased.

Each of the four BRIC countries also developed economically in an initially different but similarly changing demographic context. Demography not only has important implications for economic growth but also for the challenge of incorporating the young population into secondary and higher education. Demography also has implications for the relative payoffs for higher education. In all but India, the young population (0–14 years old) is declining, and in Russia and China, the decline is very rapid—a 38 percent decrease in Russia since 1990 and, in China, 21 percent. Even Brazil has had a 7 percent decrease in its young population. Only India has had an increase in the number of young people since 1990 (12 percent), but this is about to change—since 2000, the growth had slowed to 2 percent for the entire decade. If, as in China and Russia, young populations decline and even if economic growth rates slow somewhat, rates of return for university education could remain high because of lower relative increases in the supply of educated labor.

Especially in Russia and China, income distribution, tightly controlled and equalized under communist governments, has become much more unequal, with university graduates benefiting more from greater inequality than less educated groups because it is the higher incomes (associated with higher education) that have risen the most, at least in relative terms.[2] This also appears to be the case in India. Of the three countries, there are some initial signs that inequality is beginning to taper off in China because of a number of demographic, political, and labor market factors, including increased government investments in less developed and rural areas (OECD, 2010a). Brazil's income inequality seems to be declining slightly, also mainly because of government income policies favoring very-low-income Brazilians. Brazil's income inequality is also one of the highest in the world, so even with some reduction, differences between higher- and lower-income Brazilians continues to be greater than in Russia, India, and China. These increasing and decreasing income differences are usually reflected in higher and lower payoffs for higher levels of schooling, including university.

In addition to the impact of economic growth and income distribution, we observe from analyzing rates of return for education over time in a number of countries that rates generally fall with expanded schooling and that they fall first at lower levels of schooling as the educational system expands (Carnoy, 1972, 1995). An important explanation of this phenomenon is the "downward substitution" by employers of higher educated labor for lower educated labor as the educational system expands. The studies suggest that where there is rapid industrialization and simultaneous rapid expansion of schooling toward the universal completion of primary, then lower and upper secondary school, rates of return for various levels of schooling decline over time and tend to decline first at the primary level, then at the secondary level, and finally at the university level. There is evidence that in many countries this process has left the rates of return for university education higher than those for secondary education and those for investment in secondary education higher than those for investment in primary education (see also Blaug, Layard, and Woodhall, 1969).

We can illustrate this "staged supply" phenomenon in educational expansion by the relative expansion of human capital in BRIC labor forces. Human capital in the labor force is usually measured by the percentage of workers with various levels of schooling. These data are not generally available for the BRICs before the 2000s. But we can approximate trends in this percentage in younger age labor (25–34 years old) by using the lagged gross enrollment rate (GER) in secondary and higher education. Assume that this age group of workers was in secondary school 10–15 years earlier and in university 5–10 years earlier. Taking the GER from those earlier years gives an idea of how quickly the young labor force is becoming more schooled. That said, the GER is a controversial figure because it is not always clear what it represents, either at the secondary or higher education level. For example, secondary education often includes lower and higher secondary education, and higher education often represents sub-university vocational education as well as university education.

Table 3.1 indicates, for example, that by 1990, Brazil had only about 11 percent of the younger labor force with university education, but probably 50 percent had at least some secondary school. Further, whereas it is only very recently that the GER in higher education increased (implying that the supply of university education in the younger labor force rose considerably by 2010), the fraction with secondary school had made this leap 10–15 years earlier. By 2010, about 80 percent of young workers in Brazil had some secondary education. China and India's secondary education expansion lagged behind, and the proportion of secondary and particularly university graduates was much smaller than in Brazil in the 1990s and early 2000s (considering a ten-year lag). However, because of the high percentage of rural population in China and India, the GER data hide much higher levels of secondary and university educated persons in China and India's urban areas by the early 2000s. In India, urban males in the labor force also had much higher rates of both secondary and university education by the late 1990s than those shown in Table 3.1 because of the large male-female enrollment gap in that country. Thus, in urban China and India, by 2005 a relatively high fraction of the young labor force had some secondary education, and rates of return for that level of schooling should have begun to decline.

In Russia there was a generally high level of secondary and higher education graduates in the labor force in the early 1990s (almost 20 percent were university educated), and in the younger labor force the figure went considerably higher by 2005–2010, probably to about 30 percent. Yet the GER in higher education is overestimated during the Soviet period because part of

TABLE 3.1 BRIC countries: Gross enrollment rates in secondary and higher education, 1970–2009 (percentage)

	1970	1975	1980	1985	1990	1995	2000	2005	2009
BRAZIL									
Secondary	26	47	54	51	65[a]	80[a]	104	106	101
Higher	5	10	11	11	11	12	16	26	36
CHINA									
Secondary	28	51	46	32	38	52	62	71	80
Higher[b]	—	1	1	3	3	4	8	19	24
INDIA									
Secondary	24	26	29	35	39	45	45	54	62
Higher[b]	5	5	5	6	6	6	9	11	14
RUSSIA									
Secondary	91	94	98	99	96	90	92	83	89
Higher	47	43	45	52	55	43	55	72	76

SOURCE: UNESCO Institute for Statistics (http://stats.uis.unesco.org/unesco/tableviewer/document.aspx?ReportId=143), accessed Jan. 10, 2012.
[a]Approximated.
[b]China and India higher education enrollment rates include shorter-course tertiary degrees.

that enrollment was in postsecondary vocational "colleges," not universities. Enrollment in universities in the 1980s fell to about 25 percent, according to one estimate (Androushschak, 2011).

Thus, it is not clear whether any of the BRICs (most so, probably Russia) are at the point where the payoff for completing university begins to fall. With essentially universal secondary education in Russia and the possibility of substituting university graduates for secondary, the earnings of secondary graduates are probably under pressure to stay relatively low, which may keep the rates of return for university up. Even if not, as we suggest below, young people will continue to enroll in university because those individuals who do not do so when such a high proportion of youths attend higher education send a negative "signal" to employers.

Rising Rates of Return for Higher Education in China

As mentioned above, China (and Russia) until the 1990s were command economies with tightly regulated labor markets, although China's agricultural sector was partially "marketized" in the late 1970s. Because the communist government tightly controlled Chinese wages and income, and an important goal of the Communist Party was equality rather than market-driven "allocative efficiency," income distribution was quite equal and the payoff for education as measured by income differences was low. According to Zhang and colleagues (2005), "Although the wage scale permitted wage differentials by level of completed schooling, these differentials were very small. At the same time, the government effectively eliminated most of the direct private costs of education by waiving all tuitions and fees for college students and by providing living stipends to students from poor families" (732). Nevertheless, the government tightly controlled the number of young people attending university.

The main issue raised by economists regarding the payoff for education in the 1980s was just how low it was (Johnson and Chow, 1997; de Brauw and Rozelle, 2006; Meng and Kidd, 1997; Liu, 1998) and whether productivity differences for more-educated workers (especially college graduates) were actually much larger than wage differentials (Fleisher et al., 1996; Fleisher and Chen, 1997; Fleisher and Wang, 2005). For example, Liu (1998) used data from 1988 to show that the marginal rate of return per year of university was somewhat higher than for secondary school—about 4.5 percent per year of university versus about 3 percent per year of secondary school. A meta-analysis of rate of return studies in China concluded that the rates of return for education during this period were close to zero primarily because of the compression of wage differentials by the government (Liu, 2008). Economists further considered steadily rising returns for schooling from the early 1990s as an indicator of the degree of China's economic transition away from centralized planning (Yang, 2005). With the reduction of wage controls, rates of return rose sharply in the 1990s (Zhang et al., 2005; Knight and Song, 2003; Fleisher et al., 2005; Fleisher and Wang, 2005) and even more rapidly, according to our estimates, in the 2000s, especially for higher education (Table 3.2). This was predictable, given the higher rates of return for younger Chinese in the 1990s than for older Chinese. Older Chinese were more likely to be paid at lower rates in state-owned enterprises when they were younger, and when older they were less able to take advantage of opening opportunities offered by economic reform.

The rising payoff for secondary and higher education occurred and continued to take place in the face of a rapidly increasing flow of secondary and university graduates into the labor force as the government rapidly expanded first secondary and then higher education enrollment in the 1990s and 2000s

(Table 3.2). Zhang and colleagues point out that between 1988 and 2001, the share of college-educated workers in the urban samples they used increased from 12.6 percent to 28.1 percent (Zhang et al., 2005: 745),[3] and the wage premium for college graduates over high school educated workers still increased from 12.2 percent to 37.3 percent (Zhang et al., 2005: 745). This suggests one of several probable explanations:

- The "real" payoff for higher education graduates in the late 1980s and early 1990s was already very high, as reflected in the studies showing a large gap between productivity estimates and wages for the higher educated (Fleisher and Chen, 1997). Tight government constraints on higher education enrollment could have played an important role in driving up this "unmeasured" payoff across age groups. However, this high rate was probably an overestimate of the "true" rate because of the sizable selection bias when only 4 percent of the age cohort attended and completed university.

- Younger workers are likely to have entered the labor market during the period when labor market reforms had already been implemented and with skills more in line with the kind of work required in the new Chinese economy, so their wages are more likely to reflect the "real" payoff for education than the wages of older workers who were tied in to stable positions that offered relatively lower wages. Thus, as older workers retire and younger workers replace them, the payoff for education rises. As Zhang and colleagues (2005) report, the rates of return for education rose for workers of all ages but less for older workers.

- The demand for upper-secondary and higher-educated labor increased rapidly in the 1990s and 2000s with China's very high growth rate and a shift to financial and business services as well as more sophisticated manufacturing production and a sharp increase in private business.

- The skill intensity of work increased within firms, possibly because of increased computer use or the introduction of other technologies. This continued to favor higher-educated workers even as their supply increased much more rapidly even than the supply of secondary-educated workers.

Analysis by Zhang and colleagues (2005) and Fleisher and Chen (1997) provide evidence that the first two of these explanations are highly plausible.

TABLE 3.2 China: Estimated private annual rates of return for education, by level of education and gender, 1988–2005 (percentage per additional year of schooling)

Study	Year	Total	Total male	Total female	Total urban	Total rural	Upper secondary	Professional	University
Johnson and Chow[a]	1988	3.3			3.3	4.0			
Li[b]	1995		4.3	6.9	5.4		6.2–8.3	6.2	6.8
de Brauw and Rozelle[c]	2000					6.5[d]			
Heckman and Li[e]	2000								10.8[f]
Zhang et al.[g]	1988		2.8[h]	5.2[h]			3.7[i]	1.0[i]	3.1[i]
	1992		3.7	5.8			3.2	3.1	5.0
	1995		5.6	7.9			5.1	4.0	6.1
	1998		6.4	9.2			5.4	5.5	8.0
	2001		7.5	12.5			7.1	5.9	9.3
Loyalka[j]	2005 males						10.1	10.0	14.9
	2005 females						14.5	22.6	23.3
Calculated rates[k]	2005 males								16.7
	2005 females								17.3
Calculated rates	2005 males								27.4
Graduates employed as engineers[k]	2005 females								27.4

SOURCES: Johnson and Chow, 1997; Li, 2003; de Brauw and Rozelle, 2006; Heckman and Li, 2004; Zhang et al., 2005.

Total = Annual return per year of schooling.

[a]Based on the 1988 Chinese Household Income Project (CHIP), a national survey of urban and rural households in 10 provinces.

[b]Based on the 1995 CHIP, a national survey of 6,928 urban households in 11 provinces. RORs shown here are all based on wages—the estimates using earnings are lower. The RORs for secondary are per year of schooling compared to those with primary education (lower rate is for academic, and the higher rate is for secondary professional; the RORs for professional and for university are per year of schooling compared to those with primary schooling, so they represent average rates over 9–10 years of schooling beyond primary). Li also shows that those educated later have higher RORs.

[c]Based on a nationally representative survey of 1199 households in 60 villages in 6 provinces in rural China.

[d]They based their estimates on off-farm wages, including both local wage earnings and wages of migrants from rural areas. The ROR based on local wages is 4.3 percent per year of education and, for migrants, 7.8 percent. For those under 35 in the sample, the RORs are 8.9 and 11.7 percent for locals and migrants.

[e]Based on the China Urban Household Income and Expenditure Survey (CUHIES) for the year 2000. Data used in ROR estimates are for 6 provinces and 4,250 households. They focus on 587 individuals, mostly younger, with senior high school graduation or more.

[f]The figure here is the average treatment effect per year of university. Heckman and Li correct for selection bias, showing that the treatment effect varies across groups. The ROR for those who actually attend college is considerably higher than 11%.

[g]Based in the CHIP survey of urban households, 1988–2001. We report only some of the years here, but the paper includes all years. The authors estimate OLS regressions not corrected for selection bias. They use earnings, not wages.

[h]Gender RORs reported here for 1988–2001 are the Heckman-corrected for labor market participation RORs.

[i]RORs reported here for 1988–2001 are the marginal rates per year of schooling beyond the previous level (for example, secondary ROR is the annual ROR for individuals with secondary school compared to individuals with middle school).

[j]Based on the 1% national population survey data for 2005. The results shown were estimated using a censored least absolute deviations (CLAD) model (Powell 1984), with dummy indicator variables for level of education completed. These estimates correct for the censoring of wages at zero (i.e., the estimates account for the fact that many persons do not work and earn wages), but do not correct for other types of selection bias.

[k]Based on an assumption of private costs equal to tuition of 5,500 yuan plus earnings foregone. If we add in addition private costs, such as dorm fees and books, the rates are lower by about 2 percentage points for the total of university graduates and about 4–5 points lower for graduates employed as engineers.

Labor market reforms worked their way through the economy gradually, but ultimately did bring wages more into line with productivity differences. However, the large increase in the payoff for college education in the early 2000s is probably less related to labor market reforms than the third and fourth possible explanations. We have no evidence that this is the case, but such explanations would conform to what has been happening in the United States, for example (Katz, 1999).

Thus, the average rate of return for university education in China continues to rise (as of 2005) and to remain higher than for secondary education even though the supply of college educated labor increased substantially and more rapidly. Correcting for selection bias tends to make rates higher. Heckman and Li (2004), Fleisher and Wang (2005), Chen and Hamori (2009), and others attempt to correct for selection bias using instrumental variable (IV) strategies and generally achieve slightly higher estimates than the standard Mincer rates.[4] Heckman and Li (2004) and Fleisher and Wang (2005) also notably allow for the possibility that individuals sort themselves into and out of college based on their own heterogeneous returns from college. Our own estimates for 2005 use a large, nationally representative sample of urban and rural dwellers (as well as migrants) and correct for censoring at zero wages, but do not attempt to correct for selection bias.[5] These results, despite their significant methodological differences, all suggest a rather high and rising ROR.[6] In addition, as various authors have shown, the payoff for college is rising over time because the "new" workers entering the labor market are more likely to get wages that reflect their productivity than was the case for older workers leaving the labor market (Maurer-Fazio, 1999).

None of the earlier rate of return studies we cite in Table 3.2 estimated the rates of return for engineering education or for other specializations. However, with the large 2005 national sample, we were able to approximate the returns for engineering education. We do not have data on an individual's degree, but we used his or her reported occupation as a proxy for education. The results suggest that the payoff for engineers is even higher on average than for those who went to university and considerably higher than for those who are engaged in other nonengineering occupations. Figure 3.1 shows the age-earnings profiles for males who are employed as engineers and have B.A. degrees or higher, for all those who have B.A. degrees, and for those who have upper-secondary degrees.[7]

These age-income profiles look very different from estimates we make for Brazil and India in that they do not increase steadily with age beyond age thirty-two—that is, for workers and employees who entered the labor force in the mid-1990s. But because the cross-section estimates (at a single point of time) measure the earnings of individuals of different ages who entered the Chinese labor market at different points in time, and labor market reforms

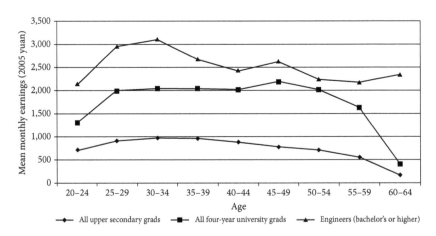

FIGURE 3.1 China: Male age-earnings profiles, by level of education and engineering graduates, 2005 (2005 yuan)

SOURCE: 2005 One Percent National Population Survey. Authors' calculations.

began to affect wages only in the 1990s, it is likely that these age-earnings profiles for all workers, but especially for higher-educated workers, are a fairly accurate estimate of future earnings in the twenty-two through thirty-two age range but underestimate future earnings at higher ages. Further, if the Chinese economy continues to grow, real earnings should rise at all ages at the same rate as real growth.

This analysis suggests that the "calculated rates of return" we estimate from these profiles may be underestimates of the true rates of return for higher education and for engineering education. However, because the earnings profiles used to determine the calculated rates do not correct for selection bias (for example, that those who complete higher education are more "able" or are more "suited" for a college education than upper-secondary-school graduates), they are biased upward. Yet the CLAD estimated rates, which are corrected for selection bias, and the calculated rates are similarly high, suggesting the payoffs for university education are well worth the 5,000–6,000 yuan required annually for parents' children's higher education and the additional several thousand yuan required for other expenses.[8] We were not able to estimate rates of return for higher education in more recent years, but given China's high and continuing growth rates, it is likely that the payoff for higher education will remain high and that the demand for places in higher education will continue to grow. This is especially true for engineering education.

Despite the apparent high returns for university education, media outlets and certain publications in China sometimes declare that graduates have difficulty finding jobs. The media reports do not seem to capture the entire story, however. Research confirms that graduates do take a certain amount of time on average to find jobs and make a relatively low starting salary (that is on average only a few hundred yuan higher than a migrant worker, for instance) but also that the wages of graduates generally rise steeply over time, thereby creating high returns (Park, Cai, and Du, 2010). Furthermore, university graduates may receive a variety of benefits that are not captured by income measures in surveys.

There may be different returns in China for different university tiers (Shavit et al., 2007) and, as we have shown, for different programs of study. Fan and colleagues (2010) use a regression discontinuity research design to measure the causal effects on future wages of attending four-year (regular) versus three-year (vocational) colleges. They find that the marginal return from a four-year college education is around 40–60 percent.[9] The returns from a college education in general and four-year institutions in particular may have continuing repercussions for widening income inequality in China. High economic growth rates and a demand bias favoring the higher educated seem to be outpacing increased supply of college graduates, driving up wages of the higher educated relative to those of workers with secondary education.

Did the rising payoffs in the mid-1990s create a level of demand for university education from the population great enough to pressure the state to expand enrollment rapidly? Alternatively, did the state leadership come to the conclusion that investing heavily in higher education would yield high economic payoffs and contribute to growth? Although we have no direct evidence of either, it is highly likely that both are true. Constraints on higher education expansion in China were largely political, as discussed above, but by the mid-1990s, with an average real growth rate of over 10 percent since the early 1980s (World Bank, 2011) and six years after Tiananmen Square, Communist Party views on threats from higher education had softened. The proportion of Chinese youths completing secondary education had increased substantially, China's population had accumulated considerable cash savings, and Chinese leadership was becoming increasingly technocratic in outlook. It is logical that these factors combined to pressure the state to begin a rapid expansion of the university system and use family savings to finance it. Perceived high rates of return for university completers, by both families and government, likely shaped policy.

Given China's political system, students and their families did/do not have much choice in the matter of the state imposing substantial tuition fees for higher education. Yet, because education is highly valued in China, there was little resistance to state tuition policies. Even so, tuition fees have not risen in the past ten years despite rising costs per student in universities, which suggests that Chinese officials are sensitive to the political meaning of universal tuition fees and the possible negative reaction to raising those fees.

Russia: Rates of Return at the Limits of Expanding Enrollment

The changes in the Russian labor market were brusquer than in China. Nevertheless, they followed a very similar pattern of shift from state control of wages, manpower formation, and employment toward a market system of wage setting, response by students to labor market opportunities through choice of courses of study, and employment by employers hiring or not hiring graduates based on market conditions. Many university graduates are still employed in the public or quasi-public sector, and the state, as in China, still sets the numbers of students that universities admit in each field. In Russia, however, the state's direct influence is over the number of "free," or fully sub-sidized, places in universities and university faculties. Universities have much more leeway in the number of "fee-paying" students they can admit. The result, as we have seen in Chapter 2, is a tremendous expansion of students paying tuition to attend public universities. The fields that have expanded through this education "market" are those that are likely to provide students the best access to employment and better-paying jobs.

There have only been a few studies estimating the impact of these changes on the payoff for higher education in Russia. Elizabeth Brainerd (1998) used data from a series of monthly cross-section household surveys conducted by the All-Russian Center for Public Opinion Research (or VTsIOM, its Rus-sian acronym) in 1991, 1993, and 1994 to estimate changes in monthly income (adjusted for hours worked) distribution in Russia in the early years of the transition. As part of her study, she estimated Mincer earnings functions for men and women in each of the three years. These yielded Mincer rates of return for years of schooling and for different levels of schooling. She shows a rapid increase in the overall rate of return for schooling in the three years and, more important, that the rise in the rate of return is driven by nominal wage declines for those with less than secondary education and nominal wage increases for those Russians who attended university. In terms of purchas-ing power, however, "real" wages fell for all education groups.[10] Much of this change in returns for education appears to come from the possibilities for university-educated workers to get jobs outside the state sector after 1991. In general, higher-educated workers had greater flexibility in responding to the drastically new conditions in labor markets. This also helps explain rising relative payoffs for university graduates as they moved out of jobs that paid government-regulated wages. A second fallout of the transition was a decline in the premium paid to seniority, as we also observed in China in the 1990s. Thus, earnings shifted up for younger workers relative to older workers, again probably because of the shift out of government wage-regulated jobs. We re-port her results for payoffs for education (unadjusted for private/public sector employment) in Table 3.3.

Gorodnichenko and Peter (2004) used the Russian Longitudinal Moni-toring Survey (RLMS) for 1994, 1996, 1998, 2000, and 2002 to estimate Mincer monthly earnings functions for those years. In addition, they used a feature of the RLMS 2000, namely a series of retrospective questions regarding jobs held in 1985 and 1990 (including earnings), to estimate similar earnings functions based on the characteristics of the same workers in 2000, and projecting their age back to 1985 and 1990. These Mincer rate of return results are also shown in Table 3.3. They are not adjusted for sector of work, but in this case, they make separate calculations for males and females and adjust for the higher wages paid in Moscow.

These estimates suggest that the payoffs for education in Russia rose rapidly with the transformation of the labor market in the 1990s and were not very different from those in China—even to the extent that women in both Russia and China faced higher rates of return for investment in education while they averaged much lower incomes than men. The payoff for university education in the mid-1990s in Russia was also very similar to the payoff in China despite a much higher proportion of university graduates in the labor force in Russia than in China. We can only hypothesize that the influence of government wage setting continued to be more influential in China than in Russia in the 1990s. One indication that this hypothesis is probably correct is the apparent big leap in payoff for Chinese university graduates in 2005. In Russia the Soviet system of the "uniform tariff grid" was used in the public sector until 2008, when it was formally replaced by a decentralized merit-pay scheme, although public administrators accustomed to the former system still tend to use it for determining their employees' pay. Even so, the process of deregulating public sector pay has begun.

Although engineering was a favored profession in the Soviet Union, with the transformation of the command economy and the corresponding decline of much of Russia's heavy industry after 1991, the demand for engineering places in universities did not increase nearly as rapidly as places in economics and business administration, associated with jobs in financial services and employment in international companies. As we show in Chapter 2, the demand for engineering education (applications/admissions ratio) was much lower than for studying economics or management.

Nevertheless, Denisova and Kartseva's (2005) estimates suggest that the payoff for technical education in specialist degrees (five years) in Russia was higher at the end of the 1990s and early 2000s than for any other course of study but economics. They also estimate payoffs for three-year professional degrees, and the returns for engineering education for those types of degrees were the highest among the major programs of study in 1998–2001.

Thus, engineering education at the turn of the twenty-first century and even under "market" conditions was a high payoff course of study. As in other countries, this does not necessarily mean that the payoff for working as an engineer is higher than in other professions. Engineers managed (and continue) to find jobs in business—the mathematical and problem-solving skills of engineers were more suited to the new realities of the labor market after 1990. Graduates with good mathematics training were employed by banks, oil companies, and foreign businesses that began investing in Russia (see, for example, Raleigh, 2006: 142–143).

Did rising payoffs for university education in the 1990s put pressure on the Russian government to expand free, budgeted places in Russian universities? Not much. Enrollment data shown in Chapter 2 indicate that higher education enrollment fell in the first five years of the decade. Between 1995 and 2000, when the payoff for university completers rose substantially, public budget places increased only by 350,000, and tuition-paying enrollment increased from zero to almost 1.5 million. Thus, the Russian state contributed only about 20 percent of the financing for enrollment expansion in this period. It promoted a market approach by universities to absorb increased demand.

Did the payoff for university education in Russia also continue to rise in recent years? There is some evidence that it may not have. The Mincer rates estimated by Androushschak and Proudnikova for this study (see Table 3.3) suggest that the payoff for university corrected for selection bias increased somewhat up to the early 2000s, but with the continued expansion of tertiary enrollment to very high levels (about 85 percent) among secondary school graduates, rates of return had declined somewhat by 2006–2008. This was also true for engineering graduates, but their payoffs still remained considerably higher than the average rate of return. Gimpelson and Kapelushnikov (2011) do not calculate rates of return, but their estimates of average earnings premiums by level of education indicate a decline in payoffs to university in 2005–2007 and a small rise in 2007–2009 (tables 1.19 and 1.20). The proportion of university graduates in the labor force in the Soviet Union as a whole was 12–14 percent in the mid-1980s (higher than in China, India, and Brazil in 2010). In the early 2000s, the proportion in Russia had increased to 25 percent and in 2008 to about 29 percent. These are very high levels even compared with more-developed countries.[11]

Because the percentage of students paying tuition has also been increasing steadily since the mid-1990s, the rates may have declined even further if we had accounted for tuition and other costs of studying among Russian university students. In Chapter 2 we show that the proportion of fee-paying students increased steadily from none in 1994 to about one-half in 2007–2008.[12]

TABLE 3.3 Russia: Estimated private annual rates of return for education, by level of education and gender, 1985–2002[a]

Study	Year	Total[d]	Total[e] Male	Total[e] Female	Vocational[f] Male	Vocational[f] Female	Professional[f] Male	Professional[f] Female	University[f] Male	University[f] Female	Engineering major Male	Engineering major Female
Brainerd	1991		3.1	5.4	1.7	3.3	5.2	6.4	3.5	6.7		
	1993		6.6	7.4	−3.0	10.1	7.5	7.6	6.2	8.1		
	1994		6.7	9.6	−1.9	9.0	5.1	11.4	6.4	10.6		
Gorodnichenko and Peter	1985	2.8										
	1990	3.9										
	1996	8.1										
	1998	9.1										
	2000	9.3										
	2002	9.2										
Denisova and Kartseva	1998										7.4	12.2
	2000										7.7	11.1
	2001										7.9	12.0
Androushchak and Proudnikova[b]	1994–1996				−0.6		5.7		5.1		3.5	
	2000–2002				1.3		6.7		6.4		11.2	
	2006–2008				0.2		3.4		5.5		10.3	
	2005[c]								8.3[g]	15.9[g]	9.6[g]	28.2[g]
									6.1[h]	10.0[h]	7.8[h]	19.2[h]

SOURCES: Brainerd, 1998, Tables 3A and 3B; Gorodnichenko and Peter, 2004; Denisova and Kartseva, 2005.

[a]Percentage per additional year of schooling.

[b]Gregory Androushchak and Anna Proudnikova of the National Research University Higher School of Economics estimated Mincer rates of return with a Heckit selection bias correction specifically for this book based on the Russian Longitudinal Monitoring Survey (RLMS)—about 4,000–4,500 households. Earnings are for full-time employees and were averaged for three annual rounds of the survey in order to increase the sample size in each age income category and data adjusted for growth of mean wages in each year within the three separate clusters of years to adjust for wage inflation.

[c]Estimates made especially for this study using the RLMS based on 4,000 households and collected in the years 2004–2006. Earnings were averaged for three annual rounds of the survey and data adjusted for inflation to 2005 in order to increase the sample size in each age income category.

[d]Annual rate of return per year across all years of schooling, controlling for gender and whether works in Moscow or not.

[e]Annual rate of return per year of schooling across all years of schooling.

[f]Annual rate of return per year of education compared to completed secondary schooling. Vocational education refers to post-basic education vocational; professional education refers to postsecondary non-university professional education.

[g]Calculated rate from age-earnings profiles (see Figure 3.2, using only income foregone as costs to make these comparable with Mincer rates for earlier years. For engineers, refers to engineering majors. Rates to those graduates who work as engineers are substantially lower for females (18.9% per year of university).

[h]Calculated rate from age-earnings profiles using income foregone, tuition, and entrance test preparation expenses as costs. For engineers, refers to engineering majors. Rates to those graduates who work as engineers are substantially lower for females (13.8% per year of university).

Androushschak and Proudnikova estimated age-earnings profiles for men and women using the RLMS data for 2004–2006 (Figure 3.2 shows the earnings for men—age-earnings profiles for women are available on request), and we used these profiles to estimate calculated rates of return that included average tuition and preparation costs for applying students.[13] Including average entrance test preparation spending (9,700 rubles paid by about 40 percent of all students applying to university) and average tuition spending (27,000 rubles for university students as a whole and 22,000 for engineering students—because a larger percentage of engineering students are accepted into state-funded slots in universities) in the 2005 "calculated" rates of return based on age-earnings profiles substantially lowers the rates of return. In Table 3.3 we compare rates estimated using just earnings foregone with those estimated using total private costs. The latter estimated rates of return for five years of university education averaged about 8 percent for men and women together compared to 12 percent when only earnings foregone are included in costs. For men, the returns for engineering education are somewhat higher, but for women, they are much higher than the average for all fields of study taken together.[14]

Official data on wage increases in manufacturing and on changes in tuition costs in 2005–2009 suggest that the wage premium for higher education has continued to stay steady (it even may have risen somewhat), whereas

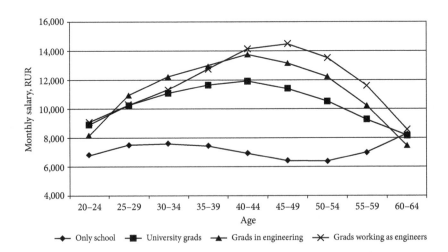

FIGURE 3.2 Russia: Male age-earnings profiles, by level of education and engineering graduates, 2005 (2005 rubles)

SOURCE: Authors' estimates based on data prepared by the National Research University Higher School of Economics from RLMS 2005 data.

tuition costs have risen less rapidly than wages. Therefore, we would not expect that the returns for higher education decreased in 2005–2009. A major factor in keeping rates of return steady has been a tremendous increase in public funding of higher education despite the economic crisis, and that has pushed down the share that families pay for higher education.

The major shift to tuition paid places in public universities in the 1995–2010 period can be at least partly explained by the rapid transformation of the labor market in the 1990s and the concomitant rise in the rates of return for higher education. The fact that such a high fraction of those students who entered tuition-paying programs went into business/economics also makes sense because the private rate of return in the early 2000s was, indeed, highest for those who completed that program of study. However, engineering graduates also did well, and there was not a particularly great demand for tuition-paying places in engineering. In recent years the availability of scores on a national university entrance test indicate that engineering students' scores are lower than in some other programs, which also suggests low demand for engineering places (see Chapter 7).

Nevertheless, if the payoff for engineering degrees is higher than average, why is demand slipping, at least as measured by the quality of applicants? If engineering education is a signal to employers of good math skills, why wouldn't secondary graduates continue to demand engineering university places? One explanation may be that the rates of return have fallen since 2004–2006. The mathematics "signal" associated with engineering may be declining in value as the mathematics scores required for engineering places decline. Another explanation is that engineering education may still have a high payoff but that the taste for engineering education is declining—in other words, the nonpecuniary costs of taking engineering education may be rising, particularly if doing so means learning skills that are seen by others as obsolete, even if the problem-solving component can be used in other types of work. Certain types of engineering training may still be glamorous, but most may be considered passé, and they probably are (Kanikov and Trunkina, 2004).

The Rates of Return for Higher Education in India

A main reason that students in India are willing to pay fees in public colleges and are willing to pay the much higher fees charged by private institutions is the relatively high rate of return for a degree. There are a number of rates of return studies for India, and these show that since the late 1970s up to the late

1990s, the private rates of return to the investment in higher education were about 11–13 percent per year of higher education (Table 3.4). This is not as high as in some developing countries, such as Brazil (see below), but it is much higher than it was in China up until recently and much higher than in the mature, developed economies, such as Europe and the United States (Boarini and Strauss, 2010).

Table 3.4 also suggests that in the past, the rates of return for secondary education were higher for women than for men, but the opposite was true for investment in higher education, and the rates of return for taking a technical diploma (a three-year degree at a technical college) suggest that a diploma was better investment than a university education in terms of payoff per dollar of income foregone for men but not for women.

Once the Indian economy began growing rapidly in the late 1990s and into the 2000s, we would have expected that the payoff for university and for tech-

TABLE 3.4 India: Estimated private and social annual rates of return for education, by level of education and gender, 1965–2006 (percentage per additional year of schooling)

Year	Secondary			University			Technical/ engineering	
	All	Men	Women	All	Men	Women	Men	Women
1965[a]	18.8			16.2				
1978[a]	19.8			13.2				
1983[b]	13.7	13.2/6.0[f]	23.8	11.6	12.2/10.0[f]	9.5	13.9	12.8
1993/1994[b]	13.8	12.6/5.4[f]	25.5	11.7	12.2/10.9[f]	10.3	15.6	12.3
1999[b]		6.1			12.3			
2006[b]		10.5	15–18.5[g]		12.0	16/13[h]	12/24[h]	16/13[h]
2006[c]					19/19.5[h]	19/18[h]	21/37[h]	30/n.a.[h]
2006[d]					14/14[h]	13/12[h]	12/22[h]	14/n.a.[h]
2006[e]					12/12[h]	11/11[h]	9/17[h]	9/n.a.[h]

SOURCES: 1965, 1978: Psacharopoulos, 1985; 1983, 1993/94: Duraisamy, 2002; 1999: Dutta, 2006; 2006: India National Household Survey, 2006, authors' calculations.
[a]Calculated rates.
[b]Mincer rates.
[c]Calculated rates, earnings foregone only.
[d]Calculated rates, earnings foregone plus tuition.
[e]Calculated rates, earnings foregone plus tuition plus public spending per student (social ROR).
[f]Second figure is recalculation by Dutta.
[g]First figure is for last two years of secondary school; second figure is for all four years of secondary school.
[h]First figure is for diploma degree; second figure is for graduate (four-year) degree.

nical or engineering degrees would have risen. We estimated Mincer rates for 2006, which are comparable with the estimates for earlier years in Table 3.4. They suggest that the payoffs for secondary schooling probably declined somewhat and the payoffs for university remained similar to those in the 1990s. For women, the payoff for secondary education declined more than for men, and their payoff for a university degree increased substantially. Indeed, in 2006, it appears that rates of return for both a diploma (three-year) and a graduate (four-year) college degree were higher for women than for men.

Table 3.4 also shows that the returns for an engineering graduate degree are much higher for men than for investing in a nontechnical college education. It should be stressed that these rates of return are not corrected for labor force participation and that this may bias them considerably, especially for women. Nevertheless, they strongly suggest that the payoff for engineering education is very high.

Figure 3.3 shows the male age-earnings profiles for the various levels of schooling. For the sake of illustration, we include the age-earnings profile for postgraduate education. The estimates show that male graduate engineers earn higher salaries than general graduates and even postgraduates (mainly master's

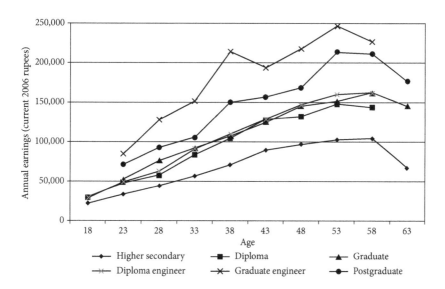

FIGURE 3.3 India: Male age-earnings profiles, by level of education and engineering graduates, 2006 (current rupees/year)

SOURCE: National Sample Survey Organization, National Sample Survey, 62nd round, 2006. Delhi.

degree holders). We have insufficient data to estimate returns for female engineering graduates (female age-earnings profiles are available on request).

The calculated rates take account of tuition costs as well as income foregone. It is important to keep in mind that students in technical higher education pay a higher fraction of the costs of their education with fees. Therefore, we estimate their private rates of return using higher fees than for diploma and graduate degree holders as a whole. Further, we estimate two sets of private rates using a lower and higher estimate of total fees in 2006 for engineering students (25,000 rupees and 40,000 rupees) because tuition fees in technical colleges vary among public and private institutions. The higher average fees are in the more expensive private institutions. We also estimate social rates of return, which include costs per student borne by the public sector in addition to private costs. The results of these estimates are shown in Table 3.4. They confirm that the private and social (including public spending per student above and beyond tuition and other fees) rates of return for graduate degrees in engineering are extremely high for males, even when tuition and other fees are included. There were too few females with engineering four-year degrees in the India national household survey to compute a reasonably accurate calculated rate of return. Even the social rate of return based on private earnings differences is 16–18 percent per year of engineering college.

When forgone earnings alone are considered, the rate of return for male engineering graduates is as high as 36.8 percent per year of college education compared to 21 percent for engineering diploma holders and 20 percent for graduates in general education. When tuition is also considered, the rates of returns for graduates engineers fall to 20–24 percent per year of higher education and those for diploma holders to 11–13 percent. When other costs are included, the rates respectively come down to 16–19 percent and 9–10 percent. If tuition and other costs are considered, the returns for diploma holders turn out to be less than the returns for general graduates. Even when only foregone earnings are considered, one does not finds much difference in the returns between general diploma/degree or engineering diploma holders. For women, the returns for engineering diploma holders, considering foregone earnings, tuition, and other costs, are either less or just about the same as diploma/degree holders in general higher education. When tuition is not included, we can observe that the rates of return are extremely high even for nontechnical higher education at both the diploma and four-year degree levels. However, at the diploma level, further increases in tuition and other family costs may reduce the rates of return to levels that could slow enrollment in technical education.

These results suggest that private rates of return for secondary education have gradually declined in India and that rates for university education have stayed fairly constant for the past twenty years. The rates of return for engineering education are higher than the overall rates of return. Because they are so high, it is not surprising that private colleges jumped into the business of higher education and focused so heavily on attracting engineering and business students (business degrees are also marked by higher rates of return). It also makes sense from a financial point of view that state governments allowed this private expansion and got students to pay a significant fraction of the costs of increased enrollment. Whether rates will continue to stay high as enrollment expands even more rapidly, as it has in the last five years, is a major question, especially with the large jump in engineering college enrollment (see Chapter 2).

The political downside of this strategy, given these high rates of return, could have been the issue of access for the mass of disadvantaged students. The state has largely diffused this issue by legislating an across-the-board affirmative action policy for disadvantaged castes, constituting about 50 percent of all college-aged youths. We discuss India's affirmative action policy in detail in Chapter 6 and again in Chapter 8.

The High Payoffs for Higher Education in Brazil

We have estimates of the payoff for education in Brazil back to 1970, and they show a clear shift, with the value of higher education increasing sharply between 1970 and 1989 and staying high in the 2000s despite rapid increases in enrollment rates (see also Griffin and Cox Edwards, 1993). The private payoff for investing in higher education doubled from about 14 percent per additional year of higher education to 28 percent at the end of the 1980s and remained close to this higher level in the 2000s (Table 3.5).

The shift in payoff is consistent with three important features of the Brazilian economic landscape in this period: (a) a rapid rate of GNP growth in the 1970s (8.5 percent) and low to moderate economic growth since; (b) a very high level of income inequality throughout this period but somewhat rising in the 1970s and 1980s; and (c) a rapid increase in the expansion of secondary schooling, particularly in the 1970s and 1980s, and continuing into the 1990s, while university enrollment remained relatively low as a proportion of the age cohort until the 2000s.

It makes sense that with a rapid expansion of secondary education but only a small increase in tertiary enrollment in the 1970s, a sharp decline in

TABLE 3.5 Brazil: Estimated private and social annual rates of return for education, by level of education and gender, 1970–2008 (percentage per additional year of schooling)

Year	Private rates of return		Social rates of return	
	Secondary school	Higher education	Secondary school	Higher education
1970	24.7	13.9	23.5	13.1
1989	5.1	28.2	5.1	21.4
2000[a]	10.0	24.4		
2001[b]	5.8	31.4		
2000[c]	12.7/13.8[g]	23.0/20.5[g]	11.1/11.6[g]	18.4/16.3[g]
2000[d]		26.5/24.3[g]		20/17.7[g]
2000[e]		21.5/19.9[g]		18.5/16.9[g]
2008[f]	1.6	24.6		

SOURCES: 1970: Psacharopoulos, 1985; 1989: Psacharopoulos, 1994; 2000, 2008: authors' estimates.
[a]Mincer rates from 2000 Census, controlling for gender and race.
[b]Mincer rates from 2001 household survey, controlling for gender and race.
[c]Calculated rates from 2000 Census.
[d]Calculated rates from 2000 Census for engineering graduates.
[e]Calculated rates from 2000 Census for computer science graduates.
[f]Mincer rates from 2008 household survey, controlling for gender and race. Thanks to Ilana Umansky, Stanford University, for these estimates.
[g]First rate is for males; second rate is for females.
For all calculated rates, tuition costs are based on a sample of private universities' posted monthly tuition costs; tuition trend data are from SEMESP, São Paulo, and from Hoper Educational Consultants, São Paulo. Public spending per student used to estimate public costs for social rates of return was estimated from INEP published data. Tuition costs and public spending costs are proportioned by the percentage of students in private and public universities in each field of study. Thanks to Mauricio Farias, Stanford University, for these estimates.

growth rates in the 1980s, and a corresponding increase in inequality between 1970 and 1989, the rate of return to investment in secondary education fell and the rate of return to investment in higher education increased greatly.

In the 1990s and 2000s, we observe a somewhat different pattern, which also conforms to demand and supply of secondary and higher educated labor and the government moves toward decreasing income inequality. Secondary education continued to expand, and as we have seen, beginning about 1995, higher education enrollment exploded, mainly through increased enrollment in private institutions.

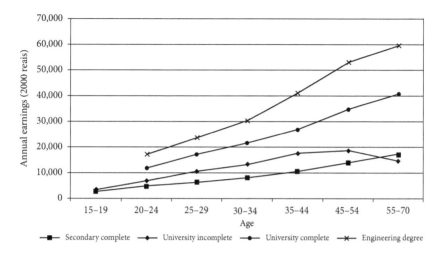

FIGURE 3.4 Brazil: Male age-earnings profiles, by level of education and engineering graduates, 2000 (current reais/year)

SOURCE: Authors' estimates prepared for this study from Instituto Brasileiro de Geografía e Estatística, Brazilian Census, 2000.

Figure 3.4 shows the estimated age-earnings profiles for men in the year 2000 (the profile for women is available on request). The difference in earnings between those who complete university and those who do not is very high for both men and women, and both male and female engineering graduates earn much more than average university graduates. From these age-earnings profiles, we estimated the calculated private and social rates for completing university education by gender and for those who complete two technical fields of study in higher education—computer science (four years) and engineering (five years).[15] Engineers have the highest private rates of return, but the rates are high for completing university overall (Table 3.5). Because these rates are for each year of university, it implies that a graduate engineer earns more than double the earnings of a secondary graduate. Other estimates using these same census data suggest that those engineering graduates who work as engineers earn considerably less, on average, than those engineering graduates who work in other occupations (Nunes et al., 2009). Thus, as we discussed in the Russian case, getting an engineering degree in Brazil is also an acquired signal that provides access to a wide range of jobs where mathematics and problem-solving skills are considered important.

With private rates of return for completing university (and other kinds of higher education) as high as they are, the demand for higher education in

Brazil should continue to be strong for many years to come. The strategy of letting private, full-fee-charging institutions absorb the pressure for access to higher education also had and continues to have a certain logic. Because those who attend public institutions pay virtually no fees and a high percentage of the students in public universities (like those attending private institutions) come from the highest-income quintile families, letting private institutions take up the bulk of new entrants is—as in India—a politically convenient way for the state to avoid investing heavily in public higher education. At least in the early 2000s, it was also a way to reduce the perverse equity effects of giving large subsidies in the form of free higher education to the already wealthy (see Chapter 8) without confronting the ideologically charged issue of paying tuition for attending public universities. However, the high rates of return suggest that the number of students enrolling and graduating from universities is constrained by financial and other barriers. The recent moves to subsidize disadvantaged groups in private institutions and to expand affirmative action in federal universities are indications of how politically charged overcoming these barriers has become. The Brazilian state is under pressure from lower-income groups to increase access to the high earnings associated with completing higher education. We explore this issue in Chapter 8.

Summing Up

The payoff for higher education over the past twenty-five years appears to have increased rapidly (China), increased (Russia), remained fairly constant at a fairly high level (India), and declined slowly from very high levels (Brazil), all in the face of increases (in most cases, rapid increases) in the absolute and relative number of university graduates. In all the BRICs, the payoff for completing university rose relative to the payoff for higher secondary school. Except for India, which has the lowest fraction of students in secondary education, the private rates of return for university now exceed the private rates of return for completing secondary schooling. This is despite the rapid expansion of higher education.

The rise in absolute and relative private economic returns for investing in higher education coincides approximately with the rapid expansion of enrollment in all four countries. This suggests that rising/high economic returns contributed to pressures on the state to invest in higher education and to create conditions in which the private sector and students' families would invest directly in colleges and universities.

Our results also suggest that it is possible for governments to charge for public education (China, India, Russia) because the private rate of return is relatively high (China, India) or, as in Russia and India, the rate of return is high for particular fields of study (business/economics in Russia and business, engineering, and medicine in India). Thus, public universities can charge students even more tuition in those fields. Furthermore, the promotion of private university education is successful in Brazil and India (and on a smaller scale in China) because of very high average private rates of return in Brazil (and China), and in India in engineering and business education. We argue that this has provided government an opportunity to shift higher education financing from general public revenues to families paying directly, and that it is quite rational in terms of getting those who stand to make substantial private gains to share in or even bear the entire cost of that investment.

We emphasize in Chapter 1 that the policy discussion should shift from the public/private nature of payment for higher education services to the income distributional/social mobility issues inherent in the way the state finances and provides higher education. The financing patterns in the four BRICs, combined with the increased differentiation between elite and mass institutions described in the next chapter, the high and sometimes rising rates of return for higher education, and the differential rates of return for engineers and business education discussed in this chapter, have important implications for the distribution of the net benefits of education. Much depends on which social class groups are, on average, getting this highly valued education and who is paying for it. The analysis in this chapter, Chapter 4, and Chapter 8 helps us begin to analyze the implications of expanding higher education in the BRICs for economic and social equity.

Furthermore, except for Russia, the relatively high and, in some cases, rising private rates of return for investing in higher education in the BRICs suggest that the demand for places in higher education should continue to rise. We should see continued rapid expansion of the percentage of the age cohort that seeks and completes university. The pressure to maintain or increase university places for engineering (and business) study should also remain high. However, this will be the case under present financing schemes only if lower social class groups can afford to pay or if governments expand publicly subsidized forms of higher education.

4   The Changing Financing of BRIC
Higher Education

I N CHAPTER 2 WE ARGUE THAT THE MASSIVE EXPANSION OF
higher education in the BRICs in the 1990s and 2000s is financially
different in two important ways from earlier expansions in developed countries: much more so than in the United States or Europe, the cost of the rapid
college enrollment growth in the BRICs has been borne by students' families
paying tuition. Second, the BRICs are expanding their university systems by
increasingly differentiating how much they spend per student in elite and mass
universities—elite universities receive increasing resources, mainly through
larger government subsidies, whereas the mass of students attend colleges and
universities that operate at low levels of funding per student, much or most of
it in the form of student tuition.

In this chapter we detail these two dominant financial features of the
BRIC higher education expansion. We also attempt to explain why, in addi-
tion to the high or rising economic payoffs to higher education discussed in
Chapter 3, BRIC states are pursuing these strategies.

The Shift to Direct Private Financing

Four decades ago two BRIC economies (China and Russia) were financing
higher education *entirely* and two (Brazil and India) *mainly* with public funds,
either from central or state-level governments. Almost every student who
was accepted at a public higher education institution incurred no costs other
than his or her earnings foregone, token tuition fees, and some direct private

expenses. In Russia and China, institutional costs were fully subsidized by the state. In many cases the student also received a stipend to offset part of the income he or she gave up to attend university.

In that financing model, higher education was considered as a pure public good, whose substantial to total support through public financing was justified by the high externalities its graduates generated for society as a whole (for a summary of this argument, see Bloom and Sevilla, 2004, and Tilak, 2008; for the argument on China, discussed earlier in Chapter 3, see Heckman, 2005, and Fleisher and Wang, 2005).

As in primary and secondary education, the implicit argument for total subsidization was that charging fees to cover much of the higher costs of university education would produce underinvestment. Without tangible collateral, such as a home, it has been inherently difficult to borrow to invest in education. Thus, cost sharing at public universities through tuition or expanding higher education through the growth of full-fee private institutions creates a financial barrier to lower-income students who could otherwise qualify for higher education. In this argument, such fees result in social inefficiency because families tend to underinvest in a good with high external benefits. In equity terms, charging tuition is also socially unfair because it distributes access to the benefits of higher education on the basis of ability to pay rather than on the basis of academic ability, hence favoring higher social class groups.

Yet for all its merits, the argument against tuition tends to ignore an evident social reality: access to higher education is usually highly inequitable even when it is tuition free. Except for Russia, four decades ago higher education in the BRIC countries was accessible to a limited few. In Brazil and India only children from families already able to invest time and money in their children's early childhood health care, nutrition, and education and in their higher-quality primary and secondary education were likely to send their children to university. Even in the Soviet Union, higher education was accessible to many but still tended to favor children of the elite—in those cases, the political elite and those among the higher educated who were favored by the regime.

The state's policy of providing free higher education was implemented to train needed professionals to run government bureaucracies and for local economic development. Eventually, everybody (meaning lower-income urban and even rural classes) bought into this university financing model, believing that ultimately their children would also benefit from this "free" good. Yet, in practice, access to universities, particularly "good" universities in Brazil,

India, Russia, and China, favored (and still favor, even in Russia) children of the more privileged.

When, in practice, only a small fraction of a nation's citizens have access to a "public" good and this fraction comes from essentially the same social class group in generation after generation, the good is hardly public. Rather, a certain class of citizens has appropriated public revenues for its private use. Contrast this with more typical public goods such as roads, low-cost public transportation (which, incidentally, charges a user fee), clean air, potable water, and publicly provided Wi-Fi.

If there are large "externalities" associated with the graduates of universities, the state can justify subsidizing privileged socioeconomic (or political) groups to earn higher incomes (or, in communist countries, access to privileges and power) at public expense, on the grounds that they also increase everyone else's well-being by becoming good doctors, good engineers, and good leaders, and that these large benefits accrue to the society as a whole, not just to the graduates themselves. We consider externalities of higher education an important argument, but it does not obviate the fact that when particular groups "privatize" public resources, they need to make the case that these resources really do produce externalities that justify the level of subsidy they receive. This they are rarely required to do, mainly because they use their economic and political power to "make the case" for them.

Today, all four countries have, in one way or another, either implemented cost share financing through tuition fees in public universities or allowed higher education to become "privatized" (or increasingly privatized, in the Brazilian case) through the expansion of publicly regulated or essentially independent private universities. The way each country has made this shift or allowed it to happen has important implications for the economic efficiency and social equity aspects of its higher education systems.

Most analyses of the shift to cost sharing have identified it as the "privatization" of the higher education system in an ideological sense—that is, a shift from believing that higher education is a public good to a new belief that is a private good. Allowing private universities a role in providing "recognized" education does mean that the private sector is in the education business. There certainly may be an ideological element in the shift to cost sharing and particularly allowing or even promoting the expansion of private institutions to absorb demand—in the sense that neoliberal market policies have become more "acceptable" politically and there is less willingness by the public to pay high income tax rates than forty years ago.

However, when the state decides to charge tuition at public universities or to allow the expansion of private universities, the main issue, we argue, is not the "privatization" of education versus considering higher education a "public" good. *It is rather whether large subsidies at public expense to students for higher education substantially benefit society as a whole and whether these public subsidies are distributed very inequitably or reasonably equitably among different social class groups.*

It is not far-fetched to claim that financing the recent enormous higher education expansion in the BRICs was borne of economic necessity: BRIC countries had lower per capita incomes in the mid-1990s when they began their leap in university enrollments than, for example, the developed European countries had in the late 1960s when they began theirs. And BRIC countries face greater hurdles in collecting income taxes (for example, much higher poverty levels and a much smaller middle class) than northern European countries and the United States faced in the 1970s.

Further, as we suggest, charging tuition in public universities or allowing part of the higher education sector to be run on a fee-for-service basis through private universities can be seen as a public financing strategy that "negotiates" the level of subsidy received by higher-educated and wealthier families. If private universities are tightly regulated by the state in terms of their fees and their "quality," the notion of "private" university also becomes less clear.

At the same time, it is the state (the public sector) that credentializes private universities, and it is the state that *may* get an important benefit—political legitimacy—from added access to higher education. It is also the state that pays a part of the cost—a dissatisfied citizenry—if the private system fails to deliver. Turning over higher education, or for that matter any education level, partly to management by the private sector also benefits the state by putting a buffer in the responsibility game—the private education provider—between the student's family and the state. If students and their families are making good or bad choices and if private universities are supplying good or bad education, there is some arm's length between the state's responsibility in meeting the education needs of the citizenry, just as in any other market-based activities.

In a secular democratic society, there are other downsides to educating a sizable proportion of students in privately run universities. For example, when universities are private, they are sometimes organized around educating a particular clientele—ethnic or religious or just very wealthy—and therefore create an environment that is homogeneous and does not try to reflect the broader national or regional mix. This can work against building a higher education system with diversity and a more tolerant society. It is also likely that private universities, if unregulated, are more likely to appeal to different strata of the social class market than publicly run universities, even in public systems that charge fees. Because most private universities have to charge fees that meet their entire costs (some that are supported by religious groups are subsidized), and that vary considerably among different institutions, this greater differentiation in the private sector usually reflects greater differences in resources allocated per student and almost certainly greater differences in quality of faculty and other inputs. This has implications for higher education systems that rely on private institutions to absorb a high fraction of increasing enrollment. They are likely to be much more unequal in the way they treat students from different social class groups able to afford different levels of tuition. It is not surprising that the Indian and Brazilian states, most reliant among the BRICs on private colleges and universities to absorb the new mass of students entering higher education, also have the more aggressive affirmative action programs to somewhat offset the inequalities inherent in their systems.

The Trend Toward Increasing Differentiation

The second, and in our view, more important feature of the BRICs expanding higher education systems is the trend toward *increasing* financial differentiation of a fraction of institutions from those that absorb the vast majority of students. The trend is not currently universal across the BRICs. Differentiation among tiers of universities is not unusual in, say, the United States or Japan. However, a widening financial gap in favor of elite institutions has not characterized previous expansions. India is the exception. It has elite universities that already receive four to five times the funding per student relative to mass institutions, but this advantage does not appear to be increasing. With the growing pressure in the BRICs and other developing countries to develop "world-class" universities, increasing differentiation is likely to dominate all the BRIC higher education systems, including India, in the coming years.

We have alluded to two types of equity issues associated with increasing differentiation. The first is that if public funding for university education is allocated to elite and mass universities in an increasingly unequal fashion, this could exacerbate the inequality of economic opportunity for higher and lower social class students. Higher social class students already have much greater access to elite institutions because they have the advantage of higher-educated, higher-income parents and are therefore more likely to attend primary and secondary schools that prepare students for elite universities.

Increasing subsidies for students attending elite institutions could be justified by an argument that economic and social externalities associated with investing in higher social class groups are increasing over time. Indeed, the implicit argument for spending heavily on developing "world-class" universities is precisely that in today's global information economy, the value of high-quality university education is much greater than in the past. If all groups benefit from the externalities, the equity implications of increasingly differentiated public spending are less clear.

The second type of equity issue arises from increasingly differentiated private higher education. In countries that rely heavily on private institutions for expanding enrollment (Brazil and India), increasing differentiation means that the more-elite institutions are able to provide "better" education by charging higher tuition. In effect, this increasingly excludes those students unable to pay. At the same time, if nonelite institutions provide education to lower social class students at ever lower tuition (so that they can afford to attend), the quality of nonelite higher education must steadily decrease. In either case, the quality of education received is increasingly differentiated on the basis of ability to pay, so access to subsequent economic opportunities is determined directly by family finances.

We observe both types of equity issues in the BRICs—mostly the first in China, a combination of the first and second in India and Brazil, and a different combination of the first and second in Russia.

The trend toward increasing differentiation can be partly explained by some of the same forces that have driven cost sharing and increased privatization. For such a large expansion in higher education enrollment to take place in relatively less developed countries such as China, India, and even Brazil, with its higher income per capita, it apparently required reducing the average cost per student in universities. We show below that spending per student fell in all three of these countries as their systems expanded. Many would argue that lower costs per student are a good thing, particularly when the ratio of spending per student for higher education is initially much greater than for primary schooling. The drop may signify economies of scale or greater efficiency rather than any reduction in quality.

Nonetheless, much of the drop in higher education spending per student in Brazil, China, and India came from a "composition effect." As the number of students enrolled increased, low-cost (and lower-quality) institutions absorbed a greater and greater proportion. In China this meant the rapid growth of second-tier public institutions and eventually low-quality private institutions. In Brazil and India in the 2000s, this took the form of the rapid increase of low-cost, generally low-quality private institutions.[1] Thus, in the three lower income per capita BRIC countries with relatively low proportions of students in universities at the beginning of their higher education expansion in the mid-1990s, the mass of "new" students was largely absorbed in low spending per student institutions, and this tended to drive average costs per student in higher education down. In China and Brazil, real (corrected for inflation) spending per student in the mass institutions in the 2000s also tended to decline. Data on total spending per student are even less reliable, but our analysis below suggests that it may have fallen earlier in the decade and is now on the upswing. Spending per student in elite public (and private) institutions in those three countries remained high and, in Brazil and China, rose sharply.

As in the argument for cost sharing and privatization, the most compelling case for this strategy is that it would have been financially difficult for these three countries to have responded to increasing demand for higher education by bringing all students into high-cost institutions. One way they could have done so is to charge much higher tuition (China and India) or, in Brazil, to charge tuition in public universities. Even though the rates of return for higher education were rising in China and were relatively high in India, increasing tuition sufficiently to put all students in higher-cost institutions was probably politically unviable. In Brazil the topic of charging any tuition in public universities is politically off limits, so expanding the public university system through tuition financing was (and is still) not an option.

Superimposed on this major expansion of enrollment at lower average cost per student was a new "imperative": increasingly, in the first decade of the 2000s, countries began to be defined in terms of the quality of their education systems, and this included the quality of their universities. International rankings defined this quality. As "world powers," China and Russia were especially sensitive to the quality of their institutions, and they began investing heavily in their elite universities to attain "world-class" status. India and Brazil are following suit. The result in China and Russia has been an increased spending per student in elite universities. Even though Russia did not fit the typical pattern of reducing spending per student as it expanded enrollment sharply in the 2000s, the divergence in spending per student between elite and nonelite institutions was similar to that of China and Brazil. As in

China, Russia was driven by a need to establish itself as having "world-class" universities.

In the sections that follow, we begin our analysis with the overall spending patterns compared with developed countries, and then move on to the considerable country-by-country variation in the cost-sharing, privatization, and financial-differentiation patterns in their expansion process.

How Much Do the BRIC Countries Spend on Higher Education?

We compare changes among the BRICs in their spending per student in absolute terms and relative to what they spend on primary schooling. These help us make inferences about how many resources these four countries are devoting to higher education and how equitable the BRICs are in their distribution of educational resources by comparing the resources spent on the relatively few youths who reach higher education with the spending on the mass of youths who take primary schooling. If spending per student over time is related to changes in quality, they also help us make inferences about the changing quality of higher education.

Estimating how much three of the BRICs—Brazil, India, and Russia—spend on higher education is not easy because a large fraction of students pay tuition, and in Brazil and Russia, individual institutions, not the government, usually set that tuition. In those two countries, tuition is largely influenced by the market, so it varies from institution to institution and by field of study. In India the situation is even more complicated because the state and central governments regulate tuition for students attending public institutions in their jurisdiction. States also regulate tuition in recognized private colleges and subsidize it for qualifying students. Some students in India also pay higher market-influenced tuition. In China students pay regulated tuition in all public and private institutions.

Thus, for each of the countries except China, we estimated public spending for students attending public universities and the average tuition paid in public and private institutions. For Brazil we did not have to estimate tuition paid in public institutions because the low student fees paid enter into the budgets of the government entities that fund public higher education, but we had to estimate tuition paid by the three-fourths of students who attend private institutions. We were able to use data collected by a private consulting firm in Brazil, Hoper Educacional, to make very approximate estimates of changes in average tuition paid to private institutions in the past decade. We also surveyed higher-prestige private institutions in Brazil to test whether their fees changed over time at a different rate from average private tuition. In Russia we were able to get data from university websites and data collected by the State University Higher School of Economics on federally funded public universities' public spending and their revenues from tuition. In India we used our student and institutional survey data, published data showing state fees set for public institutions, and the state fee regulations for private institutions. We also collected data on government funding for the Indian Institutes of Technology, the highest-prestige engineering institutions. For each country, we made approximate estimates for the first decade of the 2000s to suggest the kinds of changes taking place in spending per student in recent years. The estimates are more approximate in Brazil and India because of the large number of fee-paying students and the relatively little that is known about how much students pay privately for higher education. In any case, our estimates provide a rough idea of how much countries spend per student on higher education.

The results for the absolute spending per student are shown in Figure 4.1. The spending per student includes private tuition and public spending, and is presented in 2005 purchasing power parity (PPP) dollars; hence, it is (to the degree possible) adjusted for differences in living costs between countries. The results suggest quite large differences in the resources going to higher education in each of the BRICs. Brazil spent about the same per student as developed countries such as France, Italy, and Spain in 2000 (but much less than the United States, which spent about 2005 PPP $30,000 per student in 2008). India spends a low 2005 PPP $1,400 per student, including private tuition fees.[2] Adjusted for inflation, Brazil and China reduced average spending per student from 2000 to 2009 (Brazil sharply because of the drop in average tuition paid in private institutions and the increased proportion of students attending private institutions). India may also have reduced spending per student slightly even though it started from already very low levels. Less expensive private education expanded much more rapidly than public, tending to lower spending per pupil, but technical higher education expanded relative to humanities and science, raising average spending per student, and in recent years, largely because of the relative enrollment expansion in elite institutions, spending per student has turned up. The declines in Brazil and China leveled off even in real terms, and China's spending per student began to increase in the latter part of the decade. Russia, on the other hand, increased spending per student

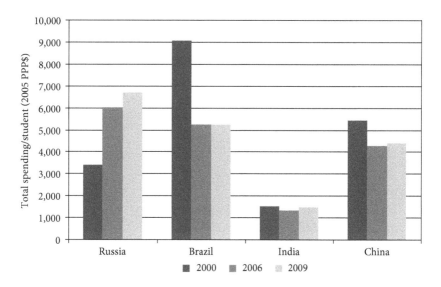

FIGURE 4.1 BRIC countries: Total of private plus public spending in higher education per student, by country, 2000–2009 (in 2005 PPP dollars)

SOURCE: Authors' estimates based on national data sources and OECD, *Education at a Glance,* 2001, 2002, 2009, 2010, and 2012.

sharply as its economy boomed in the early 2000s. Nonetheless, Russia still spends less than most European countries and was somewhat on a par with Spain in 2006–2009.

One of the reasons that India and China can supply higher education at a relatively low cost per student is that faculty salaries are very low at most universities. This is also true at many institutions in Russia. Low faculty salaries also characterize most of Brazil's private institutions, and the main reason that spending per student fell so sharply in the 2000s is that fees in private institutions have apparently declined as competition for students increased. In turn, that was probably made possible by raising class sizes in those institutions. Further, in Brazil, India, and Russia, professors often teach in multiple institutions and tutor high school and college students on the side. In India teaching in multiple institutions is not allowed, but a good number of teachers participate in private tutoring, which is also not allowed in the case of teachers in public institutions. Student-professor ratios are also high in India (see Chapter 7).

As higher education has expanded in the low initial access BRICs, such as Brazil, China, and India, not only has real spending per pupil fallen, but the ratio of this spending compared to primary education costs per pupil has

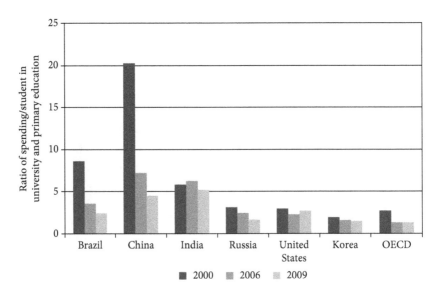

FIGURE 4.2 BRIC countries: Ratio of total spending per student on university to primary school, by country, 2000–2009

SOURCE: Authors' estimates based on national data sources and OECD, *Education at a Glance*, 2001, 2002, 2009, 2010, and 2012.

also generally declined, especially in Brazil and China, where it began at very high levels (Figure 4.2). The ratio of spending on higher education students compared to primary school students in India and China and in public institutions in Brazil is still higher than in the developed countries, but in Russia, it is similar (OECD, 2011a). One of the problems with making accurate comparisons with other countries is that these countries provide only public spending data and a high fraction of their students attend private institutions, paying fees. When we divide total public spending by the total number of tertiary students in these countries, the estimates of spending per student are likely to be inaccurate. Nevertheless, a ratio of 2:1 or 2.5:1 in higher education spending per student compared to primary (or in the case of Russia, primary and secondary combined) spending per student is fairly typical.

In Brazil the decline in the ratio of higher/primary spending per student is partly the result of a sharp increase in primary spending per pupil in the 2000s in real terms (adjusted for inflation) and partly a result of the estimated fall of tuition costs adjusted for inflation in private higher education. We show this below when we discuss the detail of Brazil's financing of its university system. In India the lack of decline is the result of a decrease in primary spending per pupil and a proportionally similarly decline in spending per student at the university level. In Russia the rise in the ratio is because of the substantial increase in spending on primary plus secondary students (the figure is combined in Russia), even as university spending per pupil also rose. In China the ratio of higher/primary spending decreased sharply, from 20.2 in 2000 to 5.3 in 2008, as (nominal) primary spending per pupil increased by more than six times and (nominal) higher education spending per student increased by less than 30 percent over the decade. At the same time, the number of primary school students decreased over the same period by around 23 percent (because of the particulars of China's changing age demographics) while the number of college students increased by over five times.

Now we turn to the detailed individual country analyses, where we focus on the shape of cost sharing and the nature of increased cost differentiation between elite and mass higher education institutions, both of which vary greatly across these four countries.

China

Of the BRIC countries, and perhaps of all the world's countries, China has made the most radical transformation of its higher education system in the shortest period of time. As part of this transformation, policy makers reduced the number of universities under the control of the central government from 345 to 111 and steadily increased the number (and size) of provincial-level public four-year institutions. Private universities have also been allowed to proliferate and offer four-year degrees since the early 2000s and now absorb about one-fifth of four-year undergraduate students (NBS, 2010). Altogether, non-elite institutions increased from about 700 (mostly public) institutions in 1996 to 2,305 institutions (720 four-year public, 370 four-year private, 929 three-year public, 286 three-year private) in 2009.

Along with these changes in institutional structure, the government radically changed the way it financed higher education. The basic sources of financing for higher education in China changed from a system that was paid for mainly by direct government contributions (83 percent of funding) in 1990 to one in which just less than half (49 percent) of the funding came from direct government contributions and about one-third (33 percent) came from tuition and other student fees in 2009.

Therefore, one major feature of expansion was the shift to cost sharing— since the late 1990s, almost all students who attend public or private higher education institutions in China pay tuition. Cost sharing was understood by policy makers to be both necessary to support university expansion and feasible since GDP per capita increased rapidly over the course of the economic transition (Min, 2004). Cost sharing was also introduced to spur the spending of the large amount of savings accumulated by families in the 1980s and 1990s. Thus, average fees in public institutions rose by approximately four to five times from 1997 to 2006. The fees in private four-year institutions also rose substantially during this time. However, in 2007, the State Council fixed tuition at 2006 levels for five years such that they would no longer increase but rather continue to differ systematically by province, by university tier, and, to a smaller degree, by major.

Table 4.1 shows the current pattern of tuition rates across different areas and university tiers. Essentially, public four-year universities (both first- and second-tier institutions) generally charge about 4,000–5,000 yuan for tuition in most provinces. Higher rates exist in Beijing, Shanghai, and more developed provinces. Private institutions usually charge more than double what public four-year institutions charge, while three-year vocational colleges on average charge somewhat more than public four-year universities.[3] The government has additionally mandated that annual dormitory fees cannot exceed 1,200 yuan in any of these institutions. Survey data for students from four-year institutions, which we collected in 2008, further show that individuals from families from the lowest socioeconomic quintile annually spend an average of 9,300 yuan on "necessary expenditures" compared to those from the upper quintile, who spend about 2,300 yuan more.[4] Personal expenditures thus vary to a limited degree across students from different socioeconomic backgrounds.

TABLE 4.1 China: Tuition charges (yuan) for different university tiers, 2009

	Beijing/Shanghai	Shaanxi	Other regions
First- and second-tier (public four-year) universities	4,200–10,000	3,500–4,500	2,500–5,500
Third-tier (private four-year) universities	11,500–18,000	8,500–10,000	6,000–18,000
Fourth-tier public colleges (three-year vocational)	6,000–7,500	4,500–6,100	1,200–7,000

SOURCE: Shaanxi Admissions Committee, 2007.
NOTES: China's State Council (2007) declared that list tuition prices must be fixed at 2006 levels for five years. Tuition prices across tiers and across provinces are somewhat higher for more-competitive majors.

Cost Differentiation

Absolute spending on higher education increased by more than five times (in real terms) from 1998 to 2010, but this huge increase went to expanding enrollment, not to increasing overall average spending per student. Discrepancies in spending per student widened across elite and nonelite university tiers, especially as different tiers expanded enrollments at different rates. That is, the spending per student in elite institutions was about 20 percent higher than in nonelite universities (about 3,200 constant [2008] yuan) in 1997, but well over double by 2008, and increased substantially in 2009 and 2010 (Figure 4.3).[5] In the 2000s the government again created space for the gradual rise of "third-tier" four-year private institutions (i.e., generally less selective than public four-year institutions), which charged high tuition fees. Such private four-year universities absorb economically better off students unable to qualify for first- and second-tier public universities.

Because tuition and other fees have been fairly similar between elite and nonelite public institutions, discrepancies in total spending per student across these institutions throughout the first decade of the 2000s were largely caused

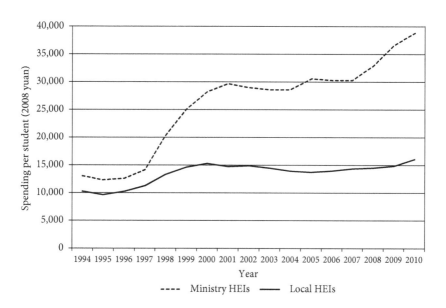

FIGURE 4.3 China: Spending per student by type of institution, 1994–2010[a] (2008 yuan)

SOURCE: NBS, various years. *China Educational Finance Statistical Yearbook.*
[a]Includes three- and four-year degree-granting higher education institutions.

by differences in the size of government allocations to each university. Policy makers have earmarked major financial support for elite institutions. The government's Project 985 has provided the designated top 9 universities in China, as well as the next 26 (in the first stage, 28 in the second stage) institutions with close to 60 billion yuan between 1999 and 2008 for improving innovation, establishing competitive fields of study, raising the quality of teaching staff, improving basic institutional conditions, and increasing international cooperation.[6] Project 211, which was initially implemented much earlier, in 1994, well before the expansion of the system, has also provided most of the 100-plus ministry-run (elite) institutions (including the Project 985 recipients) with close to 19 billion RMB (until 2011) for improving institutional capacity and developing key disciplines.[7] The 985 Project itself comprises a substantial proportion of total annual public financing for higher education since the time of higher education expansion.

Thus, discrepancies exist in total spending per student between elite and nonelite institutions, and these are increasing. Mohrman (2008) further shows how the spending patterns in top universities in China are quickly catching up to top universities elsewhere. She estimates that Tsinghua University and Peking University (the top two institutions in China) spent about 51,000 and 34,000 U.S. dollars per student in 2007 compared to 216,000, 53,000, and 48,000 U.S. dollars per student for MIT, Oxford, and UC Berkeley, respectively (adjusted for purchasing power parity). In terms of total R&D expenditure per professor/researcher, MIT spent around 131,000 U.S. in 2007 while Tsinghua and Peking spent 87,000 and 53,000 respectively (Mohrman, 2008).

As provincial-level institutions, both public and private, have had far fewer funds to work with than ministry-level institutions over the last decade of expansion (despite the fact that they have to train the majority of the college student population), they may have been motivated to keep costs per student down. There is evidence that the student-faculty ratio in Chinese higher education institutions has risen rapidly during the expansion, doubling from eight in 1993 to more than seventeen in 2008 (NBS, various years). From our survey of thirty-five universities in four provinces, we find that provincial-level universities have considerably higher student per teacher ratios than central-level institutions.[8] Further, provincial governments in more economically developed areas generally provide strong financial support to the higher education institutions under their jurisdiction, compared to those in less developed provinces.[9]

India

As discussed, a main feature of India's higher education expansion has been the growth of unaided private colleges, which rely for their financing entirely on tuition. They now account for about 93 percent of the student intake in undergraduate engineering, about 90 percent in business administration, and more than 50 percent in medicine. Overall, enrollment in private colleges is roughly 50–60 percent of total enrollment (although an accurate figure is difficult to come by). Their fees vary greatly. In addition, public institutions charge fees that vary by field of study and the fee policies of each state. Public and private aided colleges and universities use these fees to supplement funding they receive from either the central or state government (depending on their affiliation). Thus, cost sharing plays an increasing role in financing higher education in India.

However, the degree of cost sharing is very difficult to measure because of the extremely complicated fee structure in Indian higher education. Colleges and universities in each state accept students based on a state government administered college entrance examination system conducted separately by each state or nationally at all-India level. National institutions (all public), such as the Indian Institutes of Technology, the National Institutes of Technology, and the Indian Institutes of Management, conduct a separate all-India entrance examination. Students are ranked based on these tests. The students with high ranks (set by the number of admissions available that are determined by each state government), whether they join government or private colleges, pay a low fee, which is also fixed by each state government. Government colleges admit the high-rank students only and charge the (lower) government fee, which varies from state to state. The private aided and unaided colleges also admit a large number of students from this high rank, and they pay the fixed government fee. Students whose ranks are below the benchmark have to pay a higher level of fee approved separately for each college in some states. Such students join either private aided or unaided colleges.

Both government and private colleges are required to admit "designated" students from lower castes. This is the result of the government's affirmative action program, which requires all colleges in India, both public and private, to admit, as part of their allowed intake in each institution, about 50 percent of their students from such designated "disadvantaged" castes. These students get a fee subsidy, ranging from 50 to 100 percent, depending on the designated category. The fee subsidy takes several forms—scholarships, full or partial fee waivers, and fee reimbursement direct to the college by the government. On the other hand, unlike public colleges and universities, both private aided and unaided colleges and private deemed universities can accept nondesignated group students at much higher tuition fees than the fees charged by government colleges and universities. Furthermore, depending on the state, private colleges and universities can accept up to 25 percent of students at even higher fees. These students are those who obtained very low scores in the qualifying examination and have little bargaining power besides the tuition fees they are willing to pay.

Essentially all private colleges are nonprofit charitable trusts, so cannot, by law, make profits. However, as we shall show in Chapter 5, many of these charitable trusts can and do accumulate considerable surplus based on the difference between the total tuition fees they collect and their spending for faculty and other services. Most use this surplus to expand enrollment by responding to market demand and therefore accumulate more surplus in order to expand further.

Evidence of this market responsiveness is that the expansion of private colleges has been greatest in those fields of study that are most in demand and in those localities where the demand for graduates in these fields is expanding most rapidly. For example, whereas government and government-aided institutions saw an increase of barely 3.5 percent in 2000–2005, private unaided colleges expanded almost 109 percent. In 2002, 78 percent of all engineering and technology colleges were private (Tilak, 2003). In 2006 the percentage had increased to 85 percent and by 2009 to nearly 93 percent. The southern states dominate in private engineering and technology education. Andhra Pradesh, Karnataka, Tamil Nadu, and Kerala (in descending order) have the highest percentage of private engineering and technology colleges (Beteille, 2008). The only other major states where a large number of private engineering colleges exist are Maharashtra and Uttar Pradesh.

At the same time, some events point toward expansion of public universities and colleges in the future. During the eleventh five-year plan (2007–2012) period, the central government began to increase the number of Indian Institutes of Technology (IITs—by 2010, the number of IITs doubled), Indian Institutes of Science Education and Research (IISERs), National Institutes of Technology (NITs), and Indian Institutes of Information Technology (IIITs) (Planning Commission, 2008). These are all "elite," relatively expensive, highly selective, central-government-funded and public engineering/technical universities with a relatively high degree of autonomy, designed to greatly increase the high end of the Indian engineering and science cadre. However, the total number of students in all these institutions together is still small compared to the total output of India's engineering colleges.

The form of India's higher education expansion in the 2000s does not appear to be accidental. It is a conscious decision by the central state to reduce its role in financing the public expansion of undergraduate education (see Tilak, 2005, 2008; Bhushan, Malhotra, and Gopalakrishnan, 2009, Table 8) and to put more pressure on the states to take on this task. The states, in turn, are allowing expansion to be carried out by the private sector, relying less on direct state involvement through the expansion of wholly public or government-aided private institutions and more on indirect state influence through regulation of curriculum, examination standards, and how much tuition private institutions can charge. The state's motivation in encouraging private expansion may be in part the need to shift its resources to primary and secondary education. This shift from direct control to regulation is especially true in high-payoff fields such as management and engineering/computer science.

Overall, the result of this strategy in the early 2000s was a steady reduction in *public* spending per the *total* number of students in higher education until the middle of the decade, when spending per student began rising quite significantly (Figure 4.4). These data do not include the increasing private spending per student, but they do indicate that average *public* spending per the total number of students (not including tuition paid by students in public institutions) in the 2000s was about Rs 13,000–20,000 in nominal terms or USD 300–500 at the exchange rates of the time. However, public spending per student varies considerably from state to state. Public spending per student is also much higher for technical education, which is also now rising rapidly. Overall, by allowing enrollment growth to be absorbed by increasing numbers of private colleges, the public sector greatly reduced the amount it had to spend per student.

Full costs are recovered for most professional programs in private colleges and, significantly, in public colleges as well. Tuition fees remain low in central universities (usually attended by the highest-scoring students), but they are quite high in many state universities, particularly in Tamil Nadu, Karnataka, Kerala, Haryana, Punjab, and Rajasthan. In the late 1990s, nearly 50 percent or more of the operating budget of many state universities, such as Madras University (50.4 percent), Bangalore University (63.7 percent), and Punjab University (50.4 percent), came from student fees (Tilak and Rani, 2003; Beteille, 2008).

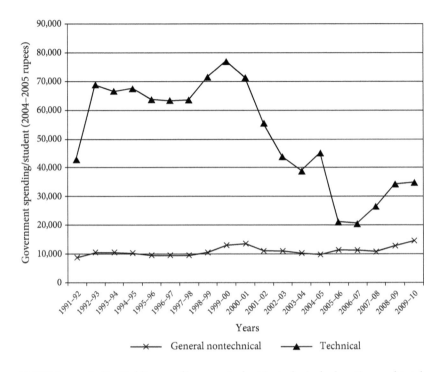

FIGURE 4.4 India: Public spending per student in technical education and total higher education, 1991–2009 (in 2004–2005 rupees)

SOURCE: Calculated from the Ministry of Higher Education and Development, *Analysis of Budget Expenditure on Education* (various years) and UGC, *Annual Reports* (various years).
NOTES: Budgets for university education cover all students other than technical students. Technical education budgets are for technical colleges and universities and cover categories of students other than just engineering and computer science—these other categories of students represented about 13% of all technical students in 2009.

We have three sources of data on fees. The first is from the websites of various Indian states, which we gathered in 2008 and again in 2012. Table 4.2 shows our estimates of average tuition fees (other fees are not included) set by several states for private unaided engineering colleges in 2006–2007 and in 2011–2012. Two of these states are in our survey (see below)—Maharashtra and Tamil Nadu. It does not appear that tuition went up in real terms in the past five years, except at the high end of the range—in some top private colleges. Because about 90+ percent of engineering students attend private unaided colleges, it appears that the cost per student in mass higher education institutions stayed rather constant when corrected for inflation. Nevertheless, in more demanded private unaided colleges, 25 percent of students—those

TABLE 4.2 India: State-prescribed annual fees for private college undergraduate programs in engineering, by state, 2006–2007 and 2011–2012

State	2006–2007 Average/range (current rupees)	2006–2007 Average/range (2011 rupees)	2011–2012 Average range (2011 rupees)
Andra Pradesh	22,000	34,200	31,000–35,000
Chattisgarh	20,000–31,900	31,100–50,000	42,300–48,300
Gujarat	30,000–36,000	46,700–56,000	30,000–59,000
Haryana	32,000–61,500[a]	70,000	
Himachal Pradesh	41,000	64,000	30,000–48,000
Jammu and Kashmir	32,000	50,000	
Kerala			35,000–150,000
Madhya Pradesh	23,300–26,000	36,300–39,000	36,000–64,000
Maharashtra	25,000	39,000	37,850–101,200
Punjab	51,500	80,000	49,000
Rajasthan	41,000	64,000	
Tamil Nadu	25,500–40,000	40,000–62,200	40,000–70,000
West Bengal			70,000–78,000

SOURCE: 2006–2007 and 2011–2012: various India state government websites. Adjustment to 2011 rupees made using consumer price index available from World Bank, various years. *World Development Indicators.*
[a]2006–2007 and 2007–2008.

who score below the cutoff on the state entrance test—may pay much higher fees because colleges can negotiate a fee above the state-mandated levels.

Our second source for tuition fees is our survey of electronic engineering/computer science students in Delhi, Karnataka, Maharashtra, and Tamil Nadu in 2008–2009. We asked students to report the tuition fees they paid. Consistent with what we would expect, average tuition fees in government and government-aided private (PA) colleges are much lower than in private unaided (PUA) colleges. Students reported paying an average of about Rs 20,000 in tuition fees in government and PA colleges, and Rs 50,000 in private unaided colleges (Rs 85,000 in one outlier). Overall, in our sample, which proportionally over-sampled government and PA colleges relative to PUA colleges (in terms of the proportion of the number of colleges), the average tuition paid was about Rs 42,000 per year or about USD 870. Total fees paid were somewhat higher, over Rs 50,000 thousand, or about USD 1,200 annually. Total fees vary greatly from institution to institution. In addition to tuition, in many cases there are other expenditures of the order of Rs 4,000–5,000, but in some cases such expenditures are much more, thus reaching the relatively high average figure reported (for the interested reader, these data are available from the authors).

The fees as reported by students are confirmed by the third source of data on fees—our institutional survey and interviews with administrators in 2008–2009 in private and public engineering colleges and universities, which also showed total fees to vary in the range of Rs 50,000–80,000 range in private institutions and about Rs 25,000 in public and private aided institutions. Related costs (housing, food, transportation, and textbooks) of attending college and additional spending by students and their families raise the total annual private costs of attending public college in 2008–2009 to about Rs 110,000 in public colleges and Rs 166,000 in private colleges.

Cost Differentiation

Because of the difficulty of gathering overall spending per student data, we limit our analysis cost differentiation between elite (public) and mass (private) institutions to engineering colleges.

Although fees vary greatly across engineering colleges, with private colleges charging average fees that are generally much higher than in public colleges, fees alone do not reflect total spending by the engineering students. In addition to fees, public colleges receive a subsidy from the state or the central government, anywhere from 0 to 98 percent of total costs per student.[10] If the average is 50 percent, as claimed by Agarwal (2006), it is likely that the average cost per student in public engineering colleges was about Rs 50,000–60,000 in 2008–2009, or about USD 1,200–1,500 per year, somewhat higher than the average for private colleges.

This is confirmed by operational cost data we gathered in our sample of almost 40 colleges and universities. Of the twenty-one institutions for which we could get operational costs, five were nonelite public (aided) institutions of engineering education. The average reported costs per student in 2009 dollars were $1,560.

Beyond the average public university/aided college, India also invests in a relatively small number of elite technical universities. The seven (which have been doubled in the past two years to sixteen) Indian Institutes of Technology produced about 7,000 graduates in 2008. Entry into the IITs is extremely limited, by special examination, and graduates are considered competitive with graduates from elite undergraduate programs in the developed countries. Spending per student in the IITs is also much higher than in other public institutions. The allocated government budget per student for the seven IITs in 2008 was Rs 154,000 per student according to government figures, or about USD 3,100 (government data collected by authors; see also Banerjee and Muley, 2007). In addition, students pay about USD 750–800 in annual fees. However, this is almost certainly an underestimate of cost per student in the IITs. We were able to get budget data from two IITs in our college/university survey and from one national institute. The average spending per student in those three institutions was about $8,000 in 2009 dollars.

As in China, then, India's elite institutions spend much more per student than those institutions that serve the mass of engineering and computer science students. The difference in India is probably relatively more than the difference in China. And in India these elite institutions subsidize students more than in China—except for the very-highest-cost Chinese institutions (such as Tsinghua University and Peking University). The IITs and NITs charge relatively much lower average fees than paid by students in India's mass private institutions because all students attending the elites are eligible for the lowest level of fees. Yet spending on operating costs per student in the IITs appears to have increased much more slowly than in elite Chinese universities even in nominal terms, and IIT spending may even be decreasing in real terms. Therefore, it is likely that the difference between the spending per student in the IITs/NITs and the much lower spending in the other aided and unaided technical colleges and universities did not increase in the past ten years when adjusted for inflation. Figure 4.5 shows operating costs per student and capital costs per student in the IITs from 1999 to 2008.

Figure 4.4, above, and Figure 4.5 suggest that average spending per student in higher education in India fell in the period 2000–2006 but may have risen since and that the difference in spending per student between elite and nonelite institutions has not changed in the past decade. The data on Brazil and Russia below indicate that this makes India somewhat unusual. India's central government-run elite institutions have many more resources per student, and students are much more heavily subsidized than in the "mass" institutions. However, the government does not appear to be increasing the resources per student to the individual elite universities, nor do we have evidence of declining average spending per student in the nonelite public and private colleges. Rather, the central government is building more elite technical institutions and is therefore providing more access to that type of university. Government has begun spending more money per student overall, but not more per student in each IIT.

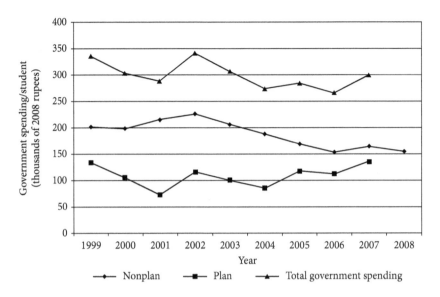

FIGURE 4.5 India: Trends in government spending per student in Indian institutes of technology, 1999–2008 (thousands of 2008 rupees)[a]

SOURCE: Banarjee, R., and V. Mulay (2007), Figure 2.34, and Ministry of Human Resource Development, various years. *Analysis of Budget Expenditures on Education.* Delhi.
[a]In addition to the government grants to IITs as shown, students pay fees that go directly to each IIT. According to Banarjee and Mulay (Table 2.12), fees represented about 10% of plan and nonplan grants in 2005 at IIT Mumbai, probably typical for IITs. There is not evidence that fees have risen in real terms since 2005 (see their Figure 2.23).

Because, as we showed above, the average tuition fees in private unaided institutions do not seem to be rising in real terms, average costs per student in these lower-tier mass institutions have stayed about the same in 2006–2011. Thus, spending differentiation between elite and nonelite institutions does not appear to be increasing, as is the tendency in the other BRICs.

Brazil

The way Brazil finances higher education is unique among the BRICs. In essence, Brazil has two higher education systems, one that is financed entirely by federal, state, and municipal governments—primarily the first two—with virtually no student tuition or other forms of cost sharing, and the second, which has been financed until just recently entirely by private sources, mainly through student tuition payments, but also with subsidies from Catholic church orders. The federal government is legally "in charge" of the private system in terms of accrediting it and keeping it "accountable" by requiring private universities to participate in student exit tests, such as the *Provão,* now replaced by the ENADE.

In Chapter 2 we show that the proportion of students attending private higher education institutions was already high in the mid-1990s but grew rapidly after 2000. Few of these private institutions have graduate programs (Nunes, de Carvalho, and Vogel de Albrecht, 2009), and few receive research monies from the government or from private sources. Hence, professors at most private higher education institutions generally do not conduct research (see Chapter 5, where we show these figures), nor are they expected to. Only 13 percent of faculty in private institutions had doctorates in 2008—about the same as in 2002—compared with 50 percent of faculty with doctorates in federal universities and 42 percent in state institutions. Although we have limited data on how much faculty are paid in private universities, what we do have suggests that almost all private institutions pay less than federal or state universities. In addition, Ministry of Education data show that the student/faculty ratio in 2008 was about 18 in private institutions, about 10 in federal universities, about 12 in state universities, and about 17 in the small number of municipal institutions. All these figures point to much lower costs per student in the average private higher education institution than in the federal- and state-funded institutions. It is important to keep this in mind when we compare the average tuition that students pay when they attend a private institution compared to what government spends on a student in public higher education.

The Brazilian government slowed down the growth of places in public universities after 2000 and essentially sanctioned the absorption of the rapid increase in new higher education students mainly in private institutions that, on average, provided that education at declining average cost. Increased privatization was not, in and of itself, the reason for the increasing differentiation between elite public institutions and the privates, because traditional, elite private institutions, according to our research, maintained their tuition rates in real terms, and some new private institutions entered the market providing very-high-cost elite education. Rather, as we shall show, by allowing lightly regulated low spending per student private institutions of dubious quality—many of them for profit—to absorb most of the new enrollment, in effect the Brazilian government increasingly differentiated the higher education received by a minority of students in elite (mostly public) institutions from the education received by the students in mass private institutions.

The fact that the government expanded engineering and computer science education in public higher education institutions relatively slowly compared to enrollment expansion in full-fee-charging private institutions has certainly made it more difficult to promote increasing numbers of graduates in these two fields (other factors, such as mathematics preparation in secondary school, which, on average, is less than adequate in Brazil, also contributed to these difficulties). Engineering is an expensive field to study in private universities even though, as we will show, the average tuition adjusted for inflation has probably declined.

Cost Differentiation

As in all the BRIC countries, tuition and cost data from the privately run part of the Brazilian system are hard to come by. In Brazil the federal government collects good data on private system student enrolment, faculty, available places, graduation, and student achievement, and even data on the tuition charged by individual private institutions for each field of study. However, there has been no systematic study of average tuition paid and how the private higher education sector is changing as it continues to accept increasing numbers of paying students.

We attempt to fill this gap by using several sources. The Ministry of Education and other websites yield current tuition information on private institutions.[11] Murakami and Blom (2008) provide information on a limited number of institutions and courses of study in 2003. As the authors note, these tend to be somewhat higher-priced institutions. Private associations have collected the best data on tuition paid over time. SEMSEP, an association of private universities in São Paulo, sampled more than 500 institutions in that state and found rapidly declining average tuition charged since 1999. Hoper Associates, a private consulting firm, collected national data and also found declining average tuition in the same period. However, these data are not weighted by field of study and may also include much lower tuition paid by students in distance education (enrollment in distance education is not included in our data shown in Chapter 2).

Weighting by field of study could alter this pattern, although probably minimally. The proportion of students enrolling in each field of study changed somewhat over time (business and law declined in relative terms), and engineering and medicine increased. But the major fields of enrollment did not change, with education, business, law, health services (largely nursing and physical therapy), engineering, and sciences (including computer science) as the main courses that students took. These ranged from 18 percent of total private enrollment in education down to 9 percent in sciences.

Total average spending per higher education student in the Brazilian system is essentially equal to the weighted (by percentage enrolled in public and private institutions) average public spending per student in public institutions—federal, state, and municipal—plus the average tuition that private higher education students pay to private institutions.[12] There are other contributions to private education budgets, namely the subsidies provided by the various church sponsors of private universities, but we have no way of getting these data. The percentage of total revenues these contributions represent is small, in any case, according to one study (Hoper Educacional, 2009). Furthermore, from our surveys in India, we know that even nonprofit private institutions can run large surpluses, where tuition paid by students exceeds the cost of running the institution. This seems to be less true in Brazil in recent years. The large excess capacity of private higher education institutions and increased competition have apparently driven down average profits, even in for-profit institutions.

Figure 4.6 shows the official figures for spending per student in the years 2000–2010 in public institutions and our estimated average tuition paid based on Hoper Educacional's data on tuition paid in 2000–2011. All the figures are adjusted for inflation. Public spending per student in public universities declined in the early 2000s but has risen steadily since 2003. Although not all public universities are elite institutions, these data suggest that spending per student in elite universities has risen in the past decade. At the same time, if Hoper's tuition estimates are correct, average private tuition is a rapidly falling percentage of public spending per public university student, from 81 percent in 2000 to 32 percent in 2010. Because almost all private institutions are mass and nonelite, this means an increasing difference in spending per student and, probably, quality between elite and nonelite higher education institutions.

There are a number of reasons that this decline in average tuition (hence, spending per student in private institutions) could have occurred, including a changing composition of low-cost and high-cost fields of study in public and private institutions, increasing numbers of private institutions in the marketplace that increased competition and drove down tuition, and possibly that expansion meant attracting lower-income students, which could have meant new institutions entering the market offering increasing lower-tuition (and lower-quality) programs for those students. Our analysis suggests that the

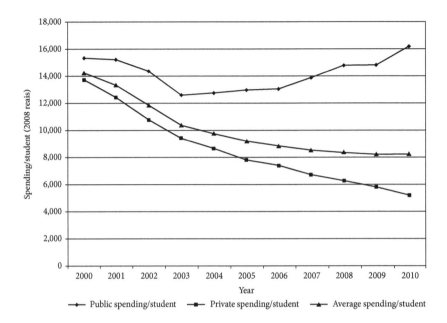

FIGURE 4.6 Brazil: Public spending per public higher education student, average private tuition in private higher education, and average spending per student, 2000–2010 (2008 reais)

SOURCE: Private tuition from Hoper Educacional, 2009. Public spending per student from INEP (http://portal.inep.gov.br/estatisticas-gastoseducacao-despesas_publicas-p.a._precos .htm), accessed Aug. 4, 2012. Average spending per student estimated by weighting public spending and private tuition per student by percentage enrollment in public and private institutions.

most likely reasons are the last two. [13,14] This implies that part of the declining costs per student in the private sector could be caused by greater efficiency, and part is probably because of absorbing increasing numbers of new students in institutions that have lowered costs by lowering quality (for example, hiring more part-time, less-prepared instructors and increasing class size).

We show in Chapter 3 why it is possible for the Brazilian government to believe that (up to now) it can rely so heavily on the private sector to meet the nation's needs for graduates in most fields of study and for greater numbers of technical graduates. The payoff is high for higher education graduates generally, including for engineers and computer scientists, even when we account for the high fraction of students who must pay full tuition costs to obtain this education. On the other hand, given that average payoffs are so high for higher education suggests that either financial barriers to entry posed by tuition are great or that the rates of return for attending lower-cost (lower-tuition) private institutions and lower-tuition programs of study in these institutions are much lower than average. It seems to be increasingly difficult to expand access to higher education for low-income secondary graduates because they cannot score high enough on entrance examinations for the public universities and cannot afford to pay tuition at the privates.

Some private institutions seem to be offering lower-cost, almost certainly lower-quality higher education to attract these lower-income students, but this implies that these students are probably getting an increasingly different kind of higher education than students who can pay much more or those who have been able to acquire the academic qualifications to get free public university education. The government has begun partially subsidizing tuition at private universities for low-income students, has recently passed affirmative action legislation to admit increasing numbers of disadvantaged black and indigenous students to federal universities, and plans to expand public university places in night courses. But even with these efforts, given the overall reliance on private institutions to expand enrollment, the average quality of higher education received by the mass of young Brazilians could well be declining.

Russia

Like Brazil, Russia still provides those secondary school students with the highest test scores on the Russian Unified State Exam (USE) a free higher education in public institutions that is totally paid for by the government (in Russia, by the federal government). Unlike Brazil, Russia has created the possibility for students who do not qualify for free places in the program of study they wish to pursue to attend a public institution as a tuition-paying student. An increasingly large proportion of Russian university students fall into this category. Thus, in Russia most paying students attend the same public universities that receive quotas of "free" students, and about one-sixth of all students attend private institutions. Those students also pay full tuition, usually less than that charged by public institutions.

The Federation Law on Education, which established the legal basis for these financing changes in 1992, also gave universities more autonomy in staffing and managing their budgets. However, as the Russian economy declined in the 1990s and government higher education funding declined even more, universities were forced to rely increasingly on tuition revenues to survive (Bain, 2001). By 1997–1998, one of five students paid tuition, and the fraction of university revenues accounted for by tuition payments during this period was as high as 70 percent in some institutions (Bain, 2001).

Bain (2001) traces the origins of Russia's tuition policy to contract training in the 1980s, when specialists were trained in higher education institutions for particular public enterprises and paid for by the future employer enterprises. With the fall of the communist regime and the command economy in the early 1990s, the pressure for admission to universities in law, business, financing, and banking increased over and above the small number of free places available in these fields. The 1992 law and the new Russian Constitution of 1993 still guaranteed free higher education but also stipulated that the free places were for students entering university for the first time and based on competition in entrance examinations. This provided the legal basis for allowing students who did not qualify for the free places to enter on a fee-paying basis, but still as a contract between a future employer and the university. A governmental decree in 1994 changed this so that students and their families could also pay tuition directly. Although the expansion of fee paying was originally tied to a student loan program, by 1996, "the clauses on student loans were omitted as a work in progress" (Bain, 2001: 67). Public higher education institutions, in turn, saw tuition as a major source of additional revenues, although in the 1990s Russian economy, there was concern that this revenue source could not expand much because fees were very high compared to Russian families' income. But as the economic situation improved in the 2000s, so did the proportion of fee-paying students. To this day, the Ministry of Education in Moscow, in conjunction with other ministries, assigns the quotas of publicly paid places in the various public universities and their programs of study nationwide.[15]

Thus, some students in public universities are subsidized, and some pay. This varies from university to university and department to department within universities. In Chapter 2 we show that more than half the students now enrolled in Russian public universities pay tuition and that about one-sixth of the total enrollment is in tuition-based private institutions. Furthermore, for 45 percent of the public university students, but only 37 percent of all higher education students, university is free, totally subsidized by the federal government. Sixty-three percent pay tuition either in public or private institutions, and tuition varies from university to university and for different courses of study. We also have anecdotal evidence that students pay different levels of tuition in the same institution and for the same field based on their USE test scores.

The Russian financing system is just one more variation of what we have seen in the other BRIC countries: an increasing fraction of students studying in universities pay fees—in the Russian case, fee-paying students study in public universities side by side with "free" students. These fee-paying students generally do not pay at a level that meets university costs per student. The reason for this lower tuition is that fee-paying students are "add-ons." In addition, many of the paying students attend courses in the evening. They generally pay closer to the marginal cost of their education than to the average cost.

As in Brazil and India, estimating how much the country is spending on higher education per student means we have to estimate the public spending per publicly subsidized student—in Russia, these students are considered in budget university places (students pay no tuition)—and how much tuition families/students are paying. In Russia about 75 percent of tuition-paying students attend public universities.

We make two estimates of public spending on higher education in Russia. Figure 4.7 shows our estimates using data that the Russian government reports to UNESCO (the proportion of GDP the public sector spends on tertiary education). The OECD reports a somewhat lower figure for 2008 in *Educational Indicators* (OECD, 2009). We use Ministry of Education figures to make a second estimate in more recent years (Figure 4.8). But there is strong agreement among those who know the system and from the different sources that spending per student went up substantially in 2000–2009. This estimate suggests that in 2005 PPP dollars, Russian government spending on government-subsidized students in the quota or "free" places in 2008 and 2009 was more than 5,000 PPP dollars, up from 2,200 PPP dollars in 2000. These data are approximate. However, the spending per budget place leveled off in real terms in 2010 even though the number of students in universities declined.

Estimating tuition paid to public institutions and to private universities over this same period of time is even more difficult. There is no comprehensive study of tuition charges in Russia over the past ten years, so we draw our figures from several primary sources: website searches, our student survey of 2,200 students from 25 technical universities in several different states (*oblasts*), and Ministry of Education data on tuition revenues for 2006–2010. To get some idea of how much tuition charges have changed in the earlier 2000s, we also used data from a survey that measured tuition paid for non-quota places in 1996–1997 (Bain, 2001). We likely overestimate the steady drop from this earlier period in real (corrected for inflation) tuition that students

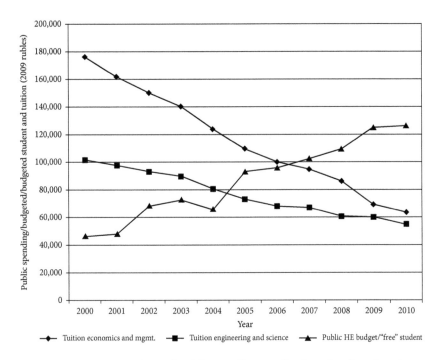

FIGURE 4.7 Russia: Estimated public spending per "budget place" student in public higher education and estimated tuition fees for fee-paying students in public universities, 2000–2010 (2009 rubles)

SOURCE: Government budget data from State Statistical Committee of Russia, 2010. Budget data divided by enrollment data for budget places from Figure 2.3. We used baseline tuition costs in the late 1990s from Bain, 2001, and tuition figures for more recent years from various sources, including Russian Education—Federal Portal (System of Federal Educational Portals). For example, see www.edu.ru/abitur/rating/rating_cost_2009.htm, accessed Aug. 4, 2012. Tuition is very approximate, as in Brazil and India.

paid because of the highly approximate nature of our baseline figure from the mid-1990s (Figure 4.7).

Tuition varies greatly by university and field of study. For example, in 2009–2010, tuition for studying in the field of economics and business management averaged 72,000 rubles outside of Moscow/St. Petersburg and 95,000 rubles in Moscow. Of course, there was major variation, particularly in Moscow, with a number of the more prestigious institutions charging 200,000–300,000 rubles tuition (USD 7,000–10,000) per year of study. In technical fields, tuition can also be much higher than the average 60,000 rubles we estimated. In Moscow one institution charges about 100,000 rubles to study a variety of technical fields.

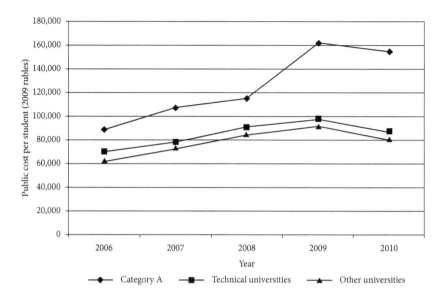

FIGURE 4.8 Russia: Estimated public spending per "budget place" student in public higher education, by category of university, 2006–2010 (2009 rubles)

SOURCE: Estimates made for this study by the Economics Department, State Research University Higher School of Economics, from data supplied by the Ministry of Education.

In real terms (corrected for inflation), tuition fell sharply relative to public spending per student for "free," or government-budgeted, places. Tuition levels were probably held down at most institutions in the 2000s by the competition to attract a dwindling number of potential new fee-paying students, as more and more students were incorporated into the higher education system. According to estimates made for this study by the Higher School of Economics (HSE) from Ministry of Education data, tuition revenues per student rose from about 160,000 to 170,000 rubles (in 2009 prices) in 2006–2008 for elite universities and about 98,000 to 105,000 rubles for nonelite, nontechnical universities. The HSE estimates suggest that revenues per paying student were higher than public spending on budget places, even though Figure 4.7 suggests that this seems to have changed in 2009 with the economic crisis and increased spending per student by the federal government. The average reported fees of 46,000 rubles in our surveys of technical students are much lower than the estimates in either Figure 4.7 or those made by HSE from the ministry data. Most of the students we sampled were outside Moscow, but it is also likely that they underreported how much tuition they pay.

Cost Differentiation

Like the other BRICs, Russia provides more public financing to elite institutions than to the "mass" universities. In addition, the large number of students paying fees is a second source of differentiation: paying students are charged higher tuition fees in the more prestigious public institutions. Thus, the elite universities not only get more public funding per student; they are also likely to have more revenues per student from tuition.

Unlike in the other BRICs, government spending per university student corrected for inflation increased in Russia, at least until 2009. Is the funding for elite universities rising more than for the mass universities? Elite institutions have always existed in Russia, but in the 2000s, the Russian government moved to officially designate one group of universities as "special." In Chapter 5 we delve more deeply into this reform. We just note here that thirty-eight Russian institutions, made up of the two traditional leading institutions—Moscow State University and St. Petersburg State University—seven federal universities (to be increased to twelve), which have been or are in the process of being formed in various regions by combining groups of existing local universities,[16] and twenty-nine universities that have been designated as National Research Universities (NRUs)[17] are in this special category and are expected to become "leading" or even "world-class" universities. Using data from the Ministry of Education prepared by the Higher School of Economics (one of the designated research universities), we were able to estimate public spending and tuition revenues per student separately for these Category A institutions, technical universities not Category A, and other universities not Category A.[18]

Figure 4.8 shows how public spending per student in the different types of universities rose in recent years but, corrected for inflation, began to decline in 2010. The estimates suggest a major change in government policy in 2008, where public spending per student in the elite universities was drastically increased relative to both technical and other "mass" universities. This is similar to what happened in China in the late 1990s, when the government changed the level of differentiation between a group of "chosen" 111 universities and others. At the same time, the pattern of tuition revenues per student did not change: Category A universities continued to collect higher fees, but their revenues per student from such fees fell slightly compared to mass universities. The data also suggest that nonelite technical universities get about the same public spending as other nonelite universities but are able to collect higher tuition revenues.

Enrollment in budgeted places fell in 2009 and continued to fall in 2010 (see Chapter 2). This contributed to the rise in public spending per student in 2009 because federal budget allocations are made on the basis of staffing and other costs, therefore sticky downward. By 2010, the federal university budget declined in real terms, and despite the falling enrollment, even Category A universities saw a small decline in spending per student. Yet the gap between Category A universities and technical and other nonelite universities continued to increase.

The Russian government is now attempting to "rationalize" the large number of public institutions developed during the Soviet era. Part of this rationalization is a proposal to allocate resources on the basis of university department "performance" on the financing model used by some of the German *Lande* (Orr, Jaeger, and Schwarzenberger, 2007). Performance budgeting requires universities to present a number of outcomes measures (graduation rates, faculty publications, etc.) to the government and to compete against other university departments and other universities for public funds. At highest risk in this competition are technical institutions connected directly to declining industries, many local provincial universities in low-population or low-economic-growth regions, and major cities' second-tier institutions facing enrollment declines in budgeted places and having difficulty attracting tuition-paying students.

Summing Up

We have made the case that in expanding their higher education systems and their technically trained labor forces, the BRIC countries have relied increasingly on user fees (tuition) to pay for this expansion. In terms of raising quality, we have argued that two of the BRICs—Russia and China—are doing so by spending a greater amount of public resources than in the past on a limited number of institutions. In Brazil there is also increasing differentiation between elite and nonelite institutions, and this is taking place partly through the declining spending per student in mass private higher education institutions, which have consolidated and have incorporated increasing numbers of new students at reduced cost per student, and partly through increased spending per student in public institutions, many of them elite. In India we have no evidence of increasing cost per student differentiation between elite and nonelite engineering institutions or that the Indian government is attempting to reduce the differentiation or to improve the quality of either elite or nonelite engineering colleges and universities.

What are the implications of these financing patterns? One is that they are made possible at least in part because of the relatively high and rising private rates of return for higher education. High rates of return have given states the clear option—signaled to them by the exploding demand for attending universities and colleges and, in all four BRICs, by the increasing supply of private university places even when government regulates tuition fees (in India and China). It is true that this increase in demand may be concentrated in certain professional fields, but this still gives governments the opportunity to tax families directly to help finance higher education expansion.

The second implication is that by charging fees in public universities or allowing part of the new enrollment in higher education to be absorbed by full-fee private institutions, BRIC governments may actually be making the distribution of public subsidies more equitable across social class groups and creating the possibility of more equitable access to universities through expansion and government affirmative action policies or other forms of direct subsidies to lower-income students. We consider these topics in Chapters 6 and 8.

On the other hand, increasing differentiation implies that expanding university enrollment, which would be expected to contribute to reductions in income inequality by incorporating increasing numbers of young people into upper levels of education, thus reducing the variance in years of schooling in the labor force, may instead be contributing to greater income inequality depending on who gets access to increasing resourced elite higher education and who gets access to rapidly expanding much less (and possibly increasingly less resourced) mass higher education. We also take on this issue in Chapter 8.

The third implication is that although the quality of university education, particularly of engineering and technical education more generally, may be increased for the relatively small number of graduates from the elite, or so-called "world-class," universities, the average quality of higher education received by the vast majority of students in the expanding system may actually be declining. As a higher fraction of the university-age population gains access to higher education institutions without access to the same level of resources as students had in the past, it is easy to imagine that the quality of the education they receive at best does not increase from already low levels, and may actually decrease. This pattern is very different from the pattern of higher education expansion in the developed countries, where even though second- and third-tier higher education institutions spent (and spend) considerably less per student than the elites, all levels of institutions had their funding per student rise at about the same rate. We explore this changing quality of education in the BRICs in Chapter 7.

5   BRIC Universities as Institutions in the Process of Change

Most analyses of university systems are institutional—that is, either they begin and end with universities as the units of observation and as the sources of change or they begin and end with a global institutional culture rooted in notions of the university. In many such analyses, university actors—usually innovators and leaders—are the principal shapers of the way universities evolve. They, in turn, are constrained by institutional and organizational cultures—often resistant to radical transformations—that serve various goals and constituencies. The institution is therefore the focus of inquiry, and change is situated in the institutions themselves, usually in the form of change agents with a "vision" of transforming the institution into some other version of itself. There are many examples of such studies (see Clark, 1983; Levy, 1980).

There are other views of how higher education functions, and we have discussed some of them in Chapter 1. In the United States, many analysts have focused on universities as influenced by market forces (for example, Kirp, 2003), by business interests (Veblen, 1918), class reproduction or elite reproduction (Bowen, and Bok, 1998), and elite culture (Stevens, 2007). Burton Clark's classic study of university organization (Clark, 1983) stressed the "triangle" of coordination—"market-like" coordination (i.e., a response to market demand from students and their families), state-induced coordination, and academic-professional coordination (the influence of the professoriate and the professional administration of universities). Later work by Clark (1998) and Kirp (2003) discussed the rapid transformation of U.S. higher education institutions into "entrepreneurial universities" concerned with their "bottom line."

In Latin America, besides the structural functionalist view of universities—that universities as institutions can be described in terms of the way these institutions function to meet the goals of the social system—and the elite reproduction view—in which universities' main purpose is to reproduce leaders who have internalized the norms of the power elite—one important analysis characterized the National University of Mexico (UNAM) as a direct extension of the ruling institutionalized political party (Ordorika, 1999). This is similar to the way universities in the Soviet Union or pre-1990 China or Cuba could be analyzed as an extension of the Communist Party. The main difference is that, unlike universities in the Soviet Union or China, the UNAM was allegedly autonomous.

Even so, in Latin America, Europe, and much of the world outside the Anglo-Saxon nations, there is generally acceptance of the notion that the institution of the university is in some form an extension of the state apparatus. The university institution has varying degrees of autonomy from any particular regime or political party, yet it is directly concerned with the goals of the nation-state regarding elite formation, scientific knowledge production, the production of high-level human capital formation, and shaping national culture through intellectual activity (Castells, 1991; World Bank, 2000). At the same time, there is acknowledged tension between the Enlightenment (even pre-Enlightenment) "tradition" of university autonomy and the state's political goals.

Consistent with this more generalized sociological-political literature and contrary to the more institution-centric education literature, we have argued throughout this book that a main driving force behind change in the BRICs' higher education system is the nation-state, and this is true even when significant proportions of universities are private and a high proportion of university students attend such institutions.

In this chapter we examine how the state in each of the BRICs has tried to influence change in universities' institutional structures during the process of great expansion, and, in turn, how higher education institutions (administrators and faculty) have responded to such state efforts. There are many factors of interest in the relationship of the state to universities and universities to the state. Here we focus on two of them—the degree of autonomy universities have in terms of the state and the financing incentives that the state or other structures, such as the market or the state bureaucracy (in terms university administrators' political advancement), provide universities to improve quality. We focus on autonomy and incentives to improve quality because we think they are important for understanding how the state is related to university actors, how decisions are likely to be made about the shape of the university system, and what objectives universities are likely to pursue.

In our study we have direct observations (administrator questionnaires and interviews) in almost forty engineering colleges and universities in India, thirty-four universities in China, and about twenty-five technical and other universities in Russia. In Brazil we draw on secondary studies of public and private universities based on a smaller number of direct observations. In their totality, these comparative data are a rich source for describing how the state in each BRIC country tries to shape the higher education system and, in turn, how various types of higher education institutions respond to changes in regulation (autonomy/state control) and financing.

We show that, in general, BRIC states not only have created multi-tier higher educational systems (more like the United States and in contrast to most European countries), but they also provide different incentives to elite and mass institutions regarding the quality of services to be delivered and even regarding the institutions' goals. Yet each of the BRIC states has its own particular relationship with its higher educational system, based on the past development of the system and the political structure of the state itself. These, in turn, condition institutional responses to the state's attempts to regulate higher education expansion and can change the institutional environment in universities.

Our analysis supports the notion that in China and Russia, the state has considerable control over universities' (including private institutions') institutional development, although there is some degree of conflict over state direction by universities (or provincial governments overseeing provincial universities) in both countries. In Brazil and India, state control is more indirect because private mass institutions absorb so much of the new enrollment there. They have enough autonomy (even with the considerable regulations imposed in India) to both pursue surplus accumulation as a primary objective and to exert pressure on the state to reduce existing and potential regulatory controls. Both public and private institutional environments change as this process evolves, with private institutions adjusting with new strategies to state regulations and public institutions shaped directly by needing to respond to demands from the state for higher quality, new forms of expansion, affirmative action, fewer or more resources per student, and, in some cases, greater accountability.

In the sections below, we provide a brief description of state-university relationships in each BRIC and how they may be changing. Once we establish this understanding of how the state and universities have viewed each other in a time of transformation, we assess the possibly changing autonomy of public and private universities and how university actors view such change. We also analyze several aspects of state efforts to shape institutional incentives in each country and the reaction of administrators and faculty to these incentives. We address five main questions:

- What are the explicit and implicit state policies to increase or reduce university autonomy?
- How are university actors reacting to state policies (if any) toward university autonomy?
- What are the explicit and implicit state policies to improve higher educational quality in each of the BRICs?
- How are university actors reacting to state incentives (if any) to improve quality?
- What are the implications of these interactions between universities and the state for the future of higher education developments in the BRICs?

China

After China's economic reforms in the late 1970s, the state initiated policies that radically transformed the institutional landscape of higher education (Wang, 2011; Tsang and Min, 1992). One major policy change was to merge the many small, highly specialized higher education institutions (HEIs) under various central ministries into more comprehensive institutions under the Ministry of Education. A result of the change was that the average size of HEIs increased by about three times over the 1990s, and HEIs benefited from economies of scale (Levin and Xu, 2005). Under the new system, students were also offered a more flexible, market-oriented training rather than the overly specialized training required by the planned economy. Graduates were similarly asked to apply for jobs in the labor market on their own rather than being assigned to positions in public enterprises under the jurisdiction of the former central ministries.

Toward the end of the 1990s and in the 2000s, the Chinese government also introduced a series of reforms that decentralized university financing. First, much of the responsibility for financing (and managing) nonelite HEIs was devolved from the central government to provincial and municipal governments. Elite HEIs would, for the most part, continue to be financed by the central government. Second, most students were required to pay college fees for the first time in 1997, and these fees quadrupled over the next decade. The government also encouraged universities to generate revenue through outside research and teaching activities (Ngok, 2006). The outcome of these financial reforms was that government and total per capita expenditure in higher education more than doubled from 1995 to 2000, while the government share declined from 70 percent to 56 percent (OECD, 2005).

Besides the large structural shifts in higher education administration and financing, the government extended the autonomy of HEIs in several areas. Public HEI administrators were granted greater control over the internal allocation of funding, personnel management, instruction, and the establishment of research programs. Private institutions, which could determine many of their own internal policies, were also allowed to proliferate and expand (albeit in a limited manner—see Chapter 2). The government also allowed public and private HEIs to provide some input into the size of annual student enrollment quotas and the selection of majors. Overall, the greater autonomy of HEIs strengthened their ability to respond to the needs of an increasingly market-oriented economy.

State Control and University Autonomy

Despite the introduction of "neoliberal" policy reforms such as decentralization, marketization, and privatization over the last three decades, HEIs in China continue to be heavily regulated and influenced by the state (H. Li, 2010). The seemingly neoliberal reforms that policy makers instituted arose from practical considerations and were not the result of changing ideological beliefs. For example, one practical motivation for decentralizing the responsibility to manage and finance HEIs to local governments was economic: decentralization allowed for greater cost sharing between central and local governments. It further allowed HEIs to focus on producing graduates with skills relevant to the needs of local economies. From the standpoint of increasing the political legitimacy of the state, local governments were also more able than the central government to manage the rapid expansion of higher education enrollments. Decentralization also allowed the central government to focus on converting a small group of elite (central) institutions into world-class universities.

The "neoliberal" reforms have also had a limited effect on institutional autonomy because the government has simultaneously instituted other policy reforms that have exerted control over the character and development of HEIs (H. Li, 2010).[1] One of the main ways in which the Chinese state has maintained a strong control over the higher education system and HEIs has been by controlling financing. Despite the shift to cost sharing since the 1990s, about one-half of total higher education financing still comes from the government (see Chapter 4).[2] The government sets tuition list prices and dormitory fees, and finances the bulk of student financial aid, thus effectively controlling net tuition fees across both public and private institutions. In most provinces the government also allocates funds based on each institution's total number of enrollments (which are also controlled by the government).[3] Policy makers determine the amount of funding allocated toward different majors (in addition to influencing their tuition prices), which can influence the expansion rates of different majors.

However, our survey and interview data from almost two dozen university financial departments in China show that the government's ability to use financing to shape institutional behavior is limited by several factors. First, HEIs lack uniform accounting standards. The lack of uniform accounting standards prevents the government from comparing financial performance (e.g., instructional costs per student) across institutions. Second, useful summaries of basic financial information are often not organized and made available even to important internal stakeholders at the university and department levels, much less to the government (see Loyalka and Zhou, 2011). Third, the lack of uniform standards and basic financial information may be exacerbated by a lack of transparency in the allocation of certain types of funds. For example, it is unclear how elite universities spend the funds that they receive from Project 985 and Project 211 (Loyalka and Zhou, 2011).

The lack of financial standards, information, and transparency at HEIs has in turn led government agencies to place stricter regulations on how HEIs use government funding. HEI administrators complain that an overwhelming proportion of government support is in the form of earmarked funds that place rules on how funds can be allocated to departments and faculty. The strictures on how to allocate government funds have been further exacerbated by the fact that Chinese HEIs use highly centralized resource allocation models to distribute funds to departments and faculty (Loyalka and Zhou, 2011). Financial regulations, both from the government and central administrations at HEIs, altogether limit the space for departments and faculty to make flexible, effective decisions. The lack of flexibility can, in turn, affect institutional quality.

One way in which HEIs (and their secondary schools/departments) in China have responded to the constraints associated with government financing (and strict regulations about resource allocation within HEIs) is by generating revenue through alternative channels. For example, many schools/departments in China have established high-fee training programs (such as MBAs, for example), attracted research funding from corporations or other "horizontal" channels, opened businesses or production and development centers, and allowed for faculty to engage in outside consulting work. As is the case in Russia (see below), Chinese HEIs and their secondary units have two sources of funding that they manage: state funding, which is strictly controlled, as well as extra-budgetary funds from which administrators can spend largely at their own discretion.

Besides financing, another area of government control involves regulations on the appointment and promotion of university administrative personnel and faculty. Shortly before the Tiananmen Square uprising, the government enforced a "dual controlling mechanism" in which the administrative staff of an HEI would officially include a group of administrators under the jurisdiction of the Communist Party. These party administrators have been involved in the daily management of faculty and student affairs, ensuring that the culture, organization, and policies of HEIs follow party/socialist lines (H. Li, 2010). Reinforced by a series of laws in the 1990s and 2000, party committees have also been established at the university level (at public and private institutions) and at schools and departments within each HEI. The hiring and promotion of the top university administrators such as the party secretary and university president (who is under the party committee) are also directly determined by the government—in fact, these positions are akin to political appointments. The leadership and administration at each institution are thus intertwined (H. Li, 2010). University administrators have strong incentives to ensure that the state's policies are carried forward. Lower-level administrators, faculty, and even students furthermore often aspire to be part of the party structure, which, among other things, can offer additional career opportunities. This is a unique feature of the Chinese higher education system, long disappeared from Russian universities, for example.

A second way in which the government controls personnel management at HEIs is through the allocation of a limited number of tenured faculty spots (*bianzhi*) at each institution. These *bianzhi* spots enable faculty to receive a basic salary and social benefits including pension, housing, residence permits (which allow faculty to send their children to schools for a reduced tuition price), and medical insurance. Although the autonomy to hire and promote professors by and large resides within public HEIs, schools, and departments, the limited number of *bianzhi* spots at each professorial rank (assistant, associate, and full professor) can limit hiring and promotion opportunities.

According to our interview data from more than thirty HEIs in four provinces, faculty and administrators (especially at lower-tier HEIs) were indeed concerned about the limited number of *bianzhi* spots. Limiting *bianzhi* spots has constrained the number of teachers who can be hired and, relatedly, the ability of departments to reduce teaching loads. Limiting spots for associate professors in first-tier and more-selective second-tier HEIs has created pressure among new faculty to publish journal articles. More generally, the tenure-like status associated with *bianzhi* spots has also prevented the hiring and promotion of new and outside talent within universities and departments. In effect, policy makers (whether consciously or not) influenced the quality of HEIs by setting the number of *bianzhi* spots at each institution.

A third way in which the government influences personnel management and higher education quality is by fixing faculty salary schedules. Specifically, policy makers at the central and local levels determine the basic salary schedules for faculty of different ranks (assistant, associate, and full professor) at public institutions.[4] The salaries are also generally regarded as being quite low. As a result of the low base salaries, almost all of our interviewees at first- and second-tier institutions mentioned the importance of acquiring research funding as a major means to supplement faculty salaries.[5] Therefore, on the one hand, the pressure to supplement base salaries incentivizes scholars to focus on research. On the other hand, the low base salaries of faculty have sometimes made it difficult for HEIs to recruit high-level talents who can earn higher salaries in the private sector or abroad.

Despite the government's controls over personnel management, our interview data indicate that HEI administrators do not find it difficult to hire new, qualified faculty. Administrators do not find hiring difficult in large part because the supply of Ph.D. students (especially in engineering) in China is fairly large (more on this in Chapter 7). Thus, there seems to be an adequate number of candidates applying for faculty positions, despite the higher salaries available in the private sector. Among the elite HEIs we visited, schools/departments noted that they hired only candidates who had graduated from top institutions domestically or abroad and had a strong research agenda.

Second-tier institutions stated that not only should potential applicants have a doctoral degree but also that their undergraduate degree should be from an elite institution in China. Only some of the third-tier institutions we visited had difficulties in hiring a candidate with a doctoral degree.

Beyond financing and personnel management, the government further influences the behavior of HEIs by categorizing them into different tiers (see Chapter 2). The categorization for HEIs into different tiers affects institutional rankings, reputation, and funding opportunities. The categorization can also influence how an HEI decides on its institutional mission. For example, first-tier HEIs, especially those that receive 985 Project funding, are slated to become world-class research-oriented universities with strong undergraduate and graduate programs. Second-tier (public) and third-tier universities (private, four-year) focus more on producing human resources to serve the needs of the local economy. Third-tier universities also have the task of absorbing excess demand arising from higher social class families who can afford high fees but whose children may not have scored high enough on the college entrance exam.

The state has controlled the development of private, four-year institutions since the early 2000s through the promotion of "independent colleges" (*duli xueyuan*). "Independent colleges" refer to third-tier, private HEIs that are primarily established by first- and second tier (public) HEIs. The sponsorship of first- and second-tier (public) HEIs enables independent colleges to receive considerable support in terms of faculty, equipment, financial, and administrative resources from their "mother institution." Further, the existence of private HEIs with clear links to established public institutions gives the state greater control over the development of private higher education.

The government also exerts some control over what is taught in public and private HEIs. Policy makers can determine the catalog of university majors that HEIs can choose from. Policy makers also set minimum requirements for the types of courses that are taught in each major. For example, subjects on communist political philosophy are still required coursework for both undergrads and graduate students. This is a powerful symbol of state control.

Despite the requirement of the government that HEIs teach a small number of specific courses, schools, departments, and faculty have considerable freedom to decide major requirements and design the bulk of the course content for each major. Most engineering schools where we interviewed were proactive in changing majors' curricula every two to four years. Some schools were required to do so at the instigation of the university administration (but not necessarily the government). Schools and faculty were also engaged in researching and borrowing from the curricula of other HEIs, both domestically and abroad.

State Incentives to Improve University Quality

Besides imposing regulations on HEIs, the state also incentivizes HEIs to improve quality. One way in which the government does this is by emphasizing the importance of university rankings and allowing HEIs to rise or fall in rank. Higher-ranked HEIs are generally allocated more government funding per student. Obtaining a higher ranking can also help a HEI attract higher-ability students through the government-controlled college admissions process. Because of the emphasis placed on university rankings, most HEIs pay attention to strengthening various indicators the government uses to rank HEIs, such as the number of key research centers and labs, the number of departments that have successfully petitioned for the right to accept master's and/or Ph.D. students, and the receipt of prestigious government research grants.

Many of the less selective HEIs in China seek to improve their university rankings, and thus to gain the notice of the government, but it is not clear whether they have the capacity to do so. One reason to doubt their capacity is that many of the less selective, "mass" institutions have had to expand enrollment by many times over the past couple of decades and may be asked by the government to continue to do so in the next decade, although this pressure may decrease because of the rapidly declining population of the college-age cohort and the restrictions on the expansion of enrollment in academic secondary schools. The budgets of less selective HEIs are also constrained by government funding. Less selective HEIs that seek to improve in rank must therefore raise resources from outside the normal budgetary revenues. Student-faculty ratios have increased since the year 2000 as these universities try to keep costs down. Thus, despite many of the signals from the state to increase quality, the dominant signal that less selective HEIs receive is to increase enrollment while maintaining acceptable quality in terms of the many regulations we outlined earlier.

Additionally, government tries to affect quality by incentivizing HEIs and departments to improve instruction and curricula. Our interview data indicate that policy makers often award and promulgate "model" examples of classes in various majors. Policy makers also monitor and rank the quality of teaching at departments within HEIs. For example, the local government in one province we visited had instituted its own instructional assessment program with assessment outcomes tied to instructors' salaries and opportunities for promotion.

With government research funding in China growing at more than 20 percent per year (Shi and Yi, 2010), the state provides substantial incentives for HEIs, schools, and faculty to produce research of increasing quality. This is especially true for first-tier and more-selective second-tier institutions, which have the resources to engage in quality research. The various research grants made available by the state are tied to opportunities for institutions and faculty to increase extra-budgetary spending as well as increase their reputation. HEIs and engineering schools thus further incentivize faculty to acquire these funds (by providing pecuniary awards or higher marks for promotion) in addition to rewarding the quantity and quality of research publications, patents, and horizontal funding. As with teaching, state incentives on research are arguably not straightforward either. The process of acquiring government-sponsored research funding can be characterized by favoritism toward certain institutions and established professors rather than being solely merit based (Shi and Yi, 2010).

Despite the extensive control of the state over many of the main aspects of higher education, university administrators and faculty do not react negatively to government regulations. Compared to their counterparts in, say, Brazil and India, they seem to accept the plethora of government regulations as part of a system in which they conform, work, and progress. Rooted in many decades of communist rule, they do not resist the rules of the system. Rather, university administrators and faculty find it important to understand the letter of the regulations imposed by the government and their own institutions as well as by social and cultural norms pervading the university workspace. Conformity has allowed the government to implement major reforms in the higher education system and expand it rapidly. It also allows for the higher education system to have greater stability on the whole. The willingness to adhere to strict regulations tends to result in fewer innovations in departments and universities regarding the organization of the institutions, courses, teaching, and (in the first-tier universities) the way research is carried out, other than those the government chooses to incentivize. Adhering to regulations makes universities and faculty innovative when the incentives are there, such as in developing external revenue sources and in seeking research funding.

However, another potential problem with readily accepting the controls and incentives provided by the state is that the market has less of a role in providing information and incentives to improve higher education quality. Further, because the government relies on input-based measures of quality to determine the performance of HEIs, university administrators rarely consider output-based measures, such as college student exam scores, dropout rates, graduate employment rates, or the impact of various research products. Government and university administrators therefore focus on pushing for good "hardware" in terms of infrastructure, equipment, and research funding, as opposed to the "software" of the quality of graduates produced, the quality of research maintained, or the degree to which an institution promotes local economic and social development. The problem of measuring teaching quality is especially difficult in China's higher education system because HEIs do not "fail" students and do not systematically track graduated students into the labor market. They are also far from considering the "value added" by universities to student learning as a measure of quality (see Chapter 7). Similar to the situation in other countries, university administrators and faculty are reluctant to be assessed on output-based performance indicators.

India

Our discussion in Chapter 2 of the development of India's higher education system suggests that since India's independence in 1947, the governance of higher education has been shaped by shifts in control of higher education institutions between the central and provincial governments. Politically, India is a federated system, and the role of higher education is important for both national and provincial politicians. They have pushed higher education policies in different directions in different periods to meet varying political goals. In recent years, with the rapid growth of private colleges under the purview of provincial governments, the issues of control and autonomy have become even more complex. How this struggle and subsequent reforms played out in each period affected the governance of universities and colleges, their autonomy, and their incentives to improve quality or pursue other goals, such as equity, access, and cost effectiveness (see Carnoy and Dossani, 2012, for details). Table 5.1 shows a brief summary of the main historical periods we discuss in Chapter 2.

The table shows that the importance of provincial governments to the system's objectives varied with time and is, as of 2011, at a peak. The states, largely through governance by local politicians (although ostensibly maintaining standards through academics at the state universities), focused on satisfying

TABLE 5.1 India: Types of higher education reform, by roles, outcomes, and period

Roles and outcomes	Major education supplier	Other important suppliers	Provincial government's objective	Impact of provincial government on objectives			
				Quality	Equity	Access	Public cost control
Colonial	Affiliated private colleges	N/A	University regulation for quality	Positive for elite quality	None	None	Positive
Nehru	Affiliated public colleges	Unitary national institutions	Expansion of universities and public colleges	Negative	None	Positive	Negative
Indira Gandhi	Affiliated public colleges	None	None	None	None	None	None
Reform period	Affiliated public colleges	Private autonomous colleges	Expansion of public colleges and enabling private colleges	Negative	Positive	Positive	Positive

SOURCE: Authors' compilation.

local demands by the upper and middle classes for places in higher education by expanding the number of colleges in each state with little or no attention to the capacity of those colleges to deliver quality education. In practice, the autonomous, nationally governed institutions have been too small to offset declining average quality driven by the growth of enrollment in the provincial (and increasingly private) institutions.

Therefore, a key influence on the governance of higher education is the locus of political governance and the objectives of politicians, rather than academics or civil society at large. As we spell out below, the growth of private institutions under the jurisdiction of state governments interested mainly in expanding access has meant an increase in de facto "regulated" autonomy for private unaided colleges, which as a group within each state have become a powerful force for influencing the conditions of their regulation so that they can realize their main goal of increasing tuition revenue while keeping costs low. Because the state governments are so focused on expansion, they appear less likely to enforce high standards on private colleges, the principal engine for that increase.

In turn, our interviews in engineering colleges strongly suggest that both public and private colleges have organized themselves to meet government regulations by delivering the required courses and laboratories and teaching students the curriculum required to pass university-designed and graded tests in each subject.

State Control and Private Autonomy

In Chapters 2 and 4 we discuss that in the Indian system, universities are the affiliating body for independent member colleges and that to offer accredited degree programs, all colleges must be affiliated with a university, which awards degrees to the graduates of the affiliated colleges as well as the students graduating from the university's departments. All aided and unaided colleges are necessarily affiliated with public universities; hence, even though not financed directly by the government, they are subject to public university controls over curriculum and the tests students must pass to get credit for the courses. The private institutions are also subject to accreditation by the National Board of Accreditation (a body of AICTE), which sets minimum infrastructure requirements and reviews curricula and teaching standards. All higher education programs are assessed and institutions accredited by a national body called the National Assessment and Accreditation Council (NAAC), although it was not obligatory until very recently for institutions to be accredited.

The states also define whether a college (private or public) can create a program of study, including the number of students to be admitted and, in public colleges, the number of faculty billets for that program. Hiring policies are subject to quotas for disadvantaged groups, so in many of the aided technical colleges where we interviewed, positions have not been filled because the college could not find someone to meet the government's quota requirements. Many faculty positions are also vacant because of inadequate availability of qualified graduates.

In addition, private affiliated (aided and unaided) and public colleges and universities are subject to government controls over their admissions policies. They must admit certain percentages of disadvantaged students by category of student. *State* governments, in turn, control the tuition paid by these disadvantaged students, whether the student attends public or private college. In varying degrees, depending on their disadvantage designation and the state's policy for tuition subsidies and affirmative action policies, students' tuition is subsidized wherever they attend. Therefore, even private unaided colleges

TABLE 5.2 India: Autonomy of departments within engineering colleges, by type of college

	Sector type of college			
Academic activities	Public	Aided	Unaided by state	Unaided by trustees
Disciplinary choices	Low	Low	High	Low
Faculty recruitment	Low	Low	High	Low
Syllabus	High	High	High	High
Textbooks	High	Medium	Medium	Medium
Assessment	Low	Low	Low	N/A

SOURCE: Authors' interviews.

receive a certain percentage of their students under the same tuition arrangements as public colleges and universities, and receive grants from the state.

The unaided colleges are also subject to significant control from trustees, who represent the ownership of the college. Our interviews with colleges revealed that such control can be significant, as shown in Table 5.2. It indicates that unaided colleges have significant autonomy from the state; however, in the case of disciplinary choices, specializations within disciplines (not shown in the table), and faculty recruitment, that autonomy is exercised by trustees rather than by departments. Such autonomy is used to respond to market conditions and enables the college to quickly change faculty and courses in response to market demand. Below, we discuss how this might be influencing the quality of instruction at unaided colleges.

Under rules established by national regulators, including AICTE, both public and private colleges of good standing may also apply for autonomy from the university. If granted, then the college is allowed greater flexibility on course selection within university-approved disciplines and will also control assessment. Thus, autonomy from the university partially frees the college from university and state controls but puts the college under central government jurisdiction. Several restrictions remain, including quotas and tuition fees for designated students, and commitments to introduce postgraduate (including doctoral) programs. The final degree awarded bears the name of both the college and the university, rather than just the university's name. The autonomous college continues to be under national regulatory standards. The autonomous college, whether public or private, is also granted greater freedom from control by the college's board of trustees, particularly in the areas of disciplinary choices, faculty recruitment, and student recruitment.

As of 2011, the national government's key strategy for improving the quality of both private and public colleges has been to get more of them to seek autonomous status as "deemed" universities because autonomy places the institution more under central government regulatory control and partially frees the college from the bureaucratic and political influences of the state. However, few colleges seek autonomy (less than 1 percent of all colleges as of 2011 were autonomous). This is true for both public and private colleges. Among private colleges, trustees are reluctant to cede control over disciplinary choices and faculty recruitment to central government officials, fearing that these will not respond to market conditions.

Therefore, it appears that both public and especially private colleges prefer the level of autonomy (and regulation) they are granted by their state governments to the central government controls and pressures to improve quality that they would incur were they to become autonomous universities. In any case, the single biggest regulation is affirmative action student admissions, and this would not change were colleges to become autonomous universities. Were a private unaided college to become autonomous, it would further have to conform to faculty hiring conditions also subject to affirmative action requirements, a much greater constraint than affirmative action in student admissions.

Our interviews with administrators in public and private colleges gave us the impression that they complained about various regulations but had learned to live with them and, particularly in private unaided colleges, were largely unencumbered by curriculum and examination controls by their affiliating university. Indeed, the more influential of the colleges were able to negotiate as a lobby with their state officials so that they could charge very high fees to the 25 percent or more of students who did not fall into the high-scoring or disadvantaged-caste regulated fee groups. In some states, such as Maharashtra, the government subsidized disadvantaged-caste students, creating an even larger market for private unaided colleges. Where it counts most for private colleges—financially—autonomy is considerable, whereas for public colleges, to the degree that states enforce regulations, most activities are regulated, including, of course, their financial autonomy.

As mentioned above, our interviews also suggest that aside from the curriculum and testing and other university controls, with the degree of autonomy in public and private colleges, administrators and faculty have considerable control over how they deal with these regulations. Many private unaided colleges we visited were meeting the minimum standards by having their professors teach whatever was required so that a high percentage of students would pass the university-set tests in each course. The administration of these colleges is mainly interested in recruiting more students to generate more revenue and supervising their faculty in delivering adequate pass rates on course tests and guaranteeing high enough completion rates to insure their "brand." As we discuss in the Brazil case below, private institutions are organized to limit professors' classroom autonomy and to exert tight control over the delivery of required curricula. Less efficient private institutions are less able to exert that control.

Public and private aided institutions have longer histories and a greater percentage of highly trained professors, so they seem to have the human infrastructure in place to deliver more-demanding courses. Their "brand" is better established. But administrators there are also concerned largely with student pass rates, although they are much more likely to rely on their (autonomous) professors to keep student completion acceptably high.

The State, Public-Private Differences, and Incentives to Improve Quality

The central state and the provincial governments attempt to influence the quality of higher education mainly through control of the curriculum, minimum teaching standards, and the instruments used to evaluate students—all potentially powerful tools to raise the quality of the education that a college delivers to its students. However, provincial governments have simultaneously allowed for rapid expansion of undergraduate places to satisfy rising demand and kept the bar relatively low on quality control. This has fed into the promotion of private college growth at the state level, increased access, and, in our observation, little incentive from market forces or from state regulations for the expanding private sector colleges to improve quality. It is also unclear whether federal government policies have been able to promote public institutions under their control to improve quality (see Table 5.3 for a summary of quality levels by type of institution).

Our interviews strongly suggested that unaided private colleges—many of them quite young—are anxious to expand their enrollment and are interested in attracting more students by improving their reputation. Their main competitors for better students are established older private aided and public engineering colleges in the same city or state. In theory, such competition should improve quality as colleges strive to produce better-prepared, more employable students. However, our interviews suggest that administrators of these colleges appear to interpret quality as sufficiently meeting standards to

TABLE 5.3 India: General characteristics of colleges, by type of college

General characteristic	Sector type of college		
	Public	Aided private	Unaided private
Ratio of Ph.D.s in faculty	High	Medium	Very low
Ratio of part-time faculty	Low	Medium	Very high
Ratio of undergraduates	Low	Medium	High
Ratio of students to faculty	Low	Medium	High
Cost/student	Medium	Medium	Low
Share of tuition/total costs	Low	Medium	Very high
Salaries/total costs	High	Medium	Low

SOURCE: Authors' interviews.
NOTES: "High," "medium," and "low" are relative terms. Even the "high"—e.g., in the case of the ratio of Ph.D.s in the institution's faculty—is only 49% in government institutions.

have acceptably high pass rates, and this means focusing on controlling their relatively less well prepared faculty to meet the minimum standards set by their university regulators. Private unaided colleges have varying success in exerting such control over their professorate, so they vary in quality.

Education trusts of unaided colleges, according to our interviews, tend to hire management and heads of institutions who may have less academic prestige than directors at public colleges but appear to be more dynamic in terms of developing new programs, marketing their universities, and motivating teachers to be successful deliverers of state university regulated curricula so that students will pass state university regulated examinations. Together, all these types of higher education institutions lobby the states to raise allowable general tuition levels (including for those who are admitted under quotas and are partly subsidized by the state).

The private unaided colleges also lobby the states to raise allowable tuition fees for those students who cannot qualify academically for the fixed proportion of lower-priced places. The proportion who can be charged the higher fees also varies from state to state and can be negotiated—another bargaining point for private unaided colleges. Our interviews suggest that the costs of running an engineering college are considerably lower than total revenues. One large engineering college estimated that management ran the college at a cost of $1,250 per student but collected average revenues of about $1,900 per student.

To summarize, Indian engineering higher education is marked by considerable competition and considerable opportunities for social entrepreneurs to enter the market for producing college graduates and accumulate surplus that could be used for expansion and improvement and also to channel surpluses into private coffers. It appears that the main use of the surplus in private unaided colleges is expansion rather than improvement, mainly because it is not easy to increase higher education effectiveness without entering into risky strategies of trying to attract better full-time professors with research opportunities and the chance to work with postgraduate students.

In addition, the supply of better professors is limited. The production of engineering and technical Ph.D.s is small in India. With such a high fraction of private unaided engineering institutions, most without postgraduate programs, and so little funding for research and development, the few Ph.D.s produced come from the IITs and NITs, themselves small in number and in graduate enrollment. Thus, even if they wanted to hire more Ph.D.s, private colleges would have to recruit them from the relatively few engineering public colleges and universities. Such recruitment would not be easy—there are simply too few Ph.D.s to go around, private colleges generally do not grant tenure, and salaries are somewhat lower than in the public sector.[6]

Contributing to the general lack of pressure to focus on improving student training, state universities regulating private unaided and public colleges seem to set quite low standards of quality and lack the capacity to regularly monitor the large number of institutions. Because public and private aided colleges have better-educated faculty and pay higher salaries, they are more likely to have staff teaching who can deliver higher-quality courses. But our interviews suggest that there is little effort to improve quality even in such colleges, in part because of qualified faculty shortages and in part because the standards set are not high. Increasing access rather than raising the academic bar is still the main priority of the state bureaucracies.

Russia

As institutions, Russian universities were indelibly shaped by seventy years of Soviet policies, which not only greatly expanded postsecondary education but also tied it closely to training manpower for particular industries. The Soviet central state tightly controlled university administrators and faculty in terms of hiring, curriculum, and ideology. Today, many of the faculty staffing higher education institutions began teaching in the Soviet era. They passed through a period of upheaval and change in the 1990s, during which universities gained considerable autonomy and had to scramble for financing because of a deep recession from 1992 to 1997. At the same time, the demand for higher education increased sharply, caused in part by the leveling off of enrollment in the last decade of the Soviet era. Most industries with feeder universities became unviable as demand for their Soviet products disappeared, yet these universities did not transform themselves.

By 2008, the major post-Soviet higher education expansion had achieved one of the highest rates of gross enrollment in the world, just as Russia's youth population began to decline. This meant, in effect, that after 2007–2008, many universities began to lose enrollment. In this context the Russian state moved to reassert control of universities, both to rationalize the system financially and to develop policies that would help universities' overall transition out of the Soviet model and help at least some to improve their quality (Sigman, 2008).

We interviewed central government policy makers and faculty and administrators in about twenty-five institutions to understand the objectives of state policies and the interplay between state objectives regarding the role of different kinds of higher education institutions and the faculty and administrators of those institutions. Not surprisingly, in a country as large and diverse as Russia, we found differing reactions to central government attempts to reform the system. The attempted reforms and institutional reactions provided insights into the considerable power of the Russian state in shaping decision making at the local university level, even though there is a great deal of "slippage" between what the central government wants to take place and what actually does take place. The power of the state is partly in the eye of the beholder: most university faculty and officials—conditioned in Soviet times—continue to look to the state for direction and financial support, and the central state, in turn, is trying to use—with varying success—its financial clout to try to change the system (Kuhns, 2011). Although many universities have significant income from fee-paying students (see Chapter 4), they see themselves as dependent on state financing to survive. In most cases they have little choice but to survive in the way that the state defines survival. There are deviations from this rule, but they are relatively infrequent. Nevertheless, there still seems to be considerable evidence that players at the local (university) level can resist change successfully, "powerful" as the central state may be.

State Control and University Autonomy

Autonomy was touted as a state goal in the early 1990s primarily because of a national financial crisis facing the country. The idea was to devolve financial and programmatic authority from federal to local control. The 1993 Law on Education legitimized the decentralization and autonomy, self-governance, and devolution of authority, and further legalized the introduction of private and nongovernmental higher educational institutions. The law confirmed academic freedom in teaching, learning, and research. Further, institutions were allowed to establish individual contracts with teachers and professors; thus, in theory, they were no longer to be considered civil servants (Zajda and Zajda, 2007).

When Vladimir Putin came to power in 2000, an important feature of his political agenda was the reconsolidation of power into federal hands. Part of this political consolidation also included recentralizing federal control over key public good and services, including the education system. In 2004 the federal government initiated a series of administrative changes that governed how higher educational institutions would be financed from the center, further consolidating higher education oversight.

Currently, the Russian Ministry of Education and Science (MOES) has oversight of both the political direction and operational management of the higher education system. According to the World Bank, a major change in MOES culture would be required in order to give more autonomy to individual institutions (Canning, 2004). Allowing autonomy would also necessitate a discussion on the devolution of control to the regions; regional authorities have indicated that they are willing to commit more resources to higher education if the system becomes more responsive to the development needs of their regions.

According to our interviews, one frustration of university rectors and local and regional government officials is that despite considerable autonomy, universities cannot accept funding from local government offices. Public federal higher education institutions report only to the MOES in Moscow and do not have to respond to local city or regional officials. This creates a communication difficulty when local governments want to include higher education institutions in the economic development planning processes. Some regional and local governments are more proactive than others and maintain good relations with the higher education institutions in their regions as well as the ministry in Moscow. The disconnect between regional needs and federal government control of university financing is compounded by the fact that all student "budget places" in universities (those slots fully funded by the federal government) are determined and rationed in Moscow, with little to no input from the regions or the universities themselves (authors' interviews).

How does autonomy play out in the details of Russia's university decision making? In terms of Levy's three criteria—appointive, academic, and financial autonomy—for judging institutional autonomy in authoritarian regimes (Levy, 1980), the picture is mixed.

Although instructors and faculty are state employees, they are hired by the university and appointed to positions of authority within the institution by election of peers or by direct appointment of the rector. In this sense, Russian universities have a fair amount of autonomy in terms of hiring, promotion, and dismissal of professors and persons of authority. While we were visiting one university, it was holding an election to choose a new rector, and the outcome was highly contested.

Academically, other than now being required by federal law to use only the Unified State Exam (USE) scores as criteria for student admission (some elite universities are allowed to use their own examinations in addition to the USE), higher education institutions have total control over their admits. They are limited by the number of government-allocated budget places, but this does not restrict them from increasing the number of commercial (privately paid) places in their institution.

There is less autonomy regarding curriculum. In the past, curriculum was entirely centrally controlled and, even today, under the Bologna rules, is about 50 percent centrally controlled for the B.A. and 25 percent for the M.A. In practice, however, this autonomy is limited to those entrepreneurial and innovative universities that are able to accept the challenge of creating their own curriculum. Only leading higher education institutions are allowed to create the new standards, although ultimate approval resides with the MOES. And while there is some effort to involve other higher education institutions in the creation process through the Education and Methodological Associations (EMAs) chaired by the lead institution responsible for a particular discipline, the process is still very much in the hands of those lead institutions.

The other important aspect of academic autonomy is academic freedom. Our interviews suggest that most Russian academics define academic freedom in terms of the freedom of mobility—the freedom to transfer from one higher education institution to another and to travel to another region to look for work. Few choose to view it as being able to teach what and how they want or to publish opinions without reprisal. If we assume that respondents tend to define freedom in terms of what they have, our interviews suggest a restricted level of individual academic autonomy. Yet, compared to the past, increased mobility can also be viewed as a major increase in autonomy.

From a financial standpoint, most public higher education institutions still depend heavily on the state for a majority of their funding, although tuition fees now represent a significant proportion of university revenues. Federal funding is strictly regulated. If funds go to one higher education institution to support a student, that student cannot take a course at another Russian higher education institution or go abroad. Tuition fees are unrestricted. As one institution reported, 55 percent of such funds went into the higher education institution's general fund, and 45 percent went to the department itself (authors' interviews). Thus, there is incentive to increase the number of commercial students in order to increase flexibility over the use of university revenues. Such extra-budgetary funds are used to support internal grant programs, student study abroad programs, salary increases, and the purchase of new equipment.

State Reforms and Incentives to Improve Quality
The Russian government has begun implementing a series of reforms intended to improve university education, at least in terms of the indicators used internationally to rank universities. The reforms are of two kinds: those almost entirely focused on a subset of universities—either already established first-tier research institutions, institutions deemed by the government as potentially first-tier research universities, or those best local universities consolidated by the federal government into larger regional institutions; and reforms aimed to improve university education more generally. However, quality reforms in Russia must be viewed in the context of the declining college-age population and the high proportion of students already attending universities. Many universities are not filling budgeted, "free" government places in a number of fields, and the government is searching for ways to consolidate the higher education system into fewer institutions. Our interviews suggest that in addition to the specific, mainly supply-side reforms discussed below, the government is counting on increased competition among institutions for a shrinking clientele to improve quality. As we discuss below in the section on the reaction to the reforms by university actors, this hope is unlikely to be realized very widely.

We have already discussed the financial priority given to the thirty-eight elite universities that the federal government hopes to turn into a community of internationally competitive universities. The state hopes that these leading universities will be a quality benchmark for others to emulate, including developing the curriculum standards for the university system as a whole.

Picking up on the last point of more general quality improvement of higher education through curriculum standards, in the 1990s and early 2000s, many higher educational institutions further specialized their fields from an already broad list inherited from the Soviet era. One reason was to differentiate themselves to attract students in an increasingly competitive higher education market. The new standards decrease the overall number of specialties, making the newly defined specialties broader in scope.

In 2009 the MOES solicited competitive proposals from the country's leading universities for the creation of the third generation of academic standards to fit these broader specialties, and the new standards would also correspond to the new degree structure under the Bologna accords. No single university would create all of the standards for all disciplines. The task is to be divided among institutions according to the strength of their department in a specific field. Once the standards are approved by the MOES, they are to be disseminated to the higher education community by those lead institutions.

The second general reform geared to improve higher education quality is the Bologna process.[7] The argument made by the government for joining Bologna is the enhanced competition for Russian higher education institutions in Europe through the convertibility of degrees, increased academic mobility, and thus the possibility to "export" Russian higher education. There is also an argument from the efficiency standpoint that competition within the European and world higher education system will exert pressure on higher education institutions in Russia to improve the quality of education and employ improved teaching methods.

The federal government is also posting the results of the USE university entrance examination by department and institution as a way to indirectly stimulate competition among institutions or, at the least, to warn implicitly those institutions that are attracting low-scoring entrants of difficulties they might face in securing future federal funding. It is unclear what most such institutions can do about attracting more highly qualified applicants in the face of a declining applicant pool and level federal financing, but the hope is that some may take steps to make themselves more desirable (for cases of U.S. institutions that acted aggressively to change their image, see Kirp, 2003).

Reactions to the New Centralized Reforms

The Russian state ostensibly has enormous control over universities through the centralized financing of significant portions of university budgets, through its power to bestow accreditation, and its control over the opening and closing of new programs of study. In contrast to the Soviet era, however, the state can now no longer resort to overt coercion; it must find different mechanisms of control over various public functions. The financing mechanism is the most obvious. For example, the creation of an elite group of publicly funded institutions that get an increasing share of resources can be seen as an effort to create "world-class" universities (and universities more generally) and therefore a way for the state to legitimize itself domestically and internationally. And in doing so, the state creates a group of educational institutions tacitly loyal and highly dependent for their excellence on increasing levels of state financing.

In contrast, the state continues to exert tight control over the rest of public and private higher education institutions through implementation of academic standards, the threat of institutional mergers, and the threat of domestic accreditation revocation. Because they will receive substantially less state funding than the elite institutions, the remaining higher education institutions will be constantly competing with one another over these remaining limited resources, hoping to eventually join the elite few.

However, there is evidence of limits on the government's ability to carry out its policies, especially if the proposed changes run into stiff resistance at the local level. Conservative administrators have little incentive to fully implement the reforms, which has further delayed the process. The Bologna reforms have been difficult to implement because the public has never fully understood why Bologna is important for the nation, and employers continue to fight against hiring "unfinished" four-year baccalaureate graduates (rather than the traditional five-year *specialists*).

Even the clear need to reduce the number of higher education institutions poses problems. There are many ways that the state can implement such a reduction. The simplest would be to eliminate the budget places allocated to certain institutions, forcing them to survive on tuition-paying students or close. But because closings entail political risk (loss of political support in some regions), it will not be easy for the state to shut down many nonelite institutions even when the number of students greatly declines. It is particularly difficult to eliminate universities where there is no alternative nearby. The public has come to expect universal access to higher education, and most families interpret such access as the right of their children to attend a local institution.

One way to classify the reaction to these reforms from university actors is in terms of the kinds of initiatives that technical universities have taken in the past five years to respond to the changing Russian higher education land-scape. Our interviews suggest three categories of technical universities along a "tradition-innovation" continuum.[8]

The first type includes universities that used to be leading institutions in the Soviet period and were most closely connected to the large Soviet military-industrial complex. They see their comparative advantage in their traditionally strong schools of engineering. The administration and staff of these universities focus on restoring their traditional position of producing more graduates in their specialties and on restoring the military industries that they used to serve. They complain of the lack of demand for their type of knowledge and still regard the military as their key customer. They lament the state's not producing as many ships and helicopters as before. Their posi-tion is passive in the sense that they are waiting for the state to turn to them ("for a miracle to come"), and even though some employers badly need the graduates that they potentially might be able to turn out for other sectors, they do not try to respond to this new demand by restructuring their pro-grams. They complain of the poorer "quality" of prospective students but do nothing to attract better students. To the contrary, they open fee-paying spe-cializations for which there is relatively less demand (which, by default, attract less talented students). Their central focus is on obtaining sufficient financial resources (mainly from the central state) to survive, without much concern for contributing to the advancement of engineering education. We call them the *WayWeWeres,* and they are the largest group of universities in Russia, cre-ated for an economic system that no longer exists and whose staffs are unable or unwilling to respond to a totally new set of conditions. To be fair, many of the staff do not have the skills to make the change.

At the opposite end of the continuum are institutions we call the *Innova-tors.* These universities seem to be ahead of the curve in terms of responding to state reforms (for example, the transition to the Bologna 4+2 plan) and state incentives (for example, grant competitions). They are more research oriented and have worked for most of the post-1991 period in close cooper-ation with public and private firms that are usually also in R&D. They are flexible and active, and they are willing to experiment with new courses and practices. In the context of general underfinancing of higher education, they are short of financial resources, but instead of waiting for the state to give them more money, they tend to be inventive in seeking new forms of fund-ing, such as forming partnerships with advanced enterprises and thus get-ting access to modern expensive equipment, and opening up attractive new specializations for fee-paying students related to their university's main mission, such as "management in R&D" and "marketing R&D." Further, they work with secondary schools to find and recruit the most talented students. Not surprisingly, there are few technical universities in this category, and they are all among the thirty-eight "leading" institutions.

Between these two poles is another category of technical universities we call *Flexible Responders*. These universities are influential in the current historical conjuncture because they are responsible for developing the new state standards. The state also counts on them to institutionalize its reforms. It is this group that implements recommendations from the state, such as appeals to create quality management systems. Many Flexible Responders are among the federal universities and NRUs, but not all. They include other local technical universities that have begun to transform their traditional roles in the Soviet system, finding ways to fit into the new economy. What they tend to lack is the capacity for cutting-edge innovation either in the research they do or changes they make in their own institutions. However, this group can be regarded as the most stable and reliable in terms of building education structures for the future. Table 5.4 summarizes the differences in attitudes and reactions to recent challenges faced by the three technical university categories.

Given the variation in institutional attitudes among the three categories of technical universities in our sample (and the considerable variation in attitudes among the staff in the middle category), it is not surprising that an overriding theme throughout our interviews was ambivalence on the part of university actors between wanting stronger leadership from the state and wishing the state would leave them to their own devices. Those institutions that look to Moscow's universities for new standards fear a lack of state leadership. The more forward-looking and entrepreneurial institutions rely on strong state support but, as self-styled educational leaders, are impatient with state controls. This ambivalence about the state's role is partly the result of the reforms having been introduced inadequately. In the resulting confusion, all three types of higher education institutions have no choice but to look to the center for guidance; otherwise, they might face penalties for not following the new rules and regulations. If the state would implement the reforms with a well-designed framework and time line, more institutions might feel confident taking the initiative because they would understand the new rules of the game. However, that is not the case and is unlikely to be the case in any foreseeable future.

TABLE 5.4 Russia: Types of technical universities, by their attitude toward and reaction to recent contextual changes and state reforms

Reforms/challenges	Technical university categories		
	WayWeWeres	Flexible responders	Innovators
Bologna 4+2	Formal, slow	Formal/partially advancing the standards	Indifferent/introduced changes when first introduced
UNE Exam + poorer quality of prospective students	Lament	Introduced adaptive courses	Combined with other mechanisms of searching for the most talented
Decline of the "parent/customer" industry	Lament	Form partnerships with more stable enterprises/focus on practical skills	Form partnerships with cutting-edge enterprises/focus on innovations
Underfinancing	Open fee-paying low-quality specializations and regional branches/focus more on vocational education	Open high-demand, fee-paying specializations related to their main mission	Rely on/recombine internal resources in an entrepreneurial manner
State competitions for resources to undertake state higher education innovations	Passive	Active, winners; advance the formal standards	Active, winners
International context	Do not participate, feel superior (traditions) and deprived (facilities)	Respond to the standards	Respond in terms of participation in international research
Deterioration of physical and technical facilities	Lament	Improve through winning competitions	Improve through winning competitions/use partner enterprises' facilities

SOURCE: Authors' interviews.

Brazil

The main features that distinguish Brazil's higher education system from those in the other three BRIC countries are the high proportion of students attending private institutions and the increasingly diverging character of private higher education from public higher education. About three-fourths of university enrollment is in private institutions, and in recent decades the private sector has begun consolidating into large enterprises run as profit-making businesses that are distinctly different institutionally from public universities. In 2007 about one-third of all private higher education institutions were "for profit," and this percentage has been increasing steadily since the beginning of the decade (Nunes, de Carvalho, and Vogel de Albrecht, 2009, Table 48). At the same time, public universities dominate high-level professional formation and graduate education. These two types of institutions have differed historically in their relationship to the Brazilian state, particularly in the past twenty years, as the private for-profit universities have grown in number and in size.

We did not carry out an institutional survey in Brazil as we did in China, India, and Russia. Fortunately, other researchers and government institutions have, and we draw on their data and work to compare how the Brazilian state relates to these different types of Brazilian universities, how the state has tried to expand and improve universities, and how they, in turn, respond institutionally to the process of change.

State Control and University Autonomy

We establish in Chapter 2 that, at least in legal terms, the Brazilian state has almost complete power over public higher education. The total dependence of public universities on state funding and the bureaucratic regulatory structure created by government legislation have allowed the state to define the role of the public universities and specialized faculties, the programs of study these universities can offer, the setting up of graduate programs, and the types of research projects that are funded. However, academics at public universities do have considerable autonomy over a great many of the internal organizational details concerning teaching and research.

There is considerable variation in the defined role of academics at different types of Brazilian institutions, and this reflects on the nature of these institutions and has some influence over their participation in decision making, although less than on whether the institution is public, private elite, or private, delivering undergraduate degrees to a "mass" clientele.

A survey of 1,200 academics in various kinds of public and private higher education institutions shows that in public research universities, about 46.1 percent of academics teach only undergraduates and another 52.3 percent teach doctoral, master's, and undergraduates—less than 2 percent teach graduates only. In public regional universities, 62.5 percent teach undergraduates only, and about 37 percent teach both graduate and undergraduate students. Teachers at private elite institutions, which include both religious (Catholic) and high-tuition secular institutions producing mainly business and economics degrees, teach largely undergraduates (64 percent), but

34 percent teach both graduate and undergraduate, and almost 6 percent teach only graduate students. Finally, for those who teach at private mass institutions, almost all (93 percent) deal only with undergraduates and only 7 percent with both graduate students and undergraduates (Balbachevsky and Schwartzman, 2011, Table 3.1).

The other side of this coin is that more than 53 percent of academics at public research universities are full researchers with external support, 27 percent in regional universities fall into this category, 25 percent at elite private institutions, and only 7 percent at private mass institutions. There also exists a small group of public research institutes in which 70 percent of the faculty are full researchers and 54 percent teach only graduate students (Balbachevsky and Schwartzman, 2011, tables 3.1 and 3.3).

Given these parameters, it is not surprising that Brazilian higher education institutions vary in the way they are organized and managed:

> [T]he departmental model, introduced in Brazil by the 1968 reform is well developed and recognized by the academic staff in the public sector. This tends to be the reference for the academics employed by the elite private institutions as well. Nevertheless, in the mass-oriented private sector, the department as the smallest relevant academic unit is not recognized. For most academics employed at these institutions, the relevant academic unit is the undergraduate program where he/she teaches. (Balbachevsky and Schwartzman, 2011: 46)

Balbachevsky and Schwartzman argue that this difference in organization is key to the perception that faculty have of how power is distributed in each institution. In the 2007 survey of 1,200 faculty at different types of institutions, faculty were asked to identify whether administrators, either at the institutional level or the academic unit level, were the main decision makers in eleven different decision areas or whether faculty were. Even though institutional authorities were always perceived to have power in decision making (they were identified as the main actor in seven of eleven areas), there was considerable variance across types of universities in how faculty answered. At public research universities and regional universities, institutional authorities were identified as the main decision makers in five and six of the eleven decision areas. However, in private elite universities, faculty saw them as dominating in eight of eleven and in private mass universities in nine of eleven (Balbachevsky and Schwartzman, 2011: 48). The opposite pattern obtains for faculty influence, where they are seen as having the most influence in four areas in public research universities, three areas in regional publics and elite privates, and only one area in the mass privates (Balbachevsky and Schwartz-man, 2011, Table 3.7).

In part, the degree of faculty autonomy in public universities was rein-forced by the reaction to the military's attempts in the 1960s and early 1970s to repress academic freedom (Durham, 2005). At the same time, however, re-sistance to military control, according to Durham, defended "a radical egali-tarianism that contributed . . . to a delegitimization of academic values related to recognizing merit and competence" (2005: 217). At the same time, research funding expanded, and research funding criteria continued to be based on faculty competency as judged by government scientific research agencies.

The leftover from this period is that, particularly when it comes to deci-sions regarding many areas of daily academic life, including faculty promo-tion, the distribution of power in research universities and research institutes is tilted toward academic committees, and collegiality is the most relevant form of power for such internal matters. In regional public universities, state authorities are seen as playing more of a role, but collegiality and individual faculty are still regarded as most important in daily academic life and in an institution's broader decision areas. Faculty in the regional public universi-ties also regard the choice of university authorities as the prerogative of fac-ulty and students, without external control or influence (Balbachevsky and Schwartzman, 2011: 52). Further, the criteria used to evaluate faculty for pro-motion are not necessarily based strictly on competence either in research or teaching (Balbachevsky and Schwartzman, 2011: 54).

On the other hand, in private higher education institutions, institutional authorities are viewed as playing a much more important role in these same academic activities:

> The most important distinction between elite- and mass-oriented institutions is the more autonomous role played by the intermediary bodies of management in the former setting. In fact, among academics from elite private institutions, unit managers are significantly associated with decisions regarding selection of new faculty, teaching and research evaluation, and setting the institution's research priorities. In the case of academics from the mass-oriented private in-stitutions, all these decision areas, except hiring new faculty are associated with the central authorities. (Balbachevsky and Schwartzman, 2011: 50)

And when it comes to institution-wide decisions in the private sector, these are tightly associated with the institution's managers, not external actors (such as the state authorities): "In the private sector, one finds a more hierarchical pattern, with less autonomy for academic initiatives and an en-larged space for management and central authority decisions. Intermediate managers are more active in elite-oriented institutions while central authori-ties seem to concentrate more power in mass-oriented institutions" (Bal-bachevsky and Schwartzman, 2011: 52).[9]

All in all, then, autonomy has a different meaning in Brazil's public and private universities. In public universities, within the context of state man-dates, faculty members have considerable autonomy, collegiate arrangements are predominant in the internal decision-making process, and these arrange-ments cover more academic areas than in the private sector. We can also in-fer that institutional authorities in public universities are likely to be directly responsive to state policies regarding staffing and other aspects of resource allocation, undergraduate admissions policies, and defining new programs because the state ultimately sets their budgets.

At the other end of the spectrum, the mass private universities, which enroll close to 65–70 percent of Brazil's higher education students, are more autono-mous as individual institutions from state control (they receive essentially no funding from the public sector) but give much less autonomy to their faculty over academic life. They are run more like businesses, "with a relatively clear chain of command radiating downward from the central authorities to the aca-demic body" (Balbachevsky and Schwartzman, 2011: 55). This is logical because most of them *are* now businesses, some very large, and engaged in an industry that is competitive and subject to medium-term constraints on the size of its market. A very high percentage of Brazilians are poor and cannot afford tuition at higher education institutions, even when that tuition may be falling in real terms (see Chapter 4). Thus, cost considerations in mass private universities are of primary concern, and this requires strong internal controls over the use of faculty time, staffing, course setting, and standardized norms for staff evalu-ation. In such a competitive environment, it is not surprising that the sector has been characterized by increased consolidation and the appearance of mega, multi-campus, multi-city private universities that are run by large, complex internal hierarchies.

The elite private universities, many of them organized to exploit niche markets, face a much less competitive environment, so intermediate manage-ment and individual faculty members have more autonomy than in the mass private universities. Nevertheless, higher-level management in the elite pri-vate institutions still has a lot more control over academic life than in public universities and is much less subject to state bureaucratic authority.

State Incentives to Improve University Quality

In understanding whether or not higher education institutions in Brazil have an incentive to improve quality, it is crucial to start with the concept that the elite and the mass institutions are largely organized differently, with different kinds of autonomy from the state and different actors with decision-making power in each sector.

One factor that differentiates state-controlled higher education institutions in Brazil from most private institutions is student selectivity. In the name of maintaining quality, federal and state universities used and still use a system of entrance examinations and *numerus clausus* to restrict the number of students able to enter the public system. By expanding the number of public university places over the past twenty years relatively slowly—much more slowly than the increase in graduates from secondary schools—the state has maintained the highly selective nature of public, particularly federal, universities. In the 2000s there were about eight to nine applicants for each place in public federal and state institutions, which translates into a 12 percent admission rate. Although the number of applicants per place in public universities has declined somewhat in recent years, it is still relatively high. To put this in perspective, the University of California at Berkeley and UCLA, premier U.S. public institutions, admitted 22 percent of applicants in 2008.

In contrast, admissions selection is not used to control quality in mass private universities. Brazilian private higher education institutions had about 1.2 applicants per place available in 2008, but that includes private elite universities, so we can assume that essentially all those who apply to mass private institutions are admitted.

Instead of rapidly expanding the public sector by creating new kinds of institutions to absorb demand, the state relaxed constraints on the requirements for private higher education institutions, and the number of these private institutions multiplied rapidly from the early 1970s onward, mainly in the form of for-profit, teaching-oriented, nonuniversity schools and colleges but also in the form of many new universities. And despite its clear "blessing" of this expansion, the ministry's bureaucratic bodies, according to Balbachevsky and Schwartzman, considered the private higher education sector as "a deformity that defaced the elegant uniformity proposed by the [1968] Reform. From this perspective, the private sector was tolerated but placed under strong controls" (2011: 38). Yet, beginning in the 1980s, the private sector was able get around these controls by forming federations of private institutions and quickly transforming them into universities, thus gaining autonomy from the

National Council (Durham, 2005). The more flexible regulatory climate of the 1980s also allowed for the major growth of for-profit private institutions.

The type of autonomy that characterizes private higher educational institutions has created problems controlling their quality. In theory, competition for students in local markets should provide an incentive for these institutions to improve quality in order to attract more students. Part of the private sector does respond to such incentives because certain institutions are competing for students whose families can pay for what they perceive to be better, more costly, higher-prestige education. However, most private institutions in Brazil increasingly compete for students who have difficulties paying the $2,000–$3,000 annual tuition, so lowering cost is a major objective for their owners and administrators, and improving quality is much less important than managing costs. Furthermore, private institutions that otherwise would be subject to stricter state controls have managed to use political influence to organize themselves into universities and "integrated faculties," which have much greater autonomy. This gives these institutions—some of them among the largest (enrollment) higher education institutions in the country—even greater freedom than other private institutions from federal oversight.

There is also difficulty in improving quality in the public institutions. As Durham has argued, the resistance to the military in the 1970s produced a tendency for faculty to reduce emphasis on "technocratic" measures of academic competence as criteria for promotion in favor of more cronyism and ideological criteria. Nevertheless, the 1931 and 1968 legislation governing public universities has been successful in influencing quality through its emphasis on developing graduate programs at public universities and research institutes (Balbachevsky and Schwartzman, 2011). The 2007 faculty survey we reported on above showed that a relatively high fraction of faculty in public universities teach graduate students as well as undergraduates, more than half at public research universities and institutes do supported research and publish, and about one-fourth at regional public universities and private elite institutions do research and publish.

The federal government passed further legislation in 1996 designed to improve quality, particularly in private universities (Durham, 2005). The law required all universities to have at least a third of the teaching staff hold a master's degree or a Ph.D. and at least a third employed full time. Although the law was strongly opposed by the private university lobby, it was passed. In the process, the requirements were reduced from one-half with graduate degrees and full time to one-third. Further, the legislation required periodic evaluations of universities for accreditation and periodic review of every higher education institution to establish the validity of its diploma.

The legislation may have been successful in raising standards. The 2007 faculty survey we have cited shows that about one-fourth of those teaching undergraduates in the mass private institutions held Ph.D.s, and this is a relatively high percentage compared to other BRIC countries. However, other data—namely INEP's census of higher education—give much lower figures for private institutions overall—only 14 percent for all privates, including elite privates, and 12 percent for nonconfessional privates, which would exclude most private research universities such as the Catholic Universities of Rio, São Paulo, and Rio Grande do Sul (INEP, 2009, Table 2.1).

In addition, to evaluate the quality of programs of study under the new 1996 legislation, the federal government created an obligatory national examination, called the *Provão*, designed for each academic program, to be taken by all students in the last year of study in every institution offering that program. The exam was strongly opposed by both private institutions and the students and professors in public institutions. The opposition in public institutions was part of the general resistance, particularly by the professors' union (and supported by students), to any evaluation that compared performance across institutions. But once the exam was applied, it gained enormous public support. It showed that students in public institutions did much better than those in private higher education, which dissipated some of the opposition among public-sector teachers and students. According to Durham, the *Provão* became "the most powerful instrument yet created in Brazil to promote and improve teaching quality because it also influences the market. Private programs with higher scores used their scores as publicity to attract students . . ." (2005: 227, authors' translation).

Beginning in the early 2000s, the *Provão* was replaced by the ENADE, which measured students' knowledge in every higher education department in Brazil at the end of the first year of study and at the end of the final year of study. Yet, even though the test results are published, there is no mechanism besides the institutional embarrassment of getting a low score to improve the outcomes on the test. The test is not a value-added evaluation, so the best approximation of departmental effectiveness is to control for the average socioeconomic background of the students entering a particular program. Doing badly on either a measure of absolute achievement level or of achievement gain would not necessarily induce institutions to make more costly hires when this could imperil bottom-line profitability in the short run. With about 70 percent of students attending mass private higher education institutions, raising overall quality in the system has been difficult. Most institutional efforts in such institutions continue to be aimed at efficiency, but an efficiency that focuses on costs and profitability rather than improving the quality of the services delivered.

The most recent efforts by the state in higher education are aimed less at improving quality than in expanding access—a politically charged issue in a country where almost three-fourths of new entrants to higher education have to pay fees. In the public institutions, this is embodied in new legislation that creates a second tier of access into public universities through evening courses developed by university departments and meant to incorporate more students who would otherwise not have gained entrance to public universities. In August 2011 the Brazilian Senate also passed long-gestating legislation to require all federal universities to admit quotas of black and indigenous students who attended public secondary schools. The quotas are based on the percentage of those race/ethnic groups in the population of the state in which the federal university is located. This effort expands past voluntary affirmative action efforts by federal and state universities that have increased the number of disadvantaged minority students who attended public secondary schools to enter federal and state institutions.

The second type of legislation intended to increase access created a program subsidizing private mass institutions to accept disadvantaged minority students who cannot afford to pay private higher education tuition. Thus, for the first time the federal government is subsidizing private institutions with the purpose of expanding higher education enrollment among those who cannot afford tuition but who also do not have the academic standing to enter public universities. This provides a clear incentive for private institutions to accept minority students who attended public secondary schools. Whether these students will succeed in these generally lower-quality institutions is another questions, but there is some incentive for the institutions to help them progress in order to keep receiving a subsidy for their education. We discuss affirmative action in Brazil further in Chapter 8.

Brief Conclusions

We have shown in this chapter that higher education institutional conditions share certain features in the BRIC countries, but because the political contexts differ so greatly, there are also major differences. In all four countries, the state has played an important role historically in defining the governance structure of higher education institutions, and this structure, in turn, defines how faculty and administrators in these institutions view their autonomy and their relation to the state. Recent reforms in China and Russia have formalized and even accentuated the tiers in their higher education systems, with implications for the degree of autonomy in upper- and lower-tier institutions. In India the historical drift toward provincial (local, state) control over higher educational governance, including over rapidly expanding private institutions, means that much of the relations that influence institutional autonomy and state regulations vary across local states—this makes India quite different from the other three BRICs, although in both China and Russia provincial governments can influence higher educational governance, including autonomy. In India the provincial governments have used their expanding influence to promote access and equity at manageable costs. Private colleges are a key instrument of expansion, accounting for the lion's share of provision in technical fields and in driving overall growth in enrollment, while privatizing costs and reducing the state's financial burden. The problem in Russia is that universities cannot accept local funding, making them much more tied to central government control. Brazil is also unique, as we pointed out, in that the main division in higher education governance is between public and private institutions, although within the public sector, there are also state and federal universities with different loci of control. The privates have much greater institutional autonomy from state influence. But faculty and administrators in the publics have much greater decision-making power than their counterparts in the privates over a broad range of governance issues.

There are major differences in political contextual factors that drive reforms in each country and the reaction to them by higher education institutions. The Russian and Chinese central states clearly have the greatest control over decisions at the institutional level, and administrators and faculty in those two countries are not only aware of that control, but shape their thinking about institutional policies in that context. That said, the situation is very different in those two countries. China's higher education system is continuing to expand, although at a slower rate, and a main issue for many university administrations is how to best achieve that expansion, how much financing they are going to get, and where they are going to get it. This is particularly true for lower second- and third-tier institutions, which get a high fraction of their funding from tuition and training contracts with firms. Even so, over the next few years, many of these universities may face the end of enrollment expansion as the number of available academic secondary school graduates starts to decline.

In Russia a main issue today is student population decline and university system contraction. University administration and staff are concerned where they fit into this downsizing.

In India there is also considerable state control over many aspects of higher educational governance—both public and private—including mandated affirmative action, curriculum, examinations, the creation of new departments, and the number of students that a college can admit into a particular course of study. Yet, with the rapid growth of private institutions (with state blessing), state control is being increasingly contested by this expanding sector, and there is increasing public pressure on the central government to expand its more prestigious public institutions.

Brazil's historical decision to have an autonomous private sector play a major role in higher education has also had a definitional impact on its higher educational reforms and, indeed, on its ability to control the shape of decision making in higher education institutions. The private sector not only now absorbs a very high percentage of students; it has also consolidated to produce a number of dominating for-profit institutions that can influence state higher education policy even more than in the past. Decision making in these mass private institutions is distinctly top down, driven largely by bottom-line profit considerations. These make them not very different from private institutions in India or, for that matter, China and Russia, except for the low degree of direct state regulation of privates in Brazil compared to the other three.

This brings us to the incentives for raising quality in BRIC higher education. We argue that the higher education governance structures and political contexts in each country shape these incentives. Russia and China, with their high degree of centralized control over the financing and governance of their university systems, have been able to define a tier of universities that will be supported with increased per student financing, higher faculty salaries, and increasing funds for research, all as part of a strategy to create "world-class" institutions, clearly incentivized to increase quality. "Mass" higher education institutions are also to be expected to increase quality but would receive relatively little support to do so. In China the main task of second-, third- (private), and fourth- (vocational) tier universities is, and would continue to be, to absorb increasing numbers of students and provide them with an acceptable level of tertiary education for employment; in Russia mass universities will not be expanding, so their main role is to "survive" in the context of a declining student population, adjusting to a host of new realities (including, possibly, the Bologna process) and relying on new curricula (academic standards) produced by the high-tier institutions.

Despite the state regulations imposed on all Indian higher education, we have shown that the most rapidly increasing sector—private unaided colleges—has little incentive to improve quality, and the Indian provincial authorities have necessarily (from a political imperative) placed much more emphasis on expansion and increasing equity through affirmative action. Further, the states produce few adequately trained engineering faculty to staff the expanding system. This has left the main options for increasing quality in the hands of the central government—expanding the number of elite, highly selective institutions, including their graduate schools, and, more generally, expanding the number of autonomous ("deemed") private and public universities, over which the national government could have considerable quality control. The government has moved forward on the first option. Progress on the second is limited because of resistance from trustees in private colleges and from the states regarding granting autonomy to public colleges.

Finally, in Brazil, where the government can directly control quality only in the public universities (and even there, because of the considerable autonomy of faculty and administrators, this control is largely exerted through finances), the main state efforts to improve quality have focused on indirect means, such as government-mandated staffing requirements in private institutions, student testing, and the publication of test results, program by program, for each higher education institution. To what degree test results induce private higher education institutions to improve quality when they have strong counterincentives to keep costs low is questionable. In both Brazil and India, there is so much excess demand for higher education places that financial constraints on families may be more important in governing the expansion of private institutions than public perceptions of their quality.

6 Who Are the Students, and How Are They Shaped by BRIC Higher Education?

W E HAVE IDENTIFIED SOME COMMON TRENDS IN THE WAY BRIC higher education systems have developed, including the rapid expansion of college enrollments, the steady rise in the rates of return for completing university, the increased share of higher education costs paid directly by students' families, greater institutional differentiation, and the changing institutional environments in colleges and universities as the systems expand and differentiation increases.

In this chapter we turn to the students attending BRIC universities and colleges. We analyze how students are selected into differentiated higher education institutions, how they are trained (with special emphasis on engineering and computer science education), and how engineering and computer science students in their last year of study feel about their education. We detail the educational pathway students take during pre-tertiary schooling, their academic readiness before college, and the process they undergo in their application and admission to university. We then describe the learning experiences of these students at different types of institutions within each country and how students regard their learning experiences and their preparation for work. As part of this analysis, we investigate how well BRIC higher education systems do with their engineering and computer science students compared to similar institutions in the developed countries. The findings of this chapter are therefore a preview and an input to our more extensive analysis of the quality of BRIC higher education systems in Chapter 7.

Little comparative research has been done on the quantity, background characteristics, and quality of students—especially engineering students—produced by the BRIC higher education systems. Research is also very limited on the policy levers available to and employed by states to improve students' experiences and learning. A few studies have attempted to make comparisons of the quantity of engineering graduates produced by China, India, and the United States up until 2006, as well as to provide some initial feedback (mostly from employers) about the quality of engineering graduates (Gereffi et al., 2008; Wadhwa et al., 2007). There have also been many general claims that China and India place particular emphasis on mathematics and science education at the pre-tertiary levels. Researchers have also documented the influx of Chinese and Indian students into science and engineering doctoral programs in the United States, which indirectly reflects on the abilities of students at the upper end of the ability distribution in these countries (Bound and Turner, 2010).

Similar to previous chapters, we highlight the dominant role of the state in shaping student experiences. In addition, we show that BRIC states seem to be succeeding in an important political goal—namely, in their quest for improving their political legitimacy through higher education expansion. For the most part, students are quite satisfied with the higher education they receive, even in how relevant it is for the job market. This appears to be true even for students who attended institutions regarded as lower quality.

In that context we are able to show that in all the BRICs, the selection process into higher education is formally based on meritocratic norms—namely, entrance examinations—and that this is especially true in the "elite" universities and colleges. Nevertheless, many if not most of the students who do well on entrance examinations have had access to "better" primary and secondary schools, which is often a matter of social class as well as academic ability. This sorting system means that a very small proportion of the age group in Brazil, China, and India is able to gain access to the top tier of institutions, and a somewhat larger but still small proportion is able to do so in Russia.

We also find that the BRIC countries are at different stages in preparing students for college. First, Russia and Brazil have high rates of upper secondary school enrollments, China has recently caught up, and India lags rather far behind. There is also substantial variation across BRIC countries in how well students are equipped with mathematics and science knowledge and skills before college. For example, results from international assessments indicate that China's pre-tertiary system seems to be producing an ample number of students who have strong cognitive skills in mathematics and science and can potentially become innovative and productive college graduates. In Russia, students on average perform somewhat lower than developed countries on international assessments. In addition, within Russia the nation's engineering students have only average scores in math on college entrance exams. Brazil and India's student pools going into engineering and science—again according to international scores and general evaluations of the quality of secondary schooling (OECDb, 2010; Wu et al., 2009; Kingdon, 2007)—appear to have significantly lower average math and science knowledge skills than secondary graduates in China and Russia, even when we account for the reduced fraction of college-age students in Brazil and India that end up in higher education institutions. In addition, as we discussed in Chapter 2, Brazil has a lower proportion of the total of university students who complete engineering programs.

Furthermore, BRIC governments often set policies that constrain students' educational opportunities and choices before and during college, a situation that has implications for the selection and quality of human capital in each country. First, China's, and to a lesser extent India's, education systems are characterized by tracking mechanisms that early on steer students from less advantaged backgrounds away from higher education. This is in addition to the wide differences in quality between pre-tertiary institutions in all four countries, which result in unequal opportunities to enter college and selective institutions. Second, unlike in the United States, students in China, India, and somewhat less in Brazil are tracked into science and engineering majors and associated occupations at various stages along an educational "pipeline"—students who stray from a relatively unidirectional path toward science and engineering careers at a particular stage have difficulty returning. Third, all BRIC countries use college entrance exams that can heavily influence what is studied in high school and act as a screen for admission into better higher education institutions. The limited number of college spots (especially in select institutions) in China, India, and Brazil creates fierce competition among eligible students to perform well on these exams. There are further widespread concerns that, in preparing for the exam, students spend much of their time engaged in rote memorization and learning narrow skill sets. Fourth, students in the four BRIC nations likely make suboptimal decisions when choosing colleges and majors, as there is little if any educational and career counseling in pre-tertiary schooling or information about institutions and majors when applying for college. Students may additionally be admitted to higher education institutions through complex and abstruse admissions rules set by the state. In the countries besides Russia, students also have few chances to transfer between institutions or disciplines once they get to college.

Finally, students in all four countries tend to have limited learning experiences in college compared to the American engineering education paradigm. BRIC engineering students face narrowly defined major offerings, a high proportion of technical course requirements (often with fewer courses in "soft skills" that engineers are said to increasingly need), and/or less practical versus theoretical training. Yet, despite all of this, as mentioned above, students who make it to college in any BRIC nation are on the whole quite satisfied with the education they receive, regardless of which type of university (i.e., elite or nonelite) they attend.

The Pool of Students Available for Higher Education

In this section we discuss broad trends in high school enrollments and graduation, educational tracking, and the content and nature of pre-tertiary schooling in each country. This helps describe the ability level and socioeconomic class of the students that universities potentially receive, which in part affects each higher education system's likelihood of producing qualified graduates.

High School Enrollment and Graduation Trends

The BRIC nations have achieved nearly universal primary school enrollment rates but have different gross enrollment rates for secondary education. Foremost, Russia's gross enrollment rate for upper secondary school has been quite high for some time, reaching 88 percent in 2009 (OECD, 2011a). In Brazil enrollment rates are also quite high, at 82 percent in 2008 (World Bank, 2011). China has rapidly expanded upper secondary school enrollments (reportedly, evenly split between academic and vocational tracks) over the last decade such that the gross enrollment rate reached 79 percent in 2009 (NBS, 2010). Chinese policy makers further expect to universalize access to upper secondary school before 2020. Finally, India has by far the lowest proportion of students attending high school, with a gross enrollment rate of 63 percent in grades nine and ten and just 36 percent in grades eleven and twelve in 2009–2010 (MHRD, 2010). A rather modest goal of the government of India (as compared to the other countries) is to universalize enrollments through grade eight as soon as possible and through grade ten by 2017.

According to the OECD (2011a, Table A2.1), 65 percent of Brazilian upper secondary graduates (or 34 percent of the age group) entered bachelor's-level higher education programs. Our estimates using Brazilian undergraduate enrollment data and the 18–22-year-old population estimate from the 2010 census show a 32 percent enrollment rate in 2010. This is probably an overestimate because of the high repetition rate in Brazilian higher education. UNESCO data suggest that a very high fraction (about 90 percent) of Russian upper secondary students attended university (formerly, all five-year programs, now gradually converting to four-year programs), or about 76 percent of the age group. In China about one-half of academic high school graduates went on to some form of higher education in 2009.[1] Slightly less than one-fourth of these graduates (about one-eighth of the age cohort) entered four-year programs, slightly more than one-fourth entered three-year programs, while approximately another one-fourth repeated the college entrance exam the next year. In India, the gross enrollment rate among 18–23-year-olds in undergraduate (B.A.-equivalent) degree education for the 2009–2010 academic year was 10 percent. The rate among 18–22-year-olds was approximately 12 percent (MHRD, 2011). Indian enrollment is increasing so rapidly that the gross enrollment rate for B.A.-type degree programs was probably about 16 percent in 2010–2011. We will later use this enrollment rate information to approximate the relative "quality" of BRIC students entering university.

Tracking
The BRIC education systems have different mechanisms when it comes to tracking students into and away from higher education.[2] China's education system begins tracking early as students who graduate with nine years of compulsory education (around age fifteen) take a high school entrance exam; the scores of this exam as well as the willingness to pay substantial tuition fees determine whether students can enter academic high schools versus vocational high schools (or the labor market). As a result, less than half of the higher-scoring junior high school graduates, generally those from more advantaged areas and backgrounds, enter the academic track (Loyalka, Wei, and Zhong, 2011). Furthermore, higher-ability and more socioeconomically advantaged students in China tend to go to key high schools that have higher rates of sending students to college and selective institutions.[3]

Students in the other three BRIC countries appear, at least on the surface, to have more choice in deciding whether or not to continue pursuing a path toward higher education after junior high school. In India students can choose to go to an academic or vocational track after grade eight, but few choose the latter track.[4] A clearer demarcation takes place either after grade ten or grade twelve, when students chose either technical/vocational schools or general/professional higher education. Students who stay in the academic track are further required to qualify for a particular subfield in grades eleven and twelve. As is the case with China, students who end up in the academic track and eventually in grades eleven and twelve are likely from families of higher socioeconomic status. In Russia and Brazil, about 17 percent and 10 percent of high school students (respectively) are in the vocational versus the academic track (OECD, 2011a; INEP, 2010a, Table 1.1). In contrast to the other two countries, students in Russia and Brazil who enter vocational school are not necessarily of lower ability.[5] Therefore, educational inequality in India, Russia, and Brazil mostly takes place as students sort between less and more selective high schools (something that additionally occurs in China).

China, India, and Brazil also track students into science and engineering majors and occupations earlier than in the United States.[6] For example, Chinese students must choose between a science track and a humanities track after the first year of academic high school (grade ten). This track choice often determines whether students take the science or humanities college entrance exam, which in turn determines whether students can enter most science or engineering majors (Loyalka, 2009). In 2009 about 1.8 million or 63 percent of Chinese students entering a four-year institution entered through the science track.[7] Similarly in India, tenth-grade graduates are filtered into science and math, commerce, or arts tracks based on their performance on the tenth-grade board exam. After completing grades eleven and twelve in a given stream, students who wish to enter a rather competitive college program in, say, medicine or engineering (such as at one of the IITs, NIITs, or a state-level institution) take one or more corresponding entrance exams. Finally, in Brazil, tracking happens a bit later as all high school students take the same courses; when high school graduates enter college, however, they must stick to a particular track (e.g., humanities, science, or engineering).

Russia's system, by contrast, does not seem to commit students to science and engineering at any point of the educational pipeline, besides about 40 percent of students who take more advanced mathematics in high school. High school graduates can generally choose in which subjects they wish to take the country's annual national college entrance exam (with the exception of Russian and mathematics, which are required of all students). These applicants choose test subjects according to the requirements of the particular universities and programs to which they wish to apply. Once in university, there are no formal restrictions on changing majors. Furthermore, according to our survey of more than 2,000 engineering students in Russia, many students graduated from secondary schools that either specialized in fields outside of mathematics or science or from schools that did not specialize in any particular field. This could be one reason that new engineering students in Russia seem to have mathematics and science ability comparable to nonengineering students. We discuss this finding further below.

Cognitive Skills

In general, the cognitive skills acquired by precollege youth differ markedly across BRIC nations. For instance, the Program for International Student Assessment (PISA), which measures the cognitive skills of fifteen-year-old students in science, mathematics, and reading across more than sixty countries, shows substantial differences in exam scores across Russia, Brazil, "average" level of development states in India (Himachal-Pradesh and Tamil Nadu), and economically developed regions of China (e.g., Shanghai, Hong Kong, and Macau).[8] In particular, among OECD and other countries, "regions of China," Russia, and Brazil/Indian states rank at the top, middle, and bottom of the score distribution respectively in each subject test (reading, math, or science). Furthermore, while Shanghai-China ranks significantly higher than all other countries in every subject, Russia tends to score below the OECD average (but not significantly different from the United States); Brazil is in the bottom quarter of the rankings, well below Russia; and India is below Brazil.

Specific results from each country shed further light on the preparedness of students before they get to college. For instance, while there is substantial variation in academic performance across the provinces of China (as much as across the entire OECD, which includes low-scoring countries such as Chile and Mexico), the country has many urban centers and provinces like high-scoring Shanghai and Hong Kong with strong educational systems, including regions such as Beijing, Tianjin, Jiangsu, Zhejiang, and Guangdong. Given that the total population of these regions is approximately 260 million (Shanghai alone has a population of 23 million), we surmise that China has a large number of students who would potentially score high on the PISA.

Among the BRIC nations that took the PISA, students in Brazil performed much worse than China and Russia but better than India. A very small percentage of students in Brazil (about 3.5 percent at level four or higher) who took the mathematics test reached the higher levels of proficiency that the

OECD says are important for producing innovative individuals who can perform well in university and lead the growth of the knowledge economy. Brazil has seen some improvements in PISA mathematics scores over the course of a decade (World Bank, 2010; Klein, 2011). However, because less than one-third of the Brazilian fifteen-year-olds tested in the PISA will end up in university, if we assume that these are the highest scoring one-third, the average math score for that group is about 460, which is still significantly below the OECD average, but not as far below as the Brazilian average of 386. In addition, as we show below, the data from the end-of-first-year general ability test (ENADE) given to most higher education students in Brazil suggests that engineering students in Brazil score somewhat above almost all other majors on that test.

Only two states in India (Himachal Pradesh and Tamil Nadu) participated in the 2009 PISA. Although regarded as above average in comparison to India's other states in terms of human development (Planning Commission, 2011), the students' scores in those states ranked at the very bottom of all countries and regions in the PISA survey. In mathematics less than 1 percent of Indian students scored at level four or higher, the level at which students have to solve complex tasks (Walker, 2011). Only a few percent in each state scored at the proficiency level (level three) (Walker, 2011). Science scores were similarly low. Furthermore, in India only about 60 percent of fifteen-year-olds (the age group tested by PISA) reach this level of secondary schooling, although in urban areas the percentage is higher. This suggests that even if only those few percent "proficient" in mathematics are the ones that end up in engineering, they enter at much lower levels of knowledge than in China (37 percent of Shanghai male students and 51 percent of female students at levels five and six) or Russia (18 percent of males and females at level four or higher) (Walker, 2011).

In addition to these results, Wu and colleagues (2009) conducted a study in which eighth- and twelfth-grade students in two states (Rajasthan and Orissa, which have a lower GDP/capita than the average GDP/capita in India and a high percentage of scheduled castes/tribes) took the TIMSS exam. The authors compared the TIMSS scores from these states to the average scores from forty-six high- and low-income countries. Results show that only 15 percent and 25 percent of students in Rajasthan and Orissa achieved the international average on 1999 TIMSS items—students from these two states had difficulties across a full range of different types of math and science questions and had greater difficulty with problems that involved complex procedures. Furthermore, grade eight students' average scores were 34 percent and 37 percent, compared to the international average of 52 percent. Grade twelve students in Rajasthan and Orissa averaged 44 percent and 38 percent, compared to the international average of 57 percent.[9] While we cannot generalize the results of the above study to students in India's more economically developed regions, there are other indications of weak pre-tertiary schooling across India, including poor reading and mathematics achievement (ASER, 2012), inadequate school facilities (Kingdon, 2007), and high levels of teacher absenteeism (Kremer et al., 2005) in primary education.

According to the PISA and TIMSS results, students in Russia appear to perform fairly well on average, albeit somewhat lower in mathematics and science than students in a number of Western European countries and the United States (but Russian students scored very high on the TIMSS 2011 mathematics test). Students who decide to study engineering in college seem to be among the average-performing students in math and science. For example, most university administrators we interviewed (e.g., deans of engineering departments as well as vice-rectors responsible for admissions, curricula, and science) complained of the deteriorating quality of engineering students admitted into universities, especially in mathematics. These findings were confirmed by the relatively average performance of first-year engineering majors on the 2009, 2010, and 2011 Unified State Exams compared to students entering social science, humanities, and medicine majors (see below).

These international comparisons suggest that China and Russia are on the whole competitive with the United States and other developed countries in producing a substantial number of high-achieving students, at least up until age fifteen. If high school education in these countries is of reasonable quality, then students entering universities on the whole are likely to be quite competitive in mathematics knowledge with, for example, U.S. students. Students in Brazil and India, on the other hand, appear to be hampered to some degree by weaknesses in the quality of (and for India also quantity of students in) pre-tertiary schooling at least through about grade eight or nine. Even when we account for the fact that a much more select group of students enters university in Brazil than the average of those taking the PISA test, this group does not seem to be on par with the equivalent groups of students in China. Even accounting for the relatively higher than average performance of engineering students in Brazil and the average performance of engineering students in Russia, Brazilian engineering students are probably less well prepared at entry than those in Russia. We do not have the data to make a similar comparison for India, but it is probably the case, given the results presented above, that the average student entering technical colleges in India is less well prepared mathematically than a comparable student in China or Russia.

High School Curriculum

It is important to ask what students are learning in high school in each of the BRIC countries because arguably the most comparable test results—the PISA scores—are for students at age fifteen (and not older). In particular, given our interest in science and engineering education, to what degree do academic high schools in these countries focus on math and science? As a partial response to this question, we examine evidence on the number and content of the math and science courses taken by high school students in BRIC countries and compare this to the United States.

The 2009 U.S. National Assessment of Educational Progress (NAEP) High School Transcript Study (IES, 2011) provides detailed information on U.S. high school students' course load and content (see Table 6.1, columns 1–3). Using a nationally representative sample of high school students, it finds that students who take a "standard" or "midlevel" curriculum complete three

TABLE 6.1 The United States and the BRIC countries: Number of courses required in high school by subject type

	United States			China	India[a]	Brazil	Russia[b]
	Standard	*Midlevel*	*Rigorous*				
Native language/ literature	4	4	4	4	4	3	2–6
Mathematics	3	3	4	4	4	3	2–4
Science	3	3	3	11 (4P, 4C, 3Bio)	2 years (9th/10th), 2P, 2C, 2S (11th/12th)	9 (3P, 3C, 3Bio)	2 + (0.67–1.67P)
Foreign language	0	1	3	4	4	3	2–4
Grades	9–12 (4 years)			9 + 10–12	9–10 + 11–12	10–12	10–11

SOURCE: U.S. statistics are from the Institute of Educational Sciences, 2011. BRIC statistics are estimates based on official documents and authors' anecdotal evidence.

NOTES: P = Physics; C = Chemistry; Bio = Biology; S = Optional.

[a]For India, the course loads apply to students who eventually enter the science stream in grades 11 and 12.

[b]For Russia, students may choose between basic and advanced curricula; hence, there is a range of possibilities. Also, three hours per week of lessons in a given year are counted as one course in Russia. High school ends with grade 11.

years of math and three years of science. The midlevel curriculum further requires that math subjects include geometry and algebra and that science courses include some mix among biology, chemistry, and physics. A "rigorous" curriculum, on the other hand, requires students to complete four years of math, including a minimum of precalculus, and at least one year each of biology, chemistry, and physics. The percentages of high school graduates in the United States who took below-standard level, standard level, midlevel, and a rigorous-level curriculum are 25 percent, 16 percent, 46 percent, and 13 percent, respectively.

Table 6.1 compares these requirements with course taking in BRIC countries. First, in academic high schools in China (column 4), we find that students from grades nine to twelve take a total of four years of math, physics, and chemistry (each), as well as three years of biology. In Brazil (column 5), all high school students are required to take the same courses from grades ten to twelve, including three years (each) of math, physics, chemistry, and biology. We have course requirement information only for the last two years of pre-tertiary education (i.e., upper secondary school) in Russia. Overall, Russian students may take less math and science courses (on average) than students in the other three countries because a significantly large proportion of students choose a basic curriculum that has less math and science electives than the advanced curriculum. The course requirements in Indian high schools, by contrast, vary considerably, not only between regions and schools but also among the specializations (e.g., humanities, business, or science) that students choose in grades eleven and twelve. Roughly speaking, most Indian upper secondary students take two years of math and science (a combination subject of physics, chemistry, and biology) in grades nine and ten. Then grade eleven and twelve students in the science stream who are planning for future studies in sciences or medicine generally take two years of math, English, chemistry, physics, or biology.

Therefore, high school students from the BRIC countries spend much more time studying mathematics and science than students in the United States. Because lower-achieving students are sorted away from the path to college (especially in China and India) and also because academic high schools emphasize math and science coursework, it could well be that academic high school students in the BRIC countries are much more prepared for undergraduate engineering studies than their PISA scores would suggest.

Of course, the level of difficulty of high school math and science education can vary greatly among schools in all four countries. While Table 6.1

illustrates the number of high school courses dedicated to math and science, it does not tell us what students actually learn in these courses. This may depend to no small degree on the nature and content of each country's college entrance examination.

College Entrance Examinations

Each country's college entrance examination system appears to have a strong influence on what students learn and how they develop in high school. For example, the college entrance exam in China is a two-day high-stakes test. Students' scores on the test largely determine into which college and major they will be admitted.[10] High school students in China have been known to prepare all day, seven days a week, for the exam, paying for extra classes and tutoring, and receiving considerable pressure from families to score well enough on the exam to get into the most selective institution possible.[11] Moreover, the curriculum in Chinese academic high schools is heavily structured around the college entrance exam. This is because most provinces in China release syllabi to high school teachers about what generally will be covered on each year's (provincial-level) exam. Whereas teachers may instruct students somewhat according to a standardized curriculum in the tenth and eleventh grades of high school, they almost entirely mold their twelfth-grade lesson plans according to this syllabus.[12]

India has been an exception among the BRIC countries in that college students in a number of fields outside of science and engineering often have not had to take an entrance exam to get into college. However, students who have qualified for grades eleven and twelve in science and who have been interested in engineering studies generally take one of three types of entrance exams to compete for selective programs: the IIT Joint Engineering Exam (JEE), the All-India Engineering Entrance Examination (AIEEE—usually for entry into one of the thirty NIITs), or one of many State Level Engineering Entrance Exams (SLEEEs—for entry into a state-level institution). It has often been claimed that the JEE is one of the hardest engineering entry tests in the world, as only about one out of forty-five applicants gain admission into an IIT.[13] Many Indian students spend a large part of their time during grades eleven and twelve preparing for one or multiple entrance exams, generally consisting of math, physics, and chemistry. There is no humanities component in these exams.

A number of criticisms have been directed at India's engineering entrance exams. Perhaps most importantly, critics claimed that student learning has become narrowly focused on preparing for the test. For instance, the exams usually required students only to show proficiency in math and basic sciences, rather than other subject areas (both within and outside of science) that may be important for training future engineers (Mohanan, 2010). Students are further encouraged, often by "coaching institutes," to recognize patterns within the exam questions rather than learn underlying scientific concepts and inquiry (Gupta, 2000). In recent years the exams also asked a large number of closed-ended (e.g., multiple choice) questions in a short period of time (three hours), favoring "surface-smartness" and efficient test taking over thinking and creativity (Mohanan, 2010). The apparent "dumbing down" of IIT applicants through the JEE has led some industry leaders to state that they would be much less likely to hire IIT graduates in the future (Srinivasaraju, 2007).

Partially in response to such concerns, the government has established several committees to suggest ways of reforming the engineering entrance exam system. One likely, notable outcome is to end the four-decades-old JEE and the other 150 engineering entrance exams by 2013–2014. In their place, Ministry of Human Resources and Development policy makers have proposed instituting a common entrance exam for students, such as the Scholastic Aptitude Test used in the United States. Furthermore, a larger weight would be given to students' marks in the qualifying twelfth examination and a relatively smaller weight to this aptitude test.

As in India, university entrance exams to enter select institutions in Brazil have traditionally been very competitive. Only a third of the age cohort now enrolls in bachelor-degree-level higher education institutions, and only 7–8 percent enter public universities. Each of the selective institutions has traditionally given its own *vestibular* (entrance exam), which also varies by department within university. To provide more standardization to the admissions process, the Brazilian government introduced a national high school final exam, *Exame Nacional do Ensino Médio* (ENEM), in 1998. In 2009 the government proposed that all federal public universities use the ENEM as a national unified entrance exam.[14] Although this exam has not universally been adopted, high school graduates can now apply for multiple institutions in the country through their registration in the ENEM system, and many public and private universities either consider students' scores in ENEM as their only criterion of selection or as one of many criteria. As the unification process continues, the expectation is that more institutions will take this test as their only selection criterion.

In Russia higher education institutions also traditionally used their own admissions tests. However, since 2003 the government recommended that institutions use results from the Unified State Examination (USE), and by 2009, policy makers mandated that all students must at least take the Russian language and math portions of the exam. Students now choose from a range of subjects based on the requirements of the universities to which they wish to apply. Students interested in engineering departments normally submit scores for mathematics, physics, IT, and Russian tests. Thus, similar to other BRIC nations, the curriculum in Russian high schools is gradually aligning with the college entrance exam.

There are many opinions but only limited research about how college entrance exams affect student learning and educational opportunities. It has been argued, for example, that high-stakes high school exit tests increase the focus of high school teaching and increase student learning (Bishop, 1997). Others claim that the competitiveness created by the exam culture causes students to be more engaged in their classes.[15] At the same time, there are concerns about the equity effects of these tests because higher social class students have access to schooling that is better at preparing students for the tests. Empirical evidence from China does suggest that students of lower socioeconomic status (e.g., from rural areas) are less likely to score as high as students of higher socioeconomic status (e.g., from urban areas), especially as one moves to the higher levels of the score distribution. About 20–25 percent of students decide to retake the entrance exam every year in China, and the repeat rate in a province is negatively associated with the level of economic development of that province (Loyalka, 2012). Retaking the exam in fact entails considerable (financial and nonfinancial) personal and social costs, including the possibility that repeat students may not make useful gains in learning in their extra year of high school.

Applying and Gaining Admission to College

Although the college applications and admissions process differs across BRIC nations, it generally tends to be high stakes and less flexible compared to the process in developed countries. In particular, beyond the competitive pressures associated with the college entrance exam and college quotas, students face informational constraints when making their college and major choices and may be matched into colleges and majors by potentially inefficient or inequitable admissions rules.

In China students lack systematic knowledge about how to choose universities and majors. For instance, students receive almost no formal career counseling in pre-tertiary schooling (Loyalka, Liu et al., 2012). Students also seemed to be immersed in exam preparation and may give little attention to college and major choices. Surprisingly, many students see the gamut of college and major choices they are eligible for only near the time they have to officially register those choices.

In addition, Chinese universities tend to provide few useful indicators of the quality of their institutions. More specifically, these institutions provide little reliable information about college outputs such as graduate employment statistics and indicators of student learning. Rather, students frequently refer to guidebooks, which list both the enrollment quotas as well as the average college entrance exam scores for the last few years for each college major combination, to fill out their college major choices. Institutions also seem to refer to last year's college entrance exam scores to determine their competitiveness in a given year. Student and institutional reliance on entrance exam scores may thus create an inertia in which higher-scoring students continually misattribute high quality to institutions with high past exam scores.

A further complication for students in China is that the applications and admission process, which takes student college entrance exam scores and college and major choices into account and then subsequently matches students into a single college major combination, can be both complex and opaque. Each province uses its own set of application and admissions rules to determine how students are matched into colleges and majors, and there is substantial variation across provinces in these rules (Loyalka, Zhong et al., 2012). For example, in some provinces students are asked to fill out their college and major choices before they know their entrance exam score or where their score fits into the overall distribution of scores that year. In other provinces students who are not accepted into their first college choice are penalized for their second college choice (i.e., points are subtracted from the student's college entrance exam score when determining entry into the second college). These types of admissions rules may prevent students from revealing their true preferences for colleges and majors or even lead students from disadvantaged backgrounds to make less optimal choices than students from advantaged backgrounds.

Once Chinese students enter a given college major, they must stick with it. We find, for example, that less than 1 percent of Chinese students in our Shaanxi sample change their major after four years of college, and no students transfer between universities. The only viable recourse for the vast majority of students in China to gain admissions to another college major is to retake the college entrance exam the next year (which usually entails going to college another full year).

In India all higher education institutions are supposed to provide detailed information about the courses they offer, about their faculty, about their fee structures, and the like. However, relatively unreliable information on all these aspects is generally available either through institutional websites or through printed materials (called "prospects") that may have to be purchased for a nontrivial amount of money. Furthermore, it is not possible for students to check the websites or brochures of a good number of institutions before they make their choices.

After finishing their entrance examinations, students in many states attend pre-counseling sessions, where the students make their final institutional and major choices in the span of a few minutes. Higher-ranking students tend to have more choices in terms of selective institutions as well as majors. Such students tend to opt for modern subjects such as electrical engineering and computer science. Students with lower rankings not only have to be content with poorer-quality, often private unaided institutions, but also may have to pay a premium to get into the major of their choice. Students who do not get into the institutions and majors of their choice often decide to repeat their entrance examination the following academic year.

Another complexity faced by students in India is that many take entrance examinations from multiple boards. Besides the few national entrance examinations through which students gain admission into the IITs and NIITs, for example, each state has its own entrance examination. High scores on these state exams also enable some students to make competitive choices.

Students are selected into Indian engineering institutions in a relatively meritocratic way. They are assigned to universities and majors based on the exam (score) rank and student preferences. During the early phases of admission, students can also attempt to move from a lower-quality institution to a higher-quality one if spots are still available. Once in college, however, students can rarely change into more-selective colleges or change majors.

With the recent expansion of the Brazilian higher education system, the programs of study available to students have multiplied. At the same time, there is no formal system of information about course requirements, graduate labor market statistics, and other factors important for student choice. The Brazilian Ministry of Education has developed a system to evaluate higher education institutions, the ENADE, which could serve as a reference about program study for prospective candidates, but the validity of the ENADE test has been challenged, particularly as a measure of institutional quality. In many institutions relatively few students take the test in each program specialization. Lacking more sophisticated information, students generally aim to obtain a spot within their state's public university or consider attending prestigious Catholic private universities as a first option. Although increasing numbers of universities have signed on to the federal government's new ENEM test—meant to be a universal national university entrance examination—most students currently still must take the examination specific to a particular program in a particular university (the *vestibular*). This means that when applying to various programs, they need to take multiple entrance examinations, some of which are scheduled at the same time on the same day. Again, like students in China and India, once Brazilian students get into college, they have little flexibility to switch programs of study as their majors are defined through the entrance exam process. Students usually have to retake the entrance exam to change their major or their university.

Brazil and India could look to Russia for the effects of a national examination system: introducing the Unified State Examination in Russia in 2009 has led to more transparent admission procedures and allowed high school graduates to make more informed choices than in the past. Also in contrast to students in China, Russian students are informed about their USE scores and then simultaneously submit these scores to up to five different universities of their choice. The admissions matching algorithm is also quite simple in Russia: students are admitted into any of the college major combinations they've chosen if they have a high enough score (given the distribution of scores and the number of available college major spots). Similarly to China, Russian institutions have started posting online the mean scores of last year's admitted students, by major. At present, these scores allow students to assess their likelihood of admission. However, there is the potential problem that students in Russia (like China) may overly rely on these scores to evaluate the quality of different universities. Nevertheless, peer test scores could certainly be used as one measure of institutional quality.[16]

A recent study by the National Research University Higher School of Economics (Moscow)[17] assessed the utility to students of available admissions information on the websites of Russian higher education institutions. As part of the study, the researchers collected data from 524 universities in 83 regions of Russia (85 percent of all state universities in the country) in 2011. Overall, they found that these institutions usually provided information about admissions regulations (97 percent of institutions), contacts and working hours for admissions offices (93 percent), alternative admissions policies for "talented"[18] students (95 percent), as well as tuition and fees (75 percent). Past scores of their admitted students were posted by more than 60 percent of institutions. On the other hand, institutions did not provide much information on course syllabi (30 percent), academic curriculum (20 percent), or professional experience of the faculty (22 percent). Therefore, while Russia has made admissions requirements more transparent, prospective students are often unable to compare the content of various programs.

Students in Russia may find it difficult to select an appropriate major or university for other reasons. For one, majors in Russia tend to be quite specific/narrow and can have abstruse names.[19] In addition, once students are admitted into a particular major, few of them switch into other fields (under 10 percent in our student sample), even though they are technically allowed to do so. It could be that the vast majority of students do not wish to change their initial majors (60 percent of the 10 percent who did switch majors in our sample reportedly did so because of changing interests), but it could also be that very specific majors in the same field teach more or less the same curriculum, obviating the need to switch majors within the same general discipline. Finally, it is also not a common practice for students in Russia to transfer from one university to another. However, it is fairly easy for students to switch to a lower-quality institution. Students who may not be able to cope with the requirements of a more rigorous educational program appear to be eagerly accepted by second-tier institutions.

The Characteristics of College Students Entering Engineering Programs

We now examine the characteristics of students entering engineering majors in each of the BRIC countries. Wherever possible, we examine the relative ability (compared to students in nonengineering majors), gender, and socioeconomic status of students in engineering majors compared to other students.

In China in 2009, about 34 percent of all new four-year university students were enrolled in engineering majors. In addition, roughly 8 percent and 10 percent of all new engineering students in four-year institutions matriculated in elite 985–211 and 211-only universities, respectively.[20] The numbers of engineering graduates coming from both the elite and four-year institutions are therefore quite high, especially considering that students' completion rates in four-year universities are close to 100 percent.

Figure 6.1 compares the ability of first-year engineering versus nonengineering entrants who came from different provinces in China in 2009.[21] In almost all provinces, the average score of (science track) students who go into engineering is not much different from the average (science track) score of students who go into nonengineering majors (including medicine, science, economics, management, and agriculture). This result holds across all college tiers separately, but especially within the first tier (results not shown). Thus, engineering students (as a whole) are not necessarily of higher ability (on average) than other students in other majors in China, and this seems to be especially true in the more economically developed regions such as Beijing, Shanghai, Tianjin, and Zhejiang.

Our random sample of approximately 7,500 local senior college students in four-year universities in one Chinese province provides further information about the composition of university students and engineering students in particular. We find that the proportion of males to females attending university (1.06) is essentially the same as the age-cohort male-female ratio in that province (1.07). For engineering majors, however, the situation is much more lopsided, with a 2.23 male to female ratio (by contrast, the next highest male to female ratios are 1.18 for agriculture and 1.16 for basic science). Engineering in China, as in other countries, is a male-dominated field. Furthermore, we find

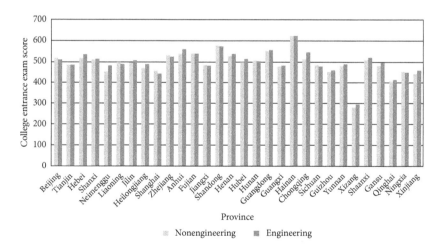

FIGURE 6.1 China: Comparison of average college entrance exam scores by province, new undergraduate enrollees in engineering versus nonengineering majors, 2009

SOURCE: Authors' estimates using data on all university students in China in 2009.

that the proportion of rural to urban students attending engineering majors in four-year institutions (1.78) is substantially smaller than the rural-urban population ratio in that province (2.84) and slightly more than the rural-urban ratio of four-year university students (1.63). In addition, while individuals from rural areas more often choose to study an engineering major than individuals from urban areas, rural students in the science track (to enter college) are represented more in second-tier (rather than first-tier institutions) and much less in expensive private (third-tier, high-tuition) institutions.

As we see in Chapter 2, about 13–14 percent of all university graduates in Russia are in engineering or engineering-related specialties. Table 6.2 shows the mean cognitive ability levels (in mathematics) of university students admitted into various majors in Russia. The estimates are based on the 2011 USE score data from a select sample of universities. From the table we see that computer engineering programs on the whole have students with slightly higher than average mathematics scores, whereas electronic engineering programs have students with slightly lower than average scores.[22]

If engineering students come from social class backgrounds similar to those of the totality of Russian university students, we would expect that with such a high fraction of youths attending universities, the socioeconomic background of Russian students measured by father's occupation should be lower than in the other BRICS, particularly in Brazil and India, where a relatively small percentage of students attend university. This is indeed the case. Our surveys of final-year students in technical universities show that 24 percent of Russian students' fathers are skilled workers (18 percent) or low-level service workers (6 percent), compared to 3 percent of students' fathers of our surveyed Indian students in those two categories. Almost 20 percent of Indian students' fathers were in business, compared to only 5 percent of Russian fathers. More Russian fathers were senior professional workers (24 percent versus 16 percent), and about the same were government officials (29 percent versus 26 percent in India). Another major difference between the parents in our India and Russian student surveys is that about one-half of the Indian mothers were identified as not working (housewives), compared to only 4 percent of the Russian mothers. In contrast, a much higher proportion of Russian mothers were government officials (18 percent versus 8 percent in India).

The income distribution of Russian students overall also suggests that the average student comes from a family of modest means. From national household survey data, the family income of Russian university students was 23,000 rubles per month in 2010, and a high fraction have relatively "middle" incomes

TABLE 6.2 Russia: Unified student entrance examination score comparison, by select majors, 2011

| | Mean USE scores (maximum 100) | |
Major	Mathematics	Russian
Machine building	48.5	57.8
Metallurgical engineering	51.4	59.7
Ship building	51.7	56.9
Vehicles	54.3	59.2
Biology	54.5	65.5
Electronic and radio engineering	54.7	60.7
Chemistry	56.4	65.1
Energetics	56.7	60.6
Instrument making and optical engineering	57.0	67.9
Nuclear technologies and technical physics	57.0	54.8
Management	58.1	69.4
Computer engineering	58.2	64.5
Chemical and biotechnologies	58.6	66.9
Automation and control engineering	58.7	63.7
Physics	59.4	64.9
Aircraft engineering (practical)	60.5	64.9
Mathematics	62.2	67.8
Economics	63.1	73.1
Business-informatics	63.5	73.4
Oil and gas engineering	67.0	76.0
Aircraft engineering (theory)	70.0	73.7

SOURCE: Authors' estimates from all higher education institutions in Russia that publish USE statistics on the Internet, 2011.

(Figure 6.2). However, our survey in seven Russian cities of 2,300 engineering students in their last year of university in 2009–2010 shows a much higher average family income (42,000 rubles) and high parental education levels—about 60 percent of mothers and 50 percent of fathers with higher professional education and another 30 percent of mothers and fathers with higher general education. These survey results likely differ because of the high percentage of

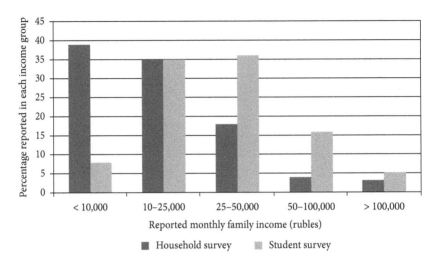

FIGURE 6.2 Russia: Family income of university students from household and student survey data, 2009–2010 (rubles per month)

SOURCE: Authors' estimates using data from the State Research University Higher School of Economics, *Monitoring of the Economics of Education 2010* (Moscow).

students (47 percent) in high-income cities (Moscow and St. Petersburg) in our sample and undersampling of higher incomes in the household survey. Engineering students likely also come from middle-class backgrounds in Russia because engineering is not a high-status program there.

Brazil provides a stark contrast to the Russian situation. The absolute number of college engineering students is quite low in Brazil compared to the other BRIC nations. As shown in Chapter 2, the number of students in higher engineering education in Brazil in 2009 was 475,000, or about 9 percent of total higher education enrollments.

We do not have data on the entrance exam performance of engineering students compared to students entering other programs in Brazil because most university departments in Brazil still give their own entrance tests. But university students are tested in the first and last years of their undergraduate study. This evaluation, called the ENADE, consists of two separate tests: one is program specific, and the second is a short test of general ability. To get an idea of the engineering students' relative academic ability, it is possible to compare their general ability scores with the scores of students in other programs in their first year of university. Table 6.3 shows that most types of Brazilian engineering majors (except for agricultural engineers) and computer science students do as well on the general ability test as science and mathe-

TABLE 6.3 Brazil: ENADE first-year university scores of engineering and other students on test of general ability, 2005 (except where noted)

University program	First-year general ability test score (mean)
Engineering I	52.6
Engineering II (electrical and electronics)	51.6
Engineering III	55.0
Engineering IV	58.1
Engineering V	60.1
Engineering VI	56.9
Engineering VII	58.6
Engineering VIII (agricultural engineering)	48.0
Computer science	52.4
Mathematics	53.1
Physics	53.8
Chemistry	50.9
Social sciences	44.5
Economics (2006)	44.5
Administration (2006)	40.8
Law (2006)	47.0
Pedagogy	48.4
History	52.8
Letters	56.2
Medicine (2007)	64.2

SOURCE: INEP, ENADE, 2005a, 2006, 2007. http://portal.inep.gov.br/web/guest/relatorio-sintese-2005, accessed Aug. 10, 2012; http://portal.inep.gov.br/web/guest/relatorio-sintese-2006, accessed Aug. 10, 2012; http://portal.inep.gov.br/web/guest/relatorio-sintese-2007, accessed Aug. 10, 2012.

matics majors and better than social science, law, economics, administration (includes business), and pedagogy majors.[23]

One possible explanation for engineering and computer science students' higher-than-average test scores is that in Brazil they come from more privileged backgrounds than students studying in other programs. Table 6.4 shows that younger students, whites, and those whose parents have a high level of educational attainment are overrepresented in electrical engineering and computer science courses. Specifically, about 38 percent and 23 percent of students who are selected to engineering and computer science courses in public and

TABLE 6.4 Brazil: Student demographics for combined engineering and computer science majors and combined all other majors, 2005

	Public higher education institutions				Private higher education institutions			
	EE and CS		Other programs		EE and CS		Other programs	
	1st-year students	4th-year students	1st-year students	4th-year students	1st-year students	4th-year students	1st-year students	4th-year students
GENDER								
Male	88.5	84.2	40.6	31.5	85.4	82.7	30.5	24.0
Female	11.5	15.8	59.4	68.5	14.6	17.3	69.5	76.0
RACE								
White	68.7	72.4	57.0	55.2	68.3	74.8	65.7	68.8
Black	4.5	2.7	7.1	6.7	6.0	3.1	7.3	5.6
Mulatto	22.9	19.7	32.8	34.7	22.1	16.8	23.9	22.8
Asian	2.7	4.0	1.6	1.4	2.4	4.4	1.5	1.5
Indigenous	1.0	1.0	1.2	1.5	0.9	0.8	1.2	1.0
FATHER'S EDUCATION								
No schooling	1.2	1.1	7.5	11.2	2.5	1.9	7.0	7.4
Grades 1–4	13.0	12.6	29.0	37.2	20.7	20.5	36.2	41.1
Grades 5–8	11.4	11.0	14.9	13.5	18.4	15.4	18.0	16.1
High school	35.4	30.7	27.7	20.8	34.5	33.0	24.2	20.7
College	38.5	44.2	20.1	16.7	23.2	28.8	13.6	14.0
MOTHER'S EDUCATION								
No schooling	0.9	0.9	5.8	9.0	2.5	1.7	6.5	7.3
Grades 1–4	10.8	11.4	25.4	33.7	18.8	19.3	33.5	38.4
Grades 5–8	12.7	11.9	15.6	14.8	19.2	17.9	19.1	17.2
High school	36.5	35.6	30.6	24.5	36.3	34.6	25.9	22.9
College	38.7	40.1	22.3	17.7	22.8	26.0	14.7	14.1
TYPE OF SECONDARY ATTENDED								
Only public	37.2	36.6	56.0	59.6	54.0	43.5	65.5	61.9
Only private	50.6	49.8	30.9	26.4	31.0	38.6	19.7	22.0
Both	12.2	13.6	13.1	14.0	15.0	17.9	14.8	16.1
SECONDARY PROGRAM								
General	78.8	70.0	69.9	50.9	66.1	56.1	57.5	44.3
Technical	18.6	28.0	11.1	14.6	26.2	39.2	13.8	16.8
Other (mostly pedagogical)	2.6	2.0	18.0	24.5	6.7	4.7	18.7	38.9
Number of observations	6,526	5,079	64,680	72,295	30,699	16,476	121,181	89,821

SOURCE: Authors' estimates using INEP, ENADE 2005 database of student survey.

private universities, respectively, have parents who have completed a higher education program, compared to 20 percent and 13 percent for students in other majors. Other data show that in the early 2000s about 60 percent of all university students came from families in the top 20 percent of income earners (Schwartzman, 2004), and although this percentage has fallen in recent years (see Chapter 8), it is still over 50 percent. Because engineering students come from higher-than-average education families, this suggests that an even higher proportion of engineering students come from high-income families. Moreover, in public universities, 84.2 percent of the graduates from engineering and computer science programs are males, compared to an average of 31.5 percent in other majors. In private universities the gender disparity is even larger: only 24 percent of the graduates from all programs are men, compared to 82.7 percent from engineering and computer science programs.

We show in Chapter 2 that the absolute and relative number of engineering students in India has been increasing rapidly, by more than 10 percent annually over the last several years, mostly through the proliferation of private unaided colleges.

We use data from our survey of almost 7,000 engineering final-year students in about forty institutions—IITs, colleges, and universities in four Indian states—to estimate the probability of attending a (relatively selective and low-tuition) public institution as a function of gender, entrance exam score, caste, and socioeconomic background. The results show that males are about 34 percent more likely than females with similar college entrance scores and similar socioeconomic background to attend public colleges. Those with higher test scores and families with higher incomes are also more likely to attend, regardless of gender. But a majority of students in our sample (54 percent) come from families where the average income is Rs. 100–500 thousand, and the average percentage of mothers with higher education is almost 60 percent (and fathers with higher education, almost 80 percent).[24] In India these students are from unusually high social status families. So perhaps the relevant way to put our results is that the 12 percent (Delhi) to 28 percent (Karnataka) coming from families with under 100 thousand rupees income are less likely to attend a public college. Students from the lowest castes are much more likely to attend public technical colleges, controlling for test score.

Thus, higher-scoring, higher-family-income males in India are more likely to attend public colleges/universities. This makes sense because government colleges/universities are cheaper, tuition-wise, and still generally more prestigious. Yet it should be remembered that as places in public institutions are limited in number, a majority of high-scoring (those who qualify for government-mandated lower tuition) students (54 percent) take admission in private colleges at the lower tuition rates (or similarly receive fee waivers/reimbursements). Further, as caste quotas and fee waivers are more strictly enforced in public institutions, lower-caste students in our sample tend to choose government colleges, even though they, too, are guaranteed lower tuition rates in private colleges (about the same as in government colleges). Finally, engineering education has traditionally been a bastion of male students, and it is only recently that female students are joining engineering in significant numbers.[25]

Our descriptions of engineering students' characteristics strongly suggest that the types of students entering higher engineering education programs differ by country. In particular, engineering students from Russia and China are not on average of higher ability (as measured by test scores) than nonengineering students, whereas engineering students from Brazil and India are on average of higher ability compared to nonengineering students. In general, engineering students in Russia come from families that have similar socioeconomic status as other university students. In China engineering students are of relatively lower socioeconomic status compared to nonengineering students, while the opposite is true in Brazil and India (with higher status in India measured more by higher caste and university-educated parents rather than income). A trend that does persist, not only across BRIC countries, but indeed all over the world, is that male students enter the engineering fields in much higher proportions than female students.

College Student Experiences

In this section we examine the course requirements of engineering majors, the time college students spend on various tasks, student perceptions of instructional practices, how much individuals believe they have gained from college, and their satisfaction with their overall educational experience.[26] In looking at course requirements in particular, we keep in mind that the globalization of some engineering professions has led to the expectation that engineering education should adhere to certain international standards, particularly the American paradigm of core science competence, fundamentals of engineering, and specialization. Moreover, the teaching/learning of "soft" skills such as foreign language abilities, management capacity, and teamwork are now stressed by engineering educators even from within the BRIC countries (e.g.,

Biswas et al., 2010; Kong and Qiu, 2007; Cha, 2009). We thus start by comparing the course requirements of undergraduate computer science (CS) departments in universities across the BRIC countries and selected institutions in the United States and England, paying particular attention to the proportion of courses dedicated to the core sciences, computer science, and soft skills.

As discussed in Chapter 5, the course requirements for college science and engineering degrees in Russia and India are established (or suggested, in the Indian case) by central agencies, while Chinese and Brazilian institutions have a great deal more autonomy to make decisions about curriculum. In Russia, the Ministry of Education and Science establishes standards for nonelite institutions for the course structure as well as the list of professional and social competences to be acquired for each major. Elite institutions in Russia (i.e., the national research universities), on the other hand, are given autonomy to develop their own standards. In India, state-level universities establish the curriculum for colleges under their jurisdiction, with considerable oversight from the All-India Council on Technical Education (AICTE). The AICTE's "model curricula" for bachelor's degrees in engineering suggests specific course requirements with details on syllabi and textbooks, as well as general assessment guidelines for each course. IITs are much more autonomous in developing their own curriculum, however, and this curriculum tends to be "oriented with a modern outlook and innovative spirit" (Biswas et al., 2010).

China's Ministry of Education does set a total number of credit hours and designates certain courses that should be studied for each major. Other course specifics, however, including the choice of curricular materials and instructional styles, are left to the discretion of individual institutions. In Brazil there is a tradition of university autonomy that grants individual institutions substantial discretion to establish their course requirements. At the same time, there are some broad policy guidelines that establish national parameters for Brazilian engineering higher education. In general, these guidelines require that all programs be divided into courses on basic skills (30 percent) and professional/specialized knowledge (15 percent). The remaining 55 percent of course requirements may be freely chosen by higher education institutions.

Table 6.5 shows the percentage of course units in various subject categories that are required to complete a computer science major in China, Russia, Brazil, and India and at Stanford University. The percentages for Russia and India are largely based on guidelines for nonelite universities from central agencies in these countries, whereas the percentages for Brazil are based on general recommendations from the country's Computer Science Society; elite

TABLE 6.5 Stanford University and the BRIC countries: Percentage of courses taken by computer science majors (bachelor's degrees) by course category

Course category	Stanford University	Brazil	China	Russia	India
Engineering fundamentals	13%		1–7%	53%	21%
Computer science	33%	63%	30–42%	—	53%
Senior project	2%		5–10%	5%	3%
Math	11%	16%	5–13%	23%	6%
Physics	4%	5%	3–6%	—	4%
Chemistry	0–2%	0%	0–1%	—	3%
Humanities and social sciences	36%	16%	12–20%	14%	9%
Other	0–2%	—	6–18%	4%	—
Period of study	4 years	4 years	4 years	4 years	4 years

SOURCES: Chinese data are from the authors' surveys. Russia's percentages are based on federal standards (and do not include national research universities). India's four-year degrees are from the AICTE Model Curriculum for Undergraduate Program (B.E./B.Tech) in Computer Science and Engineering (2000). Brazil's data are a suggested standard from the Brazilian Computer Science Society. Stanford's data are from the four-year plan for computer science bachelor's degree (unspecialized track) in 2011–2012 (www.stanford.edu/group/ughb/cgi-bin/handbook/index.php/4-Year_Plans). Accessed December 1, 2011.

universities in these countries tend to set their own, somewhat more flexible requirements. The percentage ranges for China are based our surveys of more than thirty elite and nonelite institutions.

From Table 6.5 we see that students from Stanford and the typical Chinese university are required to spend proportionally less of their time taking science and engineering/computer science courses in total when compared to university students in Brazil, Russia, and especially India. In addition, whereas India, China, and Brazil students generally take about the same number of physics and math credit hours as Stanford's students, Russian students take somewhat more. In fact, according to the standards of the Ministry of Education and Science in Russia, engineering programs should spend a substantial amount of time teaching technical courses (~75 percent). What most stands out is that Stanford computer science students take a substantially higher proportion of humanities and social science courses than their counterparts in the BRIC countries.[27]

Although Table 6.5 does not cover elite universities in Russia, Brazil, and India, we also collected information about the course requirements of computer science departments in elite institutions in these countries. Computer science courses at three first-tier universities in Russia are roughly divided along the same lines as the government requirements: professional (55 percent), mathematics and science (25 percent), and social sciences and humanities (20 percent). In India the vast majority of classes in the first and second years at IIT Madras are in the core sciences and engineering. Students take about seven humanities and social science courses, or 6 percent of their total time over the four-year period. Similarly, in the Pontifical Catholic University of Rio de Janeiro (PUC Rio), students are required to take six courses of humanities, which include philosophy, religion, ethics, and other humanities classes chosen by the students. However, students in both IIT Madras and PUC Rio are not required to take foreign language courses.

Beyond course requirements, we also examine how engineering and computer science students use their time. In Russia about two-thirds of the time that students devote to educational activities is spent attending lectures, labs, and meetings with faculty (~27 hours per week), and about one-third is spent on individual studies and homework (~13 hours per week). Students in India have a very similar allocation of time on these formal and informal educational activities (29 hours and 10 hours, respectively). According to our Indian survey, students also spent relatively little time working on their courses at home. Similarly in Brazil, computer science students are required to spend a minimum of about 25 hours per week in instructional activities and in laboratories. In contrast, however, according to a study by the *Instituto Nacional de Estudos e Pesquisas* (INEP) in 2005, about 19 percent of computer science students reported that they studied only one to two hours a week outside of class, while another 14 percent said they studied only three to four hours a week (INEP, 2005). These findings should be interpreted with caution, however, as the majority of students (51.4 percent) did not answer the time-use question of the survey. Based on a large 2011 college student survey in most four-year institutions in Beijing, Chinese engineering and computer science students allocated approximately three-quarters of their time to educational activities and another quarter to homework and studying outside of class (27 hours and 10 hours per week for engineering students, respectively).[28] The time use in the BRIC higher education institutions stands in sharp contrast with engineering/computer science training at Stanford, where typical students will be in class or laboratories 15–18 hours per week and spend about 2.5 to 3 times that number of hours working on class assignments on their own.[29]

The types of instruction that students are exposed to can directly affect what and how well they learn. A number of classroom-based instructional practices in engineering departments in China, India, and Russia aligned with those found in the United States.[30] For instance, although the majority of (senior-year) engineering students in our surveys in China, India, and Russia stated that instruction is mostly lecture based, more than three-quarters of the respondents in each country also reported that they had at least occasionally participated in technical demonstrations given by instructors and engaged in small-group discussions and work. A large majority of the respondents, regardless of the country, also noted that they had written technical research reports and given technical oral presentations. Furthermore, about one-half to two-thirds stated that they had experience developing original technical designs and discussed global economic trends in class.

Whereas it appears that classroom-based instruction is gradually becoming somewhat more flexible in these three countries, students still seem to lack practical (research and internship) experience as well as exposure to certain types of "soft skills." For example, only about one-sixth of the engineering students in our India and China samples participated in a professor's research project, compared to about one-third of students in our Russian sample. In addition, only a minority of engineering students in these countries reported having worked directly on projects with enterprises. Similarly, a minority of students participated in a leadership program or took an interdisciplinary course in the sciences. Individuals in India and Russia were also not very likely to have had an engineering internship in college. And even though the majority of Chinese students did report participating in such an internship, the basic quality of engineering internship opportunities in China is frequently questioned (Kong and Qiu, 2007; Cha, 2008).

How do students in different BRIC countries perceive their abilities to have changed after having gone through college? From our China survey, we find that the large majority of computer science and engineering students (85+ percent) believed that their abilities in technical knowledge, engineering practice, and understanding of new technologies improved at least somewhat by attending university, and this held slightly more for first-tier university students. A similar proportion of students believed they had improved at least somewhat in oral communication skills, problem-solving abilities, and the ability to collaborate with others. About two-thirds or more students believed they improved somewhat in other nontechnical areas such as foreign language ability, intercultural and entrepreneurial skills, and interest in lifetime learning.[31] Only slightly more than half of the students felt they improved at least somewhat in writing, however.

The perception of students in Russia and India was similarly positive. Over three-quarters of (senior-year) engineering students in our Russian sample, and slightly less than two-thirds of the students in our Indian sample, said that their research skills had improved over the course of their undergraduate education. The vast majority (+85 percent) of students in Russia and about three-quarters of students in India also stated that they had improved their technical knowledge and knowledge of engineering practices after coming to college. Around 60–70 percent of the respondents in India felt that their leadership, teamwork, problem solving, writing, and oral communication skills had increased. Respondents in Russia were even more positive about having improved their general academic (77 percent) and problem-solving (82 percent) abilities, although less positive about having improved in their foreign language (53 percent), leadership (56 percent), and writing (42 percent) abilities.

In the three countries where we conducted surveys, students expressed a general satisfaction with their overall higher education experience. In Russia about 88 percent of the students interviewed were satisfied with the quality of their education, compared to 67 percent in India who said they are well prepared to be engineers and computer scientists.[32] Yet only slightly under half of the Russian students said that they would study engineering if they could go back and choose their major again. This can be contrasted with the three-quarters of Chinese senior students who said that they would choose engineering again if they could and the 90 percent who thought they would work in a science- and engineering-related occupation upon graduation. In other words, students in China, Russia, and India on the whole believed that the education system had "done right by them."

Although we did not conduct a comparable survey in Brazil about student reactions to their educational experiences, secondary survey data from Brazil shows that computer science and electrical engineering students seem to have slightly mixed opinions about the instructional quality in their programs. Asked to evaluate the instructional practices of the majority of their professors, about 47 percent of the students reported that they found the practices adequate, 14 percent said they found them highly adequate, and 31 percent said that they found them only partially adequate (INEP, ENADE, 2005). Therefore, we tentatively conclude that the majority of Brazilian students seem to be satisfied with instructional quality but perhaps somewhat less so than students in the other BRIC countries.

Some Conclusions

We can draw several conclusions regarding the characteristics and experiences of students studying in technical fields in BRIC higher education institutions. First, our surveys suggest that engineering students at least in Russia, India, and China are largely satisfied with their higher education experience, regardless of the selectivity of the institution they attend. This should not be surprising because students rarely have alternative benchmarks by which to measure their academic experience outside of the variation in their own university or college. Nevertheless, the relatively high levels of satisfaction even among engineering students in second- and lower-tier institutions (i.e., the majority of students) indicate that the strategy of expansion has been successful from the perspective of state legitimization.

Second, the preparedness of students before college is undoubtedly a major factor in determining the relative quality of technical graduates across the four countries. We showed that compared to Russia and China, Brazil and especially India are producing a relatively much smaller proportion of upper secondary school students who have reasonably high mathematics and science skills. Russia has a large pool of high school graduates who attend college, and their international mathematics scores are comparable to U.S. students' scores. However, students entering engineering in Russia seem to be of average academic ability compared to students entering other majors. This is also true of China. At the same time, while there is a great deal of variation within China in how well students are prepared for technical higher education, the country is producing large numbers of students (many who go into engineering) who have a strong preparation in mathematics and science both before and during high school.

Third, some progress has been made in increasing flexible instructional practices, opportunities for students to engage in practical research, and the breadth of coursework in each country. Elite institutions in the BRIC countries, in particular, seem to be in the lead in these respects. Much more progress can still be made in each country, however, especially in nonelite institutions.

Finally, we have also shown that a number of mechanisms (generally associated with state policies) constrain students' educational opportunities and choices. These mechanisms can include tracking into and away from college and/or science and engineering education, high-stakes entrance exams, various constraints associated with choosing colleges and majors, rigid and/or complex admissions procedures (compared to those in the United States), and limits on transferring between institutions and disciplines.

Not only do the above mechanisms constrain individual choices, but they also may contribute to some of the inequities in educational opportunities that we have thus far seen for different groups of students. Namely, we observed that Brazilian and Indian students who enter elite universities and engineering majors (both of which have high economic returns) are generally from more socioeconomically advantaged families. Similarly in China, although rural students are more likely to major in engineering than urban students, we find that they are less represented in first-tier institutions as compared to second-tier institutions (both in engineering and in general). Moreover, as in the rest of the world, in all four BRIC countries women are underrepresented in science and engineering fields.

7 The Quality of BRIC Higher Education

WITH ECONOMIC GLOBALIZATION AND THE INFORMATION revolution, BRIC countries have joined in the development of value-added high technology over lower value-added traditional industries. BRIC states have paid significant attention to expanding the supply of new scientists and engineers for the high-technology sector. We have emphasized that increased global competitiveness is driving BRIC states to take steps to improve the quality of higher education—at least in a part of their university system—or to expand the number of students in higher-quality institutions. BRIC countries together now produce a significant fraction of the world's annual crop of engineering graduates (National Science Board, 2010).

Despite the huge increase in the number of technical graduates in the BRICs, demand for highly skilled labor may continue to outpace supply. The Chinese labor market will continue to have a high demand for qualified scientists and engineers in the coming years (Simon and Cao, 2008). Chinese officials have made high-profile plans to better train and attract talent to work in growing science and technology industries (Wang, 2011). In India there are concerns that the quality of work in IT service firms may stagnate because of low-quality workforce technical skills (Dossani, 2012). Some reports indicate strong demand for but short supply of medium and highly skilled labor in Brazil (Farrell, Jain, and Pietracci, 2007). In Russia the proportion of the population with a college education is one of the highest in the world, yet employers have complained about shortages in highly skilled labor (Klintsov,

Shvakman, and Solzhenitsyn, 2009). With their well-publicized effort to build a "Russian Silicon Valley" in Skolkovo and to train elite researchers and entrepreneurs there, the Russian government has also signaled its desire to ramp up high tech.[1]

Other studies have argued that the overall quality of talent in the BRIC countries has thus far been low (Klintsov, Shvakman, and Solzhenitsyn, 2009; Farrell, Jain, and Pietracci, 2007; Farrell and Grant, 2005; Gereffi et al., 2008; Levin Institute, 2010). These studies suggest that there is a shortage of quality scientists and engineers who can drive the development of knowledge-intensive products and services within each BRIC economy, and certainly not enough to meet the demands of the global labor market. This shortage, these studies claim, has resulted in increased competition between local enterprises and multinationals for technical talent.

In this chapter we explore the evolving *capacity* of BRIC higher education systems to produce highly skilled graduates, especially in the field of engineering (including computer engineers and scientists), with implications for the quality of the higher education system as a whole. Wherever possible, we compare developments across university tiers—particularly elite and nonelite institutions—within and across each country. We further examine research productivity at the national level and in university systems. Research productivity within universities is not only a key representation of quality in its own right, but seems also to be associated with the quality of human capital development in these institutions.

Nations largely define high-quality technical graduates according to the American paradigm of core science competence, fundamentals of engineering, and specialization. Yet higher education systems or institutions within a given system don't necessarily produce the same type of graduates. Despite the emphasis on developing engineers who are globally mobile, the concept of a well-trained graduate often differs according to economic, political, and social contexts. For example, operating in the more entrepreneurial environment of the United States requires different skills than the more hierarchical business environment of China. As another example, civil engineers may be more geographically constrained than computer engineers because the regulatory environments of the construction industry vary more across countries than those of the computing industry. In addition, it may well be that the Asian engineer offers advantages, such as a knowledge of design for local markets, not available to an American engineer even if the amount of learning in undergraduate education is the same.

Beyond these considerations, we expect that national higher education systems vary significantly in their essential capacity to train quality engineers and conduct high-quality research. We use the state-centered framework of higher educational change to contextualize the current quality of higher education and engineering education in BRIC countries and assess the prospects for quality improvement. A state-centered framework seems particularly useful for understanding the growth of aspiring world-class universities that intend to produce the top talent, as explicit government support is important in helping these institutions approach the level of a first-class U.S. or European-style research university (Salmi, 2009). National and local governments also regulate and financially support nonelite universities, but to a lesser degree than the elites.

Assessing and comparing the quality of education systems and their institutions is no small challenge. Quality in higher education is often indirectly measured through a number of indicators such as the cognitive ability of college entrants, assessments of student learning during college, faculty credentials, the effectiveness of instructional practices, research productivity, and the amount of research funding available to universities. However, data on some of these indicators are often not even available in developed countries. For example, in most countries, college student learning is typically not evaluated using standardized testing. The much-anticipated Assessment of Higher Education Learning Outcomes (AHELO) project sponsored by the OECD will eventually introduce standardized testing that allows cross-country comparisons of the cognitive abilities of college seniors. However, even this extensive undertaking is so far limited to measuring the "status" of student learning at the end of the combined pre-tertiary schooling and college experience and not the "value-added" contributed by an institution over the period of undergraduate study.[2]

In the following sections, we compare the quality of BRIC higher education systems through a production function type approach—that is, we examine the various inputs, processes, and outcomes associated with higher education and especially engineering education. We draw heavily on the quality-related findings from the earlier chapters on higher education expansion, financing, institutions, and students. Despite the lack of fully comparable indicators of higher education quality, our data suggest that in all four countries, a minority of graduates are getting higher-quality training in elite institutions and that many graduates from nonelite institutions are receiving less than adequate training in terms of both practical and higher-order skills.

There is substantial variation between countries in how well prepared they are to extend the scope of quality higher education. Russia still produces many engineers and has a number of elite research-oriented technical institutions of high quality. However, as traditional Russian industries declined after 1991, the engineering education tied to them also declined in quality, mainly because it was obsolete. China has made significant strides in improving curricula/instruction, raising faculty qualifications, and promoting research, and it now annually produces more engineering graduates from elite institutions than the total number of engineering graduates in the United States. At the same time, efforts to improve quality in the majority of China's nonelite institutions still appear to be quite limited. Brazil graduates relatively fewer engineers than Russia or China, but the fraction completing universities of generally reasonable quality is greater. India, on the other hand, produces masses of engineering graduates, but only a very small proportion of high-quality engineers. In addition, India faces serious short- to mid-term barriers to increasing its output of high-quality engineering graduates, and these barriers are not as apparent in the other BRIC university systems.

Current Human Resource Capacity

Overall, as shown in Chapter 3, BRIC countries, with the exception of Russia, still substantially lag behind advanced developed countries in human resource development for the population as a whole. Whereas the number of R&D personnel per 10,000 workers (in person years) is fairly high in Russia (112 in 2009 compared to 133 for Japan), it is still low in the other three BRIC countries (e.g., 28.7 for China in 2009).[3]

At the same time, the rapid expansion in enrollments and graduates as well as increased investments in developing science and technology (which we discuss below) are among the factors helping China, Brazil, and India to catch up to Russia and the OECD countries. Recent trends in the proportions of scientific researchers per thousand employed in each country reflect this general phenomenon. Although Brazil, China, and India have a much lower proportion of researchers in the employed population (about 2 per thousand employed workers in 2007–2009) than the United States (about 10 per thousand employed), the proportions have been steadily climbing over the last decade. China roughly doubled the proportion of its researchers from 2000 to 2009 and is now approaching the United States in terms of absolute numbers. Brazil has increased the proportion steadily but moderately over the same time period. India has made less progress, moving from 0.3 per thousand employed in 2000 to 0.4 per thousand in 2005. The gap between Russia and the United States, on the other hand, has widened between 1999 (8 per thousand versus 9 per thousand in the United States) and 2009 (7 per thousand in Russia versus 10 per thousand in the United States) (OECD, Main Science and Technology Indicators, various years).

Inputs

To analyze the quality of higher education in each country, we begin by assessing some of the major inputs or building blocks of a higher education system: the numbers and characteristics of enrollees, the amount of financial resources, and faculty credentials. Not surprisingly, we find that in terms of inputs, Russia, with its enormous head start in university expansion and investment in primary and secondary education, should currently be closest to producing the average quality of graduates found in developed countries. At the other end of the spectrum among the BRIC countries, India is the furthest behind. However, even in India the quality of many elite-institution graduates is comparable with high-end graduates in developed countries. How much of this is caused by the selectivity of elite Indian institutions and how much by the quality of the institutions is an important question—we suggest that it is as much the former as the latter, largely because of the low level of resources going to research in India, even in elite universities.

Students

We have already described the large and increasing numbers of college and engineering students entering each BRIC higher education system (Chapter 2). We have further discussed some student characteristics such as socioeconomic status, gender, and academic preparedness within each higher education system as a whole (Chapter 6). In this chapter we look more specifically at the changing numbers of students who attend elite versus nonelite universities and engineering programs. This provides one perspective by which to compare trends in "higher-quality" enrollments (i.e., in elite universities) versus "lower-quality" enrollments (i.e., in nonelite universities) within and across countries.

The BRIC states are at the center of determining the supply of college enrollments in elite universities either directly, by regulating quotas, and/or indirectly, through their role in higher education financing, while the numbers of enrollments in nonelite universities tend to be influenced more by market forces within each country (in addition to direct state action). In China, for instance, universities and policy makers at various levels generally negotiate enrollment changes based on a number of political and economic factors. This type of supply-driven enrollment growth might be criticized for being slow to respond to the demands of the labor market across specializations. In India state-level bodies technically regulate the number of colleges and student admission quotas for both public and private institutions. However, market pressures or social demand often guide government prescriptions. In India and Brazil, overall, market forces play a much larger role in influencing the eventual supply of private college spots, as reflected by the expansion of private college places in engineering, business, and medicine. In Russia budget places (in both elite and nonelite institutions) are subject to economic negotiation with the government, while fee-paying places are more market driven.

Figure 7.1 presents the number of university enrollments in elite versus nonelite institutions in each BRIC country over the course of the past decade.[4] From the figure we can see that the number of those enrolled in elite four-year institutions in China increased by approximately 54 percent from 1999 to 2009, while the number of entrants into nonelite four-year institutions increased by close to 600 percent. In Russia, from 2006 to 2009 the increase was only 1 percent and 5 percent in elite and nonelite institutions, respectively.[5] In Brazil the number of students enrolled in elite institutions increased fairly rapidly from 1999 to 2009 (by 71 percent) although somewhat less rapidly than in nonelite institutions (126 percent). We were unfortunately unable to locate enough data to identify the trend in India, but as an upper bound, we estimate that only about 7 percent of bachelor's degree students were enrolled in elite institutions in 2009–2010.[6]

Although the expansion of higher education has been rapid in India in the past decade, the increase in the number of spots at India's elite institutions has been relatively modest despite a major recent expansion of "nationally recognized" technical universities. Russia's elite enrollments also remained stable over the last several years. China and even more Brazil, by contrast, had a notable expansion in elite enrollments, although it is important to note that the vast majority of China's expansion was in nonelite institutions and much of Brazil's enrollment increase was also in low-quality institutions.

Two more points about Figure 7.1 are worth mentioning. In absolute terms, Brazil, Russia, and India had rather large absolute numbers of students attending elite institutions (~650,000, 850,000, and 900,000, respectively) in 2009, whereas China had more than 1.6 million. We also note that there were

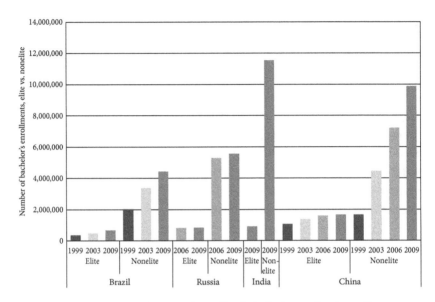

FIGURE 7.1 BRIC countries: Number of bachelor's-degree-level enrollments, elite versus nonelite institutions, 1999–2009

SOURCES: Authors' approximate estimates based on data from China: NBS (various years); Russia: MOES, 2011, and special estimates of enrollments in elite universities from State Research University Higher School of Economics; India: UGC, 2010, and data on annual college intakes through the JEE (www.jee.iitm.ac.in) and AIEEE (www.aieee.nic.in); Brazil: INEP, *Sinopse*, 1999, 2003, 2009, Table 5.1, plus enrollment data from elite state and Catholic universities.

six to seven times as many students in nonelite institutions as elite institutions in Brazil, Russia, and China in 2009. India, by contrast, had about twelve times as many students in nonelite versus elite institutions in 2009.

The number of engineering enrollments in elite and nonelite institutions in BRIC countries has also increased at varying rates in recent years (Figure 7.2). Engineering enrollments in Russia increased only slightly from 2006 to 2009 and somewhat more in elite institutions (3 percent) compared to nonelite institutions (1 percent). In Brazil engineering enrollments increased considerably faster from 2003 to 2009 in nonelite institutions (114 percent) than in elite institutions (53 percent). Similarly, engineering enrollment in Indian elite institutions increased very rapidly, by 29 percent in just two years, but enrollment in nonelite institutions increased much more rapidly, by 68 percent.[7] In China elite engineering enrollments increased slowly by 4 percent from 2006 to 2009, while nonelite engineering enrollments increased rapidly by 32 percent over the same period.[8]

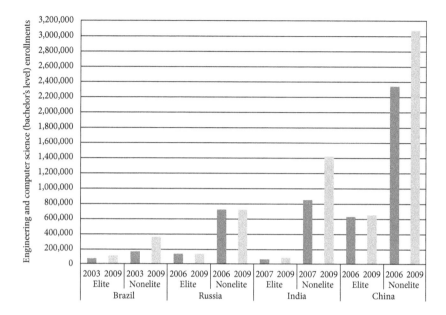

FIGURE 7.2 BRIC countries: Number of bachelor's-degree-level engineering (includes computer science) enrollments, elite versus nonelite institutions, 2003–2009

SOURCES: Authors' approximate estimates based on data from China: NBS (various years); Russia: MOES, 2011, and special estimates of enrollments in elite universities from State Research University Higher School of Economics; India: UGC, 2008, 2010, and data on annual college intakes through the JEE (www.jee.iitm.ac.in) and AIEEE (www.aieee.nic.in); Brazil: INEP, *Sinopse*, 2003 and 2009, Table 5.2, plus enrollment data from elite state and Catholic universities.

Thus, in Brazil, India, and China (in contrast to Russia), we see a decline in the proportion of elite engineering versus nonelite engineering enrollments from the mid to the late 2000s. In India, up until 2009 the expansion of elite engineering education had been less rapid compared to nonelite engineering education. From 2009 to 2011, however, the number of new engineering places available through the AIEEE increased quite rapidly, from approximately 24,500 to 35,000 students. In the absence of data on bachelor's-level engineering enrollments for 2011 and, instead, using data on bachelor's-level engineering enrollments for 2010–2011 as a base (see MHRD, 2011), we approximate that the percentage of elite engineering students in India was around 8–9 percent in 2011—still below the percentage in the other BRIC countries. Also, given its sharp rise in the last two years, the number of elite engineering enrollments in India is now larger than that of Brazil and Russia. China, on the other hand, has more than four times as many elite engineering students at the bachelor's level than any of the other BRICs.

The quality of BRIC elite institutions has received much attention (in part because of university world rankings lists). However, the larger enrollment numbers and growth in nonelite institutions highlight the importance of also understanding the quality of nonelite institutions. At least in China, empirical evidence exists that there is a continuum of quality between first-tier and second-tier institutions (Loyalka, Song, and Wei, 2012). In addition, within each country there is substantial variation in institutional quality that is likely correlated with regional development. Across countries, nonelite institutions also face different combinations of incentives and barriers to improving quality (see Chapter 5).

It is also important to remember that the college gross enrollment rates among 18–22-year olds in Brazil (32 percent in 2010), India (12 percent in 2009, probably 14 percent in 2010), and China (13–14 percent) are still relatively low.[9] Thus, it is the "cream" of the student cohorts, whether in terms of innate ability, motivation, and social status, that is attending college in these countries.[10] The efficiency of BRIC higher education systems to produce quality graduates may be affected as they gradually expand and draw relatively less able students. This will, of course, depend in part on how well primary and secondary levels prepare students for college in the future and how well tertiary institutions can adapt their teaching to a less academically elite student body. Yet because college enrollment is growing much more rapidly than we can expect pre-tertiary education quality to change, it is likely that the average quality of incoming students will decline.

Financing
In Chapter 4 we show that the total amount of money spent on higher education has increased in all BRIC nations over the last decade. Nevertheless, the average expenditures per full-time equivalent student in 2005 PPP dollars in Brazil (about $5,000, when the costs per student in private institutions are averaged in), Russia ($4,000–$7,000),[11] China (about $4,300 in 2009), and especially India (about $1,400 in 2009) are still relatively low compared to those in the United States ($30,000 in 2008) and to the OECD average (about $13,700 in 2008).[12] Because these figures are in purchasing power adjusted dollars, they must reflect either much lower salaries paid to higher education professors or many more students per professor, on average, in BRIC higher education programs.

We have also showed that there are large differences in per student expenditures between elite and nonelite institutions in each country. In China, for instance, there are substantial differences in spending all along the hierarchy of universities. In Russia the thirty-eight Category A institutions get much more state funding than other universities and collect considerably more revenue per fee-paying student. The difference also jumped considerably in 2009. Brazil's elite research universities—both public and private—and even the non-elite publics—already receive much higher levels of resources per student than the mass privates (which get essentially all their revenues from tuition). These higher resources come either directly from the government or, in the case of the elite privates, from charging high tuition and receiving public research funding. The public funding per public university student has also been increasing for the past five to six years. Finally, the top Indian Institutes of Technology receive a high level of funding per student from the central government but accept less than 10,000 first (bachelor's) degree students annually (many of whom eventually go abroad for further study and employment once they graduate). The National Institutes of Technology, which accepted about three times as many students as the IITs through the competitive All India Engineering Entrance Examination (AIEEE) as of 2011, similarly receive relatively strong support from the central government.

For most nonelite institutions in each country, higher education financing does not seem to be tightly linked to incentives to improve quality. In Russia, for example, our interviews suggest that until recently, most second-tier institutions have had little pressure and few incentives either to improve quality or reduce costs in these institutions because the central government has been increasing spending per student and allowing universities to open fee-paying programs with which to augment their revenues. In theory, such programs should increase competition among institutions, but most have, until now, relied on high demand and local monopolies rather than better quality to attract fee-paying students. However, with population decline and current government attempts to rationalize the system financially and to gain greater control over institutions, the nonelites may be forced to innovate and improve their standards just to survive. They face the looming threat of the government reducing or even eliminating their budgeted places. Furthermore, recently the Russian government has introduced more direct financial incentives to increase competition between second-tier institutions to support their strategic development programs.

In India and Brazil, because a high fraction of engineering and computer science students get their education in mass private institutions, the main issue is whether such institutions, focusing on their bottom line (and in India, generating much of their income from high-demand engineering and computer science programs), have any incentive to improve their faculties or invest in innovative programs. Our interviews in India and the available data from Brazil suggest that cost efficiency is far more crucial to the operation of these private institutions than quality improvement, although there are always some that do respond to competition by focusing on increasing productivity and raising quality. The situation may be somewhat different in China, with some nonelite institutions vying for higher rankings and associated increases in funding while others have few available resources with which to compete in this process.

Faculty

We use several indicators to examine the quality of faculty across BRIC nations. These include identifying the number of Ph.D.s in the country, the current number of professors with Ph.D.s, and the types of institutions from which professors have earned their graduate degrees. We also briefly discuss institutional constraints on hiring faculty, as well as the incentives for highly skilled talent to join engineering departments.

Table 7.1 presents the number of Ph.D. graduates produced annually in the BRIC countries and in the United States from 1998 to 2009. From Table 7.1, we can see that the annual number of Ph.D. graduates in China increased by approximately seven to eight times over the decade.[13] In addition, by 2009, roughly three-quarters of the 48,658 Ph.D. graduates (15,524 from engineering) came from elite Chinese universities. Also, from the late 1990s until 2009, Russia almost doubled the total number of Ph.D. graduates to 34,235 (7,570 from engineering) by the end of the period. In marked contrast, Brazil and India had considerably fewer Ph.D. graduates (roughly 11,000 each) in 2009, with only 1,300 engineering Ph.D.s in Brazil and even fewer in India. What may be surprising is that although Brazilian institutions more than doubled their Ph.D. output over the course of a decade, Indian institutions produced about the same number of Ph.D.s in 2009 as in 1998. This was despite a temporary increase and then fall of Ph.D. graduate output in India in the mid-2000s.

On the whole, therefore, China and Russia have a large number of Ph.D. graduates, whereas India does not. Brazil's situation is more nuanced as it has a much smaller population than either China or India, is increasing the num-

TABLE 7.1 BRIC countries: Ph.D. graduates (total and engineering only), by country, 1998–2009

Country	1998	1999	2000	2001	2002	2003	2004	2005	2006	2007	2008	2009
TOTAL (ALL HEIS)												
Brazil	3,949	4,853	5,344	6,040	6,894	8,094	8,109	8,991	9,366	9,919	10,718	11,368
Russia	18,274	n/a	24,828	n/a	n/a	n/a	29,850	33,561	35,530	35,747	33,670	34,235
India	10,408	11,066	10,951	11,296	11,544	11,974	13,733	17,853	17,898	12,773	13,237	10,781
China[a]	7,535	8,749	9,409	11,065	12,849	16,401	20,607	24,035	31,653	36,270	38,111	48,658
United States	42,638	41,098	41,366	40,737	40,025	40,759	42,118	43,381	45,617	48,130	48,763	49,562
ENGINEERING ONLY												
Brazil	n/a	492	705	765	819	1,023	1,055	1,114	1,123	1,178	1,222	1,284
Russia	n/a	n/a	6,208	n/a	n/a	n/a	n/a	7,431	7,743	7,902	7,528	7,570
India	744	696	723	778	734	779	882	968	844	1,079	1,427	1,141
China[a]	3,095	3,642	4,225	4,534	5,252	6,573	7,262	8,377	10,879	12,852	13,593	15,524
United States	5,922	5,330	5,323	5,510	5,081	5,281	5,777	6,427	7,185	7,744	7,862	7,634

SOURCES: China: MOE Stats, 2010. Russia: MOES Stats, 2011. India: MHRD and UGC Reports (various years). Brazil: Ministerio de Ciencia e Tecnologia, 2012. Indicadores, Table 3.5.2. (www.mct.gov.br/index.php/content/view/7755.html), accessed Aug. 14, 2012. United States: NSF, 2010, 2012 *Science and Engineering Indicators*.

[a]University only (does not include Ph.D. graduates from research institutes, which would add another 10–15%).

ber of Ph.D. graduates steadily, and seems to have a higher quality of graduate education (see below).[14] It is also important to note in the case of India that whereas in the mid-1990s over 75 percent of engineering Ph.D.s graduated from the IITs, only 25 percent of engineering Ph.D.s graduated from the IITs by 2005 (Banerjee and Muley, 2007). Many Indians get doctoral degrees in engineering and computer science abroad; each year approximately 1,200 students from India earn Ph.D. degrees in the United States alone (National Science Board, 2012, Figure 2-22 and Table 2-28). However, a very high fraction of these graduates obtain jobs in their host countries. Relatively few return to India (about 10 percent), and even fewer look for work in academic institutions. This lack of Ph.D. graduates, especially in the field of engineering, undoubtedly limits the quality of India's higher education system in general and higher engineering education in particular.

Closely connected to the supply of Ph.D. graduates, there is some variation across all four countries in the proportion of higher education faculty with Ph.D. degrees. Table 7.2 presents the percentage of full-time faculty who have doctoral degrees across the various countries for selected years. The highest percentage is in Russia, with 63.5 percent of professors having a "candidate" or "doctor of science" degree in 2010.[15] In China the proportion of faculty at all three- and four-year institutions with Ph.D.s has increased steadily over the last decade, from 7 percent in 2002 to almost 14 percent in 2009. If we assume that lower tiers (i.e. three-year vocational institutions) have few if any professors with Ph.D.s, however, the proportion in four-year institutions is closer to 20 percent (and higher still for public four-year institutions). In Brazil about 27 percent of professors in the higher education system have a Ph.D. However, there are currently large differences in the proportion of faculty with Ph.D.s between Brazil's public and private institutions (49.9 percent and 15.4 percent, respectively, in 2010). India's University Grants Commission (UGC, 2010) reported that the proportion of faculty with a Ph.D. *or* a master of philosophy degree in a subset of approved colleges (3,142 out of the then total of 20,677 colleges in India) was only 43 percent. Because this percentage is for approved colleges only, we approximate that the average percentage across all colleges is significantly lower—about 16 percent, and this, too, may be a high estimate. Not only is there a dearth of faculty with Ph.D.s in India, but the supply of professors itself is limited, resulting in a fairly high average number of unfilled vacancies across institutions (UGC, 2010; Banerjee and Muley, 2007).

Thus, overall, the ratio of professors with doctoral degrees teaching in the higher education system is relatively low in Brazil, China, and especially

TABLE 7.2 BRIC countries: Higher education professors with Ph.D.s, by country and type of institution, 2001–2010 (percentage of all professors)

	China			Russia		India		Brazil		
Year	All HEIs	Four-year HEIs	Public four-year HEIs	Doctor of science	Doctor of science or candidate	University (% Ph.D.)	College (% Ph.D. or Mphil)	All HEIs	Public HEIs	Private HEIs
2001	—	—	—	10.6	57.6	—	—	—	—	—
2002	7.0	9.4	9.6	—	—	—	—	21.4	38.2	12.0
2003	7.4	10.2	10.7	—	—	—	—	21.0	39.5	11.8
2004	8.2	11.4	12.3	—	—	—	—	21.6	38.9	11.8
2005	9.2	12.7	14.0	—	—	—	—	22.4	40.1	12.3
2006	10.1	—	—	12.0	60.0	76.0	43.0	23.0	42.3	12.4
2007	11.2	16.1	18.3	12.6	61.2	—	—	24.0	43.2	12.4
2008	12.3	17.7	20.2	13.0	62.4	—	—	24.0	44.3	13.1
2009	13.6	19.5	22.6	12.5	63.3	—	—	—	—	—
2010	—	—	—	12.4	63.5	—	—	—	49.9	15.4

SOURCES: China: NBS (various years); Russia: MOES, 2011; India: UGC, 2010; Brazil: INEP, *Sinopse*, various years, Table 2.4.

NOTES: For China, the estimates from the second column assume that there are no Ph.D.s in three-year vocational HEIs, and the estimates from the third column assume that there are no Ph.D.s in four-year private HEIs.

The "candidate" degree in Russia is a three-year degree (often plus dissertation) after a master's degree. The "doctor of science" degree in Russia is one level higher than the candidate degree.

The India statistics are for only a particular subset of institutions that have been assessed by a UGC-related agency as "A-rated" (140 out of 164 universities, 3,142 out of 20,677 colleges). As approximately 14,000 out of 20,677 colleges are not recognized by the UGC because of not meeting minimum quality standards, the ratios in the table should substantially overestimate the ratios in all HEIs. For example, if we assume that the percentage of faculty with a Ph.D. in the non-A-rated universities is one-half the percentage in the A-rated universities, that the percentage of faculty with a Ph.D. or Mphil in the recognized colleges is also one-half the percentage in the A-rated colleges, and that the percentage in the unrecognized colleges is one-fourth the percentage in the A-rated recognized colleges, the average percentage for 2006 would fall to 70% in the universities and 16% in the colleges. Even the latter may be an overestimate.

India. The ratio in Russia is at face value higher than that of the United States (where roughly two-fifths of faculty in all institutions or roughly two-thirds in four-year doctoral-granting institutions have a doctoral degree—see Cataldi et al., 2005). At the same time, the percentage is increasing at a steady pace in Brazil and China. And although we do not have data over time about the changing qualifications of faculty in Indian institutions, the low number of Ph.D. graduates produced by the university system every year suggests that the percentage of faculty with Ph.D.s is not increasing significantly, at least in private colleges.

Our institutional visits in various countries provide further details about the quantity and quality of engineering faculty across elite and non-elite institutions. In our China sample, which is somewhat skewed toward more-developed provinces, a much higher proportion of faculty in electrical engineering and computer science departments in four-year institutions have Ph.D.s (around 40 percent) than the average proportion in Table 7.2. In the nation's more developed provinces, a relatively large pool of Ph.D. graduates is seeking positions at engineering departments both in elite universities and in nonelite institutions. Some of the applicants for positions at the very top universities are graduates from (sometimes top) foreign institutions, whereas the applicants for positions in local (nonelite) public four-year institutions in one economically developed province tend to be graduates from elite domestic institutions or some of the more selective nonelite institutions. Overall, in China we see a trend of increasingly selective applicants vying for faculty spots.

It is also the case in India that elite engineering institutions have a high proportion of qualified faculty, while nonelite, especially private, institutions have a rather low proportion. In our sample of forty engineering colleges, the share of faculty with Ph.D.s was 49 percent for state and aided institutions and just 13 percent for private unaided colleges. A major reason why the former two types of institutions can hire more qualified and full-time faculty is that they can offer relatively higher salaries (set by the government), greater job stability, and better infrastructure for teaching and research. By contrast, the salaries are lower for faculty in private unaided institutions than in state and aided institutions. Furthermore, faculty members in private institutions have few if any opportunities to engage in research, little institutional motivation to initiate research, rudimentary lab equipment, and heavy burdens from large classes and many teaching hours.

In almost all of the universities and engineering departments we visited in Russia, our interviewees complained of the fact that academia is no longer an attractive career for a young talented specialist. Institutions offer little in the way of salary and few prospects. The problem of faculty aging is also becoming quite acute at many engineering departments, which usually hire from their own graduates to fill faculty positions.

A survey of 1,200 professors in Brazilian higher education institutions reveals that qualified professors, especially in the elite institutions, are actively engaged in teaching undergraduates (Balbachevsky and Schwartzman, 2011). The more elite the university, the more likely an undergraduate student will be taught by a professor with a doctoral degree. More generalized data from the Brazilian higher education census show that in federal universities, almost 55 percent of faculty hold Ph.D.s. This is even more likely to be true for graduate teaching (which usually takes place in elite institutions). For example, 99.5 percent of engineering professors engaged in graduate teaching have a Ph.D. degree (INEP, 2010).

There are a number of institutional factors affecting the supply and demand of qualified faculty in each country. In China, despite the growing number of Ph.D.s, the quality of a doctoral education is thought to be quite poor as programs are relatively short, curriculum is outdated, professors on average have a large number of graduate students at any given time, and faculty on the whole are not experienced enough to successfully guide graduate students.[16] As we explain in Chapter 5, many universities therefore look at where a potential faculty hire received his or her undergraduate degree, as this is apparently a better signal of the individual's academic ability. Another factor is that the Chinese government regulates faculty base salaries at fairly low levels—even in engineering—so that professors likely earn less than they could in private industry. At the more selective universities, however, base salaries are often supplemented with bonuses from extra-budgetary (e.g., research or outside training) funds. A faculty position, at least in a public institution, is also relatively stable and occasionally carries nonwage benefits such as reduced-price housing or access to high-quality and subsidized education for children.

We noted that the professoriate in Russia is on the whole aging, with many faculty having held their positions since the Soviet era. At the same time, many qualified professors left higher education in the 1990s to enter the private sector. Thus, the mid-term future of higher education in Russia may partially depend on the system's ability to recruit younger, qualified faculty. However, the quality of a doctoral education in Russia has also recently been subject to some debate. Professors have few incentives (financial or otherwise) to guide their doctoral students. Furthermore, the amount of financial aid allocated to a Ph.D. student is not sufficient for the individual to engage in his or her studies full time. Graduate students are often forced to take part-time jobs to earn a living, and those in science and engineering can earn higher salaries in industry. These problems may thus have implications for the quality of academic talent available to higher education institutions in Russia.

Policy makers in India have recently instituted regulations that affect the presence of qualified faculty in higher education institutions. These regulations have been part of a response to a drastic downsizing of the public sector (as part of economic reform policies) in the early 1990s, which led to a shortage of qualified faculty for a number of years. One important recent regulatory guideline has stated that all faculty with the position of assistant professor or higher should have a Ph.D. by academic year 2013–2014. Public universities, which tend to have a fairly high percentage of professors with Ph.D.s, are more likely to meet this guideline, as universities offer professors higher pay and occupational stability. Although individual colleges are also required to meet this guideline, college management widely believes that these policies will be relaxed in certain cases. Indeed, the regulation has not been strictly enforced thus far, given the small output of Ph.D.s in India. In some private engineering colleges, even bachelor's degree holders have been allowed to teach courses.[17]

India's regulatory environment furthermore requires that a certain percentage of faculty spots is reserved for underprivileged groups defined by law—that is, those who belong to the category of Scheduled Castes and Tribes or other "backward" castes. These spots are often hard to fill given the dearth of Ph.D.s in the country as a whole. Another aspect that is often relatively unnoticed by regulators in India, but which affects quality, is the low retention rate of faculty in mass private institutions. In several colleges we surveyed, the average length of stay was two years. This appears to be a consequence of the complex factors discussed above: low pay, an absence of incentives to conduct research, large teaching loads, etc.

Salary structures for engineering faculty in India have equalized over the last few years, subsequent to the recommendations of the government's Six Central Pay commission in 2008. These recommendations are widely followed by all institutions and have increased the average salaries of faculty at the level of assistant professor and above by more than 70 percent. However, in light of the new recommendations concerning salaries as well as the regulations for faculty to have Ph.D.s, private colleges have begun recategorizing a large percentage of faculty who were previously at the assistant professor level or above as lecturers and are continuing to pay them poorly.

Beyond looking at the proportion of faculty with Ph.D.s, there are a number of institutional factors that indicate that Brazil's higher education faculty are of relatively high quality in public (especially federal) institutions, somewhat less so in state and Catholic universities, and much less so in mass private institutions. We argued earlier that mass private institutions tend to use a high percentage of part-time faculty and employ only about 15 percent Ph.D.s. Although Brazilian government regulations of private universities legislated in 1996 have increased the proportion of Ph.D.s and full-time faculty in the past fifteen years, the private university lobby was able to keep these proportions rather low. Further, the Brazilian government's support of R&D and graduate programs (in public universities) has led to a steadily increasing proportion of faculty with a strong graduate education based on research experience. In contrast, only about one in fifteen faculty in mass private institutions engages in any research.

Student-faculty ratios in BRIC elite and nonelite institutions partly reflect faculty supply and demand, and are yet another indicator of the quality of instruction. Across all four-year institutions in China, the student-faculty ratio has hovered around 17–18 to 1 since 2003 (NBS, 2003–2010). The ratio has been only slightly lower in Brazil, at 15–16 to 1 from 2002 to 2008 (NBS, various years). In Russia the ratio was around 13 to 1 for all tertiary institutions in 2009 (OECD 2011a, Table D2.2). These ratios are quite similar to those in the United States and the OECD average (approximately 15:1) (OECD, 2011a, Table D2.2). And in India, although higher education regulators require a ratio of 15:1, the reported student-teacher ratio is 24:1 (MHRD, 2011). Furthermore, the NAAC's 2006–2007 survey of 3,412 "approved" colleges (see above) suggests that the student-teacher ratio is 20.4 in A grade colleges, 31.8 in B grade colleges, and 28.5 in C grade colleges. Furthermore, the student-faculty ratio for teachers with permanent positions is 29.8, 38.1, and 35.8 in A, B, and C grade colleges, respectively.

Processes

In this section we discuss processes that potentially promote student learning and research productivity inside the BRIC higher education systems. We first summarize some of our major observations from Chapter 5 on the interactions between the state and institutions to improve quality. We then briefly review the quality of classroom teaching according to the self-reported student data from Chapter 6. We next describe steps taken by policy makers and university administrators to strengthen international programs and exchanges for faculty and students. Finally, we examine how successful policy makers and institutions have been in attracting foreign students into their programs.

The Role of the State in Influencing Institutional Quality

In our analysis of institutions in Chapter 5, we highlight the incentives provided by the state to BRIC administrators and faculty in an effort to improve teaching and research quality at different types of institutions. All four countries' central governments have long been committed to increasing the quality of their elite higher education institutions. They have accomplished this in numerous ways, including providing relatively large amounts of funding per student, granting admission only to students who score high on admission examinations, ensuring that faculty are relatively well paid, generally requiring that teaching faculty have Ph.D.s, incentivizing faculty with accessible funding to engage in research, and basing faculty promotions on publication records (in theory at least).

We showed that in the past ten years, China and Russia particularly have pushed to create among these elite institutions at least some that would be ranked "world class," competing in prestige with the better research universities in the United States, Europe, Japan, and Australia. India has expanded its already prestigious Indian Institutes of Technology and National Institutes of Technology, and has a number of other universities, such as the Delhi School of Economics and the Indian Institutes of Management, that follow the same quality promotion model. Brazil's public federal universities, a few state research universities and institutes, and some of its private Catholic universities, with their excellent graduate schools, highly selective admissions policies, and research-oriented faculty (many trained in elite U.S. and European universities), are also powerfully incentivized to try to meet standards of high-quality institutions elsewhere.

It remains to be seen whether the elite universities in the BRICs will, in the short run, become competitive with the elite institutions in the developed countries. In all the BRICs, elite universities are given the autonomy to respond positively to incentives and, most of all, in China, Russia, and Brazil are given the funding to do so, particularly in the form of increasing salaries and research funding. The case is less clear in India, which we discuss below.

We conclude that in second- and third-tier BRIC universities and colleges, the incentives for improving quality coming both from the state and from university management are very mixed. We reviewed the many regulations that the BRIC states have legislated to maintain minimum standards at all colleges and universities. In China and Brazil, the state has added incentives such as potential rewards for raising tier status (China), legislated proportions of faculty with Ph.D.s and working full time (Brazil), and tried to increase competition among universities by publishing their graduating students' test scores (Brazil). Less directly, India has sought to offer colleges greater autonomy from supervising universities if they increase graduate training and raise standards, and Russia is promoting universities to improve courses and may move to performance-based budgeting to improve overall quality (Sigman, 2008).

At the same time, however, in all the BRICs (even in Russia, with its declining student-age population), the state and university administrations of mass universities appear to be much more focused on increasing enrollment than raising quality. Increased enrollment means increased revenues because their budgets (and surpluses/profits for the private institutions) depend directly on enrollment. Thus, for the most part, mass institutions in the BRICs organize their departments, curricula, and faculty hiring to be reasonably efficient at delivering the required quality courses to maximize the number of students they can process "successfully" to maintain demand for their "brand." For many private institutions, this means being more flexible than public institutions in creating new courses to attract more students. For most private mass institutions, it means keeping a tight rein on costs per student, lobbying governments to be less stringent in applying regulations, and competing via advertising that may have little to do with academic quality. As we have shown in the case of Brazil, to be successful then requires top-down, management-driven institutions, with little incentive to raise quality through improving faculty, lowering class size, or even recruiting higher-quality students. Many second-tier public institutions, such as those in China and Russia, could compete more effectively by raising quality, were they able to organize themselves to achieve that goal. But it is difficult to do so when trying to survive in a declining market (Russia) or trying to raise additional revenues through local contracts and to keep costs per student down (China).

Teacher Knowledge and Pedagogy

In Chapter 6 we discuss how students across the BRIC higher education systems report having had some exposure to flexible instructional practices (e.g., by engaging in small-group discussions, technical presentations, and original technical designs). We also saw how the coursework in the various countries now tends to focus not only on engineering fundamentals, math, and basic science, but also somewhat more on the humanities and social sciences. At the same time, students, especially in the nonelite institutions, seem to be less engaged in practical (research and quality internship) experiences and courses that teach certain types of "soft skills" (e.g., leadership and entrepreneurship) or cross-disciplinary knowledge.

We also discussed some particular barriers to student learning within each country. For example, students in China (especially in less selective institutions) have few incentives to perform well in college because they are essentially guaranteed a diploma after the designated time of study. Also, while four-year students complete a rather concentrated, classroom-oriented course schedule in the first three years, they are generally expected to spend the last year or semester finding a job.

In both China and India, assessment is further based on testing academic concepts rather than their application to real-world problems. The final year capstone design course in India, which is an important part of grounding the student in real-world problems, is often of little use to students because of limited access to industry. Similar problems exist in Russia, where students at second- and third-tier institutions, who have few opportunities to learn practical knowledge and skills, are often thought to put forth little effort toward their studies and rather bide their time until they receive their degrees. According to faculty reports, these students lack motivation even though, as we discussed, they themselves are mostly satisfied with their education.

In Brazil, over half of all engineering students study in rather low-quality private institutions that are characterized by high noncompletion rates (approximately 45 percent noncompletion in a six-year period). In addition, according to our estimates (discussed below) using the ENADE tests of specific engineering and computer science knowledge given in the first and last year of study, low-quality private institutions do increase students' skills over the course of study in these fields, but only up to the level of the first-year students studying in the "better" institutions. This suggests that many engineering graduates in Brazil are minimally prepared to practice in technical jobs.

Internationalization

The internationalization of higher education, including short- and longer-term student and faculty exchanges, research collaborations, and the offshoring of university services from developed countries, among others, has occupied an increasingly important position in the process of the expansion and development of higher education in BRIC countries. Beyond potentially advancing economic goals such as improving human capital and increasing innovation, internationalization also serves as a marker of the degree to which a nation is able to participate as a major player on the global stage.

BRIC governments are increasing support for programs and initiatives that encourage short- and longer-term faculty exchanges. The Chinese government has funded the short-term Young Faculty Study Abroad Program, among others, and provided a number of other publicly funded opportunities for students and faculty to either study or conduct research abroad as visiting scholars. Furthermore, China has allocated a substantial amount of money to several programs both related to and outside of higher education to attract overseas experts (especially those of Chinese citizenship or descent). The Thousand Talents program was designed to attract 2,000 high-level overseas "talents" to relocate to China; by the middle of 2010, about 662 leading scientists and entrepreneurs were persuaded to return (NBS, 2010; Simon and Cao, 2008). The government also reported that in 2009, about 480,000 foreign professionals were invited to work for short-term stays as experts (Simon and Cao, 2008). Additionally, provincial governments, especially those in the more developed eastern region, have instituted separate policies and programs to attract and train talent.

Graduate courses in Brazil have study-abroad components that aim at developing a body of highly qualified and well-trained university teachers and researchers. As of 2005, Brazil's Federal Agency for the Support and Evaluation of Graduate Education (CAPES), a foundation attached to the Ministry of Education, had provided more than 1,400 foreign study scholarships. From 2010 to 2012 the Brazilian government greatly increased the amount of funding available to CAPES for graduate training in STEM fields. Initiatives such as the Program to Promote the Retention of Doctorate Qualified Staff (PROFIX), created in 2001, provide incentives such as monthly salaries, support for participation in international events, medical insurance, and research grants, with the aim of incentivizing Ph.D.-level researchers to stay in the country and to provide overseas Brazilian academics with work links to Brazilian higher education institutions. The government has further funded numerous programs that offer benefits and work links in Brazil to highly educated and technically trained citizens abroad.

The Russian government did not provide direct financial support for exchange programs, study-abroad programs (with the exception of a few intergovernmental programs), or mobility programs for Russian and foreign academics until 2010. Recently, a group of Russians who graduated from the best international universities have suggested that the government support an ambitious program—to fund the education of up to 10,000 students a year to study abroad at the world's leading higher education institutions with the hope that these students would return to Russia upon concluding their studies to take up positions in government, business, and academia. Despite the lack of central government support thus far, however, leading Russian universities are supporting student and faculty international exchanges under a favorable regulatory framework. In fact, a fair number of students seem to spend a semester or two abroad or go abroad for their higher degrees. For instance, in 2008 approximately 40 universities (less than 10 percent) had joint-degree programs with foreign universities, and about 855 graduates received these joint diplomas. Yet the number of foreign professors working in Russian universities in 2008 was only 39. Finally, starting from 2010, the Ministry of Education and Science has been providing very generous grants (of up to US $5 million for three years) for international scholars to establish research programs at Russian universities. Such programs are considered highly prestigious and foster the internationalization of the previously isolated Russian higher education system.

In India the Ministry of Education has also introduced some short-term opportunities for Indian scholars to participate in international exchanges with initiatives such as the Travel Grant, which helps teachers and staff involved in higher education to present papers at international conferences. The ministry also promoted the Bilateral Exchange Programme, a scholar exchange program that during the 2008–2009 academic year attracted fifty-three foreign scholars and deployed ninety Indian scholars abroad. Furthermore, in general terms, the government of India has created the Ministry of Overseas Indians to encourage the return of overseas talent. On the whole, however, the number and size of initiatives and programs that encourage international exchanges in higher education itself are quite small.

In addition to the above government initiatives to promote international exchange, there has been a marked increase during the last decade in the number of qualified individuals from the BRIC countries who seek to acquire Ph.D.s in the United States and other developed countries. This has possible implications for both brain drain (in terms of some of the best college graduates leaving their home countries for study and long-term work) and brain gain (Ph.D. graduates coming back to their home countries as well-trained scholars and researchers). Of all foreign students enrolled in graduate programs at U.S. institutions in 2009, 28 percent were Indian and 20 percent were Chinese (the top one and two, respectively, among foreign nations), whereas the proportion of Brazilian and Russian students was significantly smaller (National Science Board, 2010). The largest numbers of doctoral students in science and engineering (S&E) programs in the United States come from China (10.8 percent of all S&E earned doctoral degrees between 2004 and 2007) and India (4 percent), with Brazil and Russia (each less than 0.5 percent) lagging significantly behind (National Science Board, 2010).

There are tentative signs that the prevalent "brain drain" phenomenon may be reversing for at least some of the BRIC countries. Of the above-mentioned S&E doctoral degree recipients, 9 percent of Chinese, 11 percent of Indian, and 52 percent of Brazilian students said that they planned to return home after they completed their studies in the United States. The actual number of Chinese returnees increased sharply right after 2008 (e.g., from 6.9 to 10.8 percent from 2008 to 2009), perhaps because of the recent global financial crisis (NBS and MOST, various years). Similarly, after the dot-com bubble crisis in 2000, more highly trained Indians residing in the United States were compelled to return to India. With economic crises, a longer-term shift in the global economic landscape, and increased governmental support for returnee academics, overseas students and professionals seem to be increasingly more willing to return to their home countries to work.

A nation's ability to attract foreign college students can also reflect on the quality of its higher education system. The number of foreign students in China has increased steadily each year: by 2009, the country had over 55,000 foreign students studying in bachelor's programs and an additional 15,000 in graduate programs. The numbers have also increased rapidly in India, with more than 21,000 foreign students by 2008 (NBS, 2010). While most of the foreign students studying in China and India are from other Asian countries, China has hosted an increasing number of students from the United States, the United Kingdom, and developed East Asian nations such as Japan and Korea. The number of foreign students was even higher in Russia in 2008: 70,000, with a large proportion of students coming from Asia and former Soviet nations, followed by Western Europe. This number has since increased significantly—more than 120,000 in 2010—with many crediting the comparatively low-cost yet equally high-quality training of Russian higher education institutions and Russia's involvement in the Bologna Process. Although Brazil does not keep statistics on the number of foreign students studying in the country, according to a recent article in the *Chronicle of Higher Education* (Downie, 2010), the number is comparable to India's. The premier university in the country, the University of São Paulo, reported 1,600 foreign students in 2010 (out of a total enrollment of 80,000 students). This would suggest that there are no more than 15,000–20,000 foreign students in the university system as a whole. The Ministry of Education is trying to recruit students from other Latin American countries and from Africa: "Despite those efforts, however, Brazil remains a tough sell, in large part because it has little tradition of overseas exchanges" (Downie, 2010).

Thanks largely to the Internet, international research cooperation has also become easier. The marked increase in the number of published papers written jointly by professors in developed countries and those in a BRIC country (Royal Society, 2011) suggests that collaboration has increased substantially between BRIC researchers and those in developed countries. The trends indicate that elite research institutions in Europe and especially the United States are acting as global hubs in terms of scholarly collaborations. Approximately 29 percent of the United States' research output is internationally collaborative. International collaborations that involve the United States make up 17 percent of all internationally collaborative papers (Royal Society, 2011). Yet, whereas collaboration among developing nations is also increasing slowly, the degree of cooperation among the BRICs themselves so far has been minimal (Royal Society, 2011).

Outputs

We now examine several main outputs that reflect on the quality of the BRIC higher education systems: student learning as measured through the perceptions of students who took our surveys (Russia, India, and China) as well as value-added through achievement scores (in Brazil), trends in the numbers of college graduates and their employment outcomes, and research productivity.

Student Learning

Senior college students, in at least three of the four BRIC countries (Russia, India, and China) where we conducted interviews, had positive impressions of their college learning experiences. The majority, in each country, regardless of tier, were satisfied with their educational experience overall. Most students also felt that their technical knowledge and engineering skills improved, at least to some degree. In addition, most students felt that they improved in nontechnical areas such as communication, teamwork, and problem solving. However, we were unable to collect more objective information on how much students improved their knowledge and skills during college (see Chapter 6).

Brazil is a partial exception to the lack of data on students' higher education performance. The Brazilian government gives first- and last-year college students general and specific-to-program tests. First- and last-year students take the same specific skills test in each program in each year the test is given. Students are tested in each program every three years, and different programs are tested each year. For example, the first and last years of study for electronics engineering and computer science students were tested in 2005 and again in 2008.

We were able to use these two years of data to do a quasi-value-added analysis of how much students gained in these two programs of study (Carnoy and Carrasco, 2012). The analysis was conducted at the program level (there are hundreds of programs across hundreds of institutions for both electronics engineering and computer science), not at the individual student level.

We compared gains on the general and specific subject knowledge tests for computer science students in their initial and fourth (final) years of their programs of study on the same test in 2008 (Figure 7.3 shows the results for the specific test).[18] These student performance distributions represent two different cohorts (those entering in 2008 took the initial test and those who entered at least three years earlier took the final test in 2008), so we were not comparing the same students at two different points in time. The results are biased because it is likely that students taking the final test had, on average, higher initial scores than students we did not observe who dropped out between entering several years ago and 2008. However, we were able to make some approximations for this selection bias, and the lower bound of the difference in test scores is about 0.5 standard deviations for computer science rather than the 1.5 standard deviations shown in Figure 7.3, and for electrical engineers, the lower bound of the difference in specific test scores is also about 0.5 standard deviations rather than 1.3 standard deviations when we make no corrections for selection bias.

We also compared gains for students in computer science and electrical engineering programs/institutions where the average initial test score was in the bottom half of the 2005 initial test score distribution (less selective) with those programs/institutions where average scores on the initial test were in

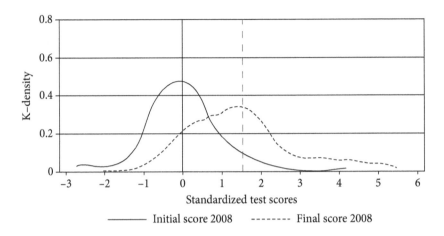

FIGURE 7.3 Brazil: ENADE computer science specific skills test, first-year kernel distribution compared to fourth-year kernel distribution, 2008
SOURCE: INEP, ENADE, 2008 (see Carnoy and Carrasco, 2012).

the top half of the distribution (more selective). These represent the same "quasi-cohort" of students taking two different tests that we "normalized" with an overall mean of zero and a standard deviation of one. Table 7.3 shows (the diagonal arrow) that although the gains are not that different for those who started in the lower or upper half of the initial test score distribution (less selective versus more selective programs), when we compare the gains on the specific knowledge test[19] for computer science students in the less selective institutions and in the more selective institutions, the average scores in the more selective programs are almost 1.5 standard deviations above the fourth-year scores of students in the less selective institutions. This is not only true for computer science students but also for electronic engineers.[20] Again, were we to correct for selection bias, this estimate would also drop—probably again to a lower bound of about 0.5 standard deviations, but we have no reason to believe that students in more selective institutions would make smaller gains than those entering less selective institutions; rather, the opposite could be the case.

We tentatively conclude that although, on average, students studying in both less and more selective institutions make gains on the specific knowledge test, the gains for those in the less selective institutions once corrected for selection bias are lower than those in the more selective institutions and bring them, on average, to a level that is probably below the first-year test score for

TABLE 7.3 Brazil: Estimated inter-cohort and intra-cohort test score gains in computer science and electrical engineering, 2005 and 2008, for students entering in least and most selective programs[a]

Year	50% least selective programs			50% most selective programs		
	Number of programs	*Initial year test score*	*Final year test score*	*Number of programs*	*Initial year test score*	*Final year test score*
COMPUTER SCIENCE						
2005	119	−0.70	1.62[a]	117	0.85	3.51
		(0.50)	(1.40)		(0.86)	(1.58)
2008	118	−0.76	0.84[b]	118	0.71	2.21
		(0.64)	(1.19)		(0.75)	(1.52)
ELECTRICAL ENGINEERING						
2005	118	−0.66	0.69	118	0.76	2.74
		(0.37)	(1.06)		(0.81)	(1.40)
2008	118	−0.57	0.60	118	0.86	2.24
		(0.42)	(0.72)		(0.72)	(1.03)

SOURCE: Authors' estimates from INEP, ENADE database.

[a]Standard deviations from mean = 0.

[b]In 2005 the average score on final year test for students in the 50% least selective programs was equal to approximately the *initial year score* of the top 20 percent of students in the most selective programs.

[c]In 2008 the average score on final year test for students in the 50% least selective programs was equal to approximately the *initial year score* of the top 40 percent of students in the most selective programs.

those in more selective institutions. In other words, if specific knowledge is an important criterion for hiring, say, in engineering or computer science, those who graduate from less selective institutions learn less and would be able to start in jobs that could be filled by first-year students in the more selective institutions. This also has implications for what it means for students to be attending less selective higher education institutions compared to raising the quality of the secondary institutions they attend.

Because of our inability to match individual students taking the initial and final tests, these results should be treated cautiously, but they suggest that computer science and engineering students attending mass private institutions in Brazil are not served particularly well by those institutions (see Carnoy and Carrasco, 2012, for more details of the analysis). The exercise also shows how a well articulated value-added analysis could inform policy makers about the "quality" of different types of institutions as defined by how much students learn in their course of study.

Graduates and Graduate Employment

Assuming that graduates of elite institutions are better prepared in their chosen field than those in nonelite institutions and that these elite graduates are the new productive labor that promotes higher growth rates, an indicator of university quality is the number of each country's graduates emerging from elite versus nonelite institutions. This quality indicator can be viewed either in terms of total graduates or, because of our particular focus on a nation's capacity to excel in high-technology production, in terms of engineering graduates.[21]

Figure 7.4a shows the number of students graduating from elite and nonelite bachelor's degree programs in each BRIC country, as well as the total number of bachelor's degree graduates in the United States, in 2006 and 2009. As expected, China and India produce more total graduates than the United States, while Russia and especially Brazil produce less.[22] The number of elite university graduates is also much greater in China than in Russia and Brazil (we were unable to divide total graduates into elite and nonelite graduates for India), but far less than the total number of graduates in the United States.

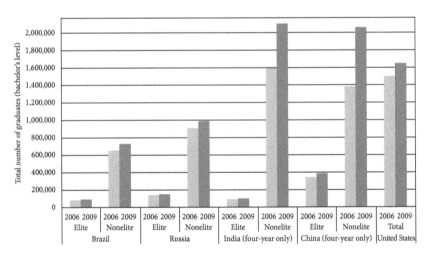

FIGURE 7.4A BRIC countries: Number of university graduates in BRICs, elite versus nonelite institutions, 2006 and 2009

SOURCES: Authors' approximate estimates based on data from China: NBS (various years); Russia: MOES, 2009, 2011, and special estimates of enrollments in elite universities from National Research University Higher School of Economics; India: UGC, 2010, and data on annual college intakes through the JEE (www.jee.iitm.ac.in) and AIEEE (www.aieee.nic.in); Brazil: INEP, *Sinopse*, 2006, 2009, Table 6.1, plus estimates of graduates from elite state and Catholic universities; United States: NCES, *Digest of Educational Statistics, 2011*. Washington, DC: National Center of Education Statistics, Table 2-1286.

Cross-country comparisons are quite different for engineering. Figure 7.4b presents the number of engineering students graduating from elite versus nonelite institutions in each BRIC country and in the United States over the past few years. Here, Chinese (four-year) and Indian institutions produce many times the number of engineering graduates as do U.S. institutions (approximately 7 and 3.5 times, respectively in 2009); Russian and Brazil institutions produce about the same and half as many as the United States, respectively. Importantly, the number of four-year university engineering graduates from elite universities in China (approximately 133,000 in 2009) is 20 percent more than the total number of engineering graduates in the United States and is also much greater than in the other three BRIC countries.[23] Elite institutions in Russia and India will each graduate about 25,000 engineers annually by 2012, about double that of Brazil.[24]

University graduates may be a good indicator of system quality, but unless they are finding productive employment, the argument for using this number weakens. With that in mind, we assess the employment situation of college graduates in each country. Are college graduates able to find employment,

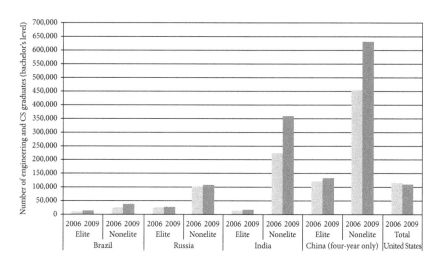

FIGURE 7.4B BRIC countries: Number of engineering (includes computer science) graduates, elite versus nonelite institutions, 2006 and 2009

SOURCES: Authors' approximate estimates based on data from China: NBS (various years); Russia: MOES, 2011, and special estimates of enrollments in elite universities from State Research University Higher School of Economics; India: MHRD, 2010, 2011, and data on annual college intakes through the JEE (www.jee.iitm.ac.in) and AIEEE (www.aieee.nic.in); Brazil, INEP, *Sinopse*, 2006 and 2009, Table 6.2, plus estimates of graduates from elite state and Catholic universities; United States: National Science Foundation, *Science and Engineering Indicators, 2012*. Washington, DC: NSF, Appendix Table 2-18. U.S. data include computer scientists.

especially related to their specializations, and right after graduation? Has the increase in the supply of college graduates in each country, especially given higher education expansion, been sufficiently absorbed by market demand? Are the knowledge and skills purportedly gained by graduates relevant to employers?

In China policy makers and the nation's media have stressed the employment challenges faced by the some six million (three- and four-year) college graduates each year, with some studies claiming that roughly 28 percent of college graduates don't find a job within the first year after graduation (Cai, Park, and Zhao, 2008).[25] Furthermore, the starting salaries of recent college graduates are also perceived to be low: the wage gap between recent college graduates and migrant labor has decreased in recent years (Cai, Park, and Zhao, 2008). Further, many (even four-year) college graduates may not be trained to skill and knowledge levels that would command higher starting salaries. According to reports, mostly from the mid-2000s, employers found the *overall* quality of Chinese graduates to be relatively low. Specific problems include a mismatch between the skills possessed by graduates and those required by companies, a lack of practical engineering experience, an absence of creativity and risk-taking behavior, as well as substandard English and communication skills (Farrell and Grant, 2005; Cha, 2009; Wadhwa et al., 2007; Simon and Cao, 2008).

However, other studies indicate that college graduates are readily being absorbed into the workforce and that the demand for highly skilled labor outstrips the supply (Park, Cai, and Du, 2010; Simon and Cao, 2008). Moreover, college graduates may start with a salary that is comparable to a rural migrant but eventually have much steeper age-income profiles over their lifetimes (Cai, Park, and Zhao, 2008). These studies are corroborated by the high rates of return to college, especially for younger cohorts and especially for those in engineering (see Chapter 3).

Despite increases in the rates of return to higher education in Russia over the past two decades, stakeholders in Russia have also expressed concern about the employment issues facing recent college graduates. In the early and mid-2000s, researchers found that between 50 and 80 percent of college graduates took jobs outside their specialties (Bydanova, 2008; Bondarenko, Krasilnikova, and Kharlamov, 2005). Moreover, there had also reportedly been substantial mismatches between university instruction and the needs of employers in the labor market—not just in terms of subject-specific knowledge but also general competencies (Bydanova, 2008; Reitor, 2005; Bondarenko, Krasilnikova, and Kharlamov, 2005). This may have been caused by the failure of higher education institutions, which used to be tied to specific industries in the time of the Soviet planned economy, to tailor their curricula and instruction to the needs of the new economy.

However, there are signs that the above-mentioned problems related to higher education quality may have relatively mild effects on labor productivity. For example, an employer survey in the mid-2000s revealed that only 20 percent of employers were dissatisfied with the quality of Russian higher education (Bydanova, 2008). The other 80 percent felt that students possessed fundamental knowledge and claimed that the other competencies were developed after working for two to three years. Our own surveys of graduating engineering students in Russia showed that engineers had little difficulty obtaining work after graduation, although admittedly they also often worked outside their specialization. Perhaps the engineering education acquired by these individuals also signaled that they were competent in mathematical skills required by other professions.

Recent college graduates in India may face more acute employment problems than in China or Russia. Unemployment rates are positively correlated with education level in India, and the rate of unemployment is highest among the population with at least some college education. Even after one year of graduation, approximately 30 percent of engineers in India remain unemployed. In the mid-2000s, this translated into nearly one million unemployed engineers (Mooney and Neelakantan, 2006). In addition, there have been a number of complaints from the industrial sector about how poorly Indian engineering graduates are prepared for jobs. For example, it has been reported that approximately three-quarters of India's technical graduates are unemployable by India's high-growth global industries, which means that many of them are underemployed (Ananad, 2011). Engineering graduates appear to be particularly weak in "soft" and higher-order thinking skills (Blom and Saeki, 2011). A few higher-paying firms are able to recruit graduates from elite universities and generally like what they get (although there are also complaints about the quality of even IIT graduates), but smaller, less well-placed firms are generally dissatisfied with what is available to them. All this could indicate that the quality of higher education is low in that it does not provide graduates with the skills and competencies they need in the labor market. At the same time, there appears to be a mismatch between college students' skills and labor market demands.

There is also some good news for college graduates in India. Our survey results indicate that the current salaries of graduates from IIT Bombay and the average Indian college are not drastically different. Given that the $6,000 earned by the average graduate in our sample is the same as the average annual wage paid by global firms such as TCS, Infosys, and Wipro, reforms have apparently succeeded in producing a graduate of acceptable quality and scale through the largely private second-tier system. It is likely that with the help of some public funding, the private second-tier system is able to attract students of high enough ability who can be trained after graduation quickly and cheaply by Indian employers. Furthermore, despite the difficulties faced by recent graduates, the average rate of return in India for having a college education (not adjusted for unemployment) remains high, especially for younger age groups (Chapter 3). There is also some evidence that these increases in returns in the early 2000s came as the demand for college-educated workers outpaced modest increases in the supply of college graduates (Azam, 2010). Thus, similar to China, it could be that college graduates in India may face employment challenges just after graduation but move up the salary scale relatively quickly compared to those without a college education.

There have been concerns in Brazil about both the shifting supply of college graduates for the labor market as well as low starting wages for these graduates (de Moura Castro, 2011). Somewhat by contrast to these concerns, however, the labor force participation rate among the college-educated has remained consistent, at about 85 percent from 1985 to 2007. Unemployment among this population has further been at a relatively low 6 percent in recent years (Menezes Filho, 2009). The rates of return for college degrees have also been extremely high in Brazil for some time, with college graduates earning significantly more than secondary school graduates, especially for those with engineering degrees (see Chapter 3). Also similar to the other BRIC countries, graduates in Brazil have complained about a mismatch between university education and occupational requirements. It could be that the rate of mismatch is comparable to developed countries, however (de Moura Castro, forthcoming).

Research

Research productivity is not only an important output of higher education, but it can also influence the quality of faculty and instruction in universities. In this section we summarize several indicators concerning the state of research and development in each country: R&D expenditures, the number of research personnel, and the number and quality of publications and patents. Although these indicators also pertain to the research produced by industry and research institutes, higher education plays a major and increasingly important role in promoting research in each BRIC economy. These indicators therefore reflect, at least to some degree, the extent to which higher education is involved in producing research in each country.

BRIC countries' R&D expenditures have increased slowly relative to GDP over the past two decades and are still much lower than in the United States, many European countries, and Japan. For instance, in 2009 the United States' R&D expenditures ($398.02 billion) were more than three times that of China ($84.9 billion), Brazil ($19.5 billion), Russia ($15.3 billion), and India ($9.4 billion) combined.[26] Gross expenditure on research and development (GERD) as a percentage of GDP has fluctuated between 2.5 percent and 2.8 percent in the United States and between 2 percent and 2.4 percent in the OECD countries (on average). BRIC countries spend a much lower proportion of their GDP on research and development than the OECD average and well below the United States. India had only a slight increase in the GERD to GDP ratio over the past 15 years, from 0.75 percent to 0.9 percent, with a slightly larger increase for Brazil (0.75 percent to 1.1 percent). Russia's ratio increased from the early 1990s until the early 2000s and has declined steadily since, from 1.3 percent to about 1 percent. China, by contrast, has experienced a continuous increase in the ratio since the mid-1990s, almost tripling since 1996, from 0.6 percent to 1.5 percent.[27] However, all four countries have invested far less money than the United States has in basic versus applied sciences; this trend, if allowed to continue, could arguably affect the long-term efficiency of R&D spending in these countries (Simon and Cao, 2008).

BRIC governments are increasingly promoting the development of research, especially in science and technology in universities but, with few exceptions, almost entirely in elite institutions. In China government research funding in general has grown at more than 20 percent per year, and the state has created some competition among elite HEIs for this funding (Shi and Yi, 2010). Some selective nonelite universities in China also tend to obtain (mostly applied) research grants from both central and local governments as well as nonpublic entities. The Russian state similarly has its top tier of national research universities compete for substantial funding (albeit less than China and Brazil, as we show below), with the hopes of improving research and achieving a higher level of commercialization in R&D. Starting from 2009, Russian policy makers also permitted higher education institutions to create innovation enterprises that could accept funding from nonfederal-government sources and give a space for local and regional governments to direct research efforts within local higher education institutions. Brazil's government also works closely with public research universities and institutes—which already have a strong capacity in terms of qualified faculty and well-run graduate programs—to set research priorities. In India government support for research exists in key institutions but is less than in the other BRIC countries.

Figure 7.5 shows the total amount of R&D spending in higher education by country in 1999 and 2009 (in 2005 PPP dollars). In absolute terms, R&D spending in higher education in China, and to a lesser extent in Brazil, is comparable to the United Kingdom and Germany, while Russia and India trail quite far behind.

Figure 7.6 shows R&D spending per student in bachelor's-level higher education for 2010 (in 2005 PPP$) in each of the BRICs and several developed countries. Spending on research per student in Brazil (PPP $1,337) is comparable to that of Korea but is still less than half that of the United States. China's spending per student is half that of Brazil, whereas Russia and India

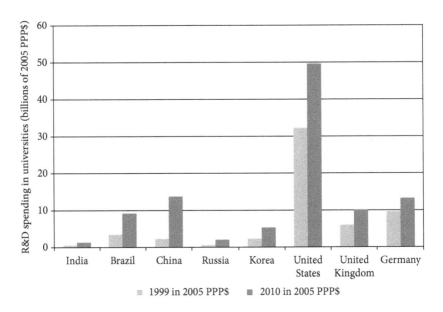

FIGURE 7.5 BRIC and comparison developed countries: Total R&D spending in higher education, 1999–2010 (in billions of 2005 PPP dollars)

SOURCES: OECD, various years, *Main Science and Technology Indicators*. India and Brazil statistics are from UNESCO Institute of Statistics, various years.
NOTES: India's statistics are for 1999 and 2007; Brazil's statistics are for 2000 and 2010; U.S. statistics are for 1999 and 2009.

are far lower at PPP \$149 and PPP \$91, respectively. It seems reasonable to conclude from these figures that Brazilian faculty and students are exposed to a more intensive research environment (as also attested by strong graduate programs), while Chinese students are considerably less exposed, and Russian and Indian faculty and students are generally lacking in research programs. Furthermore, research funding is much higher in the elite institutions in each of the BRICs. For example, IIT Bombay and IISc Bangalore spent about PPP \$29,000 and PPP \$51,500 per professor per year on research, compared to PPP \$110,000 in MIT (Banerjee and Muley, 2007). The research funding per faculty in the very top few universities in China is also comparable to that in top universities in the United States.

The number of publications in science and technology is also an important indicator of the research productivity of higher education systems. Table 7.4 shows the number of S&T papers in the Science Citation Index (SCI),

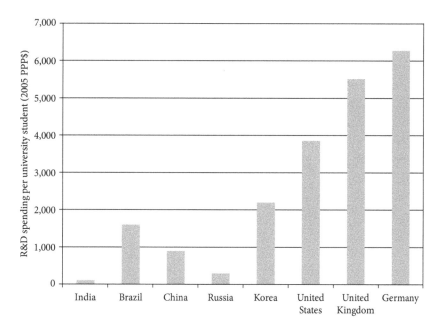

FIGURE 7.6 BRIC and comparison developed countries: R&D spending per student, 2010 (2005 PPP$)

SOURCES: OECD, various years, *Main Science and Technology Indicators*. India and Brazil statistics are from UNESCO Institute of Statistics. Enrollment data are from UNESCO Institute of Statistics, Tertiary 5A enrollment (http://stats.uis.unesco.org/unesco/TableViewer/document.aspx?ReportId=198&IF_Language=eng), retrieved Aug. 15, 2012.
NOTES: India's statistics are for 2007; U.S. statistics are for 2009.

TABLE 7.4 United States and the BRIC countries: S&T papers indexed by SCI, EI, and ISTP, 2009

	SCI		EI		ISTP	
Country	Papers (10,000)	Rank	Papers (10,000)	Rank	Papers (10,000)	Rank
World total	144.2	—	40.9	—	42.8	—
China	12	2	9.3	1	5.2	2
United States	39.8	1	6.9	2	10.5	1
Russia	3.2	15	1.1	13	0.7	14
India	4.5	10	1.6	8	0.8	10
Brazil	3.5	13	0.6	17	0.7	12

SOURCE: National Bureau of Statistics and Ministry of Science and Technology (NBS and MOST), 2010. *China Statistical Year on Science and Technology.*

the Engineering Index (EI), and the Index to Scientific & Technical Proceedings (ISPT) produced in total by researchers in each country. In terms of the total number of scientific articles published per million of the population, China ranked second behind the United States in 2009 in terms of S&T papers indexed by SCI or ISTP rankings and first in the EI ranking. India, Brazil, and Russia were ranked tenth, thirteenth, and fifteenth, respectively, in the SCI rankings (and had similar rank order in the other rankings).

Perhaps more important than these absolute numbers is the progress made by each country over time in producing publications in science and technology. China more than doubled its output from 2004 to 2009 in all indices, including SCI (120,000 papers in 2009), EI (93,000 papers in 2009), and ISTP (52,000 papers in 2009).[28] India and Brazil are also making steady progress in SCI (45,000 and 35,000 papers in 2009, respectively), EI (16,000 and 6,000 papers in 2009, respectively), and ISPT (8,000 and 7,000, respectively). India's turnaround is particularly remarkable as its SCI-indexed publication output did not increase much in the 1980s and 1990s but nearly doubled from 2000 to 2007 (King, 2008a). Russia has a comparable number of S&T papers in each index but has actually seen a reduction in publications in recent years.

China has thus outpaced all other BRIC nations by ranking first or second in each index internationally. However, the statistics presented in Table 7.4 do not reflect the number of professors working in elite universities (who do the lion's share of research in each country) or the overall quality of publications. It is difficult to measure the number of S&T professors in the elite universities, but using student enrollment numbers (Figure 7.2b) as an indicator, China produces about the same ratio of S&T publications compared to Brazil as the ratio of students enrolled (4:1). In terms of quality, the impact of scientific publications from all four BRIC countries, for example, ranks below the world average (as rated by Thomson-Reuters), with Brazil maintaining the highest relative impact among BRIC nations at 63 percent from 2004 to 2008 (King, 2009). China has made steady growth in the number of its "high-impact" papers (defined as among the top 1 percent cited), from 73 in 1998 to 511 in 2007 (King, 2008b).[29] India has also made some progress in this indicator, although not nearly as much as China. According to another indicator of publication quality—Elsevier's Scopus citation database—China also ranked lowest among the top twenty publishing countries (behind India and Brazil) on citations per article (CPA) in 2009; citations per article in fact fell from 1.72 to 1.47 in China from 2005 to 2009.

Our last set of indicators examines the number of patents produced by each nation. These indicators not only can reflect the quality of research being produced but also the ability of governments, researchers, and industry to convert research into socially beneficial products and services. The annual growth in the number of patents in the triadic patent family[30] from 1990 to 2007 suggests that the BRICs are far behind the United States. Specifically, the United States had 15,883 such patents in 2008 (out of 51,990 total internationally) compared to China's 587 (the highest of the BRIC nations). China and India are also steadily increasing the number of such patents in contrast to Brazil and Russia.

The growth in the number of patents under the international Patent Cooperation Treaty (PCT) paints a similar picture. China has made the most progress according to this indicator as well, with 7,010 PCT patents compared to the United States' 43,129. India has also made some progress in this area in the last decade, but not nearly as much. As with the quantity of scientific publications, indicators on the number of patents provide limited information about research quality and innovation. In India, for example, innovations are limited mostly to the pharmaceutical and IT industries, with most of the innovations coming out from multinationals operating in each country (Mani, 2010).

Altogether, three of the BRIC countries, with the exception of Russia, have shown steady progress in terms of research outputs. Brazil, India, and China have increased the numbers of their publications, with China on track to surpass the United States in a few years (Royal Society, 2011). Yet none of the

BRICs have made significant strides in terms of the quality of their research outputs. Brazil's universities perhaps have the most intensive research environment, with relatively strong graduate education and attention to quality research in the elite institutions. There are clear warning signs that China's researchers on average have been incentivized to produce (especially applied as opposed to basic) research *en masse,* with little regard for the quality of that research. India is making some progress in terms of quality as well, but is also starting from fairly low levels in terms of quantity and productivity, lacks strong financial support for research, and has relatively underdeveloped graduate education. Russia has in fact shown a significant decline in the quantity and quality of research outputs, with little government financial support over the 2000s. As we mentioned, however, the national universities in Russia are starting to receive some further research funding and incentives from the federal government in a (still fairly weak) effort to reverse this trend.

State Plans to Increase Higher Education Quality

We close this chapter by examining published government plans in each BRIC country to improve higher education quality over the coming years. These plans may provide some indication of how the state regards its capacity to successfully develop its university system. Over the past two decades, all four countries have produced medium- to long-term strategies for improving higher education.

The Chinese state's "National Guidelines for Medium-Term and Long-Term Educational Reform and Development (2010–2020)" (hereafter known as the "2010–2020 Plan"), for example, seeks to transform China from a nation with a mass higher education system into a "higher education power." The main emphasis of this plan concerning higher education appears to be on improving quality, particularly through financially supporting a number of the nation's top institutions to become truly competitive, world-class universities, as well as through strengthening its relatively weak local universities in less-developed central and western provinces. Beyond these rather general guidelines, there are no specific strategies indicated for how these goals will be realized.

The 2010–2020 Plan also sets several secondary numerical targets in terms of enrollments. For instance, higher education is to expand by about one-fifth, from roughly 30 to 36 million total enrollments (undergraduate and graduate) from 2009 to 2020. As a result, the country's gross enrollment ratio in higher education should increase from 24 percent to 40 percent over the same period, caused mostly by changes in population and age demographics. The proportion of the working population with a higher education is also set to approximately double, as a result, from 10 percent in 2009 to 20 percent by 2020.

Because of the importance of scientific and technological (S&T) development to China's long-term growth in the global economy, the government had also earlier established the "Medium- and Long-Term Plan for S&T Development (2006–2020)" to steer the country toward the goal of becoming an "innovative nation." Some of the general stipulations in this plan have been to adjust the structure of the talent pool, raise talents' innovative capabilities, better use existing talents, as well as implement more-liberal policies on attracting foreign talents and conducting talent exchanges (Wang, 2011). Specifically, the government plans to greatly increase investments in education and R&D to reach 4 percent (by 2012) and 2.5 percent (by 2020) of GDP, respectively. The hope is to increase the number of R&D professionals to 3.8 million (or 0.43 percent of the population) by 2020 (compared to 1.356 million in the European Union and 621,700 in the United States in 2009) (Wang, 2011).

Russian higher education is currently at a turning point, and the 2012 entering government announced plans to adopt a new strategy for higher education development. An influential government think tank has noted several major problems with higher education, including that it is not relevant enough to labor market needs; that many second- and third-tier institutions, as well as distance education programs, are of low quality; that research productivity and innovation are low in the higher education sector; and that there is a significant disparity in the allocation of higher education services across regions.[31]

Although many domestic experts advise simply to cut the number of publically budgeted student places and to regulate access to tuition-based places, the think tank by contrast has suggested addressing the above problems through (1) offering a three-year applied baccalaureate degree to equip graduates with competencies demanded by the labor market and generally broaden the curriculum to increase student choice, (2) setting a minimal entrance exam score for universities to increase the quality of entering students, (3) increasing the financial and academic autonomy of universities by allocating government funding on a per student basis, (4) increasing the public accountability of universities by strengthening the power of governing bodies and opening these governing bodies to public and industry representatives,

(5) continuing the process of merging weaker universities into stronger ones, (6) introducing a standardized graduate exam for undergraduate programs to increase the quality of lower-tier institutions, (7) supporting the development of modern distance education programs on a more competitive basis, (8) supporting the expansion of joint research and innovation projects with industry on a competitive basis, and (9) raising the salaries of university professors by 150 to 200 percent to attract and retain higher-quality faculty. The latter measure will require increasing the share of GDP for higher education from 0.06 percent to 0.12 percent.

We discussed earlier that in India, college autonomy remains one of the national government's key strategies for achieving the quality goal. Under new legislation, the central government provides incentives for private unaided colleges to get out from under state university control and, by implication, to be separated from control by state politicians. The government seems to be hoping that over time, the provincial university system would become irrelevant as a regulator or, at best, be an incubator to help strengthen the weakest private colleges. Provincial politicians oppose these new powers. Most private colleges—as we discuss in Chapter 5—appear, because they prefer the states' emphasis on enrollment expansion, to be more comfortable with the present system than putting themselves under central government quality control as autonomous universities. It is not clear as of 2012 that the current proposed legislation will become law.[32]

What about plans to improve the future quality of Indian technical/ engineering education? There are few long-term goals that have been set so far by the central government regarding engineering education. The government has begun to increase the number of IITs, IIMs, India Institutes of Science and Engineering Research (IISERs), National Institutes of Technology (NITs), and India Institutes of Information Technology (IIITs) (Bagla, 2011). These are all elite, relatively expensive, and highly selective and autonomous technical universities designed to greatly increase the high end of the Indian engineering and science cadre. However, the total number of students in all these institutions together is and will continue to be small compared to the total output of India's colleges of technical education. The government has also discussed plans to establish and fund 30 new central universities and 14 innovation universities across the country, as well as to support states financially to open 374 colleges for general education in the less developed districts that have low proportions of college-age youths attending higher education. These plans appear to be on hold, however.

In 2011 the Brazilian Ministry of Education launched a strategic educa-tion plan (*Plan Nacional de Educacão 2011–2020*) to meet twenty targets by the end of 2020. The plan includes increasing the gross enrollment rate in higher education institutions to 50 percent and the net rate to 33 percent (for 18–24-year-olds). The government has further pledged to improve infrastruc-ture, increase financing, raise program completion rates, promote free public education, and include historically disadvantaged groups in the expansion of the higher education system. There are also plans to raise the number of graduate school entrants, increase graduate research opportunities, and en-courage national and international research collaborations. The government moreover intends to improve the quality of higher education by increasing the proportion of faculty with graduate degrees (master or doctorate) to at least 75 percent, with a minimum proportion possessing Ph.D.s. The national sys-tem of higher education evaluation and supervision will further be strength-ened partially through measuring the value added by undergraduate programs.

Summing Up

Our analyses in this chapter provide insights into the changing quality of elite and nonelite institutions in the BRIC higher education systems. First, the elite institutions in all four countries seem to produce graduates of fairly high quality on average. This is because each country's elite institutions benefit, al-beit to different degrees, from a combination of factors: a competitive process by which a select group of high-ability students are admitted, relatively high per student expenditures, and relatively highly qualified faculty. The state not only plays a large role in managing these factors but has also helped elite institutions (again to varying degrees) improve their curricula and instruc-tional practices, increase their international exposure and collaboration, and urge faculty to concentrate much more on research activities than in nonelite institutions.

The Chinese government has apparently been the most aggressive state in terms of emphasizing the development of elite institutions. The Chinese state has strategically implemented parallel strategies: greatly expanding both undergraduate and graduate enrollments, markedly increasing funding for elite institutions and research funding in general, creating quasi-market in-centives for university administrators and faculty to improve institutional rankings and research productivity, and promoting internationalization in its various aspects. As a result, China produces a much larger quantity of elite enrollments and graduates, especially in engineering, than the other BRICs. China's elite institutions have also made great strides in increasing the *quantity* (but not necessarily *quality*) of research publications over the last decade, having far surpassed the other three countries.

The other three BRIC countries are, to different degrees, making similar efforts to promote elite institutions. Russia is close behind China in the race to promote elite universities and has the benefit of starting from a much broader and stronger base in higher education. The Russian state has begun providing strategic support to a small number of elite institutions in recent years. These first-tier institutions are competing fiercely under policy-based incentives to produce high-quality graduates and research, even though research productivity and financial support for research are still well below those of China and Brazil. The Brazilian government has also taken steps to expand elite enrollments fairly rapidly during the last decade and can rely on a strongly established base of public (and a few private) elite institutions that have strong faculty, research, and graduate education. Only India, out of the four BRIC countries, seems to have a disproportionately low proportion of elite enrollments and graduates (despite having absolute numbers that are comparable to Brazil's and Russia's). India's elite institutions have, on average, also received less support from the government in terms of per student allocations of research funding and may have greater difficulty than the other three countries in finding quality faculty to staff these institutions. Whereas China and Russia have promoted the idea of building "world-class" universities for some time, Brazil and India have been less aggressive in such projects.

Because the number of nonelite enrollments exceeds the number of elite enrollments by at least six times in any one of the BRICs, the question of the relative quality of the nonelite institutions is arguably of even greater importance. That is, the degree to which the nonelite institutions can produce capable graduates is a key measure of the capacity of the state to make deep and long-term changes to the higher education system as a whole.

Russia, with its high gross enrollment rate in both academic high schools and universities, relatively strong performance in international assessments, reputable math/science preparation in high school, and long history of university education with a high percentage of qualified professoriate, is perhaps best positioned to extend quality improvements to nonelite institutions. However, as we discussed, certain historically based institutional factors, such as the disconnect between nonelite institutions and the needs of industry, as well as lack of clear incentives until now for nonelite institutions to make improvements, have resulted in considerable inertia. In addition, the lack in Russia of access to research funding and research productivity likely dampens the progress of these institutions. Fortunately, there is some movement by the federal government toward providing autonomy and greater incentives for nonelite institutions, as well as efforts to merge the least selective nonelites into more selective institutions.

In China, at least the top layer of nonelite universities seems capable of producing quality graduates, especially in engineering and science. These institutions are often situated in China's more developed provinces, where local governments have relatively more resources with which to support the development of higher education. As discussed in Chapter 6, all nonelite four-year institutions in China also select from a small, competitive pool of students (13 percent of the age cohort) who are well prepared in math and science in pre-tertiary education. Furthermore, nonelite institutions can hire new faculty from an ample pool of Ph.D. graduates. Even though there is some concern about the quality of Ph.D. graduates, the more select of the nonelite institutions seem to have little trouble finding competitive candidates who graduated from elite institutions, especially in the fields of science and engineering. However, the remaining mass of China's nonelite institutions still lags behind in terms of quality in a number of areas (e.g., relatively low financing, low professor qualifications, outdated instructional methods, and little research). Perhaps because of this, the central government has noted the need to improve the quality of nonelite institutions, especially in China's less developed areas, and plans to increase funding for these institutions in the near future. Whether it does so will be a good indicator of the state's capacity to effect change.

In contrast to its elite institutions, nonelite institutions in Brazil are of generally low quality. Part of the reason is the relatively low quality of prospective college students who, despite improvements over the last decade, still do not perform as well on international assessments as students in developed countries and in China and Russia. A second reason is that, despite government regulations requiring the mostly private nonelite institutions to hire more faculty who are full time and with Ph.D.s, the proportion of such faculty in mass institutions is rising slowly, even though there is a reasonable supply of Ph.D.s in Brazil. The government has also mandated that students take a test in their first and final years that can potentially be used to measure the value added of different programs, but until now, value-added measures have in fact not been estimated and disseminated.

Of the four BRIC countries, India seems to be the least equipped to improve the quality of higher education on a broad scale. First, the proportion of elite enrollments, even in engineering, is still relatively smaller than the other countries. This is even after accounting for the steep increases in IIT and NIT enrollments from just 2009 to 2011. The number of Ph.D.s being produced is, relative to the number of undergraduates, much smaller than in the other BRICs. This is especially true in technical fields such as engineering. In addition, private institutions that have proliferated in India have few incentives to improve quality. We discussed how these institutions, like the lower-tier institutions in Brazil, seem to receive little pressure from market forces to do more than keep per student costs below revenues. Further prohibiting private institutions from making improvements is the shortage of qualified faculty in the country in general as well as the lack of external (e.g., research) funding. Perhaps as importantly, India still lags far behind the other three countries in terms of the quality of its pre-tertiary education both in terms of its low high school gross enrollment rate and the very low average educational achievement of its students.

8   BRIC Higher Education and Social Equity

O NE OF THE PROMISES OF EXPANDING EDUCATION IS greater social mobility and therefore greater social equity. In theory, as increasing numbers of young people get access to higher education, bright youths from lower social class backgrounds are able to compete for the higher-paying jobs associated with a university degree and move upward economically. Further, as the number of college graduates expands, the relative payoff for college should fall, equalizing the distribution of income. Indeed, countries with a high proportion of youths attending and completing higher education generally have relatively modest payoffs for higher education and for education in general (OECD, 2008; Boarini and Strauss, 2010). Many of these countries also have fairly equal income distributions.

It is easy to imagine how expanding higher education in the BRIC countries could contribute to greater equity. For example, the high proportion of Russian youths completing university and the relatively high proportion of the labor force with university degrees are associated with relative income equality,[1] and the relatively low proportion of Brazilian youths completing university and those in the labor force with university degrees are associated with high income inequality. Expanding higher education in Brazil could make income distribution more equal, as in Russia. However, higher education institutions in all the BRICs are differentiated into tiers of varying selectivity and are becoming increasingly so. It is just as easy to imagine how the expansion of higher education under such circumstances could contribute to greater inequality.

In this chapter we discuss three aspects of this complex relation between higher education expansion and inequality.

The first aspect is how the expansion of higher education can pull in one direction in contributing to greater income equality and social mobility, and differentiated spending on elite and mass higher education institutions can pull in the opposite direction in contributing to greater income inequality and social class reproduction.

The second aspect is how state policies regarding the distribution of fees and subsidies among types of institutions can affect the social class distribution of economic benefits for higher education in each of the BRIC countries. Although we focus on the relationship between higher education *expansion* and inequality, it is important to note that a main driver of social inequality is the unequal access to quality education more generally—that is, the reproduction of social class differences through the unequal provision of public services, including health care, early childhood education, primary schooling, secondary education, and, finally, access to better resourced public higher education institutions by selection mechanisms that favor those who can invest more heavily in themselves at lower levels.

Thus, the third aspect is how the state in Brazil and India—the two BRIC countries with the least access to higher education for students from low-income families—is using affirmative action to increase the university enrollment of those disadvantaged groups. Affirmative action is in contrast to other institutional regulations, such as those established by policy makers in China, which sort students away from higher education or selective higher education institutions and which contribute to social inequality.

We reach no definite conclusions on whether the massive expansion in higher education enrollment and the rising proportion of higher-educated workers in the labor force are contributing in and of themselves to greater income equality in the BRICs, but our analysis does suggest indirectly that, at least in China, the expansion probably added to greater income *inequality* and that in the other BRICs, the effect of the expansion on the income distribution—either in making it more equal or unequal—was probably small.

Our analysis of how various groups in BRIC societies have benefited from the financing of higher education is much clearer. We estimate public benefits by income group for two "extreme" cases, Brazil and Russia. In both countries, a high fraction of students pay user taxes (tuition fees), but the main difference between them is *not* that in one case the fees are paid to public institutions (Russia) and in the other case (Brazil) the fees are paid to private institutions. The distinguishing feature affecting how public subsidies (free places) are distributed is not that tuition is paid to a public or private institution. Rather, it is the social class distribution of students getting publicly funded "free" places in public universities. That distribution is much more equal in Russia than in Brazil. Brazil is trying to offset the stark socioeconomic inequality in the distribution of high-cost public university places with affirmative action programs in public and private higher education institutions, and our analysis suggests that this seems to be having a small positive effect in making the distribution of public subsidies more equal. Although the data are not available for either India or China to estimate the distributional impact of public funding, based on other information on the social class of students attending university, we suggest that the Indian distribution of public benefits would look more like Brazil's despite India's national affirmative action policy and that China's would look more like Russia's.

These estimates support our claim throughout this book that how much and how public funding for higher education is distributed across social class groups relative to the direct (income) and indirect taxes they pay are the most important elements in understanding the equity implications of university expansion. We try to show here the political and economic logic of shifting the so-called "public good" discussion of higher education to a debate over the distribution of net benefits associated with higher educational finance. By taking that step, equity issues come into much sharper focus; indeed, as should hopefully become clear in the sections below, the traditional public good/private good discussion can totally obscure the more important issue of whom the public sector serves by providing "free" or relatively inexpensive public education to only a small (and high social economic class) part of the youth population.

Higher Education Expansion, Income Distribution, and Social Mobility in the BRICs

The Broader Debate on Changing Income Inequality

A nation's income distribution is historically related to many factors, particularly the distribution of wealth—both physical (land and other physical capital) and human (education and skills). In market economies the more equally these assets are distributed, the more likely that the fruits of production will also be distributed fairly equally. Furthermore, in societies where a large proportion of assets is owned by the state or the state is able to tax income heavily and distribute those taxes among various income groups through state spending, state incomes policies can become a decisive factor in determining the way income is distributed (OECD, 2007, Chapter 1).

In theory, the distribution of earnings from employment and from labor-intensive self-employment should be closely related to the distribution of education. Early work on income distribution by Simon Kuznets (1955) and Adelman and Morris (1973) suggested that in very-low-income, low-average-education, mainly agricultural societies, income is more equally distributed because most workers have very low levels of education and are engaged in subsistence agriculture. Incomes are concentrated at low levels, and that concentration dominates the distribution of income. As the level of education rises, the distribution of education becomes more unequal, these societies become more urbanized, and income distribution tends toward greater inequality both because of differences between urban and rural incomes and greater income inequality within urban areas, where worker skills and the payoff for skills tend to vary more than in rural areas. Finally, according to Kuznets, as average education in societies reaches very high levels, the distribution of education becomes more equal again, and the income distribution tends to become much more equal. Adelman and Morris attempted to support Kuznets' "inverted U" theory of income distribution by plotting the Gini coefficient (a measure of income distribution) against gross domestic product per capita. They showed that countries with very low levels of gross domestic product (GDP) per capita had, on average, smaller Gini coefficients (greater income equality) than countries with middle-level GDP per capita and that countries with high GDP per capita also had lower Gini coefficients than middle GDP per capita countries.

Yet Adelman and Morris's confirmation of the "inverted U" theory does not seem to hold up in individual countries or groups of countries over time. Even when economies have gone through major changes in the economic sector and educational structures of their labor forces, income distribution has changed little, or, at least, the changes do not seem to be the result of these structural shifts. For example, Korea has had a profound transformation from a substantially rural society in the 1950s to a highly industrialized, high-income, highly educated economy in the 1990s, with little change in income distribution during that period. Those changes that have occurred appear to have been more related to government incomes policies than to production and labor force structural changes (Nam, 1994). Another example that contradicts Kuznets's and Adelman and Morris's notion of rising and then falling inequality as economies develop is the United States. Income distribution in the United States became more equal in the 1930s–1940s, then stayed at that level of equality until the early 1970s despite rapid equalization of the distribution of education, then steadily became more unequal from the mid-1970s until the present even as education distribution continued to equalize (Carnoy, 1994). As in Korea, the main explanations for changing income inequality in the United States seem to have little to do with the distribution of education.

Economists disagree on the reasons for increasing income inequality in many developed and developing countries since the 1970s (Piketty and Saez, 2003; Bourguignon, Ferreira, and Lustig, 2004; Kahhat, 2008; Carnoy, 2011). The two main positions are the "new technologies" argument, in which the earnings distribution has become more unequal because the returns for higher education (higher-level skills) have risen rapidly in the past generation, caused mainly by new technologies that put premiums on higher-order reasoning skills associated with completing college and graduate education (e.g., Murphy and Welch, 1989; Katz, 1999), and the "incomes policy" argument, in which the earnings distribution has become more unequal because of incomes policies—specifically, minimum wage policies, monetary policies that kept unemployment rates higher, and trade liberalization and immigration policies—that reduced the relative earnings of low-wage workers (e.g., Freeman, 1994; DiNardo, Fortin, and Lemieux, 1996; Farber and Western, 2002). Others (e.g., OECD, 2007) have made the case that fiscal (taxation and spending) policies also play a major role in changing income distribution. Another version of the fiscal argument is Piketty and Saez's "changing social norms" explanation for the steep increase in top U.S. incomes in the past thirty years. In addition, and most relevant to our analysis, Esquivel (2008) as well as Lopez-Calva and Lustig (2009; 2010) argue that in some Latin American countries, income distribution has become more equal in part because of declines in wage differences between skilled and unskilled workers.

Thus, the main discussion points surrounding income distribution over time are whether educational policies have had a significant effect on income distribution, whether the changing payoffs for different levels of education because of technological change or other market forces have overwhelmed changes in the educational distribution when the latter has become more equal, or whether incomes policies, which also can change the payoff for different levels of education, have been more important in shaping income distribution over time than educational policies, technological change, or even changes in labor supply and demand.

The Relationship Between Education Expansion and Earnings Inequality

A major gap exists between studies that try to assess the role of the distribution of education in income distribution across countries and studies of changes in income distribution over time within countries. The former have devoted little attention to the changing payoff for education in a country, so much at the center of the wider debate on income distribution. The latter do assess changing wages between skilled and unskilled workers but touch less on the implications of the changing amount of resources that the state invests in different levels of schooling and specifically to our interest, in the elite and mass tiers of higher education. As we have shown in Chapters 3 and 4, there have been important changes in the BRICs in both of these variables. In this section, we present an elemental model to assess how expansion of education and changing labor market conditions may have influenced income distribution in the BRICs over the past few decades.

The standard underlying model for analyzing the relationship between the quantity of schooling in the labor force in a country and the income distribution is the human capital model (see, for example, De Gregorio and Lee, 1999):

$$\log Y_S = \log Y_0 + rS + e \tag{1}$$

where Y_S = the income (Y) of an individual with S years of schooling;

Y_0 = the average (constant) income of individuals with no years of schooling;

S = schooling level;

r = the rate of return to investment in a year of schooling;

e = the error term (including other unobservable factors that influence income but that are assumed to be independent of S and r).

A simplified version of the distribution of earnings can be written as the following, for heuristic purposes (De Gregorio and Lee, 1999):

$$\text{Var} (\log Y_s) = \text{Var} (rS) + \text{Var} (e)$$

$$= \bar{r}^2 \text{Var} (S) + \bar{S}^2 \text{Var} (r) + 2\bar{r}\bar{S} \text{Cov} (rS) + \text{Var} (e) \tag{2}$$

The variance of the log of income in a given country is therefore a function of the variance and level of education, S, in the labor force.

A number of analysts have used cross-country data to estimate the relationship between the variance of the log of income (income inequality) in a country and the level and variance of schooling in that country. In most, the rate of return for education is considered constant and independent of S.

These studies generally find that inequality in the income distribution is negatively related to S, as measured by years of schooling, and positively related to the variance of S (for example, Winegarden, 1979, and De Gregorio and Lee, 1999). However, Ram (1989, 1990), using a model that includes population growth, finds that S and $Var\ (S)$ are not significantly related to income inequality.

None of those models deal with variation in the rate of return for schooling or the covariance of S and r. They also generally measure the labor force or population's schooling in years rather than in some other value that reflects, for example, differences in inputs going into each year. It is more logical to assume that the rate of return for education is not constant and is partly a function of the growth rate, the composition of growth, and the change in the supply of educated labor relative to demand (Carnoy, 1972; Lopez-Calva and Lustig, 2009; 2010). Thus, the average level of the rate of return as well as the variance in the rate of return can change with these factors. Economists have typically assumed that the average rate of return falls as years of schooling in the labor force increase, that the variance in the rate remains constant, and that the Cov (r,S) is negative—that is, as at higher levels of schooling, the average rate of return for schooling declines (Psacharopoulos, 1986). However, the sign of Cov $(r,\ S)$ may be positive if, as shown in Chapter 3 for China in the 2000s and Brazil in the 1980s, rates of return for higher education rise relative to the rates to secondary education with increases in the average level of schooling.

The above types of specifications can bias estimates of the effects of expanding education on the distribution of income for two main reasons: the first is that, as suggested in Chapter 3, the rates of return for different levels of education have generally changed over time in a way that has increased the relative value of higher education to lower education even as the number of higher education graduates expands. Our data suggest that the changes in rates vary from country to country. In the BRIC countries, the changes in the relative rates for higher and secondary education were likely influenced by the rate of increase of secondary and higher education graduates (as well as the differential increase between them), economic growth, the transformation of the economy to a market system (China and Russia), and state income policies (all the BRICs). In any case, the rising rate of return for higher education (r) likely contributed to increasing inequality even as the average level of schooling (S) increased.

The second reason is that even if the rate of return were constant over different levels of schooling, measuring schooling (S) by average years in the labor force does not reflect differences in the "quality" of education across countries, within a country over time, and across levels of education within a country at a single point in time. Therefore, omitting a measure of educational quality probably biases the contribution of schooling to earnings variance in the traditional studies that use cross-country data.

Let us assume that higher spending per student represents a greater investment (and, in some sense, higher schooling quality).[2] High-income-inequality countries generally spend less (public and private contributions) per student on education in PPP$ than low-inequality countries and have lower average scores on international tests than low-inequality countries (Adamson, 2010). This suggests that the negative coefficient of S in the log income variance estimates discussed above is smaller than the international studies suggest. Furthermore, higher-inequality countries tend to spend more per student on higher education relative to primary and secondary education, suggesting that the positive coefficient of Var (S) (the inequality in schooling) usually estimated by typical international cross-sectional studies is also biased upward.

Now we can apply some of these notions to our analysis of higher education in the BRIC countries. Bringing the costs of education into the measure of S as a proxy for educational "quality," and considering changes in spending over time in the BRICs, we observe that the spending on education per student increased substantially in Russia, thereby increasing the "investment value" of a year of schooling in both secondary and higher education. This suggests that using years of schooling as a measure of the increased education in the Russian labor force would underestimate the "true" increase in S, at least for the youngest group in the labor force (Figure 8.1 and Figure 3.1). In Brazil the situation is mixed, with spending per student rising for primary and secondary schooling, the levels pertaining to the vast majority of Brazilian students,[3] and spending per student declining for higher education (see Figure 3.1). It is likely that for the younger cohorts going into the labor force, the "investment value" of secondary education increased while that of higher education decreased. For India and China, it seems that the investment value of an average year of schooling stayed approximately the same.[4] Thus, years of schooling are probably a good proxy for the increase in education in these two countries but may underestimate the increase in the quantity of education in Russia, if we think that the value of a year of schooling improves with greater spending per student, and may also underestimate the increase in the quantity of education in Brazil, particularly because spending per student is rising in those levels attended by most students—primary and secondary schooling.

We have no evidence on how international test scores are changing in China or India because China participated for the first time in an international test in 2009 and India only in a partial survey in two states in 2009. However, we do have test scores for Russia over a sixteen-year period on the TIMSS and nine years on the PISA. The mathematics scores show some gain in this period on TIMSS and no significant decline on the PISA. Brazil, to the contrary, made significant improvements (beginning at a very low level) in mathematics on the PISA since 2000. Therefore, from an output standpoint, the very modest increase in the average years of schooling in the Russian labor force since 2000 may be a good representation of S in equations 1 and 2, whereas in Brazil the greater increase in years of schooling in the last ten years is likely to be an underestimate of the "true" increase in S, were we to adjust those years for "quality."

Tables 8.1 to 8.3 summarize the estimated changes in the BRIC countries for the key variables in Equation 2. Table 8.1 shows income distribution, as measured by the Gini coefficient. Distribution is most unequal in Brazil (a higher Gini coefficient) but is gradually becoming somewhat more equal. It is most equal in India but is gradually becoming more unequal. China has a higher level of inequality than in India, but this appears to be leveling off because of government spending in rural areas and greater increases in the wages of lower-skilled labor compared to those of higher-skilled labor (which

TABLE 8.1 BRIC countries: Income distribution, 1980–2009 (Gini coefficient × 100)

Country	1980– 1985	1986– 1990	1991– 1995	1996– 2000	2001– 2003	2005	2008– 2009
Brazil	58	61	60	59	59	57	55
China	30	32	38 (45[a])	40	43	42	—
India	32	31	32	36[a]	—	33	—
Russia	—	24	48 (40[a])	43	38	38	41

SOURCES: Deininger and Squire, 1996; World Bank, *World Development Indicators* (http://data bank.worldbank.org), accessed Dec. 14, 2012.
[a]Chotikapanich et al., 2007, Table 2. For Brazil in 1993 and 2000 as well as for China, India, and Russia in 2000, the estimates of Chotikapanich et al. do not differ from the WDI Gini estimates. However, Chotikapanich et al., 2006, Table 3 suggests that China's income distribution was somewhat more equal but definitely becoming more unequal (Gini coefficients × 100): 1985–28; 1991–31; 1995–35; 2000–35; 2003–40.

TABLE 8.2 BRIC countries: Average years of schooling in the labor force and standard deviation of years of schooling, 1980–2008

Country	1980	1985	1990	1995	2000	2005	2008
AVERAGE NUMBER OF YEARS OF SCHOOLING IN LABOR FORCE							
Brazil	3.41	3.64	4.03	4.32	4.63	4.93	5.11
China	4.76	4.95	5.84	6.10	6.36	6.66	6.84
India	3.29	3.63	4.11	4.53	5.06	5.53	5.80
Russia	—	—	—	9.77	10.04	10.31	10.58
STANDARD DEVIATION OF YEARS OF SCHOOLING IN LABOR FORCE							
Brazil	3.41	3.56	3.65	3.73	3.87	4.02	4.10
China	4.36	4.37	4.36	4.36	4.34	4.42	4.44
India	5.15	5.24	5.35	5.44	5.44	5.44	5.44
Russia	—	—	—	3.34	3.42	3.50	3.50

SOURCES: Fan, 2005. See also Thomas et al., 2003. Authors' estimates for 2008.

TABLE 8.3 BRIC countries: Private rates of return for secondary and higher education, 1980–2008 (percentage per year of schooling)

Country/level of education	1980	1990	1995	2000	2005	2008
Brazil secondary	16	12		12		2
Brazil university	20	25		23		25
China secondary		4	5	6	10	
China university		3	6	9	20	
India secondary	20		14	6[b]	12	
India university	13		12	12[b]	12	
Russia professional[a]			6	7	3	
Russia university		5	5	6	10	6

SOURCE: Chapter 3.
[a]Postsecondary, nonuniversity.
[b]Males only.

in turn is caused by a growing shortage of cheap rural labor in the country) (Cai, Park, and Zhao, 2008). According to the data shown in the table, Russia's income distribution changed drastically toward greater inequality in the early 1990s, when the transformation from the command economy occurred, but became more equal again in the early 2000s and is now gradually headed again toward greater inequality.

What is the likely contribution to the income distribution trends in Table 8.1 of the steady expansion of years of schooling in these countries' labor forces? Table 8.4 shows how the various components (as summarized in tables 8.2 and 8.3) of the right side of Equation 2 changed in the past twenty-five years.[5] The analysis in Table 8.4 suggests that in all four countries, the positive change in the covariance term—reflecting the relative increase in the payoff for university compared to the payoff for lower levels of schooling as higher education expanded—contributed to greater income inequality during this period. In Brazil the increase in the variance of r times the rising average level of schooling also contributed to increased income inequality, but the falling average rate of return, driven by the declining payoff for secondary education, combined with the increased variance in years of schooling in the labor force, helped decrease inequality. It would seem that all in all, the expansion of education and the behavior of rates of return in Brazil probably either contributed somewhat to decreased income inequality (as per Lopez-Calva and Lustig, 2009) or had little effect on it. In China, however, all the components (rates and increased years of schooling in the labor force) contributed to increased income inequality, and in India only the covariance component contributed to greater inequality. Hence, because income inequality increased in India, it probably came from somewhere else, not the rapid expansion of average schooling in the labor force. Finally, in Russia it appears that the educational expansion, even though there were only small changes in rates of return, did contribute in a small way to increased income inequality. Again, as in India, the main change in income inequality must be coming from somewhere else.

TABLE 8.4 BRIC countries: Contribution of components of educational change to changes in income distribution, 1980–2008

Country			*Direction of change in variables, 1980–2008*		
	r	*S*	*Var (S)*	*Var (r)*	*Cov (r, S)*
Brazil	Negative	Very positive	Very positive	Positive	Increasingly positive
China	Very positive	Very positive	Negligible	Positive	Negative to increasingly positive
India	Small negative	Very positive	Small positive	Small negative	Negative to zero, hence positive
Russia	Negligible	Positive	Small positive	Small positive	Somewhat negative to positive

SOURCES: Tables 8.2 and 8.3.

As noted, we may be overestimating or underestimating the size of the expansion of schooling (S) in a given country because the quality of a year of schooling may be decreasing (possibly India) or increasing (probably Brazil). In theory, this should be reflected in a decreasing or increasing rate of return for schooling, but it may not be because other factors could keep wages the same despite higher productivity (the U.S. labor market in the past twenty years is a good example). If, for example, we underestimate S in Brazil because of increasing educational quality, as reflected in higher international test scores, this would underestimate the increase in S multiplied times the variance in the rate of return. However, if the increase in quality comes largely from increasing the quality of lower-performing students, not including a quality index would imply that we are overestimating the variance of S, which would reduce the contribution of that component to income inequality.

Biases in the measure of schooling (S) aside, an important lesson from the exercise in Table 8.4 is that the rising payoff for higher education relative to secondary schooling (relative to professional postsecondary education in Russia) that we reported in Chapter 3 for all four countries and summarize in Table 8.3 can have an important influence on the distribution of income. This is accentuated when average rates of return are rising over time, as in China. The potential contribution to income inequality of rising relative rates of return for higher education in the face of educational expansion reflects an inescapable logic. Higher-educated labor can be and is substituted for less-educated labor as the schooling system expands. If this downward substitution helps raise the payoff for the highest level of schooling relative to the payoff for secondary schooling, the expansion of average education in the labor force increasingly favors those at the top of the income ladder. This is what we have observed in all four BRIC economies. However, if this continued school expansion contributes to driving down the *average* rate of return to schooling (r), as it seems to have done in Brazil, at least one component of Equation 2 (r^2Var [S]) may help push down income inequality.

Increasingly Differentiated Spending on Elite and Mass Higher Education Institutions

The conventional wisdom is that in countries with relatively high rates of return for higher education, expanding higher education should lower the payoff for those who complete university and should contribute to the equalization of incomes. But if there is a large variation in how much is invested in students attending different kinds of universities, and high-cost institutions expand much more slowly than low-cost institutions, even if the rate of return for attending one or another of these institutions is *initially* similar (which may or may not be the case), the income distribution could become more unequal as more students enter and complete higher education because rates of return would likely decline more to those attending lower-cost institutions. This trend would be exacerbated were the average spending per student (and implicitly the quality) to decline in institutions absorbing a high proportion of the increase in university enrollment compared to the spending per student in elite universities.

We show in Chapter 4 that in Brazil, China, and Russia, elite institutions are being increasingly differentiated cost-wise from mass institutions—in China and Russia because elite institutions are receiving increasingly more funding from the government than publicly funded mass institutions, and in Brazil because the mass private institutions are spending less per student, on average, as the private system expands. If *increasing differentiation of spending* among higher education institutions is the dominant trend in the developing countries, even as higher education enrollment expands, the overall rate of return for completing university can continue to hold constant or even rise (mainly from declining earnings to high school completers and those who do not complete university), but the absolute *return* (not the *rate* of return) would rise differentially for those who attend lower-tier, lower/declining-cost-per-student universities and those who attend higher-tier, higher-cost-per-student universities. Under certain circumstances, this could contribute to greater income inequality even as the higher-educated labor force increases rapidly.

We can test this proposition in terms of the components in Table 8.4. If, for the sake of argument, we assume that the rates of return for students completing different types of universities were essentially equal,[6] and we were to account for the increasingly differentiated spending per student (hence allegedly increasingly differentiated quality) in elite and mass universities, we could find a potentially larger than observed variance in S (measured only in years of schooling) once we weighted those with a completed university education by the cost of their education. In Brazil average rates of return appear to be falling. This should contribute to decreased income inequality through the first term of Equation 2. In China, because r is increasing, this increased differentiation probably contributes even more to income inequality than not accounting for the increased spending differentiation in elite and mass universities. Again, the lesson we discussed above is crucial: if expanding the level of schooling in the labor force is accompanied by falling rates of return to education, school expansion contributes to greater income *equality*. However, if expanding the level of schooling is accompanied by rising rates of return, as we have seen in China, then expanding education increases income *inequality*.

This does not settle the larger issue of why the rate of return to education increases (and also, possibly, the variance in the rates of return) as schooling levels in the labor force increase. Is it the result of exogenous technological change or state incomes policies or major changes in the organization of the economy, such as the transition from state to market capitalism in Russia and China? In any of these cases, national states can play an important role in offsetting increased income inequality. They can keep increasing education levels and improving educational quality, especially for disadvantaged young people, and hope that this eventually drives down the average payoff for higher education. They can also use state fiscal (tax and spending) policies to equalize posttax, post-spending income, or invest in less-developed regions (as in China), all possible ways for state policies to contribute to income equality.

The Distributional Consequences of BRIC Higher Education Financing Systems

Before getting into the possible distributional consequences of each BRIC country's particular higher education financing, we can make some overarching observations about all four countries. In general, when the cost of higher education is borne largely by the state, as it has been traditionally in all but Brazil, the main beneficiaries of that state financing have been higher social class students because they are much more likely to attend university. When higher education is differentiated into higher- and lower-cost institutions, as it has been in all four countries, higher social class students are collectively more likely to get the highest subsidies because they tend to get greater access to the higher-cost institutions (Hansen and Weisbrod, 1969; Tilak, 1989). Of course, the families of higher-income students are also more likely to pay higher taxes; therefore, it could be argued that they are entitled to more and better public services (see Pechman, 1970; Barbaro, 2004).

Thus, even in countries such as Russia and China, which still retain the influence of their years as strict communist (or state capitalist) societies, students from more-developed regions and from more highly educated families have more access to higher education and to "better" (and more highly sub-sidized) universities within the higher education system. Nevertheless, as we show below, this unequal social class access, characterizing virtually all the world's university systems, is more accentuated in Brazil and India, which despite considerable expansion in recent years and even the existence of affir-mative action in both, have limited numbers of students from less-educated, low-income families attending. As a consequence, little of the state's subsidy for higher education reaches lower-income groups in Brazil and India, though the situation is improving significantly over the years in India[7] (we could make similar statements about Chinese higher educational expansion).

The implications of such unequal distribution of public funding in favor of higher social class students is particularly hard to justify when the aver-age private rates of return for higher education are high, as they are in Brazil (and, more recently, China). With high private rates of return for investing in university, subsidizing those groups that can afford to pay, rather than using funding to give bright lower-income students increased access, is a good way to reproduce social class inequality but not very efficient economically, unless policy makers can show very high externalities to subsidizing higher social class students to attend high-cost universities.[8]

Given its already highly unequal social and income structure, the Brazil-ian higher education system seems to be at an extreme in the way it distrib-utes public financing, and we can show that inequality quite clearly, given Brazilian higher education data. Because India has a relatively smaller frac-tion of the age cohort attending higher education institutions, it also tends to distribute public resources to higher education largely to students from higher-educated, higher-income urban families. This occurs despite its exten-sive affirmative action requirements for college admission. In China students from the urban richer regions are also favored with subsidies. And Russian students of more humble background have, within a system of unequal access to public subsidies, the most equal access to public funding among the BRIC countries.

With that in mind, we now attempt to support these claims empirically by examining the individual BRIC cases.

Brazil

If we use the latest data on the socioeconomic background of Brazilian higher education students enrolled in private and public institutions, estimating for each family income category group the subsidy provided by the public system,

TABLE 8.5 Brazil: Estimated net public subsidies per student in higher education, 2002 and 2007 (2008 reais)

Income category	Private higher education			Public higher education			Total
	% in income group	Number of students	Subsidy/ student (reais)	% in income group	Number of students	Subsidy/ student (reais)	Net subsidy/ student (reais)
2002							
Bottom 40%	0.034	82,552	0	0.073	76,796	14,374	6,927
Next 20%	0.057	138,396	0	0.11	115,720	14,374	6,546
Next 20%	0.19	461,320	0	0.25	263,000	14,374	5,219
Next 10%	0.235	570,580	0	0.215	226,180	14,374	4,080
Top 10%	0.485	1,177,580	0	0.352	370,304	14,374	3,439
		2,430,428			1,052,000		4,342 (average)
2007							
Bottom 40%	0.077	280,203	0	0.126	156,366	13,861	4,965
Next 20%	0.1	363,900	0	0.134	166,294	13,861	4,347
Next 20%	0.256	931,584	0	0.239	296,599	13,861	3,347
Next 10%	0.239	869,721	0	0.202	250,682	13,861	3,101
Top 10%	0.335	1,219,065	0	0.299	371,059	13,861	3,234
		3,664,473			1,241,000		3,507 (average)

SOURCES: Authors' estimates based on Schwartzman, 2004, and Eckert Baeta Neves, 2009, plus enrollment data from Chapter 2 and public cost per student data from Chapter 4.

we can get an approximate idea of the direct benefits the public sector provides to higher and lower socioeconomic groups (see Table 8.5).

The estimates in Table 8.5 assume that students in the highest socioeconomic group enter the same cost/student fields of study in public universities as students in the lowest socioeconomic groups. This is probably not the case. It is much more likely that higher socioeconomic students study in higher-cost fields in public universities, hence receive higher subsidies than lower socioeconomic background students who enroll in public institutions.

Because so many more students enroll in private institutions and pay fees (therefore are not subsidized), and because a higher proportion of students enrolling in private institutions are from the highest-income groups, it appears that under our simple assumption of equal subsidy received, no matter the social class of the student, the highest social class students end up receiving a smaller subsidy *per student* and the lowest social class students end up receiving a higher subsidy *per student.* That is, such a high fraction of all higher social class students enrolls in private higher education (about 75 percent of the top quintile SES group in both 2002 and 2007) that despite the fact that the same group dominates enrollment in public higher education, that group ends up receiving a lower net subsidy per student enrolled in university. At the other end of the spectrum, about one-half of the lowest 40 percent SES group was enrolled in private higher education in 2002 and 64 percent in 2007. Thus, the subsidy received by the much smaller numbers in that group enrolled in university was higher per student (Figure 8.1).

The other point made by the estimates in Table 8.5 and Figure 8.1 is that because of the rapid expansion of the private sector and the corresponding gradual shift to incorporating more lower-income students in private institutions, the net subsidy to lower socioeconomic background students tended to fall much more than to higher socioeconomic class students between 2002 and 2007. The overall picture is that the expansion of the private sector and the need to attract more (lower-income) students through lowering the real price of enrollment has reduced the net subsidy received per student in lower relative to higher socioeconomic groups.

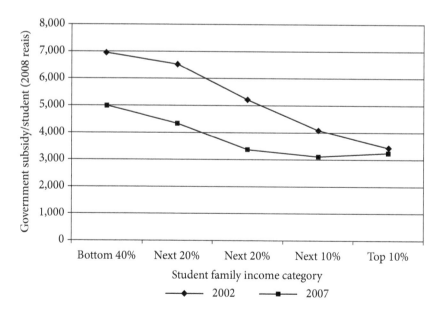

FIGURE 8.1 Brazil: Public spending on higher education per student, by student's family income category, 2002 and 2007 (2008 reais)
SOURCE: Table 8.5.

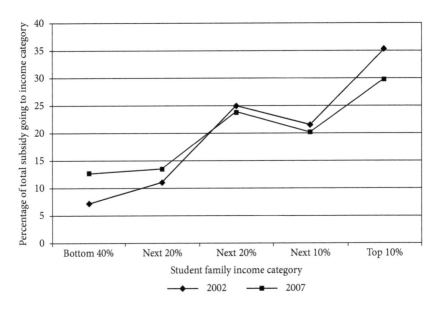

FIGURE 8.2 Brazil: Distribution of total public subsidy on higher education by student's family income category, 2002 and 2007 (percentage)

SOURCE: Table 8.5.

At the same time, the proportion of the *total subsidy* for those enrolled in public institutions has become somewhat more equalized among social class groups. In 2002 students from families in the top 10 percent of income earners got 35 percent of the total subsidy provided to public higher education students, and in 2007 this dropped to 30 percent. Again, this assumes that these students were in the same average cost fields of study as everyone else, although it is likely that they were in higher-cost fields and therefore had a higher fraction of the total subsidy. Students from families in the bottom 40 percent of income were the beneficiaries of 7 percent of the total subsidy in 2002 and 13 percent in 2007 (Figure 8.2).

Therefore, government gives a high fraction of its spending on higher education as a subsidy to students from the highest-income families in Brazil, but that same highest 10 percent of income families are also even more likely to attend private institutions. Therefore, they receive a lower subsidy *per student* in higher education than the lowest social class groups. The government could therefore argue that even though it heavily subsidizes the rich with its tuition-free public higher education, its policy of allowing higher education enrollment to expand primarily through the growth of tuition-charging private institutions ends up taxing the rich and subsidizing the poor.

Government can make a further case that the rich also pay more taxes, and that is partly right. One estimate of the distribution of the total tax burden (direct income taxes and all indirect taxes) by income group in Brazil showed that 40 percent of the tax burden was borne by the highest decile income group, 16 percent by the next decile, 11 percent by the eighth decile, 9 percent by the seventh decile, and so on down to 2 percent by the bottom decile (Baer and Fialho Galvão Jr., 2005, Table 7). If we include these tax revenue data in the estimates, it suggests that the top decile of income earners got less in benefits (30 percent) in 2007 than the proportion of taxes paid (40 percent), but the ninth decile and the fourth quintile got a greater benefit from higher education subsidies—20 percent and 24 percent, respectfully—than taxes paid—16 percent and 20 percent of total government tax revenue, respectively. The bottom 40 percent of income-earning families, even with an active affirmative action policy in public universities, got slightly less benefits than taxes paid (12.7 percent versus 13 percent). All this suggests that at the very top, Brazil's higher education financing policy is progressive (assuming that youths from the highest-earning 10 percent of families do not specialize in the most expensive courses of study in public universities) but becomes regressive for families below that top decile (higher-income families get more proportionately more benefits than taxes paid).

Nevertheless, the strategy to expand higher education mainly through the expansion of private, full-tuition institutions is running out of steam. In order for private mass higher education to have expanded in the past seven or eight years, it has had to keep prices down and recruit larger numbers of lower-income students. This means that an increasing proportion of the relatively few low-income students enrolling in higher education institutions had to pay tuition despite the implementation over the past five years of affirmative action schemes in a number of public universities and government programs to subsidize the poor who are attending private universities. The net effect of falling tuition (adjusted for inflation) and the incorporation of more lower-income students into private institutions has been, as we have shown (Figure 8.1), a much more rapid fall in the net subsidy per student for lower-income students than for higher-income students.

The response of the private sector has been to lobby for government-backed student loans, and the response of the government has been to push for subsidizing the private sector directly to admit lower-income students under affirmative action.

India

We do not have similar global data for India on the distribution of spending and taxes as for Brazil. However, our survey of 7,000 final-year engineering and computer science students in almost 40 Indian technical colleges and universities can give us some insight into who benefits more from low-cost places and how much this benefit is worth. Further, a survey from 2004–2005 that estimates the gross enrollment rates in India's colleges and universities by income quintile (UGC, 2011, Table 5.06) shows that despite a major affirmative action effort, a very unequal distribution of enrollment among young people from lower and higher social class backgrounds. Based on those figures, students from families in the bottom 40 percent of the income distribution represent about 11 percent of students enrolled, and students from families in the top income quintile were 58 percent of those enrolled in 2004–2005. This breakdown is very similar to the proportions in Brazil in 2007 (Table 8.5). Because the gross enrollment rate in India increased from 14 to 18 percent in 2008–2010 (using 18–22-year-olds as the reference group), the proportion coming from low-income groups should also have increased (as it also almost certainly did in Brazil because of a similar expansion since 2007).

Thus, Indian higher education shares two important features with higher education in Brazil: a very high fraction of students in Indian and Brazilian higher education comes from relatively well off and highly educated families, and the state in both systems has implemented affirmative action programs. In India, this initiative is large, mandatory, and comes directly from the central state; in Brazil, the program was voluntary until 2013, was up to individual public universities, which shaped the program according to university taste, and recently was extended to private universities through federal scholarship incentive programs and made mandatory in federal universities.

Our results from the student survey of engineering students in India (see Chapter 6) show that students with higher entrance test scores, who are males, and who have higher family income are more likely to attend lower-tuition, more-prestigious public colleges/universities. Thus, they are likely to be more subsidized than middle-family-income students. On the other hand, because of affirmative action, lower-income students (to the extent that disadvantaged castes are lower income) are also likely to be subsidized regardless of whether they attend public or private colleges.

As we have discussed in other chapters, private engineering colleges finance essentially their entire budget from tuition and other fees (many make a surplus). With spending per student in the range of US $1,000–$1,500 in 2009, private engineering colleges should be averaging a minimum of 45,000–68,000 rupees in tuition per student. More than one-half of students are supposed to be admitted under some sort of controlled tuition scheme, either through affirmative action or as a high-scoring student (whom private colleges desire to admit to raise their status), and their tuition is fixed in the 25,000–40,000 rupee range (see Chapter 4). This suggests that many students who did not fall into these categories paid 70,000–100,000 Rs. tuition in 2009.

At the other end of the spectrum, students attending elite, high-cost technical institutions are heavily subsidized even if they are from the highest castes. For example, the cost per student in an IIT is US $5,000–$9,000 annually, compared to about $1,000–$1,500 annually in a higher-quality unaided private engineering college. Regular tuition at an IIT is about 15 percent of the lower-end $5,000 cost and a lower percentage of higher-cost IITs, such as IIT Mumbai. The assumption in this level of subsidy is that the Indian government should be promoting the development of the best and the brightest because of possibly high social externalities associated with these individuals when they go into the labor market, even if they go into the U.S. labor market. As their supply increases with the recent opening of many more IITs and NITs, it might be argued that increased numbers will stay in India, teach, do research, and contribute much more than they earn through their creativity and innovation.

In our survey of engineering and computer science students, we were able to estimate tuition fees as a function of caste, college entrance test scores, and type of college. Our results suggest that, indeed, students with higher test scores and those from disadvantaged castes pay lower tuition. The latter pay lower tuition even when their test scores are higher. Higher socioeconomic background students, where socioeconomic background is measured by mother's and father's education, pay higher tuition. As expected, controlling for the caste and test scores, those students attending private colleges pay higher fees. These results also suggest that government affirmative action policies do result in disadvantaged castes paying less to take engineering education and do result in those of higher socioeconomic background paying higher fees, controlling for caste and test score. Therefore, it appears that from an equity standpoint, government policy regarding lower-caste access at lower fees does offset at least part of the advantage going to higher social class students in terms of their likely scoring higher on entrance tests. A ten-percentage-point higher entrance test score is associated with Rs. 5,000 less tuition, but disadvantaged castes pay about Rs. 20,000 less, on average, with the most disadvantaged paying about Rs. 30,000 less.[9]

Approximately 30 percent of students attending engineering colleges come from disadvantaged groups, as per our survey of the students of the final year before graduation: 8 percent are scheduled castes, 2 percent are scheduled tribes, and 19.6 percent are other backward classes (OBCs). This is less than the affirmative action policy officially requires. It might suggest that some students drop out before reaching the final year.[10]

In sum, the current financing of the Indian higher education system seems to be generally efficient (those who pay the highest fees, on average, are in the fields that have the highest private payoffs) and generally provides for considerable equity—some say too much equity (Kochar, 2010)—except at the upper end of the test score distribution, where the government heavily subsidizes very high scoring (and generally very high social class) students to attend highly selective technical (IITs), business/public management (IIMs), and other institutions, such as the Delhi School of Economics. The size of this subsidy is large—at least $3,500 per student, and perhaps as much as $7,500–8,000. But a much higher fraction of higher social class students in engineering fields pays high fees to attend college, and a substantial proportion of students in colleges and universities comes from relatively modest backgrounds. They are also subsidized, to the tune of about $500–$1,000 per student (in 2009).

Russia

More than any of the other BRICs, Russia has made higher education available to students across the social class spectrum. This resulted first from the long-term expansion of the Soviet higher education system, which increased even further after the creation of the Russian Federation in 1991 and now enrolls about 85 percent of the age group (see Chapter 2). Second, it results from years of highly equal income distribution during the communist era. That distribution has become much more unequal in the past twenty years, but because of the expansion in higher education, the distribution of access to university places is now much more equal than income.

As discussed in Chapter 2, Russia's universities achieved their large increases in enrollment in the past two decades mainly by allowing public universities to charge students who did not qualify for budgeted, or "free" places, tuition fees. These fee-paying students now represent more than half of the total of students in public universities. In addition, about 8 percent of students attend small (in terms of enrollment) private universities. Many analysts believe that it is mainly low-income students who pay fees to attend public universities and who attend private institutions, which are much lower in quality than the publics. The argument is that students from high social class backgrounds are likely to attend better primary and secondary schools and have more resources at home to prepare for college entrance examinations. However, despite this logic (and, as in Brazil), lower-income students appear less likely than higher social class students to pay fees to attend university. We have no data on the social backgrounds of students in private institutions, but we do have detailed information on the average fees paid by students from families with different levels of monthly income. Average fees paid by students who pay fees increase as students' family income increases, and so does the proportion of students paying fees (Table 8.6). The pattern suggests that higher-income students either are more likely to pay for places at universities

TABLE 8.6 Russia: Estimated average higher education public subsidy per student by per-member family income of students, 2010

Reported per-member family monthly income (rubles)	Average fee paid (rubles) by those students paying fees	Share of fee-paying students in income group (percentage)	Average fee paid per student in income group (rubles)	Estimated total cost per student, including student fees in public institutions (rubles)	Estimated average subsidy per student in each group (rubles)
Less than 4,000 rubles	50,368	24	12,088	125,000	112,912
4,000–7,000	44,511	23	10,238	125,000	114,762
7,000–10,000	50,283	36	18,102	125,000	106,898
10,000–15,000	42,954	40	17,182	125,000	107,818
15,000–20,000	63,017	48	30,248	125,000	94,752
20,000–30,000	68,237	51	34,801	125,000	90,199
30,000–40,000	65,541	66	43,257	130,000	86,743
40,000–50,000	67,734	51	34,544	135,000	100,456
50,000–100,000	72,810	49	35,677	140,000	104,323
> 100,000 rubles	80,570	54	43,508	145,000	101,492

SOURCE: National Research University Higher School of Economics, *Monitoring of the Economics of Education, 2010.*

or attend universities/programs that charge much higher fees. This is a logical outcome because higher-income students are probably less likely to be willing to accept a budgeted place in a less prestigious program (such as engineering) and would opt to pay to enter a more prestigious program or a more prestigious university. Further, as our engineering student survey suggests, many students in urban areas (few of whom are from lower-income families) have parents with at least some higher education (see Chapter 6).

Data are available for the distribution of students by "per member family income" as a basis for an estimate of the distribution of state subsidies among students coming from lower and higher social class backgrounds. Another basis for such an estimate is the average cost of university education in Russia (see Chapter 4). The third basis is estimates of average fees paid by students from different family-income backgrounds to attend public universities.

The estimates in Table 8.7 show that the average subsidy per student declines as student family income rises. This is consistent with our estimates in Brazil. In the Russian case, we assumed that the cost per student in the universities attended by higher-income students is somewhat higher—that is, we assume that they are more likely to attend universities in the main cities and to attend an elite institution. Furthermore, unlike our Brazil data, where we had to assume that higher social class students pay the same amount in fees

TABLE 8.7 Russia: Income distribution, distribution of students by income group, and distribution of government higher education subsidies by income group, 2010

Reported per-member family monthly income (rubles)	Percentage of population in income group	Percentage of students in income group	Average subsidy per student in income group (thousand rubles)	Percentage of total government HE subsidy going to each income group
< 5000	23	14	113	15.3
5,001–10,000	45	26	111	27.8
10,001–15,000	19	17	108	17.7
15,001–25,000	9	18	92.5	16.1
25,001–45,000	3	15.5	91	13.6
45,001–60,000	1	3.3	103	3.3
> 60,000	0	6.2	104	6.2

SOURCES: Data on income distribution from Russia Longitudinal Monitoring survey, RLMS-HSE, conducted by the National Research University Higher School of Economics. Data on student distribution by income group from *Monitoring of the Economics of Education, 2010.* As noted in Chapter 6, higher incomes are likely underrepresented in the RLMS-HSE survey.

as lower social class students, in Russia we have estimates from the household survey of actual fees paid by students from each income group.

In Table 8.7 and Figure 8.3, we estimate the total public subsidy going to students from each quintile of *per family member* income distribution. Overall family income distribution is reported, but we have only the distribution of students based on per family member income. The main takeaway from Table 8.7 and Figure 8.3 is that the distribution of total subsidies for the approximately 85 percent of Russian students attending public universities (nonpaying and paying) is more equal than in Brazil, even though higher-income students get a high fraction of total subsidies paid out, just as in Brazil. In Russia, students coming from families in the bottom 40 percent of the income distribution received 26 percent of the public subsidies for higher education in 2010, twice the percentage for that income group in Brazil. The fourth quintile and the next decile got less than in Brazil, but the top decile in Russia in 2010 got a somewhat higher proportion of the total than in Brazil in 2007. Students

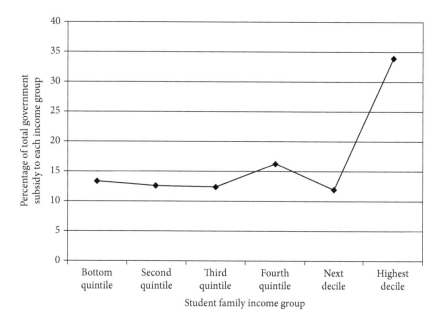

FIGURE 8.3 Russia: Distribution of total public subsidy on higher education by student's family income category, 2010

SOURCES: Table 8.7 and authors' calculation using Russian income distribution data from Russia Longitudinal Monitoring survey, RLMS-HSE, conducted by the National Research University Higher School of Economics.

from the top 20 percent in Russia got 45 percent of subsidies, only somewhat less than the 50 percent in Brazil.

Other analysts have stressed the unequal access to higher education in the Soviet Union and post-Soviet Russia (Shavit et al., 2007), but in comparison to the other BRICS, not only is access more equal, but so is how much lower- and higher-income families get in the form of subsidized costs of their children attending. As we have argued, this is influenced by the fact that so many young Russians go to university and that the spending on tuition increases with students' family income. We have, of course, assumed a certain degree of equality in the costs per student in the public universities attended by the poor and rich in Russia. This almost certainly underestimates the subsidy received by students from higher-income families, particularly in the last several years, when public spending on elite universities rose sharply.

The Russian case illustrates a higher education system in which initial conditions of relatively high levels of parents' education and relatively equal income distribution combined with considerable expansion of the system to produce apparently somewhat greater equality in the distribution of public resources than in the other BRICs. Further, this has taken place without the benefit of affirmative action policies, in part because under these conditions, the number of families pressing for affirmative action is relatively small. Should the Russian government begin making access to higher education more difficult by closing local institutions, the reaction from students denied service and equal access to higher education could be significant.

China

The Chinese government has made tremendous strides in terms of improving educational opportunities for disadvantaged students in the last two decades. For instance, Wu and Zhang (2010) use 1990 and 2000 census data as well as 2005 mini-census data to show that rural students (i.e., those with a rural as opposed to urban residential permit) and females were much more likely to attend and complete junior high school in 2005 than in 1990. In addition, they show that although female students were less represented in all colleges and four-year colleges in 1990 and 2000, they were essentially equally represented by 2005. Unfortunately, while Wu and Zhang (2010) also found that rural students were much less represented than urban students in college and four-year colleges in 2000, they did not have similar estimates for 2005.

To better understand the educational opportunities of students from disadvantaged backgrounds, Loyalka, Liu, and colleagues (2012) examined administrative data from 2001 to 2010 on all students who took the high school and college entrance exams in one northwest province in China. They show that while the proportion of rural students taking the college entrance exam in this province has increased over the last ten years, the proportion of rural students gaining admission into various levels of college has stayed low and relatively constant over the decade. In addition, by 2010, the percentage of rural students taking the college entrance exam was higher than the percentage of rural students gaining admissions into college, which in turn was higher than the percentage entering selective tiers of college. These phenomena were reflected in the fact that rural students performed less well than urban students on the college entrance exam, especially at higher ends of the score distribution. This is something we will discuss again in the context of affirmative action below.

Beyond the urban-rural gap, Loyalka, Liu, and colleagues (2012) also found disparities between more and less economically developed counties even within a single province. On the one hand, they found that college entrance exam attendance, as well as college and selective college admission rates, increased markedly over the last ten years for students in both poor and nonpoor counties, paralleling higher education expansion. However, even by 2010, students from poor counties were much less likely than students from nonpoor counties to attend the high school entrance exam, high schools, or elite high schools. Thus, students from poor counties were much less represented in the college entrance exam, colleges, and selective colleges. More specifically, in 2010 students in nonpoor counties were 70 percent more likely to be admitted to tier 1 and 2 colleges and 63 percent more likely to be admitted into elite institutions than students in poor counties.

Consistent with the findings of Wu and Zhang (2010), Loyalka, Liu, and colleagues (2012) show that female students have been much more equally represented in higher education over the course of the last decade. By 2010, females were overrepresented or equally represented in high school, key high school, the college entrance exam, colleges, and even selective colleges when compared to males.

We also use our 2008 random sample of college seniors from more than forty colleges in Shaanxi to look in more detail at the representation of students from different backgrounds in the Chinese four-year colleges.[11] In particular, we find that individuals in the first tier (especially those in 985 institutions) are of a somewhat higher socioeconomic background (as measured both by rural versus urban residential status as well as by an asset-based measure of socioeconomic status—see Loyalka, 2009) than those in the second tier and that both are of a lower socioeconomic background than students in the third tier. This validates the notion that students from more-advantaged families are entering better institutions (from which they may potentially earn higher returns in the long term) as well as private four-year institutions that charge high tuition fees. We also find that local urban students overall have a much greater chance of entering into university than local rural students and that lower social class and rural students are much less represented in the most selective tier and universities compared to their proportion in the cohort as a whole.

We now turn to the issue of how Chinese students from different backgrounds are subsidized across the higher education system. Chapter 4 points out that elite universities in China spend much more per student than nonelite universities and that there were even substantial differences between different levels of elite universities. What is more, the central government also tightly controls tuition list prices and related university fees across tiers. Table 4.1 shows how the two most selective university tiers charge about half the amount in tuition fees of less competitive third-tier (four-year private) institutions. However, the institutions in the fourth tier are more similar in list price to first-tier public universities. Tuition fees also vary across different provinces and different universities, and can differ across majors even within the same university.

Given the fact that elite universities have relatively low tuition prices yet spend much more per student (especially at the most elite universities), it is clear that on the whole, lower social class students receive a much smaller subsidy per student than higher social class students.[12] The gap in subsidies between higher and lower class students is also potentially increasing, given the increasingly differential spending in 2000s between elite and nonelite institutions and the fact that tuition rates have stayed the same over the last several years. Furthermore, while it is true that the Chinese government has paid considerable attention to ameliorating the economic burden of affording college for disadvantaged families by greatly increasing the amount of targeted financial assistance since 2007, the allocation of total aid does not change the overall pattern of tuition prices that students face across university tiers (Loyalka, 2009). That is, the current distribution of financial aid combined with the college fee structure maintains an implicit advantage for first-tier over lower-tier students. Students in third-tier universities also seem to bear a disproportionate burden (in terms of prices relative to their level of

SES) compared to students in other tiers.[13] At the same time, Loyalka, Wei, and Zhong (2011) further discuss how additional financial aid does not seem to have much of a direct impact on either four-year college access or dropout, even for students from economically disadvantaged backgrounds.

Tuition fees, net of financial aid, likely keep a substantial percentage of lower social class students from attending the third tier of private, four-year institutions. The substantial fees also make it such that high school seniors from disadvantaged backgrounds have to score much higher on the college entrance exam in order to qualify for a four-year university that they can afford. This is indicated by the fact that higher socioeconomic background and urban students within our Shaanxi sample are more likely to attend local third-tier (private) institutions than lower socioeconomic background and rural students even after controlling for college entrance exam scores. Furthermore, because exam scores are correlated with socioeconomic background, lower social class and rural students probably score more within the third-tier range (proportionally) than higher social class and urban students.

In addition, unequal spending per college student across more and less economically developed provinces, combined with other important differences between provinces (including the fact that four-year and selective college quotas are allocated more to economically developed provinces, something we discuss further below), further affect the degree to which students from different backgrounds are subsidized across the higher education system. For example, because high social class students are likely to be in Beijing, Shanghai, or developed coastal provinces and attend more-elite, high-cost institutions than students from the interior of China, the public subsidies for high social class students will be higher than low social class students even in non-elite (public) institutions. This is only partially offset by the fact that students from more economically developed areas have to pay higher tuition rates on average than students from less economically developed areas.

Do Affirmative Action Policies in Higher Education Work?

A policy used in many countries to equalize opportunity in higher education is to reserve places for "disadvantaged" groups. In the Soviet Union and other countries under communist governments, youths from working-class and peasant families officially received additional points on university entrance tests to increase the likelihood that they could gain admission. In China affirmative action policies have also revolved mostly around adding bonus points to the high school and college entrance exams and are often determined by each provincial government. Some provinces, such as Ningxia, Xinjiang, and Inner Mongolia, provide fairly significant college entrance exam bonuses for students from poor areas or from minority ethnic backgrounds. However, a number of provinces have few significant bonuses that could be widely applied to the population of economically disadvantaged students. In India quotas in public jobs and universities for the lowest castes in Indian society (scheduled castes and tribes) emerged soon after Indian independence (1947) and eventually, in the 1990s, to other backward classes and in 2005 to private institutions for both scheduled and other backward classes (Weiskopf, 2004). In 1973 the Malaysian government reserved the majority of places in public and private universities for Malays at the expense of the Chinese and Indian minorities. In the United States, beginning in the early 1970s, both public and private "white" universities—pushed by broader federal government equalization policies—voluntarily pushed for racial diversity, particularly for African Americans (Bowen and Bok, 1998). Affirmative action quotas in Brazilian public universities began in the early 2000s and have more recently been promoted in private universities through government incentives. In August 2012, after years of debate, the Brazilian Congress passed an affirmative action bill that, as in India, reserves half the places in federal universities for disadvantaged public high school graduates, with those places to be distributed among black, mixed-race, and indigenous students in proportion to the racial makeup of each state. The Supreme Court had ruled earlier in the year that it was constitutional for Brazilian universities to use racial quotas.[14]

Affirmative action programs based on quotas are highly controversial, and all have involved their nations' high courts in considering their constitutional legality. At the base of the controversy is whether nations interested in promoting "progress" should displace more "meritorious" young people from the best higher education institutions in order to promote greater diversity or to "compensate" victims of past discrimination with favored treatment in the present. To what extent should "forced" equalization penalize students who are higher achievers but not members of a disadvantaged group?

There are other critiques made of these equalization programs. One is that despite their broader intent to better incorporate the highly disadvantaged into the mainstream of society, they mainly benefit only the already very advantaged of the disadvantaged—known as the "creamy layer" in India—and even that the benefited group comes from a higher socioeconomic background than the displaced group. Another argument is that those from the disadvantaged group who are admitted into universities under affirmative action are "fish out of water." They do poorly, are less likely to succeed, and may even end up doing worse than if they had not been given extra "points" for their disadvantage.

Because the admission requirements in terms of scores in the prequalifying examinations and ranks in the entrance examination are relaxed a little bit for the disadvantaged students compared to the nondisadvantaged groups, critics also raise the issue of whether it is good to trade off merit for equity.

We review affirmative action programs in the two BRICs, India and Brazil, that have programs based on quotas (and in Brazil, subsidies to private universities to take disadvantaged students). We have seen that access to higher education in Russia is broadly available even to lower social class groups, in part because of the high proportion of youths who attend universities and in part because of Soviet policies of greatly equalizing the quality of primary and secondary education, which despite some changes after 1991, still retains many of the aspects of the earlier era. Perhaps for that reason, there is less pressure for affirmative action in Russia, although very low social class groups are clearly disadvantaged in accessing higher education. In China there are not as sharp divisions in access as in India and Brazil. Yet because of similarly restricted access to four-year universities as in India and Brazil, because upper secondary enrollments are regulated by policy makers to be roughly equal in academic and vocational high school tracks, because academic high school is (as opposed to vocational high school) dedicated to preparing students for college, and because access to academic high schools is unequal across urban-rural divisions and across social classes (Wu and Zhang, 2010), higher social class urban students from richer provinces continue to be highly over-represented in universities. Until now, China has been able to avoid greater equalization, perhaps because of the promise of continued rapid expansion of places and a rapidly declining youth population. Within the next ten years, the Chinese project that almost 40 percent of youths will have places in higher education, and 24 percent in four-year universities.

India

As noted, India has a long history of affirmative action policies in university access (and the job market) for the lowest castes in Indian society. More recently, in the early 1990s, under considerable political pressure and devolution of major control of higher education to the state governments (Weiskopf, 2004; Carnoy and Dossani, 2012), quotas for other backward classes were instituted, bringing the total quota for affirmative action students up to 50 percent in both public and private colleges and universities (22 percent for scheduled cases and tribes, 27 percent for OBCs). The quota also applies to faculty hiring in public institutions.

Students admitted under the quota who score lower on entrance tests (much lower for scheduled castes and somewhat lower for OBCs), along with high-scoring students, are awarded low-fee places (places that the government defines as qualifying for state government-set minimum fees, even in private colleges), and the disadvantaged students end up paying relatively low fees. Both government and private colleges are required to admit a certain percentage of "designated" students from lower castes based on their rank (within each caste category). These students get a fee subsidy, ranging from 50 to 100 percent, depending on the designated category. The fee subsidy takes the form of a lower fee, a fee waiver, or a direct payment to the college by the government under the fee-reimbursement scheme in some states. As noted earlier in this chapter, our survey of students in their final-year studies in engineering and computer sciences indicates that many of these backward-caste students would not have attended engineering colleges had it not been for affirmative action and the policies of the state governments to subsidize these students' tuition. What happens to the less than highest scoring Brahmins who want to attend engineering institutions? They end up attending private colleges more than they would have otherwise and paying much more tuition if they cannot get into a competitive private unaided college through a government-subsidized place.

Our survey results can speak to only one critique of affirmative action, namely, whether backward-caste students in their final year of engineering studies get significantly lower-income job offers than nonaffirmative action students. This is not the case in our sample. However, when it comes to expected income for students who have not yet gotten a job, income *expectations* are higher as reported family income increases.

There are other empirical studies that focus directly on the effects of affirmative action as outlined above. Bertrand, Hanna, and Mullainathan (2010) used a regression discontinuity analysis for a census of all applicants to engineering colleges in 1996 in one Indian state to estimate whether affirmative action actually admitted lower social class students, and took a follow-up sample of those applicants eight to ten years later to test whether students admitted just above the examination cut line in each caste designation did better economically than those who scored just below the cut line. They surveyed both the applicant and his or her parents to gauge life outcomes, including income and occupation, job satisfaction, social networks, and caste identity. In terms of admissions, they found that

> [C]ontrary to the arguments of some critics, caste-based targeting does result in the targeting of individuals who are more economically disadvantaged. For example, under a reasonable set of assumptions, the parental income among upper-caste students displaced by the affirmative action policy is Rs 14,088, compared to Rs 8,340 among the displacing lower-caste students. Similarly, 41% of displaced students come from a household in which the head holds at least a master's degree, compared to only 14% of displacing students. Fifty-nine percent of displaced students attended an English private school, compared to only 35% of displacing students. (Bertrand, Hanna, and Mullainathan, 2010: 3)

Do scheduled and backward-caste engineering students who are admitted with lower test scores perform worse in life than students admitted into unreserved slots? Bertrand, Hanna, and Mullainathan find that attending engineering college raises salaries for lower-caste students by 40 to 70 percent over those who did not attend—the same rate of return as for upper-caste students. However, the returns to lower-caste students are driven by higher returns for those lower-caste students from higher socioeconomic backgrounds, a result that coincides with the analysis of expected earnings in our sample of final-year engineering students. Further, Bertrand, Hanna, and Mullainathan show that attending engineering college for the upper-caste students "displaced" by affirmative action raises their income by Rs. 5,000 more than it increases the monthly income of the (displacing) lower-caste members. Thus, although there is no "mismatch" for lower-caste members in attending engineering college (they increase their earnings by as much in relative terms as higher-caste engineering students), they do not gain as much as would displaced upper-caste students.

Yet the question is whether upper-caste students are truly displaced by affirmative action from an engineering education or are rather just made to pay higher fees in a private college because they are moved back in the admissions queue. If the latter, then we would need to know how much their earnings are decreased by this move in the queue. The results from our survey suggest that there is a future earnings penalty for not attending a government college, but, as noted, students belonging to higher social class and/or with higher entrance test scores earn significantly more no matter which type of college they attend.

Bagde, Epple, and Reddy (2010) also examine the argument that admitting students under affirmative action creates a "mismatch" between the capacity of the quota students to do academic work and the difficulty of the institution (and the competition from the other students). They study a sample of 214 engineering colleges of different quality levels in one Indian state and find that affirmative action increases attendance for members of disadvantaged castes, that affirmative action improves priority in college selection for the disadvantaged castes, and, in turn, that improved access to institutions with, on average, higher-scoring students increases achievement for students from disadvantaged castes. In a simulation of the effect of affirmative action on the first-year test score rank in theory subjects of various caste groups, they show that the predicted difference for lowest-caste groups is largest and that the effect declines with increases in entry rank of students in each caste group. Thus, students at the lowest end of entry rank benefit most from affirmative action. At the same time, they find students who are not eligible for affirmative action suffer an achievement loss because of affirmative action.

A different perspective is reflected in Kochar's study (2010) of three cohorts of students in one engineering college in India. Kochar focused on peer effects. By looking across programs of study within the same college, she estimated the impact of greater diversity of entrance exam scores on the mean score of different caste groups of students in the program. Her study suggests that "all students are adversely affected by the variance of student ability within a classroom. Students differ, however, in their response to mean (initial) ability, with students at the top and bottom of the ability distribution within a classroom being most adversely affected by the affirmative action policy. As a consequence, the benchmark case of a pure meritocracy, without any quotas, would improve learning for *all* castes, including scheduled castes and tribes" (Kochar, 2010: 6).

If taken as all valid in their results, these Indian studies show that affirmative action improves outcomes for members of lower castes by greatly increasing their access to higher education institutions and to higher-ranking institutions than they would otherwise attend were they to go to college. There are also negative impacts of affirmative action on those higher-scoring, higher-caste students displaced by affirmative action quotas. In addition, there may be a negative impact of increasing diversity on students within institutions. How one views these tradeoffs depends largely on the weight given to equity concerns versus economic efficiency. If reducing differences among traditionally highly stratified groups in society has a high value, then the negative impacts are a necessary price to pay in order to achieve greater social coherence, which, in turn, may have positive effects on economic growth in the longer run.

Brazil

Beginning in the early 2000s, a number of public universities implemented various versions of racial quotas to admit black and indigenous students under more favorable conditions. By the end of 2004, fourteen state and federal universities already had racial quotas in operation (dos Santos, 2005). According to *the Chronicle of Higher Education* (Downie and Lloyd, 2010), by 2010, 150 institutions had adopted affirmative action programs that included race-based quotas as well as social class quotas (based on whether students attended public high schools). A recent study by the Universidade do Estado do Rio de Janeiro found that 70 percent of Brazil's public universities—both federal and state—have adopted some form of affirmative action (Smith, 2010).

These affirmative action programs vary somewhat from university to university, but they all have the characteristic of developing separate ranking lists based on *vestibular*[15] results for different categories of candidates, although not all affirmative-action-qualified candidates necessarily place themselves into the affirmative action competition.

Further, in 2005 the Lula government began a scholarship program at private institutions called the University for All Program, or *ProUni,* in which private universities and professional schools accepting Afro-Brazilians and students from low-income families get tax breaks.

All of these affirmative action programs are currently voluntary on the part of HEIs. But in 2008 a bill passed the lower house of the Brazilian Congress that would reserve 50 percent of all new places in Brazil's fifty federal higher education institutions for black, mixed-race, and indigenous students who attend public primary and secondary schools. In August 2012 the Brazilian Senate also passed the bill, and it will become law for the 2013 academic year. The law allocates these reserved places by the percentage of the population reported in each minority group in each state's federal university. For example, if 30 percent of the population of a state identifies itself as black or mulatto, 30 percent of the places would be allocated in that state's federal institutions to black/mulatto students who had attended public secondary schools. The law will have a major effect on admission policies into the country's leading HEIs, even if they already have affirmative action admissions in place, and would set a precedent for all publicly financed higher education institutions.

There have been several studies that have evaluated the impact of Brazil's affirmative action policies, both on admissions and on the college performance of students admitted under affirmative action programs. In aggregate, Table 8.5 shows that students coming from the bottom 40 percent of income families increased their share of students attending public higher education institutions from 7.3 percent in 2002 to 12.6 percent in 2007. We don't know whether this is the effect of affirmative action policies. However, more detailed studies do suggest that affirmative action policies have had a significant impact on college attendance of black students. In a series of papers that research the impact of quotas on university admissions in one Brazilian university that adopted an affirmative action policy early on, Andrew Francis and Maria Tannuri-Pianto show that at the Federal University of Brasilia (UFB),[16] racial quotas did, indeed, raise the proportion of *pardos* (brown-skinned) and *pretos* (black-skinned) applicants admitted, and that despite their lower entrance examination scores, affirmative action admits had only slightly lower academic performance in their university studies (Francis and Tannuri-Pianto, 2010a, 2010b, 2010c). Sixty percent of the "displacing" (those who would not have been admitted without affirmative action but were admitted) were *pardos* and 36 percent *pretos*. Of the "displaced" (those who would have been admitted but were not), 53 percent were whites and 43 percent *pardos*. The displacing students also tended to come from lower-income, less-educated families than the displaced (Francis and Tannuri Pianto, 2010a, Table 2). Unlike Ferman and Assunção (2005), who found that black students residing in states with a university adopting racial quotas were likely to score lower on entrance tests and that this was evidence of decreased effort due to quotas, Francis and Tannuri-Pianto suggest that affirmative action at UFB may have increased effort (at least among black secondary students in one state, the Distrito Federal). They also suggest that using quotas for public secondary school students would raise socioeconomic diversity more than do racial quotas and that quotas for low-income students would raise socioeconomic diversity even more.

It is not surprising that racial quotas increase the proportion of targeted students (blacks and lower social class students, regardless of race, depending on the particular university's objective). Also as would be expected, Mulholland (2005) reported that the distribution of affirmative action admits across programs of study is somewhat skewed toward humanities and social sciences and away from engineering and medicine. In addition, he argues that the University of Brasilia has a particularly strict system of checking the validity of affirmative action applications (see endnote 16), but in other universities not using this audit process (again, not surprisingly), there has been considerable abuse of self-identification. The abuse of quotas for low-income students could be even greater because monitoring family income reporting is more difficult than monitoring racial identity.

Brief Conclusions

The major expansion of higher education in all the BRIC countries has contributed to higher educational attainment and greatly increased the supply of university graduates, including engineering and computer science graduates. In theory, this should have had a positive impact on reducing income inequality and increased educational and economic mobility for lower social class students.

Several counterforces have worked against such a tendency to equalize opportunities and incomes, such as rising rates of return for higher education, as in China, driven by rapid economic growth, and the increase in spending by government on elite universities relative to mass universities. Both these factors may have tended to lower the economic mobility of students from lower social class groups—even those attending universities.

On the other hand, affirmative action programs, such as those in India and Brazil, contribute to greater social mobility for lower social class groups. The arguments that affirmative action leaves students worse off and that going to a more elite institution is a "mismatch" for affirmative action students appear not to be true in either India and Brazil. Nevertheless, there are concerns that quota systems for lower-income students may have negative consequences for "displaced" students and perhaps for all students with large numbers of disadvantaged students in their classes.

All these tendencies are crystallized in the degree of subsidy that government pays various social class groups to go to universities. Highest social class groups and advantaged among the disadvantaged groups get the lion's share of government subsidies to attend college and universities (Russia is an exception to some extent) because they tend to study in expensive higher education institutions and, overall, tend to pay about the same fees for their studies as students in less expensive mass institutions. Highest-income families also tend to pay a higher proportion of taxes, so they bear a higher fraction of the costs of running government, including supporting public higher education. In Brazil, however, our estimates suggest that except for the highest-income families, the balance between government subsidies and taxes paid benefits higher-income families more than lower-income families. We were not able to estimate the benefit-tax incidence differences for the other BRICs.

Thus, access to higher education is still fairly restricted to children from higher-educated families in all but Russia. In addition, the BRIC states tend to provide greater indirect support for the education of students from higher-income families because such students are likely to attend public institutions with no or low tuition and elite institutions receiving higher levels of state subsidies. But in India and Brazil, the state also supports a sizable number of disadvantaged students, offering at least some offset to bias in favor of subsidizing children from higher socioeconomic backgrounds.

9 What Do BRIC Higher Education Strategies Imply for the Future?

THE ENORMOUS EXPANSION OF HIGHER EDUCATION IN BRAZIL, Russia, India, and China has important implications for all countries in a highly interdependent world economy. Forty percent of the world's young people live in the BRICs, which means that any expansion of their educational systems generates big numbers of graduates compared to other places in the world. Just as important, the increase in BRIC higher education has created a rapidly increasing *proportion* of young people with university degrees in each of these countries. This translates into gradually increasing average levels of education in their labor forces, with all that implies for increasing domestic productivity, potential innovation, and entry into new product and service markets.

All four BRIC countries have developed a large cadre of engineers, computer scientists, and other higher educated technical personnel for their and the world's knowledge economies. Because the payoff in the BRICs for those who graduate in these fields remains high, the number of technical graduates should continue to swell. These computer scientists and engineers could be the next generation of high-tech producers and innovators, accelerating the shift in the production of high-value technology goods and services away from the developed countries. Even if that were not to happen, emigrating BRIC engineers and scientists could come to dominate the high-skilled labor forces of the developed countries. This could have a potentially positive impact in developed economy markets on output and profits but potentially negative effects on the wages of highly skilled workforces in the United States, Europe, and Japan.

We undertook our research to gain insight into these rapid changes and what they might imply for the future of the world economy. We wanted to see into the future through the lens of BRIC states transforming their education systems and their labor forces. Most studies of changing university systems focus on higher education institutions themselves, using the implicit underlying argument that autonomous universities are the main source and shapers of changes in the system. We began this study by challenging that traditional institutional approach to analyzing higher education. We don't deny that measuring higher educational change requires observing universities and colleges as institutions as well as analyzing global institutional culture. However, in the BRIC countries the role of the state is key to understanding higher educational change. University autonomy varies from country to country, and the lead institutions in all four societies are public, highly dependent on government funding, and tightly bound to the political system. The nonelite institutions, whether public or private, are subjected to direct interventions from policy makers. BRIC states often directly or indirectly steer them in one direction or another, depending on shifting political considerations.

Thus, we proposed a different starting point for understanding change in BRIC higher education systems. We put the national state in each BRIC country at the center of a confluence of forces and analyzed how the state shaped the university system in response to the various economic and political pressures on the state itself. In this approach BRIC higher education systems are a reflection of historical, economic, and political forces as filtered through the political prism of their national states. We were interested in the answers to five major questions:

1. What were the forces driving the BRIC states to expand their higher education systems in the ways they have, and how did they respond to those forces to shape the expansion?

2. How effectively have BRIC states resolved the issue of raising university quality while pursuing other economic/political goals of expanding access to higher education and developing greater social class equity in access?

3. What is the quality of computer science and electrical engineering education and graduates in the BRIC countries compared to the United States and other developed economies?

4. What is the revealed capacity of each of these states to transform their universities into twenty-first-century institutions that combine research, social inclusion, high-quality teaching, and the creation of innovative, highly skilled students for the new workforce?

5. What are the policy implications of our findings concerning the future role of the BRIC economies as centers of innovation and production in the global knowledge economy?

Forces Driving State Policies and State Responses to Those Forces

Forces Behind the Expansion

This study suggests that higher education expansion in the BRICs was a response to many forces. Major among them were the rising private economic payoffs for investing in university education—influenced in turn by the opening up of all four BRIC economies to world market forces in the 1980s and 1990s—and the increasing number of secondary school graduates as pre-tertiary education systems in these countries expanded. In turn, the expansion of the pre-tertiary school system—which took place in Russia several decades ago, in China and Brazil in the 1980s and 1990s, respectively, and even more recently in India—also must be ascribed partly to the demand in labor markets for higher skilled labor, particularly in Russia and China, but also in the two-decades-old liberalized Indian and Brazilian economies.

Expansion of enrollment at successive levels of education is therefore consistent with the state's assessment of economic systems' "needs" for increasingly skilled workers. A good case can be made that the rapid shift in the past two decades to a knowledge economy—driven by the information-communications technology revolution, the globalization of the financial sector, and the lowering of barriers to free trade and increasing international movements of highly skilled labor in the 1980s and 1990s—pushed this demand up into the skills associated with university education (Castells, 1997).

By expanding higher education (especially in the face of high rates of return for university graduates), BRIC states have sought to promote economic development—particularly economic development based on a highly trained professional workforce—and to gain increased political legitimacy indirectly through showing their commitment to high-tech, innovative economic growth through the rapid increase in the number of university graduates, and, particularly in China and India, to the rapid increase of graduates in technical fields of study.

Even were all these higher educated graduates not viewed as necessary fuel for economic development, we argued that BRIC states would be under pressure to invest in universities because families perceive higher education for their children as a valuable commodity, socially as well as economically. This perception turns into active demand for access to higher education when more youths begin completing secondary school. Hence, in addition to an indirect impact on legitimacy through the public perception of university expansion's role in knowledge-intensive economic growth, expanding the university system likely contributes directly to the legitimacy of the state as more families see their children gaining access to higher education. The state acts in its own political interest to raise and spend public monies on increased enrollment. The timing of developed country states' expanding higher education access—in the United States after World War II with the G.I. Bill and in Europe with the growth of spending on universities after the 1960s' student unrest—is consistent with the direct legitimacy argument.

We also suggested that legitimacy based on higher education investment acquires a global dimension. States tend to adopt notions of what it means to be a modern nation (Meyer, Ramirez, and Soysal, 1992), and, in today's world, the definition of a modern nation-state includes having a high proportion of youths enrolled in secondary school and a growing proportion completing university (World Bank, 2000; OECD, 2008), of which a significant part should be in science and technology fields. In addition, some of those universities should be of comparable quality to the "best" in the world, organized around eminent, highly productive researchers and large numbers of graduate students.

Because of the short period of time involved, it is impossible to measure empirically whether university expansion in the BRICs has actually contributed to the political legitimacy of BRIC states in the past twenty years. All four nations have been characterized by political stability and generally strong economic growth as well as rapid expansion of their higher education systems. The state's perceived success in promoting economic growth certainly played an important role in this stability and even contributed to the popularity of government policies in Brazil, probably in China, and maybe in Russia until recently. But we are not able to assess whether the public views the great increase of university graduates by the state as an important factor in helping spur economic growth. Further, we are unable to measure whether the continued expansion of higher education in the BRICs has had any direct impact on government's popularity. Yet our student interviews suggest that BRIC governments are probably succeeding in absorbing the demand for more education and thus satisfying students and their families in their quest for social mobility, even if that social mobility for many of them may be quite limited. Interviews with employers suggest a more varied level of satisfaction with the technical graduates they hire (Blom and Saeki, 2011), but the fact that there are so many more graduates to select from probably contributes positively to the way that employers view state policies.

How States Shaped Their Higher Education Systems in Response to These Forces

This study has shown that BRIC states expanded their university systems in many different ways, yet there are certain commonalities. The BRICs are low- and middle-income countries, and in all of them higher education is relatively expensive compared to lower levels of schooling. Even while seeking political legitimacy through greatly increasing university enrollment, BRIC states—because of the high and rising private payoff for higher education and the high demand for university places created by more secondary school graduates—could and did shift much of the cost of the expansion to students and their families. In the cases of India, Russia, and Brazil, they shifted costs especially to students wanting to prepare for perceived high-payoff occupations, such as those we focus on in this study—engineering and computer science—and business, economics, and medicine. Although public universities are still completely or almost "tuition free" for many students in Russia, Brazil, and India, many of the new students enrolling in higher education there have had to pay tuition either in public (Russia) or private (Brazil and India) universities and colleges. Even in China, where a significant fraction of the expansion was financed by tuition covering part of the costs of education in public universities, the government in recent years has gradually allowed the expansion of fully tuition-dependent private universities to absorb some of the new enrollment.

In addition to making families bear a significant share of the costs of higher education expansion, three of the BRIC states—Brazil, China, and India—absorbed a high fraction of the increased demand for university places in relatively low-cost mass institutions. These were increasingly differentiated in terms of cost per student and function (particularly research and selectivity) from *elite* higher education institutions. Increasing differentiation simultaneously lowered the average cost per student—especially the public cost per student—as enrollment grew and simultaneously served to legitimate the state at home (expanded mass higher education) and globally (raising the quality of a small number of internationally visible institutions). In China and Russia, the elites became part of the state's effort to create "world-class" universities—institutions that receive much more public funding per student than the "mass" higher education institutions absorbing the vast majority of college enrollment. In Brazil and India, there was less focus on developing "world-class" institutions. Nevertheless, the Indian government put most of the new public money invested into increasing the number of elite engineering and business schools, and the Brazilian government put renewed emphasis on expanding graduate education and sending more graduate students abroad for training, particularly in science and technology, as well as increasing research funding for elite universities.

The strategy was very different from that followed in the United States' university enrollment growth in the 1950s and 1960s (see, for example, Douglass, 2000), the European expansion of the 1960s and 1970s, and even the Japanese expansion after the late 1960s.[1] In those earlier expansions, states picked up most if not all of the cost of higher education through general taxation. This may have been caused by the ideological context of the times, particularly in Europe. Along with old-age pensions, support for the unemployed, general education, and (in all but the United States) health care coverage, public university education was generally viewed as an important element in the basket of social investments made by developed states. A strategy of expanding higher education at public expense may also have been aided by the willingness of income earners in Europe and the United States to pay higher taxes then than now, providing their governments with the revenues needed for expanding university systems without charging tuition in public universities or relying on private universities to pick up the slack.

Not one of the BRICs financed its recent expansion of higher education in that way. Again, the ideological context—the push by the United States, other individual countries, and the World Bank to convince developing-country governments to reduce public spending and to "privatize" higher education—has played a role in the new strategy. However, it is likely that global economic change raising the payoff for higher education (see Chapter 3) and the pressure on BRIC states to prepare their youths to participate in the high-tech knowledge economy pushed them to expand higher education more rapidly than they could "afford"—at least in terms of providing higher education mainly at government expense. The "richest" of the BRIC countries—Brazil and Russia—had considerably lower gross domestic product (GDP) per capita in PPP dollars (about PPP $6,000) in the late 1990s, when their university enrollment were expanding rapidly, than developed countries such as France, Japan, or the United Kingdom in the late 1970s, when their systems were expanding (about PPP $9,000). The lowest-income BRIC countries are China and India, which had GDP per capita of less than PPP $4,000 in the mid-1990s, although urban GDP per capita is much higher in both countries. It is mainly the urban populations that attend universities, especially in India.

The BRIC states either did not wish to increase income taxes or they had a difficult time raising large amounts of public revenue through direct taxation to expand their public higher education (OECD, 2008). Thus, in addition to a different ideological context today than forty to fifty years ago, a much weaker capacity of the state to finance education through general revenues (this was probably also true in post–World War II Japan), and perhaps a weaker capacity to organize the delivery of higher education through the state bureaucracy help explain why the BRICs turned to "user taxes" in China and Russia, and why Brazil and India turned to the private sector to provide much of the increased access to universities and colleges. Weaker financial capacity could also explain why all the BRICs limited the resources they devote to increasing higher educational quality for a small minority of students.

On the other hand, it is possible that high rates of return to university education—especially certain programs of university study—provided an "opportunity" for BRIC states to charge user taxes (tuition) for higher education services and that this was a sensible form of collecting revenues even by "strong" states such as China and Russia, which may have had greater difficulty doing it in more indirect ways. Again, the new ideological context of the 1990s, in which it was not considered heresy to charge tuition fees in universities, probably helped, but there were also sound economic efficiency and equity arguments for user taxes. The strategy of allowing a rapid increase in private higher education in Brazil and India is more suggestive of a "weak state" argument, and we explore this notion further below.

Improving Quality and Increasing Enrollment: Are Some Strategies Better Than Others?

Quality Improvement Strategies in the Face of Increasing Demand for Higher Education

The efforts to improve university quality in the BRICs while rapidly expanding higher education enrollment provide important examples of how effective these states are in reaching economic development and legitimacy goals. The Chinese and Russian states have moved aggressively to create groups of universities that are intended to be "world class." These universities have been funded at increasingly higher levels per student and given research monies earmarked for raising faculty publication rates. The hope in both China and Russia is that by raising the quality of these "elite" institutions, other universities will also improve. In Russia, the designated "elite" research universities have been given the responsibility to develop curriculum standards for the university system as a whole. Thus, the Russian and Chinese states are giving this relatively small group of universities considerable incentives to raise quality.

Russia also increased the resources per student going to mass universities until 2009, in part because the number of budgeted places in these universities stopped growing a half a decade ago while the overall budget continued to increase. But despite (perhaps because of) these increases in resources, the incentives to improve quality in mass institutions in Russia are very indirect, vaguely related to the threat of future closings. The main preoccupation of most nonelite institutions is to find more students, particularly paying students, in an economy marked by a declining youth population. In China enrollment in "mass" universities has risen astronomically, and the real spending per student going to those institutions is not rising. In some of those provincial universities, the faculty is encouraged to do research, but as we document in Chapter 5, the incentives in most nonelite institutions to improve quality are not strong. Instead, administrators in such institutions are necessarily more motivated to increase enrollment (on which their budgets depend) and to raise "extra" revenues by contracting with local public and private enterprises for various services, such as special evening courses and training sessions.

India and Brazil have followed a different path to improve quality from China or Russia. India increased the number of elite institutions (which are all small in scale), particularly in technical fields and economics/management, but, based on the limited data we have, India does not appear to have significantly increased resources per student (including R&D spending) in these elite institutions. Brazil expanded undergraduate (and graduate) enrollment in its research universities but much more slowly than overall enrollment expansion. However, unlike India, Brazil is gradually increasing real spending per student in elite institutions. In addition, Brazil has much higher R&D spending per student than India and is continuing to invest in graduate education to produce the Ph.D.s needed to staff expanding universities at all levels. This suggests that Brazil is attempting to build quality through beefing up its graduate programs and training higher-quality faculty, whereas India is relying mostly on student selectiveness of these institutions to ensure quality, which means keeping the number of graduates small, even after the state doubles elite enrollment over the next few years.

Mass institutions in India and Brazil are of low quality, mostly private, concerned mainly with accumulating surplus and keeping costs low. Mass institutions in India are in an especially disadvantaged position to improve quality because of the relatively small number of Ph.D.s available to teach in mass institutions. The supply of Ph.D.s relative to undergraduate students is greater in Brazil, but private mass institutions hire relatively few of them.

The Brazilian state is promoting measurement of institutional and program "quality" as an indirect way of making all institutions "accountable" to the public. The hope is that if the public has more information about student achievement levels and even the "value added" of various programs of study in each university, it will exert pressure on both public and private higher education institutions to improve in order to keep attracting students. The combination of increasing the minimum degree levels required of professors in all higher education institutions and the measurement of outcomes is intended to improve quality throughout the system. It may turn out be an effective strategy, but there is no hard evidence from elsewhere that such a strategy has worked at lower levels of schooling without strong enforcement (see, for example, OECD, 2003, for an evaluation of Chile's similar strategies to improve primary and secondary education, and Carnoy and Loeb, 2002, for the possible effects of accountability systems on student performance in the United States).

All four BRIC states are therefore responding in their own particular ways to improving higher educational quality. At the same time, they are all expanding enrollment, mainly in mass institutions that have little incentive to invest in better faculty and other measures to raise institutional value added. We argue in Chapters 4 and 5 that these approaches to higher educational quality are partly shaped by the historical political conditions in each country but also by "global" conceptions of university excellence. In the case of China and Russia's focus on developing "world-class" universities, the approaches are shaped by both a particular interpretation of how to achieve rapid economic growth (invest heavily in an elite cadre of graduates) and global legitimacy as a "developed nation" (produce highly ranked universities). More indirectly, the approach the Indian government has taken reflects a similar reliance on the notion that a relatively few elite cadres are crucial to future economic development and that expanding Indian Institutes of Technology and National Institutes of Technology, with their international prestige, expands India's "star power" on the world stage. Of the BRICs, Brazil is the most focused on raising higher education quality system-wide, but its approach is also influenced by an external—in this case, more "market"-oriented competition—concept of how to achieve higher quality. Publishing the average test scores of university students by program as a form of accountability to induce programs to raise quality is a favored technique of the Anglo-Saxon countries and the OECD's expanding testing program. Brazil is even moving to a "value-added" approach (now being promoted worldwide as an "advanced" measure of educational output) to testing the quality of higher education programs. The effort is one more example of the state seeking legitimacy—in this case, through overt, widely publicized pressures to increase institutional quality—yet with little or no evidence that simply displaying test score data has the desired effect.

Balancing Equity with Quality Improvement

Our study suggests that among the BRICs, the Russian state is probably under the least pressure to be concerned about equity in its higher education system, for two important reasons: first, during the Soviet era, Russia implemented affirmative action policies (well before this was tried in any other country) in higher education, promoting at least some access to the children of workers and peasants; and second, because Russian higher education has expanded so much that today it is widely accessible to almost all socioeconomic groups. Even so, we showed that public funding going to the highest-income university students is a high proportion of total public funding for universities. Currently, the Russian state does not have affirmative action on its agenda, rather focusing on reinforcing elite universities and the problem of distributing reductions in student places among second-tier institutions as the overall student population declines.

Similarly, China's state is not engaged in the equity of access issue in any meaningful way, also focusing heavily on producing world-class universities to compete quality-wise in the global higher education rankings race. The sharp and growing inequalities in higher education (and elite institutional) access between different social classes in China exacerbates concerns about income inequality, political legitimacy, and possibly longer-term growth (the latter even if China's efforts to create high-ranking research universities were to pan out). Some of the pressure on Chinese policy makers to increase access to higher education will be ameliorated over time by the decreasing size of its college eligible population. Furthermore, while the public has clearly expressed dissatisfaction with policies that limit the access of students from disadvantaged regions to college and elite institutions, it seems placated for the time being by the use of merit-based high school and college entrance examinations. These give the appearance of a "fair" chance at higher levels of education. However, over time the high and increasing degree of sorting of students of lower social classes away from universities and selective institutions all along the pathway to college in pre-tertiary education will likely continue. Even the estimated 40 percent of the age cohort projected to matriculate higher education by 2020 is to be stratified among institutions of greatly varying quality and function (e.g., about 45 percent of these enrollees will be in two- to three-year short-cycle courses, implying that only 24 percent of the age cohort is projected to attend bachelor's degree programs). Thus, the lack of attention to unequal access to universities in general and four-year and first-tier universities in particular will likely complicate efforts to reduce social inequality and discontent.

Brazil and India's states are more traditional democracies, and this subjects them to considerable pressure to provide more equity in access to universities and colleges for the high proportion of the population that is disadvantaged economically and academically. Such pressure may translate into potential difficulties for the Brazilian and Indian states in increasing higher educational quality, even in a small number of institutions. They are also hampered by low-quality pre-tertiary education, which results in relatively low achievement levels even for the limited group of young people that gets access to bachelor's degree programs. Brazil and India will need to devote considerable resources and energy to improving pre-tertiary education in tandem with expanding higher education, particularly if they hope to give a higher proportion of low-income students access to reasonable quality universities and colleges.

The very nature of university selection processes, as we show in Chapter 6, makes it likely that in all but Russia, where most college-age young people attend university, a high proportion of university students comes from higher-educated and higher-income families. India has passed strong affirmative action legislation that applies to all colleges and universities, private and public, in which 50 percent of all places are reserved for disadvantaged castes (see Chapter 8). Brazil recently put into law a blanket affirmative action policy that should expand access for black, mixed-race, and indigenous students to the country's federal (public) universities, which are among its most elite institutions. The government has also implemented a financial incentive program for private universities to admit, with reduced tuition, students from disadvantaged backgrounds.

In the short run, India and Brazil may suffer in their higher education quality improvement efforts as they try to resolve the equity of access issue, even though there is little evidence that affirmative action is reducing the overall quality of university output in those two countries. As noted above and in Chapters 6 and 7, a critical issue is that, on average, even high social class students in India and Brazil are not achieving at high levels. Nevertheless, in the longer run and from a macro-political standpoint, the economic development payoff for making university education more accessible to bright youths from lower-income families may be great. Although we do not have any direct evidence for Brazil and India, it is possible, even probable, that affirmative action policies, which contribute to greater and more equitable access to high-payoff higher education, along with other policies, such as conditional cash transfers (in Brazil), contribute to reducing income inequality (World Bank, 2006).

Focusing on equity now could also have major positive implications for long-term political stability. Like the Brazilian state, the Indian state is highly sensitive, in the context of an unequal society and broader democratic political pressures, to issues of access to higher education for socially disadvantaged groups. Increased access for the disadvantaged has important implications for political stability; in that context, India and Brazil's higher education strategies may have a positive impact on state legitimacy that is lacking in China, which is largely ignoring issues of unequal access to universities.

The Quality of Engineering and Computer Science Graduates

What do the alternative strategies for improving higher education imply for the quality of the BRICs' university and college graduates? The total number of first-degree engineering graduates just in China (four-year) and India (four-year) in 2009 was much larger—760,000 and 350,000–400,000, respectively—than the almost 500,000 engineering graduates in the developed countries. When we add the 130,000 engineering graduates in Russia and 50,000 more in Brazil, the total output of engineers in the BRICs is two-and-a-half times as much as in the developed countries as a whole. However, a high percentage of these graduates is not trained to the same level as engineers in the United States, Europe, or Japan.

Nevertheless, given the resources and attention the BRIC governments have lavished on their elite institutions in recent years, we speculate that by their very selectivity and the quality of their faculty, the top half of engineering graduates from the BRICs' elite universities are probably as well prepared technically as the top half of the engineering graduates in developed countries. More specifically, the close to 100,000 engineering graduates from elite programs in the BRIC countries each year are comparable to the top 50,000 engineers receiving bachelor's degrees from U.S. colleges and universities, the top 150,000 engineering first degrees annually in the European Union, and the top 50,000 engineering first degrees annually in Japan.

The large supply of qualified engineering graduates from the BRIC countries undoubtedly has a large impact on their domestic production of high-technology products. As the supply of elite engineering program graduates from the BRICs continues to grow (as it is growing, especially in India) and as nonelite engineering programs gradually increase in quality (as they seem to be in China and have the potential to in Russia), engineering graduates from the BRIC countries could also ultimately overwhelm production of and innovation in high-technology products and services in the world's developed countries. This is especially the case because the growth of engineering graduates in developed countries is low, and the potential for the growth of qualified engineering graduates in the BRIC countries is especially large as these countries continue to rapidly develop their economies and education systems.

State Capacity to Transform Education, Economy, and Society

Early on in our study, we claimed that by studying changes in higher education in the BRICs, we could gain insights into the BRIC states and, with those insights, make some judgments about the capacity of each state to "guide" the economy and society from "developing" into "developed" status. In each part of the study, we tried to show how the evolution of these higher education systems reflected actions and inactions by the state.

Increasing differentiation between "elite" and "mass" institutions varies among the BRICs but seems to reflect the capacity of the state in all four countries to deal, on the one hand, with domestic pressures for greatly increasing enrollment and, on the other, to meet perceived human capital requirements for competing effectively in a global information economy dominated by developed-country university graduates.

In our analysis in Chapter 7, we try to evaluate the degree to which the BRIC states are realizing this second goal by using a number of indirect benchmarks of higher educational quality. We came away from this exercise convinced that graduates from the elite institutions in the BRICs were relatively well prepared in engineering and computer science, although not necessarily well prepared in the more creative and entrepreneurial aspects of their skills—those that are more likely to be a feature of technical education in the better-developed-country institutions. The sheer number of these elite institutions' graduates in China suggests that this nation could potentially develop massive information technology production.

At the same time, when we analyzed how little BRIC governments spend on basic research in their higher education system as a whole compared to developed countries and how relatively few Ph.D.s teach in all but the elite technical colleges and universities (other than in Russia), and the probable low quality of many of those Ph.D.s, the picture—at least in the short to medium term—becomes less optimistic. This is especially the case when it comes to supplying local markets with a wide range of high-quality science-based products and services and creating the many new firms that would produce those products and services. Obviously, ten years from now, major transformations may have taken place. These are most likely in China, where elite students' relatively high pre-tertiary achievement, the increasing R&D resources provided by the state to a limited number of institutions, and the large numbers of graduates from these elite institutions could provide the critical mass to develop an indigenous high-tech innovation sector competitive in the global economy.

Beyond these commonalities of massive system expansion, cost shifting to students and their families, and the new focus on developing higher educational quality, we have noted that there are considerable differences in the approaches taken by each country. These differences, not surprisingly, are strongly influenced by the initial conditions in each country. The political-economic histories of each of the BRICs and the role played by higher education within those histories are very particular, as we have described in detail throughout the book. It would be unusual if these particularities did not have a major effect on current policies even in the face of common global economic conditions. One reason, for example, that India has not reacted the same way as China to expanding its higher education system is that over the past half-century, the Indian system became highly decentralized to the state/provincial level. One reason that Brazil has relatively less direct control over its higher education system is the historically important role of private institutions and, in a more recent history, the political struggle of the universities against the military regimes of the 1960s and 1970s. One reason that Russia is faced with drastically changing much of its technical higher education system is that many such institutions in the Soviet period were organized to train engineers for particular industries now in steep decline. One reason that China's higher education is relatively tightly controlled is the centralized power of the Communist Party, with its strong hierarchy and legacy of close watch over intellectual activities.

Current political conditions are also important factors in shaping differences. Brazil and India are democracies; Russia, although ostensibly a democracy, is dominated by a complex authoritarian state-capitalist regime; and China is officially a communist state that allows a large free-market sector to operate within its state-capitalist economy. A compelling argument can be made that these political conditions help explain why China and Russia are less concerned about the equity impact of their approaches to higher education expansion and quality than are Brazil and India.

There are other variables at play here as well—for example, the much greater historical inequality in Brazilian and Indian society and in the educational system than in China and Russia. However, inequality in China has increased greatly in the past twenty years, yet Chinese policy makers seem willing to ignore how China's various education policies affect students' ultimate access to higher education and how putting so much emphasis on "world-class" higher education institutions may be contributing to inequality.[2] As we show in Chapter 8 as well, despite the relatively equal access to universities in Russia, the government's financial policies still subsidize higher-income students much more than their lower-income counterparts. Yet the Russian government, if anything, is pursuing university rationalization policies that could affect lower-income university students more adversely. Were China and Russia more democratic, it would be more difficult to ignore the equity impacts of higher education policies.

What does our analysis tell us, then, about the capacity of BRIC states to develop high-quality university systems and, beyond universities, to transform their nations into innovative knowledge economies? Let's briefly summarize our conclusions for each of the BRIC countries.

China: Can the State Keep Getting It Right?

China began its current fifteen-year-old expansion with a tiny fraction (approximately 3 percent) of its age cohort in higher education. The Chinese state was able to expand the number of four-year university graduates from 380,000 in 1997 to about 2.5 million in 2009, just twelve years later. This included a jump from 175,000 to 750,000 four-year engineering graduates. Although almost all this increase was in nonelite, mass institutions of generally not very high quality, the very fact that the state could organize such an expansion with about one-third of the cost borne by families through tuition payments is an impressive feat. In addition, graduate education in China has kept pace with undergraduate enrollment. Although the ratio of engineering Ph.D. graduates to engineering four-year graduates in 2009 in China (2 percent) is lower than in Brazil (2.7 percent), much lower than in Russia (5.7 percent), and far lower than in the United States (approximately 11 percent), China is doing much better than India (less than 0.5 percent) on this score.

An important feature of China's expansion, and one possible advantage of its small university sector in 1995, is that the state decided early on (1997–1998) to invest significantly more in a limited number of universities, relegating the rest of the system to absorb the massive increase in enrollment at relatively low cost and financed much more by student tuition. Early on, then, the Chinese committed themselves to develop elite, research-oriented universities that would be competitive with developed-country institutions in producing scientific and technological innovations and graduates who would, in turn, be the next generation of intellectual and technical cadres.

This strategy suggests a high level of state capacity to imagine and invest in a future in which China is a world economic leader. However, there are elements of this strategy that are not as positive. We have already mentioned that Chinese researchers in many fields work in an intellectual culture—also inherited from the past, but sustained by the current hierarchical political and social structures—that probably dampens innovation and creativity, even in allegedly "objective" hard sciences. In Chapter 5 we argue that Chinese higher education institutions are characterized by *both* market-like incentives to perform well in sciences (especially in the Soviet-style academy of sciences and elite institutions) and nonmarket forces that allow professors to sit around and not exert much effort.

Further, China and Russia's university systems are controlled by large bureaucracies. China (but not Russia) still maintains a dual-control system in universities where the Communist Party requires parallel leadership, so two administrators are involved in running each institution, one of them from the party. Most universities are also characterized by nontransparency/cronyism, as noted in our discussion of the allocation of research funding (Shi and Yi, 2010). Spending and budgeting of public resources in higher education, including the giving of many earmarked funds from the government to universities and from universities to departments, are also very nontransparent. For example, nobody knows how the 211/985 financing—the major funding going to elite universities—is actually being spent to improve quality. Because of its governance style, China's state is also very guarded in allowing the quality of its education to be measured and allowing those data to become available to outside scrutiny. Such honest evaluations and accountability are important for improving higher education, and they are currently lacking. We know that China is recruiting high-scoring students into its best universities and spending increasing funds on faculty and research there, but without any measures of student outcomes, we cannot say whether this is improving the amount of learning that students achieve during their university years.

China has become a fairly unequal society, and the way that the higher education system growth is organized, with unequal social access to higher education institutions and considerable and possibly increasing division between elite and nonelite institutions, is probably contributing to that inequality rather than reducing it. Further, most Chinese university graduates are getting their training in (nonelite) institutions, many of questionable quality, some with declining public spending per student, artificially high graduation rates, and faculty that do little if any research. China's central and provincial policy makers have not yet taken meaningful steps to correct these weaknesses in higher education. In the long term, the implications of poor preparation and greater inequality for economic growth will probably be important. Whether the state is not aware of these downsides to the current expansion or is politically unwilling to take steps to correct them, its inaction suggests that there are potential weaknesses in a state that appears to be a powerful effective apparatus for planned change.

Russia: Inept Oligarchy or Scientific Powerhouse?
How does the centralized Russian state of the 2000s measure up to China's ability to expand and improve its university system? Despite going through a major economic downturn for much of the 1990s, Russia was able to greatly increase university enrollment with a major contribution from tuition payments in public universities for programs in high demand. This strategy relied

heavily on Russia's universities to mount these programs and recruit students. In a sense, the state got out of the way during the first part of the expansion. Yet this has changed, as the state has focused increasingly on quality improvement through consolidation and attempts at greater control of what takes place in universities themselves—especially in nonelite universities. Russia got into the quality improvement effort in higher education almost a decade later than China. The concept is the same—to select and fortify a group of elite universities to produce high-quality research and future cadres—but consolidation has been difficult, as we discuss in Chapter 5.

Russia has the advantage of a highly developed university system and a very high fraction of its young people attending higher education institutions. The state has a different set of issues from the other BRICs in that the youth population is declining and university enrollment will likely fall over the next fifteen to twenty years. Like China's central state, Russia's also has considerable control over the higher education reform process and, from that standpoint and the fact that a high fraction of its youth is already in universities, could make the kinds of changes that could produce the cadres needed for rapid economic growth in the knowledge economy. On the other hand, research productivity appears to be declining steadily over the past decade, the state invests relatively very little in university R&D, and, like China, the state is pursuing policies that, by definition, pay little attention to quality in the mass higher education institutions.

Furthermore, the Russian state, despite its legacy of centralized power, has not been particularly effective in implementing university mergers, although it has been able, partly because of the slowdown in enrollment growth, to increase sharply the resources per student going to universities. Like China, Russia inherited (and has not shed) a legacy of bureaucratic control that stifles innovation and creativity. In addition, the Russian state has developed a cronyistic model of state capitalism that rewards insiders and makes life difficult for outsiders—not a recipe for innovation-led economic growth. Similar arguments have been made for China. The picture that emerges from Russia is one of a powerful state that, on the one hand, because of history has little innovative energy to draw on from universities but, on the other, is not particularly effective in implementing the needed changes to shock the system from the outside. With all its advantages as a highly educated society and a generally more equal society with less poverty than the other BRICs, there are real questions whether the state, as now organized, has the capacity to recreate a progressive university system and a high-tech Russian economy.

Brazil and India: Will Market Energy Overcome Weak State Direction?
Brazil and India, the two democratic (and more financially and administratively decentralized) BRIC states, have structurally less power to directly control the expansion of their higher education systems. These are states that can be viewed as inherently "weaker" than the Chinese and Russian states in their capacity to control change in their universities. We therefore have to judge them more by their capacity to "steer" the system through their financial control of the central/federal universities and their capacity to incentivize and regulate the rest of the system to develop in ways that best serve the nation's economic and social development (de Moura Castro, 2011).

Brazil inherited a highly decentralized education system, but, historically, the central government was given legal responsibility for higher education. That means that it has the legal power to regulate private universities. In practice, as we showed, private higher education has successfully resisted most government control, but in the past ten years, the state has been successful in legislating some quality controls, such as faculty degree requirements and participation in a higher education evaluation system (ENADE). Even so, quality in most of the private education sector is very low. On that score, the Brazilian state has shown relatively little capacity to oversee the private provision of higher education even as enrollment in that sector exploded. However, the state has been successful in maintaining what appears to be relatively high quality in its more slowly expanding elite sector. The state has been able to mobilize more resources for graduate training and a high level of per student university R&D. It has been less successful in producing large numbers of engineers and computer scientists in part because of the poor quality of math education at lower levels of schooling. The state has been able to promote affirmative action for historically disadvantaged groups, although Brazilian higher education, along with Indian, remains highly unequal and state subsidies for higher education in Brazil go overwhelmingly to the nation's richest families. This all suggests that the Brazilian state, for all its accomplishments, gets mixed reviews for its capacity to successfully steer the expansion and improvement of the university system and, by implication, the economic development process as it moves into post-commodity dependency.

Similar to Brazil, India shares a dynamic private sector, with many dynamic entrepreneurs, but the Indian state must still play a creative role in aiding and abetting Indian development. India is a much poorer country per capita than the other BRICs, with a rapidly increasing bachelor's level of higher education enrollment. The Indian state has been weak in expanding public university enrollment in part because the control of much of the public higher education sector is with the states, not with the central government. The states, in turn, have turned expansion over to the private sector, which has focused largely on offering programs of study that yield high private returns to students and for which they are willing to pay relatively high fees. The main role of the states has been to regulate fees and, along with the central state, to legislate favored access to disadvantaged castes. These are important interventions. But at the same time, the Indian state has done little to implement quality controls besides allowing individual universities (and to a lesser degree national agencies such as the AICTE) to regulate curriculum and examinations for colleges under their jurisdiction, including the private unaided colleges. R&D spending is low; the number of Ph.D. graduates per B.A. graduate, especially in engineering, is abysmally low and probably decreasing; and spending per student is very low except in the relatively few elite institutions. Furthermore, the private colleges have little or no incentive to invest in higher quality. This all paints a pessimistic picture for the longer-term development of the Indian higher education system and for the capacity of the Indian state to steer the system toward higher quality. One path is to give much more autonomy to private colleges, hoping that they will generate the innovations needed to raise quality; the other is for the central state to take a much more aggressive role in expanding high-quality universities and colleges. Neither appears very likely in the immediate future.

Do States or Markets Develop More Innovative University Systems?

Given the contrast between China and Russia's centralized control of their higher education expansion and Brazil and India's relatively decentralized, market approach, what do the BRIC states' experiences tell us about the advantage of market-style autonomy versus strong state direction in developing more innovative higher education systems? Is state direction or market competition more likely to make universities centers of innovation and, in turn, more likely to produce higher-quality scientists and engineers? We should be able to draw insights on this issue from the contrast between, say, Brazil, with its large, financially autonomous, market-driven private higher education sector, at one extreme, and the highly directed Chinese public higher education system at the other extreme.

Before discussing this question, we need to say a few words about what we mean by a "more innovative higher education system." In Chapter 7 we discuss several components of university quality that reflect inputs into innovation (spending per student on research and development funding going to universities) and outputs (publications in scientific journals and impact of scientific publications). These are indicators of how much the state promotes innovation and how productive researchers are. We concluded that Brazil and China were both higher than Russia and India in all three of these components.

Nonetheless, there are broader measures of national innovation systems. In all such measures, the underlying definition of innovation is similar: namely, creating better products and services, finding better ways of making and delivering them, or simply creating good ideas. The INSEAD business school and the Boston Consulting Group publish separate annual Global Innovation Indices using different measurement criteria and different methodologies. The INSEAD version uses five input elements—institutions, human capital and research, infrastructure, market sophistication, and business sophistication—and two output elements—scientific and creative—to construct the index. Brazil ranks twenty-first in the INSEAD index, China, thirtieth, Russia, fifty-sixth, and India, sixty-second.[3] The BCG version of the index interviews 1,000 business executives to try to measure the "innovation friendliness" of different countries. In that index, out of 110 countries, China is twenty-first, India, forty-fourth, Russia, fifty-first, and Brazil, seventy-second.[4] The major discrepancy is in Brazil's position, and this is probably because of the emphasis in the BCG index on government's policies toward innovation, such as immigration, tax incentives, education, and intellectual property, and on the *business* outcomes of innovation.

Thus, whether a society/economy is considered "innovative" can depend on how innovativeness is measured. From these two indices, we could conclude that Brazil and China on average do not differ greatly in their innovation levels. We reached a similar conclusion in estimating the innovation components in these two university systems. It is likely that neither the more autonomous Brazilian university system nor the more directed Chinese system has a particular advantage in innovating its way toward higher levels of quality in the mass part of their systems.

In Chapter 5 we argue that most Brazilian private institutions, aside from the elite private research universities, are organized to train masses of undergraduates in a top-down, directive fashion that focuses on financial efficiency and meeting specifications. The main argument in favor of such institutions when compared to second-tier Brazilian public institutions (such as many of the state universities and the municipal institutions) is that the large, for-profit privates might be more financially efficient than the publics, mainly because in Brazil the publics are governed in part by autonomous faculties. However, none of these institutions are organized to improve quality. The state has made efforts to monitor them, but logically this would have little impact when the private mass institutions are concerned with their financial bottom line and the lower-tier publics are focused on faculty autonomy and control. The main creativity of private, for-profit institutions in Brazil is channeled into marketing their institutions to fee-paying students, including building attractive campuses in some cases, and being more flexible than public institutions in developing new programs that will attract students. Students and their families can use ENADE results to make comparisons among competing institutions, but because policy makers have not tied additional incentives to these results, institutions have little reason to reorganize themselves to get higher results.

Could China's state shape the quality of its mass public institutions more easily than Brazil could shape quality in its mass (mostly private) institutions? Possibly, although in China, too, it would be difficult to change institutional culture in universities organized to mass-produce graduates at rather low cost per student. As in Brazil, there is variation among China's public mass institutions. Some are more quality oriented than others, and some have graduate education, making it more likely that their faculty are concerned with their status in the national academy. China, much more than Brazil, could increase funding and research conditions in a high percentage of mass institutions as Chinese institutions are still mostly publicly controlled. It is doubtful that either China or Brazil will undertake this strategy in the near term. China's central state, for at least the time being, has still left such moves mainly to the provinces, as has Brazil's federal government left them to public and private universities themselves. China's central government has recently stated its intention to provide greater public financial support to local institutions. At the same time, Brazil's federal government is attempting to improve the quality of second-tier higher education by expanding enrollment in high-quality federal universities through night courses to be organized on a voluntary basis by academic departments and designed to incorporate students who would normally not qualify for entry to those departments. These night courses would be free of tuition, and so they would compete directly with second-tier private institutions and state universities. Whether the federal universities will provide higher-quality education because of their "higher-quality" teaching staffs is yet to be seen, but it is an interesting experiment in trying to improve higher educational quality.

At the elite level, Brazilian universities would seem to have an advantage in producing high-quality, innovative scientists because of the considerable autonomy of Brazilian university faculty and the considerable academic freedom and the critical thinking culture that pervade the upper reaches of the Brazilian academy. China may have an advantage in science and technology because of the sheer numbers of researchers and because of the higher levels of mathematics achievement in the high school pool, but at these elite levels, these differences may not be meaningful. Brazilian research universities have considerable research funds (as do Chinese), and their staffs have a high fraction of Ph.D.s and large numbers of selected graduate students (as do Chinese, although in both countries, many of these Ph.D.s are of doubtful quality). Whether the Brazilian government will be as aggressive as the Chihese in investing in elite universities is another question, but this has little to do with the directive versus the autonomy/decentralization issue.

What Are the Implications for BRICs Becoming Centers of High-Tech Innovation?

What are the prospects for this huge expansion in engineers and computer scientists to shift information and communications technology production from the developed countries to the BRICs? Much depends on the innovation climate in the BRICs, and as we discussed above, there are different rankings of the BRICs in different surveys of innovation climates. There seems to be some agreement that China sits among the highest two of the BRICs and that Russia and India among the lowest in innovation. But these rankings could change in the next ten years. Is that likely?

Currently, the largest stock of high-quality engineers and computer scientists is in China, and the quantity of patents is rapidly increasing but from exceedingly low levels. Is the climate for innovation in China and Russia changing radically from the pre-1990s government-dominated, military-oriented Academy of Sciences model? Innovation requires room for experimentation, error, and a freedom to criticize and overthrow existing paradigms—the antithesis of control. Further, investing heavily in "world-class" institutions while mass institutions produce the vast majority of graduates with low-quality training may have negative implications for long-term productivity growth as the Chinese economy moves into the postindustrial phase of development. This should not imply that this model is incapable of important results, as China has shown in alternative energy innovation and production.

There is evidence that the research systems in China are changing and that the academies of science and elite universities are highly motivated to produce more and higher-quality research (see Chapter 7). Also, there appears to be much less control over the research process by government bureaucrats, although there is an overarching system of political control in China and Russia that could still influence the degree of critical research in fields such as the social sciences.

Russia is also at the beginning of a major effort to create a high-tech innovation center in Skolkovo, near Moscow, which includes SkTech, a new graduate university being built in partnership with the Massachusetts Institute of Technology and headed by Edward Crawley, an MIT professor of aeronautics and astronautics. The new institution intends to bring together Russian, U.S. and other scientists and engineers to produce a new breed of innovative and entrepreneurial researchers and to conduct basic research for high-tech start-ups. The effort is very much in the model of a centralized state attempting to create the innovation center itself rather than the legal and cultural context that would stimulate innovation, but some would argue that the U.S. Defense Department played a similar role in the growth of Silicon Valley and Route 128 in the 1960s with its purchases of new technology for military purposes. Whether Skolkovo will, indeed, become a Russian Silicon Valley will depend very much on its being able to attract foreign firms such as Microsoft and Google, but under the right conditions, the initiative could flourish.

However, for the time being, if innovation centers in information and communications technology—especially software and including efforts such as Skolkovo—are expected to emerge in the BRICs, they will probably be mostly as parts of developed-country investment and control.

Is the situation different in the more "open" societies of India and Brazil? Perhaps, but for their size, both countries produce relatively few high-quality engineers and computer scientists, and some of these go abroad. Both countries certainly aspire to become new innovation centers, but India has the tremendous drawback of investing very little in R&D, and although Brazil has produced some important players in commercial aircraft production, ATM machines, and other products (including software), it seems a long way from competing with the United States, Europe, or even Israel.

The Indian case is interesting because India is the world's largest exporter of outsourced IT services after the United States. The Indian IT industry employs more than two million engineers. Although led by the few very-high-quality engineers and computer scientists produced by its elite institutions, the overwhelming majority of the Indian IT workers are graduates of the mass educational system. That India has been able to do so is often taken as proof of the high quality of its engineers. The reality, as Indian IT firm leaders openly admit, is that the type of IT work done in India is at the lowest end of the value chain because of the poor quality of its workforce. NASSCOM, the Indian IT industry's trade body, estimates that less than 25 percent of engineering graduates are employable (NASSCOM, 2009).

Everything can change in the longer run. A large stock of high-quality human capital can generate innovation and create new economic dynamics—in the right conditions. In the shorter run, the much more likely scenario is that many of the most innovative people in China, India, Russia, and Brazil will continue to emigrate to the United States, Europe, Japan, Australia, and Canada to take advantage of the opportunities for innovation and economic success in innovation industries. In turn, some of the successful emigrants will invest in innovation industries back in the BRICs. This has happened in India (Saxenian, 1996) and is now happening in China. At the same time, the availability of skilled engineers and computer scientists in the BRICs has shifted U.S., European, and Japanese investment and production in information technology (including some of the research) from the developed countries to the BRICs.

In terms of labor supply in the U.S. and European markets, the impact of the increase in BRIC engineering graduates has been very positive for universities (in the United States, half of university engineering professors are foreign born) and high-tech producers but has probably lowered wages for U.S. and European professionals competing for information technology jobs. Clearly, increasing the supply of the world's highly qualified technical personnel helps increase the output of new technology products, lowering prices and benefiting consumers worldwide.

Triumph of the BRICs?

In the beginning of this study, we argued that by analyzing how states in these four societies organized the expansion of their changing higher education system, we would be able to gain perspective on the overall prospects of these societies for long-term economic and social development. For those used to economists' views on these issues, the notion of studying the state in order to understand prospects for economic development may seem strange. Freeing up markets has played an important role in unleashing economic growth in all four BRICs. A good case can be made that freeing up markets even more in Russia would help the economy. That said, however, a well-organized state is absolutely crucial even in market economies, and the contrast between China and Russia is good support for that argument.

So what have we learned?

Our study suggests that, for all the flaws in China's political climate and its possible ramifications for creativity in that society, China's state has carried out a major transformation of its higher education system, and (based on international test scores) it appears that the highly selected students coming into Chinese universities are well prepared educationally in pre-tertiary education. It also appears that China's elite universities are probably improving in quality, at least as measured by research publications. Although China's state has not done much to develop quality second-tier institutions, all of this tells us that it has been quite effective in carrying through this huge reform. It suggests that China's development process should continue to transform its economy into a highly developed powerhouse over the next generation. Whether this means that Chinese engineers and scientists will be at the center of an indigenous innovation economy in the next few decades is less clear. Until now, we have seen little evidence that China's state is capable of developing an innovation system beyond forming the human capital to potentially fuel it or, more important, that any highly directed state system could be any more than a supportive force for this type of economy.

The case for Russia is less clear. The Russian state is just in the early stages of trying to reorganize its higher education system, and it has not been nearly as systematically well organized as China in doing so. The Russian state is also exerting more centralized control over the process than China, and it faces the unusual situation of being near capacity in drawing more of its population into universities when that population is declining. Russia's state also seems less unilaterally committed to transforming Russia's economy from oil dependence and, despite the very high human capital levels that it inherited from the previous communist state, has done little to improve the quality of its pre-tertiary system. Thus, our analysis suggests that although Russia has a big advantage in the depth of its university-trained human capital and the quality of its qualified engineering and technical labor force, the state has not shown the capacity to organize Russian society to compete in the global knowledge economy.

Brazil, like China, has elements of an innovative society, creating new products and high-quality research in universities, investing more per student than the other BRICs in R&D, and facing great possibilities for future development. If it can continue to reduce inequality and to incorporate the 40 percent of its population that is poor and extremely poor into the mainstream of its economy, it may be able to maintain high growth rates and greatly reduce population growth and poverty over the next decades. In our analysis of higher educational change, the state receives mixed reviews. It has accomplished rapid expansion of access to higher education and has increased access for the poor. Yet it is only just beginning to address the rather low quality of its pre-tertiary education system, which produces poorly prepared students for universities, and the very low quality of most of its higher education system, which is private and over which the state has legal influence but has done little to exert pressure on those mass institutions to change. Even public institutions do not seem to be headed toward much improvement. On the other hand, the state has moved to strengthen graduate education, which is almost all public, and that could have an important positive effect in the future. Thus, if the effectiveness of the state in higher education reform is crucial to Brazil's future development, the jury is still out on whether the current level of Brazil's economic and social energy can be maintained.

Our analysis draws the most pessimistic picture for India. This runs counter to much of the optimism around the economic surge India has witnessed in the past fifteen years. Nevertheless, like Brazil but with even greater issues confronting it, the Indian state has had difficulty attacking the problem of how to expand education, including higher education, while increasing quality. One of the great issues confronting the Indian state is the very low quality of Indian pre-tertiary public education, and this has been a major problem for decades. Enrollment in higher education is increasing rapidly, but almost all of it in very-low-quality institutions, many of them private and, as in Brazil, with little if any incentive to improve. Unlike Brazil, however, India is investing very little in graduate education in technical fields, despite its enormous growth of undergraduate enrollment. So even if engineering institutions wanted to increase quality, they can draw on very little human capital to make these improvements. If our analysis of the situation in higher education is an accurate reflection of state capability to provide support for economic development, it does not portend well for India's development future. This is especially the case because India, in part because of past policies, faces enormous problems with rural and urban poverty, gender disparities (which are gradually being reduced), health care, and the universal provision of primary and secondary education.

Although much remains to be seen about how ably BRIC states will help the development of higher education over the next decade, we may ask what the current and future development of the BRIC systems portend for the United States, the nations of Europe, and other developed countries. A number of articles and reports have debated the competitive threat that the BRICs potentially pose to the continuing hegemony of the United States and Europe in higher education. Generally speaking, these articles have examined the sheer quantity of college enrollments in, say, engineering and science in China and India (e.g., Gereffi et al., 2008) as well as the relative performance of pre-tertiary students in math and science (Lowell and Salzman, 2007). They have not examined the recent quality of university education in the BRIC countries in detail.

From our perspective, China and Russia, and to a lesser extent Brazil and India, are increasingly positioned as real competitors both in terms of the quantity of science and engineering graduates and their quality. China's elite institutions produce more than twice as many engineering graduates each year as the entire U.S. higher education system, whereas elite institutions in the other three BRIC countries altogether produce about one-and-a-half times as many engineering graduates as the United States produces in total. Given the strong pre-tertiary education of Chinese graduates as well as the general state of Chinese elite institutions, it seems that China is already quite competitive with the United States in producing engineers at the elite undergraduate level, both in terms of quality and certainly quantity. China has some momentum in increasing the quantity of science and engineering research, although it remains to be seen to what degree and how rapidly China will be able also produce high-quality research at a significant scale. Russia also can take a competitive position if it continues to promote its elite institutions, is able to induce its nonelite institutions to make marked progress, and is able to put more funding into research and to create a legal, financial, and political climate that promotes innovation and private investment in innovation. Although student performance in pre-tertiary education is fairly weak compared to Russia and China, Brazil can leverage its strong graduate education, increases in research funding, and established (and growing) elite institutions to greatly increase its competitiveness. India seems the least equipped to directly compete with the United States and Europe anytime soon. Yet the upper echelons of its large, young population will continue to be a sought-after source of highly skilled labor in the coming years.

Macroeconomic forces also seem to relatively favor China and perhaps the other BRIC nations in terms of competitiveness in higher education. Both the global financial crisis in 2008 and Europe's current economic troubles may increase the tendency for postgraduates to return to the BRIC countries from the United States and Europe. Institutions in the West, in response to tighter budgets at home and global market forces, are themselves actively strengthening their ties with institutions in the BRIC countries through branch campuses, research collaborations, and visiting professors and students. BRIC institutions on their own are attracting greater numbers of foreign students and faculty, sending more students and faculty abroad, and leveraging increased funding, especially for research.

On the other hand, many BRIC engineers and computer scientists will continue to be recruited to study and work in the developed countries, where they could help fuel high-tech innovation and economic growth. The fact that so many reasonably high-quality engineers and scientists are now graduating from BRIC universities will have an enormous impact on the supply of technical talent. Whether the graduates end up working at home or abroad, they should have a huge effect on scientific and innovative productivity. They may also dampen wage growth of high-tech professionals in the developed countries, just as in the past thirty years, the growth of blue-collar wages in the United States, Europe, and Japan was affected by the development of a skilled factory workforce in China, India, Brazil, Korea, Taiwan, and other developing countries.

How will all this serve the mass of nonelite university students and the overall well-being of ordinary members of BRIC societies? Will the 40 percent of the world's population living in the BRICs reach high levels of consumption and social satisfaction in the next four decades? If the BRIC economies are able to maintain reasonable growth rates over the next two decades, harnessing their newly growing university-educated workforce, they should be able to mobilize the resources needed to begin improving the quality of even their nonelite institutions and to organize their pre-tertiary education systems. They should thus be able to better prepare a high fraction of their youths for entry into university and to find higher-paying, more productive jobs when they graduate. Steadily rising incomes per capita and more equitable distribution of those incomes should also reduce poverty and improve the nutrition and health of children generally, also contributing to higher school achievement and higher-quality university graduates.

Again, attaining these goals depends on the capacity of public bureaucracies to make the right decisions, including being able to effectively educate their populations to the increasing levels of knowledge required in the rapidly changing twenty-first-century economy.

REFERENCE MATTER

Notes

Chapter 1

1. Another dramatic change in higher education is taking place in China, India, and Russia. In the past ten years a growing (state-sanctioned) private university sector emerged to absorb excess demand for higher education places, creating a new tier (usually low quality) of mass universities. In Brazil this private sector was already well developed in the 1980s, and it has expanded greatly in the 2000s.

2. In China the government purportedly charged fees for higher education to stimulate spending of accumulated household savings as well as to reduce unemployment pressure in the economy by delaying young people's entry into the labor force.

3. However, others think that U.S. universities are themselves influenced by global competition (Clotfelter, 2010).

4. Another aspect of quality is that every great university today includes a strong component of the science and engineering (S&E) professions. The large majority of the *Times* Higher Education and the Academic Ranking of World Universities rankings includes universities that are strong in some field of S&E (even Harvard, in medicine), while including several that are focused on S&E, such as Caltech and MIT. This reflects and may be caused by the growing realization among people and their governments that a professional education is a must. There is, understandably, a stronger belief among poorer countries, with declining opportunities for generalists in the job market (partly due to government shrinkage). It is also an outcome of private entry: although encouraged by the state for various reasons discussed above, an unexpected outcome (at least in India) is how this is beginning to change the composition of graduates in favor of professional education.

5. Many years ago, Mark Blaug, Richard Layard, and Maureen Woodhall (1969) studied the paradox of Indian universities. Graduates seemed to suffer high rates of unemployment, yet the demand for university education continued unabated. They

found that although the rate of unemployment was indeed high among university graduates, it was even higher among secondary-school graduates. This helped push secondary-school graduates to go on to university. In the past twenty-five years in the United States, the real incomes of male college graduates have risen very slowly, but the real incomes of male high school graduates have fallen sharply, again raising the college income premium and increasing enrollment in higher education. Globalization may therefore benefit university graduates only in *relative* terms, but the implications for general educational investment strategies are the same as if university graduates' incomes were rising more rapidly than incomes of those young people with less schooling.

6. Private rates of return measure the gains captured by individuals compared to their own investment, and social rates measure the gains captured by individuals plus the payoffs to society of higher levels of education in the population (externalities) compared to the sum of public and private costs—see Chapter 3.

7. As we emphasize throughout this book, these numbers depend heavily on how the relevant "age cohort" is defined. For example, in Brazil, a high percentage of higher education students are over the age of twenty-two because of many factors. Thus, the 35 percent figure shown here, based on the age cohort of eighteen to twenty-two, may be a vast overestimate of the true gross enrollment rate.

8. It is worth noting the anomaly (at least in India and Brazil) that the best primary and secondary schools are overwhelmingly private, while the best colleges and universities are usually public. One reason may be differences in spending per student. Public primary and secondary schooling is entirely funded by the provinces/states in India (state and municipalities in Brazil), which tend to have far fewer resources, while the best higher education is funded by the national government, which allocates adequate resources.

9. For a critical comparison of the Shanghai and *Times* rankings, see Levin, Jeong, and Ou, 2006.

Chapter 2

1. For Russia, this leap in enrollment was its third, after a higher education expansion during the Soviet industrialization of the 1930s and again in the late 1950s, when Russia expanded and modernized its manufacturing base.

2. Nevertheless, in Brazil, by the mid-1960s, with a wave of military governments in Latin America, political activity in universities was severely repressed. The children of the elite were not spared.

3. Of course, the Chinese used tests for centuries to determine access into the imperial civil service, and Napoleon introduced the French *baccalauréat* examination in 1808 as a requirement of secondary school graduation.

4. Three of the four countries have also greatly expanded their "vocational" or "professional" degree programs, which require less than four years to complete. The number of China's three-year vocational high education graduates has ex-

panded enormously over the last several years. India produces very large numbers of engineer/technicians with "diploma" (three-year) degrees. Russia has always had a large postsecondary vocational degree program, but unlike the others, it appears to be in decline, as fewer students are interested in entering such programs. Brazil, on the other hand, is considering expanding its program: http://cshe.berkeley.edu/publications/publications.php?a=47

5. This includes 5.4 million students earning undergraduate degrees in adult higher education institutions (including Web-based undergraduates).

6. Through government policies such as Projects 985 and 211, for example, which we discuss further in the next chapter.

7 These statistics are estimated by dividing four-year university student enrollment data in 2009 (using individual-level national data) by the number of nine-year-olds in each province in 2000 (using 2000 population census data).

8. However, the recent (2009) performance of a sample of Shanghai students on the international PISA test calls for a closer look at assumptions about the overall quality of learning in Chinese high schools.

9. As always, this is a complex calculation. We use the number of undergraduates as a percentage of the eighteen- to twenty-two-year-old age group. Indian estimates (MHRD, 2010, for example) calculate the GER as 15 percent as well, but those calculations are based on the total of undergraduates and postgraduates as a proportion of the eighteen- to twenty-three-year-old population. The estimates for different states shown below are based on this latter type of calculation.

10. Other statistics worth noting: the gross enrollment ratio for women is much lower than for men, 17 percent for men versus 13 percent for women in 2009–2010. Only 11 percent of scheduled-caste young people are enrolled, and 10 percent of scheduled tribes.

11. Of the 2.86 million students reported by the University Grants Committee (UGC, 2012) in engineering and technical colleges and universities in 2010–2011, about 250,000 were reported as diploma-level and postgraduate students, and of the 17 million total students in India, about 1.7 million were diploma and postgraduate students. Thus, undergraduate engineering and technical students represented about 16.5 percent of total students. A much higher fraction of students in engineering and technical colleges are diploma students than in other fields of study. However, other data reported by the Ministry of Human Resources and Development (2011) show a much higher number of diploma students in engineering, so we think that the undergraduate enrollment in engineering/technical colleges reported by the UGC appears too high.

12. The states are Gujarat, Haryana, Karnataka, Kerala, Maharashtra, Orissa, Rajasthan, Tamil Nadu, and West Bengal. According to Banerjee and Muley, 2007, Table 1.9, engineering college intake in these states together represents about 60 percent of the national total. We were not able to get data for Andhar Pradesh and Uttar Pradesh, two states with more than 25 percent of total engineering student intake. But we do not think that the pattern there is greatly different.

13. We limited our "count" of institutions and places to those granting bachelor's in engineering (B.E.) and B-Tech degrees. Most of these institutions also grant diploma (three-year) degrees, and there are large numbers of polytechnics in each state that do not grant B.E. or B-Tech degrees. We did not include those polytechnics.

14. Schwartzman (2004) estimated that the "net" rate (number of students eighteen to twenty-four years old enrolled in higher education as a fraction of all eighteen- to twenty-four-year-olds in the population) of enrollment in 2002 was only 9.8 percent. This is compared to a 16.6 percent "gross" rate, which compares all students enrolled with the eighteen- to twenty-four-year-old population. The "net "enrollment rate is similar to that in India.

Chapter 3

1. Another historical phenomenon—the increasing number of countries where the majority of university graduates are women—can also be explained by the higher payoff for women of finishing university. Women may make bigger gains in income by taking more education, even though their absolute incomes are lower than men's at all levels of schooling. If women perceive that they earn even less compared to men by *not* attending university—that their opportunities are even more limited in the types of jobs requiring less than higher education—they should be more motivated to continue on to university and complete their studies. Apparently, this is what is happening worldwide. As job opportunities for women have opened up more generally, women seem to have a better shot at more equal paying jobs the more education they take. An important reason for this is that in many countries, government jobs are more gender equalized and more open to women than jobs in the private sector, and a large fraction of government jobs require higher education.

2. In some cases, such as the United States in the 1980s/early 1990s, salaries of (male) university graduates did not rise in real terms, but those of secondary graduates fell, which still had the effect of sharply increasing the payoff for university graduates (Carnoy, 2000). In Russia university graduates' real wages fell drastically in the early 1990s and stayed lower throughout the decade, but they fell less than the wages of workers with lower levels of education. University graduates had greater flexibility in adapting to the new economic conditions. Again, this increased income inequality and the payoff for investing in university.

3. Unless the average age of Zhang's sample declined significantly, this increase in the proportion of university graduates seems unlikely by 2001 (see our Table 3.2).

4. The meta-analysis of rate of return studies in China by Liu (2008) finds that IV estimates are about four percentage points higher than OLS estimates. See Card (2000) for possible explanations of this finding.

5. Correcting for selection bias in ROR studies is extremely difficult without using more rigorous research designs; most of the strategies tried thus far (including instrumental variable strategies) have potential difficulties (such as finding a viable instrument).

6. Liu (2008) finds that 40 percent of the variability in rate of return for schooling studies in China is explainable by different model specifications.

7. For the sake of space, we do not show age-earnings profiles for females in any of the BRIC countries. However, they are available from the authors. The differences in earnings between female secondary graduates and both university-educated females and females who work as engineers are larger than the corresponding differences for males, even though females earn less at all education levels.

8. Gross domestic product per capita in China in 2005 was about 12,000 yuan, but in urban areas the figure was higher. Even so, tuition represents a high fraction of the average Chinese family's income.

9. One problem with Fan and colleagues' identification strategy is that it relies on surveyed individuals remembering their college entrance exam achievement results from up to twenty or more years prior. Loyalka (2009) shows that only 75 percent of randomly surveyed senior-year college students can accurately report their college entrance exam scores.

10. Real monthly earnings in Russia fell precipitously in the early 1990s from about 18,000 rubles (in 2009 prices) in 1990 to 5,000 rubles in 1992. They rose gradually to 1997 to about 9,000 rubles, dropped back in 1998, then recovered steadily to 22,000 rubles in 2008.

11. For example, among OECD countries, only seven had 25 percent or more in the 25–64-year-old labor force in 2006 who had attained Type A (university) or more. See OECD, *Education at a Glance*, 2008, Table A1.1a.

12. With the decline of the youth population, the near "saturation" of the proportion of youths attending university, and no decline in the number of "free" places allocated by the government to universities, the percentage of fee-paying students had fallen by 2012 to about 40 percent of total public university enrollment.

13. The 2005 cross-section age-earnings profiles shown in Figure 3.2 are not unlike the profiles in China (Figure 3.1), except, predictably, they turn down at a higher age (early forties) than in China, reflecting the earlier marketization (1991–1992) of the Russian labor market. It is also interesting to note that older workers with only secondary schooling earn as much as younger workers, reflecting the much more equal wage structure of the Soviet period. Furthermore, during the decade of 1995–2005 there was a shift of the peak of the age-earnings curve for university-educated workers. In the mid-1990s, the peak was at about thirty-five years of age, whereas by the mid-2000s, it had moved above forty-five years of age.

14. Women have a much higher payoff for higher education than do men, probably because the jobs available to Russian women with only secondary education pay much lower wages than are available to men with secondary education completed. This is similar to the structure of rates of return in many developed countries (see OECD, 2009) and, as we have reported, similar to RORs in China.

15. We also estimated rates of return for other fields of study, namely medicine and economics.

Chapter 4

1. We study the question of institutional quality in the next three chapters.

2. As in the Brazilian case, we were able only to approximate changes in tuition fees over time for India. Unlike Brazil, there is no evidence that tuition fees declined in India over time.

3. After accounting for financial aid, (net) tuition rates take on the same pattern across university tiers as gross tuition rates. For more information, see Chapter 8 on equity in the BRIC higher education systems.

4. Our data are from a simple random sample of more than 7,000 senior college students in all four-year universities in a noncoastal province.

5. However, we should note that many public higher education (central and provincial level) institutions actively took out large loans during the last decade to meet their various objectives and associated financial obligations. The spending from these loans is not included in any of the financial figures in this chapter as this information is not easily available. Likewise, later estimates of per student spending are underestimates.

6. Specifically, 27.5 billion yuan was allocated in the first stage (1999–2001), 30 billion yuan in the second stage (2004–2008), and an as yet undisclosed amount in the third stage (2010–onward) of the project.

7. See http://english.people.com.cn/90001/6381319.html, September 2011.

8. However, it is important to mention that the central government has announced plans to further increase spending for all four-year institutions (and perhaps equalize spending between the elite and nonelite institutions). But the budgetary allocation set aside for this project has not yet been released (as of September 2011). See www.edu.cn/html/rd/r/project.shtml (in Chinese).

9. At the state level, there have not necessarily been special efforts toward financing engineering and technical undergraduate education. Before 2008, per student government allocations were awarded to institutions based on their overall type (i.e., five categories, including humanities/finance, comprehensive/technical, medical, agricultural/normal, and arts). At least for ministry-run institutions as of 2007, comprehensive/technical universities received only slightly higher amounts than humanities/finance universities and substantially less than agricultural/normal or especially arts universities. After 2008, the government decided to weight per student allocations depending on majors (and not institutions) (Ministry of Finance and Ministry of Education, 2008).

10. In a small survey of public universities, Forbes shows that there is enormous variation in the percentage of total costs per student recovered through fees—anywhere from 2 percent to 100 percent (Forbes, 2011: 8).

11. See, for example, the Ministry of Education website (http://prounialuno.mec.gov.br/consulta/cursos/#) and a second site for medical school costs (www.escolasmedicas.com.br/mensal.php).

12. Hoper Educacional's study of spending and revenues in Brazil's private education sector shows that in 2009, 85–90 percent of revenues came from tuition.

13. The number of empty places is increasing rapidly (see Table 2.3). Between 2001 and 2010, the number of unfilled places in private institutions rose from 31 percent to 49 percent, implying a much more rapid expansion of capacity than enrollment. If the market is functioning normally in the private education sector, this should have put downward pressure on tuition. There is also evidence that states with more competition, such as São Paulo and Rio de Janeiro, have lower tuition rates—both in 2000 and 2010—despite higher than Brazil average earnings per capita. The most logical explanation is more competition in those states than in the rest of Brazil. São Paulo and Rio had about 56–59 percent of unfilled places in private institutions overall in 2010, whereas Rio Grande do Sul, a high-income state in the South, had the highest level of average tuition and a smaller percentage of unfilled places, 50 percent. The northeastern states have relatively low levels of income per capita, lower levels of unfilled places (52 percent in 2010), and higher levels of tuition than in richer São Paulo (Hoper Educational, 2009).

14. We tracked the tuition rates of the twenty-one largest private institutions in the country. They had almost one-third of all the private education students in 2008. The tuition they charged for night courses in the five main courses of study went down in 2000–2008, but much less than the total estimated average tuition across the sector. This suggests that at least part of the decline in tuition is caused by new institutions coming into the market aiming to attract low-income students.

15. A pilot program exists in Tomsk where the regional government makes suggestions to the ministry on how many budget places it needs and in what fields. The program does not replace the central planning idea but attempts to make it more applicable to the local circumstances.

16. Federated universities are to be established in each of the eight federal districts and would be responsible for organizing activities that would support the economic and social development programs in these districts, including preparation of a highly qualified workforce; creation of scientific, technological innovations through fundamental and applied research; practical implementation of research results; and creation of conditions for improved academic mobility domestically and internationally. The first two federated universities were created in Krasnoyarsk and Rostov-on-Don by merging several local universities. The remaining six federated universities are currently in the process of being formed, either through merging existing higher education institutions or creating brand-new institutions.

17. Universities must compete for this status by submitting a detailed plan of their disciplinary advantages and their research and infrastructure development plans. The designation of NRU status is usually for five years, renewable for another five based on success on following the initial plan. The first five years of funding also require a 20 percent cost share on the part of the institution. The goal of an NRU is to conduct actively other educational and research activities, integrating both of these functions within the institution. The NRUs are supposed to conduct a wide spectrum of fundamental and applied research that would lead to efficient transfers of technology to the national economy.

18. Detailed data on spending for different types of universities and tuition revenues are available only for these years.

Chapter 5

1. Central ministries (especially the Ministry of Education) in China set policies for the higher education system as a whole and directly manage elite HEIs, while local (e.g., provincial and city) level agencies are responsible for local HEIs.

2. As we mention in Chapter 4, this statistic does not include the debt held by universities, which may be borne to a large degree directly or indirectly by the state now or at some point in the future.

3. Performance-based financing of HEIs is still relatively rare in China.

4. By contrast, private HEIs have greater autonomy to hire faculty and determine their own salary schedules.

5. Many of our interviewees emphasized how low faculty base salaries were and how professors and their departments had to rely on research funding (both vertically from the government as well as horizontally from nongovernmental sources) to be able to afford living in large cities.

6. The University Grants Commission in India has attempted to address the problem of a shortage of qualified faculty in universities through several programs. For example, the UGC has encouraged higher education institutions to use academicians employed in research institutes (which are outside the university system). Some of these research institutes have also been allowed to offer orientation and refresher courses to existing university faculty. Partial relaxations in the minimum conditions—such as having a M.Phil or Ph.D.—were also granted for varying periods. Finally, the UGC has offered approximately 15,000 fellowship opportunities of various types for professors to continue to acquire an M.Phil or Ph.D. degree.

7. Under the Bologna Reform, which Russia signed onto in 2003, the old system of a five-year specialist degree will change to a two-tiered system of four-year baccalaureate degree followed by a two-year master's program. The system was supposed to have been implemented by the 2010–2011 academic year; however, the adoption was delayed because of the lateness in the creation of new national standards. Although many technical institutions that were visited by the authors have instituted the new 4+2 system, they are opting to continue a parallel five-year specialist program because, as they assert, most technical employers do not understand what a baccalaureate degree is and do not wish to hire what they perceive to be underqualified individuals.

8. Because we interviewed mainly in technical universities, we do not generalize to all universities. Yet there are many similarities, and there are nontechnical universities also in the WayWeWere category because they have difficulties changing the way they teach economics, for example, to make it more relevant to the current context. However, technical universities were especially likely to be tied to particular industries, many military dependent, that were hard hit by the economic transformation in the post-Soviet era.

9. This accords with Richard Ruch's (Ruch, 2001) analysis of for-profit universities more generally. He argues that administrators in for-profits supervise the work of faculty directly; take responsibility for creating new programs in response to market demand and the profitability of such programs; make rapid changes, again in response to profit criteria; and are sensitive to the students' satisfaction. This should make for-

profits much more nimble in responding to market changes, but it is unclear that this nimbleness is organized to produce higher-quality education for clients. Market advocates claim that it does because institutions that do not deliver quality will fail to attract students. However, this assumes that students and their families can observe educational quality and that for-profit institutions know how to increase quality.

Chapter 6

1. We estimate this as follows. According to official statistics, the ratio of the total number of new entrants admitted into higher education (about 6.4 million) over the total number of academic high school seniors (about 8 million) equals 77.6 percent (NBS, 2010). However, the numerator includes those who had already taken the college entrance exam (and who thus graduated academic high school) in previous years as well as (the minority of) vocational high school students who got into college. Repeat exam takers in particular constitute about 20–25 percent of all exam takers in a given year and generally have higher likelihoods of entering college than nonrepeat test takers (Loyalka, 2012). If we assume, therefore, that 25–30 percent of the some 6 million entrants into college in 2009 are repeat exam takers, then the rate of going to college for first-time exam takers is about 53–56 percent. In addition, it seems that about one-quarter (or less) of first-time exam takers go into four-year institutions (i.e., given that about 45 percent of all college entrants go into four-year institutions).

2. There is some empirical evidence across countries that early tracking may have an overall positive effects on cognitive achievement of young adults (Ariga and Brunello, 2007) but also likely increases inequality in achievement (Hanushek and Woessman, 2006).

3. Students within academic high schools are often further tracked into "fast-track" or regular-track classes.

4. Although vocational education and training were a relatively small part of the education system in the past, the government of India plans to increase vocational education and training opportunities so that an additional 500 million persons receive training by 2021.

5. Brazilian students, for example, have options to study in prestigious federal vocational institutions and later attend higher technical institutions. Many of the students who enter vocational school in Russia do so because it allows them access to university without taking the USE national entrance test and, for males, helps them postpone military service.

6. Researchers have found that entry into STEM majors and careers in the United States is quite fluid and not according to a pipeline model (see Xie and Shauman, 2003).

7. We use 2009 data on all students entering college to estimate these figures. Note that two provinces do not have the science-humanities track distinction, but rather have students take a comprehensive exam.

8. These PISA scores serve as indicators of the knowledge and skills learned by children both inside and outside of school until age fifteen (OECD, 2011b). However,

the PISA test is not linked to national curricula, so, for example, Russia students do considerably better on the Trends in International Mathematics and Science Survey (TIMSS) eighth-grade mathematics test, which is more closely linked to the mathematics curriculum. Russia scores above the TIMSS average, and on the 2011 TIMSS was among the top scoring countries in eighth-grade mathematics.

9. The TIMSS test has been criticized for sampling different kinds of students (especially in terms of age) in each country, however, and this potentially undermines the comparability of results across countries. Yet the PISA test has been criticized for sampling students of the same age across grades, which means that some students may have had a year less of subject matter than in other countries, depending on starting age requirements in first grade, promotion policies, etc. The fact that Russian students do relatively better on the TIMSS test than the PISA test provides an interesting contrast between what each test measures.

10. Although different provinces have different exams, the science-track exam generally consists of a comprehensive science component (40 percent of the total score) as well as math, foreign language (usually English), and Chinese literature subject tests (each 20 percent of the total score).

11. The university tuition fee structure in China, where the first two tiers of public universities have relatively low tuition compared to the third tier of private institutions (or the fourth tier of vocational colleges, which have somewhat higher fees and likely lower returns [Fan et al., 2010]), no doubt reinforces the desire to go to more-selective colleges.

12. In fact, the general purpose of the tenth- and eleventh-grade curriculum is also to prepare students for the college entrance exam.

13. About 530,000 students registered for and 485,000 students took the JEE test in April 2011 to compete for 9,618 seats in 16 IITs and the ISM Dhanbad (jee.learninghub .com/news, accessed Apr. 24, 2011). In 2011 about 1.11 million students registered for and 1.05 million students took the AIEEE (AIEEE, 2012).

14. In terms of content, the ENEM covers a broad array of subjects. In 2009 the federal government reformulated the ENEM tests so that they would be composed of 180 multiple-choice questions, equally divided into four areas of knowledge: languages (plus a written essay), human sciences, natural sciences, and mathematics. Similar to China, students take the test over two days (for a total of 620 minutes of test time).

15. For example, a report from the OECD (2011b) notes that junior high school students in Shanghai are fully engaged in classes, perhaps as a result of the competition created by the high school entrance exam.

16. Students in Brazil can consult the ENADE scores of first-year students in particular programs the previous time the ENADE was given in that program, which may have been two or three years before. They also face the issue of whether they should consider such scores as a measure of quality. As we suggest in Chapter 7, average student scores in Brazil do not necessarily reflect "value added," but they are correlated with other indicators of institutional quality.

17. The research team was headed by M. Dobryakova. All results are published on the HSE website: www.hse.ru/ege.

18. A student can be admitted to a university if he or she wins an academic competition (called "Olympics") in the relevant subject. Such competitions are held for high school students, everyone is free to participate, and the tasks are more creative and difficult than on the USE tests.

19. This has started to change after the introduction in 2011 of a new classification of majors, but the trend has remained intact so far.

20. Calculations are based on administrative data on all students who entered four-year colleges in thirty out of thirty-one provinces in 2009.

21. These calculations (using administrative data on all students who entered four-year colleges in 2009) are made for the approximately two-thirds of students who took the science entrance exam test and went to college.

22. Although the 2011 USE data used to construct Table 6.2 includes only the subsample of universities that posted their average mathematics scores on the Web (and therefore does not include all universities and majors), we also examined the rankings of specializations using average scores across all test subjects (which were reported by all universities) and came to similar conclusions. One problem with the latter data, of course, is that students applying to different majors may have taken different subject tests besides mathematics; therefore, the average USE scores are not comparable across institutions. At the same time, the fact that the mathematics and total scores across both samples have a correlation of 0.9 lends credence to our basic conclusions.

23. The standard deviations of scores on the general ability test are high (17–23 points), but sample sizes are also large (for example, 10,000 for Engineering II), so these differences in mean scores between, say, engineers and social science majors are statistically significant.

24. See above for the comparison of these figures with the sample of Russian engineering students, whose fathers are less likely to have completed university than the fathers of students in our Indian sample despite the far higher average higher level of education in Russia a generation ago and now. The fact that Indian students have parents with similar education levels as those in our Russian sample suggests how relatively elite Indian engineering students are in the context of their society.

25. Readers interested in the details of these estimates can obtain them from the authors.

26. In the United States, various attempts have been made to measure the quality of student educational experiences. The National Survey of Student Experiences (NSSE) seeks to do this from the perspective of college students themselves. The limitations of the NSSE in determining college quality have been recently and duly noted (Porter, Rumann, and Pontius, 2011). Other research organizations such as the OECD are attempting to measure the "value added" of different higher education institutions using university entry and exit exam scores.

27. "Other" for China includes a fairly high proportion of political and sports classes, rather than humanities and social science courses per se.

28. We thank Professor Po Yang, one of the researchers involved with the 2011 Beijing Undergraduate Survey, for estimating these figures.

29. We did not have comparable information from China.

30. Unfortunately, we were unable to conduct a comparable survey in Brazil.

31. Results were similar in the aforementioned 2011 Beijing College Student Survey.

32. More than half of the Indian students also noted that the quality of their education was good or better, whereas 3 percent said it was poor or very poor. The rest were unsure how to answer the question or were neutral in their answer.

Chapter 7

1. See, for example, http://masterrussian.com/russia/skolkovo.htm. Accessed Feb. 3, 2012.

2. And only a handful of studies attempt to measure the causal impacts of going to college or selective colleges on student or graduate outcomes (see Loyalka, Song, and Wei, 2012). We do have data for Brazil approximating value added in all electrical engineering and computer science departments thanks to the ENADE examination applied to cohorts in 2005 (end of students' first year of study) and 2008 (end of students' fourth year of study). We present a summary below of our analysis of student gains in more elite and more mass universities.

3. These statistics are from the OECD, *Main Science and Technology Indicators,* various years, and the Ministry of Science and Technology, China (MOST), various years.

4. We defined Russian elite institutions as the thirty-eight Category A institutions (these include Moscow State and St. Petersburg State, a number of federal universities and national research universities), which receive much more state funding than other universities (and collect considerably more revenue per fee-paying student), and Chinese elite institutions as 985 and 211 institutions (generally under the central government), including Peking University, Fudan, and Tsinghua. These definitions are fairly standard and widely accepted. We defined Brazil elite institutions by taking 80 percent of students in federal universities and adding in the students attending the elite private Catholic universities (PUC São Paulo, PUC Rio Grande do Sul, and PUC Belo Horizonte), plus the students attending the University of São Paulo (state university) and the state university of Campinas. For India, we first estimated the proportion of engineering students who entered university through the JEE and AIEEE exams over the total number of engineering students over the last four years; we then multiplied this proportion by the total number of bachelor's degree enrollments in the country to arrive at the number of elite students for all majors. While the specifics of the definitions for Brazil and India may be debatable, the overall picture about what is happening between highly selective, high-quality and less selective, lower-quality institutions in these two countries will likely be the same across the range of viable definitions.

5. We unfortunately do not have Russian data before 2006 on elite versus nonelite university enrollments.

6. We were able to find Indian data for select years only. Furthermore, as mentioned above, we made an educated guess on the India statistic by multiplying the total number of bachelor's degree enrollments by the proportion of elite engineering enrollments: that is, adding the number of students admitted through the JEE and AIEEE from the 2006–2007 to 2009–2010 school years and dividing this by the number of engineering (bachelor's degree) enrollments in 2009–2010. We also estimated a lower bound on the percentage of elite enrollments by aggregating the number of undergraduate entrants at top ten colleges and universities in arts, commerce, science, medicine, and law in 2011 with the number of JEE and AIEEE entrants in 2011, and dividing this by the projected number of total (bachelor's degree) enrollments in 2011. However, this lower bound estimate of enrollment in elite institutions turned out to be only 1 to 2 percent of total university enrollment in elite institutions.

7. We used the data from the University Grants Commission (UGC) *Annual Reports* for both total enrollment and engineering enrollments in figures 7.1 and 7.2. The Ministry of Human Resources and Development (MHRD) (2010, 2011) estimates higher numbers, particularly for engineering and technical enrollment. We went with the lower number of the UGC.

8. In China we approximate the number of engineers enrolled in elite versus nonelite institutions by multiplying the number of engineering enrollments in four-year universities in a given year by the percentage of new engineering enrollments in 211 or 985 institutions (essentially all managed by the central government) in that year.

9. These 2009 statistics were either directly taken or estimated from various government statistical sources (e.g., NBS [2010]; MHRD [2011]); Brazil (INEP [2010] and the Brazilian 2010 census, population by age); Russia, population data from 2009 by age group, the enrollment figures from Chapter 2, and the OECD (2011a). In particular, India's GER, which usually looks at the proportion of college enrollments (which usually include graduate students and students in three-year "diploma" programs but not those in distance education) over the number of 18–23-year-olds in the population (which turns out to be 10 percent in 2009 for B.A.-level undergraduates only) was adjusted to account for the number of 18–22-year-olds instead, bringing it to 12.1 percent. The denominator of Brazil's GER was similarly adjusted from the number of 18–24-year-olds to the number of 18–22-year-olds. China's GER statistic above includes only four-year college (bachelor's degree) students; if we use both three-year (vocational degree) and four-year college students, the GER would be increased to around 24 percent. At the same time, we recognize that there is some debate about these GER statistics, even within each country (e.g., see de Moura Castro, 2011; Tilak, 2010).

10. All four national states influence quality between elite and nonelite institutions by controlling which types of students (in terms of cognitive ability) enter college through the admissions process. The fairly extreme sorting of the highest scorers into elite universities through a highly competitive admissions exam process (see Chapter 6) may result in peer effects being significantly larger between students in elite versus nonelite universities. This lack of positive peer effects in nonelite universities

may not be particularly serious, however, if it is easier for departments in these institutions to hone instruction toward students of more similar (albeit lower) ability. We do not have any direct evidence about tracking and college peer effects; however, we did frequently hear administrators in lower-tier universities cite the low quality of incoming students as a serious problem and voice their desire to improve their institutional ranking to attract higher-achieving students.

11. Russian spending per student estimates shown here vary according to estimates of student private spending on fees. In the lower estimate, we assume that fees are based on university website analysis; the higher figure is based on Ministry of Education reports of revenues per fee-paying student in various types of universities, which tended to be considerably higher than public spending per "free" place student (see Chapter 4).

12. The United States and OECD numbers are from *Education at a Glance* (OECD, 2011a, Figure B1.1a) and are estimated based on public institution data only, including research costs. The BRIC numbers were calculated using each country's statistical data, and the details are in Chapter 4. Note that including or excluding R&D spending has a negligible effect on the above estimates. Also, as discussed in Chapter 4, the China figures do not include (unreported, but perhaps substantial) university debt.

13. Specifically, Chinese universities produced 48,658 Ph.D.s (15,524 engineering Ph.D.s) in 2009, while research institutes produced another some 9,500 Ph.D.s (3200+ engineering Ph.D.s) (NBS, 2010).

14. In addition, the percentage of engineering Ph.D.s versus total Ph.D.s in either India or Brazil is smaller than in either China or Russia.

15. A "candidate" degree requires three years of study (and a final exam) after a master's degree—it also includes a dissertation, although according to government statistics, only approximately one-third of candidate degree graduates complete their dissertation. The "doctor of science" degree is a higher degree (that also includes a dissertation) than the candidate degree.

16. A commonly held perception is that that best undergraduate students end up going abroad for graduate degrees or into the most competitive public or private sector jobs rather than acquire a graduate degree in China.

17. A related problem regarding faculty is that most Ph.D.s in India are awarded by lower-quality institutions. The limited supply of quality faculty either comes from overseas (usually the United States) or from a few quality institutions such as the IITs (which have been mandated to increase their output of Ph.D.s, without much effect as of 2011).

18. The results are similar if we use the 2005 test—it has a similar score distribution as the test given in 2008 for both the initial and second general and specific tests.

19. Students also made (smaller) gains on the general knowledge test.

20. However, it should be noted that electronic engineering is a five-year program, so the students taking the second test in 2008 are almost all fifth-, not fourth-, year students. This means that they are not the "same" group of students who took the initial test in 2005.

21. The number of students graduating from various undergraduate programs may not mirror the number of students enrolling in these programs (see Figure 7.4a). This is because the length of time to obtain a degree can vary across and within university systems: Chinese, Indian, and Brazilian programs offer three- and four-year degrees (and in Brazil, some five-year degrees, as in engineering), whereas Russian students now are beginning to graduate with either a four-year or (still mostly) five-year degree (which was the standard until Russia joined the Bologna process). Furthermore, as we have discussed in earlier chapters, dropout rates differ across countries. Dropouts are especially low in China, where degrees are essentially guaranteed after the designated period of study, and are higher in India, Russia, and especially Brazil, caused partially by stricter graduation requirements that "weed out" less academically prepared students.

22. Although China has a larger number of total higher education enrollments and graduates than India overall, it has a lower number of "bachelor degree" graduates (as defined by each country).

23. The 2009 figures are an underestimate as they account only for students from thirty out of thirty-one provinces (data on Jiangsu students were not available).

24. We estimate the India graduate figures by directly using the number of JEE and AIEEE entrants in 2008 (and not accounting for dropouts). Under the same reasoning, India should have about 45,000 graduates by 2015.

25. Because college administrators are "graded" to some degree on the ability of these graduates to find employment, they generally report unrealistically high employment rates (often 95 percent or higher in our institutional surveys).

26. The sources for these figures are NBS and MOST (2010); OECD *Main Science and Technology Indicators* (2011/12); MCT, Brazil (2012); UNESCO Institute for Statistics (various years); authors' calculations.

27. It is important to note that the 2008 financial crisis took a big toll on Russia, resulting in 7–8 percent negative economic growth from 2008 to 2009. By contrast, Brazil's GDP remained relatively unchanged over the same period of time, whereas India and China both grew substantially (although at a rate somewhat below that of previous years).

28. SCI (Science Citation Index) and EI (the Engineering Index) are popular indices managed by Thomson-Reuters and Elsevier, respectively. ISPT (Index to Scientific & Technical Proceedings) is also a scholarly database that includes materials on international conferences.

29. Brazil's impact is especially high in engineering (only 5 percent below the world average), with China and India quickly improving their impact in this field as well. According to Thomson-Reuters, China is strong in material science, physics, and math. India is strong in multidisciplinary fields (5.47 percent), materials science (5.45 percent), agricultural sciences (5.17 percent), chemistry (5.04 percent), and physics (3.88 percent).

30. Triadic patents are a series of corresponding patents filed at the European Patent Office (EPO), the United States Patent and Trademark Office (USPTO), and the

Japan Patent Office (JPO) for the same invention by the same applicant or inventor. The Patent Cooperation Treaty (PCT) is an international patent law treaty from 1970 that provides a unified procedure for filing patent applications to protect inventions in each of its contracting states (see http://en.wikipedia.org/wiki/Triadic_patent, accessed Aug. 12, 2012).

31. This is a key group with experts from the State Research University Higher School of Economics and the Academy of National Economy and was established in December 2010.

32. See Tilak (2010) for a comment on some of the education bills that have been introduced in the Parliament and some that are in the pipeline.

Chapter 8

1. According to OECD *Education at a Glance* (2011, Table A.1.3) figures, 21 percent of the Russian labor force in 2002 had completed university degrees. It is likely that by 2011, with the great increase in university graduates after 2002, the proportion of the younger labor force with university degrees reached more than 25 percent, the OECD average.

2. Note that some analysts argue that educational spending per pupil is not a good indicator of educational quality because much of the money used in education goes to teacher salaries, and higher salaries do not necessarily result in higher-quality teaching (see, for example, Fuchs and Woessmann, 2007). That argument is made more complex by the fact that in countries such as the United States, where the demand for good mathematics skills is high, spending more on teacher salaries (hence, per student) could attract better mathematics teachers and improve the quality of education (Carnoy et al., 2009).

3. If we were able to include spending at the secondary level on private education, which still absorbs about 20 percent of secondary students in Brazil, it is possible that spending per student may have fallen in this period because private secondary schooling is more expensive than public and the fraction of students attending private education declined somewhat.

4. Private spending (from households, for example) has increased markedly in China, and we have not accounted for this, so the investment cost of education in China may also have risen.

5. We approximated the change in Var r by observing the divergence or convergence of secondary and university rates (professional and university rates in Russia) in Table 8.3. The sign on the Cov (r, S) term is taken as negative when the secondary rate is higher than the university rate and positive when the university rate is higher than the secondary (or professional in the Russian case). In all but Brazil, the lower level of schooling has the higher payoff in earlier years, and this either disappears (India) or reverses itself (China and Russia). Thus, the change in the covariance is positive. In Brazil the covariance becomes increasingly positive over time.

6. It could be argued that the rate of return for lower-tier university education is lower because the quality of education in lower-tier universities is lower, but we could

argue that the rate of return per dollar spent per student is the same in lower-tier universities and that lower quality (hence absolute payoff for students) is reflected in lower spending.

7. For example, contrast the present situation with the late 1970s (Dasgupta and Tilak, 1983).

8. Higher SES students also have access to the highest tiers because in the BRICs they have more money to go to better schools early on, which is reflected in higher college entrance exam results—and these students can already afford higher education and selective institution fees.

9. Interested readers can obtain these regression estimates as well as those estimating students' expected earnings from the authors.

10. The special fee-reimbursement scheme was introduced in Maharashtra (and Andhra Pradesh) but not in Delhi. In Delhi such a scheme has been implemented at school level since 2003–2004. All state governments have scholarship schemes, some of which target disadvantaged groups.

11. It is important to examine within-province higher educational inequality in China as each province has its own separate college application and admissions system (see below). Although we do not have data from each province, we arguably have the best data on this topic so far in China (i.e., either randomly sampled or administrative data covering all students of the related population). Furthermore, using data from these two northwest provinces likely provides an upper bound on inequality within provinces in China.

12. Here we again assume that high social class students enter the same cost/student fields of study as low social class students; in fact, tuition prices are fairly similar between most majors within a given university in China.

13. In Shaanxi specifically, we find that the net college prices (tuition and dorm fees net of nonloan financial aid) of going to a first-tier institution make up only about 40 percent of the annual per capita disposable income of urban households as compared to 160 percent for rural households. The average net college fees of going to a third-tier institution are roughly 90 percent of annual per capita disposable income for urban households as compared to a formidable 360 percent for rural households (see Loyalka, 2009).

14. The program is to be discontinued after ten years. See http://latino.foxnews.com/latino/news/2012/08/08/students-will-benefit-from-affirmative-action-bill-approved-in-brazil, retrieved Aug. 15, 2012.

15. The *vestibular* is the examination that secondary school students take to gain entry to universities. Each department in each university gives its own *vestibular.*

16. In June 2003 the University of Brasilia adopted a plan called "Objectives for Ethnic, Racial, and Social Integration," based on a quota of 20 percent of places in all undergraduate courses for black applicants, the admission of increased numbers of indigenous students, and supporting the local public school system (Mulholland, 2005). Those who chose the quota system (4,194 out of 27,397 applicants in the second semester of 2004) were required to indicate their color and whether they considered themselves black. A photograph was part of the application. According to

Mulholland, "A commission composed of faculty, staff, student, and external members evaluated the applications. It concluded that 212 (4.7%) of the quota applicants did not meet the stated criteria. They could, however, appeal the commission's decision. Thirty-four did so, presenting their arguments. All were submitted to recorded interviews. A second commission reviewed the appeals and re-admitted 21 appellants to the quota system. The other 13 were then transferred to the universal system. All applicants took the same entrance exams at the same time, without regard to the admission system chosen. All exams were corrected in the same way. Minimum scores for each exam and for the compound final score were observed. These minimum scores eliminated 40% of the universal system applicants and 57% of the quota system applicants. Quota system applicants were then ranked to fill the quota vacancies and the remaining quota applicants were transferred to the universal system where they competed with the universal system applicants. Finally, the universal system vacancies were filled with universal and quota applicants, jointly ranked by final score. In this way, quota applicants had two chances for admission, and the 20% quota became a minimum rather than a maximum participation for black students in the admission process. Quota applicants filled 378 of the 392 quota vacancies. . . . In six of the 61 courses, quota students had the highest scores. In another six, the quota students' final scores would have passed them without the quota system. In fifteen courses, no quota students would have been approved without the quota system. In the rest of the courses, quota and non-quota applicants had overlapping scores. Overall [in the second semester of 2004], 60% of the quota applicants benefited from the quota system. Forty percent would have been approved without it. There were relevant social differences between the quota and universal system students approved though the admission process. The modal family month income of the universal system students was R$ 5,000.00 or over (24% of cases). For the quota students, the modal income was in the R$ 750.00 to R$ 1,500.00 bracket (21% of cases), considerably lower. Whereas 33% of the universal system students were from public schools, this was the case for 56% of the quota students."

Chapter 9

1. The expansion of the Japanese higher education system in the 1960s was based on unregulated growth of private institutions and increased differentiation between these private institutions and the elite public universities. In response to declining quality in the private sector and violent student political demonstrations in the late 1960s and early 1970s (fueled by dissatisfaction with overcrowding and high tuition in the private universities and the anti–Vietnam War movement), the state reformed the higher education system and began financial support and regulation of private universities. It also halted all expansion of private universities for five years (1975–1980). Today, about 60 percent of students attend private institutions, most heavily subsidized by the state. As in Brazil, there is a distinct differentiation between prestigious public plus a few elite private universities and the mass private universities.

2. At the same time, Chinese policy makers have paid more attention to alleviating inequality in other ways. One example is by greatly extending social security coverage and benefits, especially in rural areas, over the last decade (Loyalka, Liu, et al., 2012). Also, because China now faces a shortage of labor from rural areas, the wages of low and unskilled labor have risen greatly in the last several years, probably helping to reduce income inequality.

3. See www.insead.edu/media_relations/press_release/2011_global_innovation_index.cfm; http://en.wikipedia.org/wiki/Global_Innovation_Index_(INSEAD). Accessed July 31, 2012.

4. See http://en.wikipedia.org/wiki/Global_Innovation_Index_(Boston_Consulting_Group). Accessed July 31, 2012.

References

Adamson, Frank. 2010. How Does Context Matter: Comparing Achievement Scores, Opportunities to Learn, and Teacher Preparation Across Socio-Economic Quintiles in TIMSS and PISA. Unpublished Ph.D. dissertation, Stanford University School of Education.

Adelman, Irma, and Cynthia Morris. 1973. *Economic Growth and Social Equity in Developing Countries.* Stanford: Stanford University Press.

Agarwal, Pawan. 2006. "Higher Education in India: The Need for Change." Indian Council for Research on International Economic Relations (ICRIER), Working Paper No. 180.

All India Engineering Entrance Examination (AIEEE). 2012. *Welcome 2012.* http://aieee.nic.in/aieee2012/aieee/welcome.html. Accessed Aug. 10, 2012.

Altbach, Philip. 1998. *Comparative Higher Education.* Westport, CT: Ablex.

Altbach, Philip, Liz Reisberg, and Laura Rumbley. 2009. *Trends in Global Higher Education: Tracking an Academic Revolution.* Chestnut Hill, MA: Boston College Center for International Higher Education.

Ananad, Geeta. 2011. "India Graduates Millions, but Too Few Are Fit to Hire." *Wall Street Journal*, Apr. 8. www.prlog.org/10695114-educated-unemployment-need-for-skill-based-education-system.html.

Angrist, Josh, and Alan Krueger. 2001. "Instrumental Variables and the Search for Identification: From Supply and Demand to Natural Experiments." *Journal of Economic Perspectives* 15: 69–85.

Ariga, Kenn, and Giorgi Brunello. 2007. "Does Secondary School Tracking Affect Performance? Evidence from IALS." Institute for the Study of Labor (IZA), Discussion Paper No. 2643.

Ashenfelter, Orley, and Alan Krueger. 1994. "Estimates of the Economic Return to Schooling from a New Sample of Twins." *American Economic Review* 84: 1157–1174.

Ashenfelter, Orley, and Cecilia Rouse. 1998. "Income, Schooling, and Ability: Evidence from a New Sample of Identical Twins." *Quarterly Journal of Economics* 113: 253–284.

Assessment Survey Evaluation Research (ASER). 2012. *Annual Status of Education Report (Rural) 2011*. New Delhi: Pratham. http://images2.asercentre.org/aserreports/ASER_2011/north_east_report_final_for_mail.pdf. Accessed Aug. 10, 2012.

Ayalon, Hanna, and Yossi Shavit. 2004. "Educational Reforms and Inequalities in Israel." *Sociology of Education* 77(2): 103–120.

Azam, Mehtabul. 2010. "India's Increasing Skill Premium: Role of Demand and Supply." *B. E. Journal of Economic Analysis & Policy* 10(94). www.bepress.com/bejeap/vol10/iss1/art94.

Baer, Werner, and Antonio Fialho Galvão Jr. 2005. "Tax Burden, Government Expenditures, and Income Distribution in Brazil." Champagne-Urbana: University of Illinois. www.business.uiuc.edu/Working_Papers/papers/05-0129.pdf.

Bagde, S., Dennis Epple, and Raj Reddy. 2010. "The Effects of Affirmative Action on College Admission and Academic Achievement in India." Carnegie Mellon University.

Bagla, Pallava. 2011. "Faculties Wither as Higher Education System Rapidly Expands." *Science Magazine*, Apr. 29: 524.

Bain, Olga. 2001. "The Costs of Higher Education to Students and Parents in Russia: Tuition Policy Issues." *Peabody Journal of Education* 76(3–4): 57–80.

Balbachevsky, Elizabeth, and Simon Schwartzman. 2011. "Brazil: Diverse Experiences in Institutional Governance in the Public and Private Sectors." In W. Locke et al. (eds.), *Changing Governance and Management in Higher Education*, Vol. 2, Part I. Dordrecht, NL: Springer, 35–56.

Banerjee, Rangan, and Vinayak Muley, 2007. *Engineering Education in India*. Mumbai: Energy Systems Engineering.

Barbaro, Salvatore. 2004. "Tax Distortion, Countervailing Subsidies and Income Redistribution." Department of Economics, University of Goettingen, Working Paper No. 121.

Bastid, Marianne. 1984. "Educational Policies in the 1980s and Economic Development." *China Quarterly* 98: 189–219.

Becker, Gary. 1964. *Human Capital*. Chicago: University of Chicago Press.

Bertrand, Marianne, Rema Hanna, and Sendhil Mullainathan. 2010. "Affirmative Action in Education: Evidence from Engineering College Admissions in India." *Journal of Public Economics* 94(1–2): 16–29.

Beteille, Tara. 2008. "India's Higher Educational Expansion in the Global Knowledge Economy." Stanford University School of Education (mimeo).

Bhushan, S., S. P. Malhotra, and S. Gopalakrishnan. 2009. *Facing Global and Local Challenges, Country Report: India*. New Delhi: National University of Educational Planning and Administration.

Bishop, John. 1997. "The Effect of National Standards and Curriculum-Based Exams on Achievement." *American Economic Review* 87(2): 260–264.

Biswas, Gautum, K .L. Chopra, C. S. Jha, and D. V. Singh. 2010. *Profile of Engineering Education in India: Status, Concerns and Recommendations*. New Delhi: Narosa.

Blaug, Mark, Richard Layard, and Maureen Woodhall. 1969. *The Causes of Graduate Unemployment in India*. London: Allen Lane.

Blom, Andres, and Hiroshi Saeki. 2011. "Employability and Skill Set of Newly Graduated Engineers in India." World Bank Policy Research, Working Paper No. 5640.

Bloom, David, and J. Sevilla. 2004. "Should There Be a General Subsidy for Higher Education in Developing Countries." *Journal of Higher Education in Africa* 2(1): 137–150.

Boarini, Romina, and Hubert Strauss. 2010. "What Is the Private Return to Tertiary Education." *OECD Journal of Economic Studies* 4(1): 1–25.

Bondarenko, N., M. Krasilnikova, and K. Kharlamov. 2005. "Demand for Labour Force—View of Employers." *Monitor Economics of Education* 1. Moscow: State Research University Higher School of Economics.

Bound, John, and Sarah Turner. 2010. "Coming to America: Where Do International Doctorate Students Study and How Do US Universities Respond?" In Charles Clotfelter (ed.), *American Universities in a Global Market*. Chicago: University of Chicago Press.

Bourguignon, F., F. Ferreira, and N. Lustig (eds.). 2004. *The Microeconomics of Income Distribution Dynamics in East Asia and Latin America*. Washington, D.C.: The World Bank and Oxford University Press.

Bowen, William, and Derek Bok. 1998. *The Shape of the River*. Princeton: Princeton University Press.

Brainerd, Elizabeth. 1998. "Winners and Losers in Russia's Transition." *American Economic Review* 88: 1094–1116.

Bydanova, Lisa. 2008. "Graduate Employability in a Transitional Economy." International Labour Process Conference, Mar. 18–20, 2008.

Cai, Fang, Albert Park, and Yaohui Zhao. 2008. "The Chinese Labor Market in the Reform Era." In Loren Brandt and Thomas G. Rawski (eds.), *China's Economic Transition: Origins, Mechanisms, and Consequences*. Cambridge: Cambridge University Press.

Canning, M. 2004. *The Modernization of Education in Russia: World Bank Report*. Moscow: World Bank Russia Office, 51.

Cantwell, Brendan, and Alma Maldonado-Maldonado. 2009. "Four Stories: Confronting Contemporary Ideas About Globalisation and Internationalisation in Higher Education." *Globalisation, Societies, and Education* 7(3): 289–306.

Card, David. 2000. "Estimating the Returns to Schooling: Progress on Some Persistent Economic Problems." Cambridge, MA: National Bureau of Economic Research, Working Paper 7769.

Carnoy, Martin. 1972. "The Political Economy of Education." In Thomas LaBelle (ed.), *Education and Development in Latin America and the Caribbean*. Los Angeles: UCLA Latin American Center.

———. 1974. *Education as Cultural Imperialism*. New York: David MacKay.

———. 1984. *The State and Political Theory*. Princeton: Princeton University Press.

———. 1993. *Universities, Economic Development, and Innovation Systems*. Washington, D.C.: World Bank.

———. 1994. *Faded Dreams: The Politics of Race in America*. Cambridge: Cambridge University Press.

———. 1995. "Rates of Return to Education." In Martin Carnoy (ed.), *The International Encyclopedia of Economics of Education*. Oxford, UK: Pergamon.

———. 1998. "The Globalization of Innovation, Nationalist Competition, and Internationalization of Scientific Training." *Competition and Change* 3: 237–262.

———. 2000. *Sustaining the New Economy*. Cambridge, MA: Harvard University Press.

———. 2005. "ICT in Education: Possibilities and Challenges." Stanford University (mimeo).

———. 2011. "As Higher Education Expands, Is It Contributing to Greater Inequality?" *National Institute Economic Review* 215: R34–R47.

Carnoy, Martin, and Rafael Carrasco. 2012. "Achievement Gains in Brazilian Universities: The Case of Engineering and Computer Science Programs." Stanford University School of Education (mimeo).

Carnoy, Martin, and Rafiq Dossani. 2012. "The Changing Governance of Higher Education in India." *Journal of Higher Education* (forthcoming).

Carnoy, Martin, and Susanna Loeb. 2002. "Does External Accountability Affect Student Outcomes: A Cross State Analysis." *Educational Evaluation and Policy Analysis* 24(4): 305–331.

Carnoy, Martin, and Joel Samoff. 1989. *Education and Social Transition in the Third World*. Princeton: Princeton University Press.

Carnoy, Martin, et al. 2009. *Do Countries Paying Teachers Higher Relative Salaries Have Higher Student Mathematics Achievement?* Amsterdam and East Lansing, MI: TEDS-M, International Education Association (IEA).

Castells, Manuel. 1991. "The University System: Engine of Development in the New World Economy." World Bank, PHREE.

———. 1997. *The Power of Identity*. Volume 2 of *The Information Age: Economy, Society, and Culture*. London: Blackwell.

Cataldi, Emily Forrest, Mansour Fahimi, Ellen M. Bradburn, and Linda Zimbler. 2005. "2004 National Study of Postsecondary Faculty (NSOPF:04): Report on Faculty and Instructional Staff in Fall 2003." U.S. Department of Education. Institute of Educational Sciences. NCES 2005-172.

Cha, Jian Zhong. 2009. "Status of Engineering, Science and Technology Education in China: The Need and Demand Among Young Students." UNESCO Project Report. Paris: UNESCO.

Chang, Parris H. 1974. "The Cultural Revolution and Chinese Higher Education: Change and Controversy." *Journal of General Education* 16(3): 187–194.

Chen, Guifu, and Shigeyuki Hamori. 2009. "Economic Returns to Schooling in Urban China: OLS and the Instrumental Variables Approach." *China Economic Review* 20: 143–152.

Chotikapanich, D., D. S. P. Rao, W. E. Griffiths, and V. Valencia. 2007. "Global Inequality: Recent Evidence and Trends." United Nations University, World Institute for Economic Development Research, Research Paper No.2007/01.

Chotikapanich, D., D. S. P. Rao, and K. K. Tang. 2006. "Estimating Income Inequality in China Using Grouped Data and the Generalized Beta Distribution." United

Nations University, World Institute for Economic Development Research, Research Paper No. 2006/134.

Clark, Burton. 1983. *The Higher Education System; Academic Organization in Cross-National Perspective.* Berkeley: University of California Press.

———. 1998. "The Entrepreneurial University: Demand and Response." *Tertiary Education and Management* 4(1): 5–16.

Clotfelter, Charles, ed. 2010. *American Universities in a Global Market.* Chicago: University of Chicago Press.

Dale, Stacy B., and Alan Krueger. 2002. "Estimating the Payoff of Attending a More Selective College: An Application of Selection on Observables and Unobservables." *Quarterly Journal of Economics* 107: 1491–1527.

Dasgupta, A. K., and Jandhyala B. G. Tilak. 1983. "Distribution of Education Among Income Groups: An Empirical Analysis." *Economic and Political Weekly* 18(33): 1442–1447.

de Brauw, Alan, and Scott Rozelle. 2006. "Reconciling the Returns to Education in Off-Farm Wage Employment in Rural China." Stanford University (mimeo).

De Gregorio, J., and J.-W. Lee. 1999. "Education and Income Distribution: New Evidence from Cross-Country Data." Centro de Economía Aplicada, Departamento de Ingeniería Industrial, Facultad de Ciencias Físicas y Matemáticas, Universidad de Chile, Serie Economia No. 55.

de Holanda Barbosa Filho, F., and S. Pessôa. 2008. "Retorno da Educação no Brasil." *Pesquisa e Planejamento Econômico* 38: 97–126.

Deininger, Klaus, and Lyn Squire. 1996. "A New Data Set Measuring Income Inequality." *World Bank Economic Review* 10: 565–591.

de Moura Castro, Claudio. 2011. "How Well Do Brazilian Universities Respond to the Needs of Society?" First Lemann Dialogue, Columbia University, Nov. 17–18 (mimeo).

Denisova I., and M. Kartseva. 2005. "Advantages of Education in Engineering: Estimates of Returns to Educational Epecialization in Russia." Moscow: National Research University Higher School of Economics, Working Paper WP3/2005/02.

DiNardo, John, Nicole Fortin, and Thomas Lemieux. 1996. "Labor Market Institutions and the Distribution of Wages, 1973–1982: A Semiparametric Approach." *Econometrica* 64(5): 1001–1044.

Dossani, Rafiq. 2012. "A Decade After Y2K: Has Indian IT Emerged?" In Dan Breznitz and John Zysman, (eds.), *Re-examining the Service Revolution.* New Haven: Yale University Press.

Dos Santos, Renato Emerson. 2005. "Política de cotas raciais nas universidades brasileiras—o caso da UERJ." Trabalho apresentado na 1.a Conferencia Internacional da Rede de Estudos de Acão Afirmativa Rio de Janeiro, 3 a 7 de janeiro de 2005, Universidade Candido Mendes.

Douglass, John. 2000. *The California Idea and American Higher Education: 1850 to the 1960 Master Plan.* Stanford: Stanford University Press.

Downie, Andrew. 2010. "Brazilian Universities Find Challenges in Internationalization." *Chronicle of Higher Education.* http://chronicle.com/article/Brazilian-Universities-Find/124312. Accessed Aug. 14, 2012.

Downie, Andrew, and Marion Lloyd. 2010. "At Brazil's Universities, Affirmative Action Faces Crucial Tests." *Chronicle of Higher Education.* http://chronicle.com/article/At-Brazils-Universities/123720/http://chronicle.com/article/At-Brazils-Universities/123720. Accessed Aug. 14, 2012.

Duraisamy, P. 2002. "Changes in Returns to Education in India, 1983–94, by Gender, Age-Cohort and Location." *Economics of Education Review* 21: 609–622.

Durham, Eunice. 2005. "Educacão Superior, Pública, y Privada." In C. Brock and S. Schwartzman (eds.), *Os Desafios da Educacão no Brasil.* Rio de Janeiro: Editora Nova Fronteira.

Dutta, Puja V. 2006. "Returns to Education: New Evidence for India, 1983–1999." *Education Economics* 54: 431–451.

Eckert Baeta Neves, Clarissa. 2009. "Using Social Inclusion Policies to Enhance Access and Equity in Brazil's Higher Education." In Jane Knight (ed.), *Financing Access and Equity in Higher Education.* Rotterdam: Sense, volume 17, 169–188.

Esquivel, Gerardo. 2008. "The Dynamics of Income Inequality in Mexico Since NAFTA." Background paper prepared for the project "Markets, the State and the Dynamics of Inequality: How to Advance Inclusive Growth." United Nations Development Program.

Fan, Elliot, Xin Meng, Zhichao Wei, and Guochang Zhao. 2010. "Rates of Return to University Education: The Regression Discontinuity Design." Institute for the Study of Labor (IZA), Discussion Paper No. 4749.

Fan, Xibo. 2005. "Measuring Education Inequality: Gini Coefficient of Educational Attainment." Background paper for UNESCO, *Human Development Report 2005: Reshaping International Co-Operation: Aid, Trade And Security in an Unequal World.* Paris: UNESCO.

Farber, Henry S., and Bruce Western. 2002. "Ronald Reagan and the Politics of Declining Union Organization." *British Journal of International Relations* 40(3): 385–401.

Farrell, Diana, and Andrew Grant. 2005. "Addressing China's Looming Talent Shortage." New York: McKinsey Global Institute.

Farrell, Diana, Roshni Jain, and Bruno Pietracci. 2007. "Assessing Brazil's Offshoring Prospects." *McKinsey Quarterly* (special edition).

Federal Service for Government Statistics. 2011. *Russian Statistical Yearbook.* www.gks.ru/bgd/regl/b11_13/IssWWW.exe/Stg/d2/07-56.htm. Accessed Aug. 3, 2012.

Fermin, Bruno, and Juliano Assunção. 2005. "Affirmative Action in University Admissions and High School Students' Proficiency." Working paper, Department of Economics of PUC-Rio.

Fleisher, Belton, and Jian Chen. 1997. "The Coast-Noncoast Income Gap, Productivity, and Regional Economic Policy in China." *Journal of Comparative Economics* 25: 220–236.

Fleisher, Belton, Keyong Dong, and Yunhua Liu. 1996. "Education, Enterprise Organization, and Productivity in the Chinese Paper Industry." *Economic Development and Cultural Change* 44: 571–587.

Fleisher, Belton, Klara Sabirianova, and Xiaojun Wang. 2005. "Returns to Skills and the Speed of Reforms: Evidence from Central and Eastern Europe, China, and Russia." *Journal of Comparative Economics* 33(2): 352–370.

Fleisher, Belton, and Xiaojun Wang. 2005. "Returns to Schooling in China Under Planning and Reform." *Journal of Comparative Economics* 33(2): 265–277.

Forbes, Naushad. 2011. "India's Higher Education Opportunity." Stanford University: Stanford Center for International Development, Working Paper No. 438.

Francis, Andrew M., and Maria Tannuri-Pianto. 2010a. "Racial Wage Inequality in Brazil: Preliminary Evidence on Quotas in University Admissions." Working paper, Department of Economics, Emory University.

———. 2010b. "The Redistributive Efficacy of Affirmative Action: Exploring the Role of Race and Socioeconomic Status in College Admissions." Working paper, Department of Economics, Emory University.

———. 2010c. "Using Brazil's Racial Continuum to Examine the Short-Term Effects of Affirmative Action in Higher Education." Working paper, Department of Economics, Emory University.

Freeman, Richard B. (ed.). 1994. *Working Under Different Rules*. New York: Russell Sage.

Freeman, Richard B. 2010. "What Does Global Expansion of Higher Education Mean for the United States?" In Charles Clotfelter (ed.), *American Universities in a Global Market*. National Bureau of Economic Research Conference Report. Chicago: University of Chicago Press.

Fuchs, Thomas, and Ludger Woessmann. 2007. "What Accounts for Differences in Student Performance? A Re-examination Using PISA Data." *Empirical Economics* 32(2–3): 433–464.

Gereffi, Gary, Vivek Wadhwa, Ben Rissing, and Ryan Ong. 2008. "Getting the Numbers Right: International Engineering Education in the United States, China, and India." *Journal of Engineering Education* 97(1): 13–25.

Gimpelson, Vladimir, and Rotislav Kapelushnikov (eds.). 2011. *The Russian Worker: Education, Occupation, Qualifications*. Moscow: National Research University Higher School of Economics.

Gorodnichenko, Y., and K. S. Peter. 2004. "Returns to Schooling in Russia and Ukraine: A Semiparametiric Approach of Cross-Country Comparative Analysis." University of Bonn, Institute for the Study of Labor (IZA), Discussion Paper No. 1325.

Gramsci, Antonio. 1971. *Selections from Prison Notebooks*. New York: International.

Griffin, Peter, and Alejandra Cox Edwards. 1993. "Rates of Return to Education in Brazil: Do Labor Market Conditions Matter?" *Economics of Education Review* 12: 245–255.

Gupta, Vijay. 2000. "Joint Entrance Examination: A Critique." *Infocell* 3(4). www.iitk.ac.in/infocell/Archive/dirjuly3/cover_story.html. Accessed Apr. 24, 2011.

Hannum, Emily, and Claudia Buchmann. 2003. *The Consequences of Global Educational Expansion*. Cambridge, MA: American Academy of Arts and Sciences.

Hansen, H. Lee, and Burton Weisbrod. 1969. "The Distribution of Costs and Direct Benefits of Public Higher Education: The Case of California." *Journal of Human Resources* 4(3): 176–191.

Hanushek, Erik, and Ludger Woessmann. 2006. "Does Education Track Affect Performance and Inequality? Differences in Differences Evidence Across Countries." *Economic Journal* 116(510): C63–C76.

Heckman, James. 2005. "China's Investment in Human Capital." *China Economic Review* 16(1): 50–70.

Heckman, James, and Xuesong Li. 2004. "Selection Bias, Comparative Advantage, and Heterogeneous Returns to Education: Evidence from China in 2000." *Pacific Economic Review* 9: 155–171.

Heckman, James, Lance Lochner, and Petra Todd. 2006. "Earnings Functions, Rates of Return and Treatment Effects: The Mincer Equation and Beyond." *Handbook of the Economics of Education*, Vol. 1. London: Elsevier, 307–458.

Hoper Educacional. 2009. "Análise Setorial do Ensino Superior Privado do Brasil." São Paulo.

Institute of Educational Sciences (IES), United States Department of Education. 2009. *Evaluation of Evidence-Based Practices in Online Learning: A Meta-Analysis and Review of Online Learning Studies.* Prepared for the US DOE by SRI International. Washington, D.C.: IES.

Institute of Educational Sciences, National Center for Educational Statistics (NCES). 2011. *Results of the 2009 NAEP High School Transcript Study. The Nation's Report Card.* Washington, D.C.: U.S. Department of Education, National Center for Educational Statistics, Institute of Educational Sciences. (NCES 2011-462).

Instituto Nacional de Estudos e Pesquisas Educacionais (INEP). 2009. *Resumo Tecnico, Censo de Educação Superior 2008.* Brasilia: INEP.

Instituto Nacional de Estudos e Pesquisas Educacionais Anísio Teixeira (INEP). 2005, 2006, 2007. *Relatórios Síntese ENADE 2005, 2006, 2007.* http://portal.inep.gov.br/web/guest/relatorio-sintese-2005, accessed Aug. 10, 2012; http://portal.inep.gov.br/web/guest/relatorio-sintese-2006, accessed Aug. 10, 2012; http://portal.inep.gov.br/web/guest/relatorio-sintese-2007, accessed Aug. 10, 2012.

———. 2005a. *Resultados ENADE 2005.* http://portal.inep.gov.br/planilhas-enade. Accessed Aug. 10, 2012.

Instituto Nacional de Estudos e Pesquisas Educacionais Anísio Teixeira (INEP), Diretoria de Estatísticas e Avaliação da Educação Superior. 1999, 2000, 2003, 2005, 2007, 2008, 2010, and 2011. *Sinopse Estadistico da Educacão Superior.* Brasilia: INEP.

James, Estelle. 1993. "Why Do Different Countries Choose a Different Public-Private Mix of Educational Services?" *Journal of Human Resources* 28(3): 571–592.

Johnson, Emily N., and Gregory C. Chow. 1997. "Rates of Return to Schooling in China." *Pacific Economic Review* 2: 101–113.

Johnstone, D. Bruce. 2003. "Cost Sharing in Higher Education: Tuition, Financial Assistance, and Accessibility in a Comparative Perspective." *Czech Sociological Review* 39(3): 351–374.

Kahhat, Jaime. 2008. "Markets and the Dynamics of Inequality: Theoretical Perspectives." Background paper prepared for the project "Markets, the State and the Dynamics of Inequality: How to Advance Inclusive Growth." United Nations Development Program.

Kanikov, F., and O. Trunkina. 2004. "Orientation of High School Students Towards Education in Engineering." *SocIs* 11: 111–115.

Kapur, Devesh. 2010. "Indian Higher Education." In Charles Clotfelter (ed.), *American Universities in a Global Market*. Chicago: University of Chicago Press.

Katz, Lawrence. 1999. "Technological Change, Computerization, and the Wage Structure." Harvard University and National Bureau of Economic Research.

King, Christopher. 2008a. "India's New Millennium in Science." Sept./Oct. Thomson Reuters, National Science Indicators. http://sciencewatch.com/ana/fea/08sepoctFea.

———. 2008b. "With Output and Impact Rising, China's Science Surge Rolls On." July/Aug. Thomson Reuters, National Science Indicators. http://sciencewatch.com/ana/fea/08julaugFea.

———. 2009. "Brazilian Science on the Rise." July/Aug. Thomson Reuters, National Science Indicators. http://sciencewatch.com/ana/fea/09julaugFea.

Kingdon, Geeta Gandhi. 2007. "The Progress of School Education in India." *Oxford Review of Economic Policy* 23(2): 168–195.

Kirp, David. 2003. *Shakespeare, Einstein, and the Bottom Line: The Marketing of Higher Education*. Cambridge, MA: Harvard University Press.

Klein, Ruben. 2011. "Uma re-análise dos resultados do PISA: problemas de comparabilidade." *Ensaio: avaliação da politica pública de Eduç@o* 19(73). http://dx.doi.org/10.1590/S0104-40362011000500002. Accessed June 15, 2012.

Klintsov, Vitaly, Irene Shvakman, and Yermolai Solzhenitsyn. 2009. "How Russia Could Be More Productive." *McKinsey Quarterly*, Sept. 2009. www.mckinseyquarterly.com/Europe/How_Russia_could_be_more_productive_2435.

Knight, John, and Lina Song. 2003. "Increasing Wage Inequality in China: Extent, Elements and Evaluation." *Economics of Transition* 4: 597–620.

Kochar, Anjini. 2010. "Affirmative Action Through Quotas. The Effect on Learning in India." Stanford Center for International Development, Working Paper No. 43.

Kong, Hanbing, and Yangqiong Qiu. 2007. "Rethinking of Engineering Education in China." In *Meeting the Growing Demand for Engineers and Their Educators 2010–2020 International Summit, 2007 IEEE*, Nov. 9–11, 1–7.

Kremer, Michael, Nazmul Chaudhury, F. Halsey Rogers, Karthik Muralidharan, and Jeffrey Hammer. 2005. "Teacher Absence in India: A Snapshot." *Journal of the European Economic Association* 3(2–3): 658–667.

Krueger, Alan, and Mikael Lindahl. 2001. "Education for Growth: Why and for Whom?" *Journal of Economic Literature* 39(4): 1101–1136.

Kuhns, Katherine. 2011. Globalization of Knowledge and Its Impact on Higher Education Reform in Transitioning States: The Case of Russia. Unpublished Ph.D. dissertation, Stanford University School of Education.

Kuznets, Simon. 1955. "Economic Growth and Income Inequality." *American Economic Review* 45(1): 1–28.

LaFraniere, S. 2009. "China's College Entry Test Is an Obsession." *New York Times*, June 12. www.nytimes.com/2009/06/13/world/asia/13exam.html. Retrieved Aug. 2, 2012.

Lemann, Nicholas. 1999. *The Big Test: The Secret History of the American Meritocracy.* New York: Farrar.

Levin, Henry M., D. W. Jeong, and D. Ou. 2006. "What Is a World Class University." Teachers College Columbia (mimeo).

Levin, Henry M., and Zeyu Y. Xu. 2005. "Issues in the Expansion of Higher Education in the People's Republic of China." *China Review* 5(1): 33–59.

Levin Institute. 2010. "The Evolving Global Talent Pool: Lessons from the BRIC Countries." *Report by the Levin Institute,* State University of New York.

Levy, Daniel. 1980. *University and Government in Mexico: Autonomy in an Authoritarian System.* New York: Praeger.

———. 1986. *Higher Education and the State in Latin America.* Chicago: University of Chicago Press.

Li, H. 2003. "Economic Transition and Returns to Education in China." *Economics of Education Review* 22: 317–328.

Li, Haizheng Z. 2010. "Higher Education in China—Complement or Competition to US Universities?" In Charles Clotfelter (ed.), *American Universities in the Global Marketplace.* National Bureau of Economic Research Report. Chicago: University of Chicago Press.

Li, Wang. 2010. "Higher Education Governance and University Autonomy in China." *Globalisation, Societies and Education* 8(4): 477–495.

Liu, E. 2008. Essays on Development Economics in China. Ph.D. diss., Princeton University.

Liu, Z. 1998. "Earnings, Education, and Economic Reform in China." *Economic Development and Cultural Change* 46: 697–726.

Lopez-Calva, L., and N. Lustig. 2009. "The Recent Decline of Inequality in Latin America: Argentina, Brazil, Mexico, and Peru." ECLINE, Working Paper Series, WP 2009-140.

Lopez-Calva, L., and N. Lustig (eds.). 2010. *Declining Inequality in Latin America.* Washington, D.C.: The Brookings Institution.

Lowell, Lindsay B., and Harold Salzman. 2007. "Into the Eye of the Storm: Assessing the Evidence on Science and Engineering Education, Quality, and Workforce Demand." Washington, D.C.: Urban Institute.

Loyalka, Prashant. 2009. Three Essays on Chinese Higher Education After Expansion and Reform: Sorting, Financial Aid, and College Selectivity. Unpublished Ph.D. dissertation, Stanford University School of Education.

———. 2012. "The Benefits and Costs of Retaking Competitive Entrance Exams: Evidence from China." CIEFR working paper.

Loyalka, Prashant, Chengfang Liu, Yingquan Song, Hongmei Yi, Jianguo Wei, Xiaoting Huang, Linxiu Zhang, Yaojiang Shi, James Chu, and Scott Rozelle. 2012. "Can Information and Counseling Help Poor, Rural Students Go to High School? Evidence from China." Stanford University, unpublished paper.

Loyalka, Prashant, Yingquan Song, and Jianguo Wei. 2012. "The Effects of Attending Selective College Tiers in China." *Social Science Research* 41: 287–305.

Loyalka, Prashant, Jianguo Wei, and Weiping Zhong. 2011. "Mapping Educational Inequality from the End of Junior High School Through College in China." CIEFR working paper.

Loyalka, Prashant, Weiping Zhong, Juan Zhou, and Jianhong Bi. 2012. "The Impact of College Applications and Admissions Rules on Disadvantaged Students' Access to Four-Year Colleges." CIEFR working paper.

Loyalka, Prashant, and J. Zhou. 2011. "Resource Allocation Models in Chinese Universities." Peking University, CIEFR working paper.

Lucas, Samuel. 2001. "Effectively Maintained Inequality: Education, Transitions, Track Mobility and Social Background Effects." *American Journal of Sociology* 106(6): 1642–1690.

Mani, Sunil. 2010. "Are Innovations on The Rise in India Since the Onset of Reforms of 1991? Analysis of Its Evidence and Some Disquieting Features." *International Journal of Technology and Globalization* 5(2): 5–42.

Marginson, Simon, and Imanol Ordorika. 2008. *Global Hegemony in Higher Education and Research*. New York: Social Science Research Council.

Maurer-Fazio, Margaret. 1999. "Earning and Education in China's Transition to a Market Economy—Survey Evidence from 1989 and 1992." *China Economic Review* 10: 17–40.

Menezes Filho, N. 2009. "Employment and Inequality Outcomes in Brazil." Paper presented for the OECD Seminar on Employment and Inequality Outcomes: New Evidence, Links and Policy Responses in Brazil, China and India. Paris: OECD.

Meng, Xin, and Michael Kidd. 1997. "Labor Market Reform and the Changing Structure of Wage Determination in China's State Sector During the 1980s." *Journal of Comparative Economics* 25: 403–421.

Meyer, John, Francisco Ramirez, David J. Frank, and Evan Shofer. 2005. "Higher Education as an Institution." Stanford University (mimeo).

Meyer, John, Francisco Ramirez, and Yasemin N. Soysal. 1992. "World Expansion of Mass Education, 1870–1980." *Sociology of Education* 65(2): 128–149.

Min, Weifang F. 2004. "Chinese Higher Education: The Legacy of the Past and the Context of the Future." Chapter 3 in Philip G. Altbach and T. Umakoshi (eds.), *Asian Universities: Historical Perspectives and Contemporary Changes*. Baltimore: John Hopkins University Press.

Mincer, Jacob. 1974. *Schooling, Experience and Earnings*. New York: Columbia University Press for National Bureau of Economic Research.

Ministerio de Ciencia e Tecnologia (MCT). 2012. *Indicadores*. Brasilia: MCT. www.mct.gov.br/index.php/content/view/7755.html. Accessed Aug. 14, 2012.

Ministry of Education and Science (MOES). 2009. *Education in Russia, 2008 Statistical Bulletin*. Moscow: MOES.

———. 2011. *Education in Figures (Russian), 2011*. Moscow: Federal Service for State Statistics.

Ministry of Human Resource Development (MHRD). Various years. *Analysis of Budget Expenditure on Education*. New Delhi: Bureau of Planning, Monitoring & Statistics.

———. 2010. *Statistics of Higher & Technical Education, 2008–09*. New Delhi: Bureau of Planning, Monitoring & Statistics.

———. 2011. *Statistics of Higher & Technical Education, 2009–10*. New Delhi: Bureau of Planning, Monitoring & Statistics.

Mitchell, B. R. 1978. *International Historical Statistics: Europe*. New York: Palgrave.

———. 2003a. *International Historical Statistics: Africa, Asia, and Oceania, 1750–2000*. New York: Palgrave, Table I2.

———. 2003b. *International Historical Statistics: The Americas, 1750–2000*. New York: Palgrave, Table I2.

Mohanan, K. P. 2010. "Entrance Examinations for Science and Technology." *Current Science* 99(10): 1321–1323.

Mohrman, Kathryn. 2008. "The Emerging Global Model with Chinese Characteristics." *Higher Education Policy* 21: 29–48.

Mooney, Paul, and Shailaja Neelakantan. 2006. "Foreign Academics Question the Quality of Their Countries' Engineering Programs." *Chronicle of Higher Education,* Sept. 8, 2006.

Mulholland, Timothy. 2005. "Quota System for Blacks at the University of Brasília." University of Brasilia, Jan. 4.

Murakami, Yuki, and Andreas Blom. 2008. "Accessibility and Affordability of Tertiary Education in Brazil, Colombia, Mexico, and Peru Within a Global Context." World Bank Latin America and Caribbean Region Human Development Sector, WPS4517.

Murphy, Kevin, and Finus Welch. 1989. "Wage Premiums for College Graduates: Recent Growth and Possible Explanations." *Educational Researcher* 18(4): 17–26.

Nam, Young-Sook. 1994. Women, Schooling, and the Labor Market: Changes in the Structure of Earnings Inequality by Gender in Korea, 1976–1991. Unpublished Ph.D. dissertation, Stanford University School of Education.

National Association of Software and Services Companies (NASSCOM). 2009. *Perspective 2020: Transform Business, Transform India*. New Delhi: NASSCOM.

National Bureau of Statistics (NBS) of China. Various years. *China Educational Finance Statistical Yearbook*. Beijing: China Statistics Press.

———. 2010. *2009 China Educational Finance Statistical Yearbook*. Beijing: China Statistics Press.

National Bureau of Statistics and Ministry of Science and Technology (NBS and MOST). Various years. *China Statistical Yearbook on Science and Technology*. Beijing: China Statistics Press.

National Science Board. 2010. *Science and Engineering Indicators 2010*. Arlington, VA: National Science Foundation (NSF). www.nsf.gov/statistics/seind10.

———. 2012. *Science and Engineering Indicators 2012*. Arlington, VA: National Science Foundation (NSF). www.nsf.gov/statistics/seind12.

Ngok, K. 2006. "Globalization and Higher Education Reform in China." In N. Sun-keung Pang (ed.), *Globalization: Educational Research, Change and Reform*. Hong Kong: Chinese University Press.

Nunes, Edson, Marcia de Carvalho, and Julia Vogel de Albrecht. 2009. "A Singularidade Brasileira: Ensino Superior Privado e Dilemas Estrategicas da Politica

Publica." Observatorio Politico, Universidade Candido Mendes, Rio de Janeiro, Brazil. Working Paper No. 87.

Offe, Claus. 1973. "The Capitalist State and the Problem of Policy Formation." In Leon Lindberg, Robert Afford, Colin Crouch, and Claus Offe (eds.), *Stress and Competition in Modern Capitalism*. Lexington, MA: Heath.

O'Neill, Jim. 2001. "Building Better Global Economic BRICs." New York: Goldman Sachs, Global Economics Paper No. 66.

Ordorika, Imanol. 1999. Power, Politics, and Change in Higher Education: The Case of the National Autonomous University of Mexico. Unpublished Ph.D. dissertation, School of Education, Stanford University.

Organization for Economic Cooperation and Development (OECD). Various years. *Main Science & Technology Indicators*. Paris: OECD. http://stats.oecd.org.

———. 2003. *Review of National Policies in Education: Chile*. Paris: OECD.

———. 2005. *Higher Education Finance and Quality. IV.18. Governance in China*. Paris: OECD.

———. 2007. *Latin American Economic Outlook 2008*. Paris: OECD.

———. 2008. *Higher Education to 2030*. Paris: OECD.

———. 2009. *Education at a Glance*. Paris: OECD.

———. 2010a. *Economic Surveys: China*. Volume 2010/6. Feb. Paris: OECD.

———. 2010b. *PISA 2009 Results: What Students Know and Can Do—Student Performance in Reading, Mathematics and Science* (Volume 1). Paris: OECD. http://dx.doi.org/10.1787/9789264091450-en.

———. 2011a. *Education at a Glance 2011: OECD Indicators*. Paris: OECD. http://dx.doi.org/10.1787/eag-2011-en.

———. 2011b. *Lessons from PISA for the United States, Strong Performers and Successful Reformers in Education*. Paris: OECD. http://dx.doi.org/10.1787/9789264096660.

———. 2012. *OECD Factbook 2011–2012: Economic, Environmental and Social Statistics*. Paris: OECD. http://dx.doi: 10.1787/factbook-2011-en.

Orr, Dominic, Michael Jaeger, and Astrid Schwarzenberger. 2007. "Performance Based Funding as an Instrument of Competition in German Higher Education." *Journal of Higher Education Policy and Management* 29(1): 3–23.

Park, Albert, Fang Cai, and Yang Du. 2010. "Can China Meet Her Employment Challenges?" In Jean Oi, Scott Rozelle, and Xuegang Zhou (eds.), *Growing Pains: Tensions and Opportunities in China's Transformation*. Stanford: Stanford Asia-Pacific Research Center.

Pechman, Joseph. 1970. "A Review of Hansen and Weisbrod's 'The Distribution of Costs and Direct Benefits of Public Higher Education in California.'" *Journal of Human Resources* 5(3): 361–370.

Piketty, Thomas, and Emmanuel Saez. 2003. "Income Inequality In The United States, 1913–1998." *Quarterly Journal of Economics* 118(1): 1–39.

Planning Commission. 2008. *Tenth Five Year Plan 2007–2012*. New Delhi: Government of India.

———. 2011. *India Human Development Report 2011*. Oxford: Oxford University Press.

———. 2012. *Approach to the Twelfth Five Year Plan 2012–2017*. New Delhi: Government of India.

Porter, Stephen R., Corey Rumann, and Jason Pontius. 2011. "The Validity of Student Engagement Survey Questions: Can We Accurately Measure Academic Challenge?" *New Directions for Institutional Research* 150: 87–98.

Poulantzas, Nicholas. 1980. *State, Power, Socialism*. New York: Verso.

Powell, J. L. 1984. "Least Absolute Deviations Estimation of the Censored Regression Model." *Journal of Econometrics* 25: 303–325.

Psacharopoulos, George. 1985. "Returns to Education: A Further International Update and Implications." *Journal of Human Resources* 20: 583–604.

———. 1994. "Investment in Education: A Global Update." *World Development* 22: 1325–1343.

Psacharopoulos, George, and Harry A. Patrinos. 2004. "Returns to Investment in Education: A Further Update." *Education Economics* 12(2): 111–132.

Raftery, Adrian, and Michael Hout. 1993. "Maximally Maintained Inequality: Expansion Reform, and Opportunity in Irish Education, 1921–75." *Sociology of Education* 66(1): 41–62.

Raleigh, D. J. (ed.). 2006. *Russia's Sputnik Generation: Soviet Baby Boomers Talk About Their Lives*. Bloomington: Indiana University Press.

Ram, Rati. 1989. "Economic Development and Income Inequality: An Overlooked Regression Constraint." Illinois State University (mimeo).

———. 1990. "Educational Expansion and Schooling Inequality: International Evidence and Some Implications." *Review of Economics and Statistics* 72(2): 266–274.

Rosen, Stanley. 1985. "Recentralization, Decentralization, and Rationalization: Deng Xiaoping's Bifurcated Educational Policy." *Modern China* 11: 301–346.

Royal Society. 2011. "Knowledge, Networks and Nations: Global Scientific Collaboration in the 21st Century." RS Policy document 03/11.

Ruch, Richard. 2001. *Higher Education, Inc.: The Rise of the For-Profit University*. Baltimore: Johns Hopkins Press.

Russian Independent Agency in Education Research (Reitor). 2005. "Which Universities Prepare the Best Graduates?" Presented at the annual meeting of the Association for Public Policy Analysis and Management, Washington, D.C. www.reitor.ru/ru/analitic/job/index.php?id19=106.

Salmi, Jamil. 2009. *The Challenges of Establishing World-Class Universities*. Washington, D.C.: World Bank.

Saxenian, Annalee. 1996. *Regional Advantage: Culture and Competition in Silicon Valley and Route 128*. Cambridge, MA: Harvard University Press.

Schwartzman, Simon. 2004. "Equity, Quality, and Relevance in Higher Education in Brazil." *Annals of the Brazilian Academy of Sciences* 76(1): 173–188.

Shaanxi Admissions Committee. 2007. *2006 Higher Education Institution Student Recruitment Plan*. Xi'an, China: Northwest University Press.

Shavit, Yossi, Richard Arum, Adam Gamoran, and G. Menahem (eds.). 2007. *Stratification in Higher Education: A Comparative Study*. Stanford: Stanford University Press.

Shi, Y. G., and R. Yi. 2010. "Editorial: China's Research Culture." *Science*, 3 Sept. 2010: 1128.

Sigman, Carole. 2008. "Higher Education in Russia: Potential and Challenges." Institut Français des Relations Internationales, Russie Nei Visions.

Simon, Denis Fred, and Cong Cao. 2008. "China's Emerging Science and Technology Talent Pool: A Quantitative and Qualitative Assessment." In H. S. Rowen, M. G. Hancock, and W. F. Miller (eds.), *Greater China's Quest for Innovation*. Stanford, CA: Walter H. Shorenstein Asia-Pacific Research Center.

Smith, Amy Erica. 2010. "Affirmative Action in Brazil." *Americas Quarterly*, 21 Oct. www.americasquarterly.org/node/1939.

Somers, Marie-Andrée, Patrick McEwan, and J. Douglas Willms. 2004. "How Effective Are Private Schools in Latin America?" *Comparative Education Review* 48(1): 48–69.

Srinivasaraju, Sugata. 2007. "Coaching Factories Are Dumbing Down the IITs." *Outlook India.com*, Apr. 27. http://outlookindia.com/fullprint.asp?choice=2&fodname=20070430&fname=IIT+(F)&sid=1. Accessed Aug. 10, 2012.

State Council of China. 2007. *Opinions on Establishing and Improving the Policies for Subsidizing Students in Universities of Regular Undergraduate Education, Postsecondary Vocational Schools and Secondary Vocational Schools from Families with Financial Difficulties* Beijing: State Council of China (in Chinese).

State Statistical Committee of Russia. 2010. *Finance of Russia, 2010*. Moscow. www.gks.ru/wps/wcm/connect/rosstat/rosstatsite/main/publishing/catalog/statistic Collections/doc_1138717651859. Accessed Aug. 4, 2012.

Stevens, Mitchell. 2007. *Creating a Class: College Admissions and the Education of Elites*. Cambridge, MA: Harvard University Press.

Thomas, V., Y. Wang, and X. Fan. 2003. "Measuring Education Inequality: Gini Coefficients of Education for 140 Countries (1960–2000)." *Journal of Educational Planning and Administration* (New Delhi) 17(1).

Thorat, S. 2006. "Higher Education in India." Mumbai: University of Mumbai, Nehru Memorial Lecture, Nov. 24.

Tilak, Jandhyala B. G. 1989. "Education and Its Relation to Economic Growth, Poverty and Income Distribution: Past Evidence and Further Analysis." Discussion Paper No. 46. Washington, D.C.: World Bank.

———. 1999. "Emerging Trends and Evolving Public Policies on Privatisation of Higher Education in India." In P. G. Altbach (ed.), *Private Prometheus: Private Higher Education and Development in the 21st Century*. Westport, CT: Greenwood, 113–135.

———. 2003. "Higher Education and Development." In J. P. Kleeves and Ryo Watanabe (eds.), *The Handbook on Educational Research in the Asia Pacific Region*. Dordrecht: Kluwer.

———. 2005. "Are We Marching Towards Laissez-faireism in Higher Education Development?" *Journal of International Cooperation in Education* 8(1): 153–165.

———. 2008. "Transition from Higher Education as a Public Good to Higher Education as a Private Good: The Saga of Indian Experience." *Journal of Asian Public Policy* 1(2): 220–234.

———. 2010. "Policy Crisis in Higher Education: Reform or Deform?" *Social Scientist* 38(9–12): 61–90.

———. 2011a. "Higher Education Policy in India in Transition." Presidential Address, Comparative Education Society of India, University of Hyderabad (16–18 Nov.).

———. 2011b. "Private Sector in Higher Education: A Few Stylized Facts." In K. N. Panikkar, Thomas Joseph, G. Geetha, and M. A. Lal (eds.), *Quality, Access and Social Justice in Higher Education*. New Delhi: Pearson/Longman, 11–33.

Tilak, Jandhyala B. G., and Geetha Rani. 2003. "Changing Pattern of University Finances in India." *Journal of Services Research* 2(2): 5–46.

Trow, Martin. 1973. *Problems in the Transition from Elite to Mass Higher Education.* Berkeley: Carnegie Commission on Higher Education.

Tsang, Mun, and Weifang Min. 1992. "Expansion, Efficiency, and Economies of Scale of Higher Education in China." *Higher Education Policy* 5(2): 61–66.

UNESCO. 2005. *Education for All Global Monitoring Report 2005: Education for All: The Quality Imperative.* Paris: UNESCO.

UNESCO Institute for Statistics. Various years. Available at www.uis.unesco.org. Accessed Aug. 12, 2012.

University Grants Commission (UGC). 2006. *Annual Report 2005–06.* New Delhi: UGC.

———. 2009. *Annual Report 2008–09.* New Delhi: UGC.

———. 2010a. *Annual Report 2009–10.* New Delhi: UGC.

———. 2010b. *Strategies and Schemes During Eleventh Plan Period (2007–2012) for Universities and Colleges.* New Delhi: UGC.

———. 2011. *Annual Report 2010–11.* New Delhi: UGC.

———. 2012. *Annual Report 2011–12.* New Delhi: UGC.

Veblen, Thorsten. 1918. *The Higher Learning in America: A Memorandum on the Conduct of Universities.* New York: Huebsch.

Wadhwa, Vivek, Gary Gereffi, Ben Rissing, and Ryan Ong. 2007. "Where the Engineers Are." *Issues in Science and Technology*, Spring: 73–84.

Walker, Maurice. 2011. *PISA 2009 Plus Results Performance of 15-Year-Olds in Reading, Mathematics and Science for 10 Additional Participants.* Australian Council of Educational Research (ACER) Report. Victoria: ACER Press.

Wang, Huiyao. 2011. "China's National Talent Plan: Key Measures and Objectives." http://ssrn.com/abstract=1828162 or doi:10.2139/ssrn.1828162.

Weiler, Hans N. 1983. "Legalization, Expertise, and Participation: Strategies for Compensatory Legitimation in Educational Policy." *Comparative Education Review* 27(2): 259–277.

Weisbord, Burton. 1962. "Education and Investment in Human Capital." *Journal of Political Economy* 70: 106–123.

Weisskopf, Thomas. 2004. *Affirmative Action in the United States and India: A Comparative Perspective.* New York: Routledge.

Winegarden, C. R. 1979. "Schooling and Income Distribution: Evidence from International Data." *Economica* 46: 83–87.

World Bank. 2000. *Higher Education in Developing Countries: Peril and Promise.* Published for the Task Force on Higher Education and Society. Washington, D.C.: World Bank.

———. 2004. *World Development Report. 2005: A Better Investment Climate for Everyone.* Washington, D.C.: World Bank.

———. 2006. *World Development Report 2006: Equity and Development.* Washington, D.C.: World Bank.

———. 2010. *Achieving World Class Education in Brazil: The Next Agenda.* Washington, D.C.: World Bank.

———. 2011. *World Development Indicators.* Washington, D.C.: World Bank.

———. 2012. *World Development Indicators.* Washington, D.C.: World Bank. http://databank.worldbank.org/ddp/home.do. Accessed Aug. 4, 2012.

Wu, Kinbing, Pete Goldschmidt, Christy Kim Boscardin, and Deepa Sankar. 2009. "International Benchmarking and Determinants of Mathematics Achievement in Two Indian States." *Education Economics* 17(3): 395–411.

Wu, X. G., and Z. N. Zhang. (2010). "Globalization, Changing Demographics, and Educational Challenges in East Asia." *Research in Sociology of Education* 17: 123–152.

Xie, Yu, and Kimberlee A. Shauman. 2003. *Women in Science: Career Processes and Outcomes.* Cambridge, MA: Harvard University Press.

Yang, Dennis T. 2005. "Determinants of Schooling Returns During Transition: Evidence from Chinese Cities." *Journal of Comparative Economics* 33: 244–264.

Zajda, Joseph, and Rea Zajda. 2007. "Policy Shifts in Higher Education in the Russian Federation." *European Education* 39(3): 16–38.

Zhang, J., Y. Zhao, A. Park, and X. Song. 2005. "Economic Returns to Schooling in Urban China, 1988 to 2001." *Journal of Comparative Economics* 33: 730–752.

About the Authors

Martin Carnoy is the Vida Jacks Professor of Education and Economics at Stanford University. He is former president of the Comparative and International Education Society and is a fellow of the National Academy of Education and of the International Academy of Education. He graduated from the California Institute of Technology with a degree in electrical engineering and from the University of Chicago with a Ph.D. in economics. He has been a research associate of the Brookings Institution, has been a visiting professor at a number of universities, and has served as a consultant to the OECD, World Bank, UNESCO, UNICEF, and other international agencies. Most recent among his more than thirty books on education and economic development are *Sustaining the New Economy: Work, Family and Community in the Information Age* (2000), *Cuba's Academic Advantage* (2007), *Vouchers and Public School Performance* (2007), and *The Low Achievement Trap: Comparing Schools in Botswana and South Africa* (2012).

Prashant Loyalka is a Center Research Fellow at the Freeman Spogli Institute for International Studies, Stanford University. He has also held appointments as a lead academic researcher at the Institute for Educational Studies, Moscow Higher School of Economics, and as an assistant professor at the China Institute for Educational Finance Research, Peking University. Loyalka is a specialist in the economics of education whose research focuses on policy and program evaluation in large transitioning countries. His recent work explores ways to improve the educational outcomes of disadvantaged populations, the quality and equity of access to upper secondary and higher education, and issues related to education and health. He was trained at Stanford, earning a Ph.D. in international comparative education in 2009; before that, he earned bachelor's and master's degrees in economics.

Maria Dobryakova is currently a research associate and the director for portals at the Center for Monitoring Quality Education at the Higher School of Economics, Moscow. In 2008, the Russian government awarded her a prize for her work in education research, which includes analyzing quality ratings for newly admitted groups of students into Russian institutions of higher education. Dobryakova received her candidate of science degree from the Institute of Sociology of the Russian Academy of Sciences. Her dissertation considered the local community as an object of sociological research on social stratification. She received her M.A. at the Moscow Higher School of Social and Economic Sciences in 2000 and her specialist degree from the Komi State Pedagogical Institute in 1997, focusing on philology and the teaching of foreign languages.

Rafiq Dossani is a senior economist at RAND Corporation. His research interests include higher education, South Asian security and regionalism, technology policy, and corporate governance. Until 2012, he was a senior research scholar at Stanford University's Shorenstein Asia-Pacific Research Center and director of the Stanford Center for South Asia. Dossani also worked for the Robert Fleming Investment Banking group, first as CEO of its India operations and later as head of its San Francisco operations. Additionally, he served as the chairman and CEO of a stockbrokerage firm on the OTCEI stock exchange in India, as the deputy editor of *Business India Weekly,* and as a professor of finance at Pennsylvania State University. He holds a B.A. in economics from St. Stephen's College, New Delhi, India; an MBA from the Indian Institute of Management, Calcutta, India; and a Ph.D. in finance from Northwestern University.

Isak Froumin is a mathematician and educator by training and the director of the Institute for Educational Studies at the National Research University Higher School of Economics in Moscow. He is also an advisor to the university's president on strategic planning and international cooperation. From 1999 to 2011, Professor Froumin was the leader of the World Bank education program in Russia. His World Bank experience extended to projects in Kazakhstan, Kyrgyzstan, Afghanistan, Nepal, Turkmenistan, and India. In 2011, he was named to cochair the Russian government's expert group on the "new school" for Russia's Strategy 2020. Most recently, he was made advisor to the minister of education on educational reform. Froumin is the author of numerous books and articles on educational theory and educational reform.

Katherine Kuhns received her M.A. from the Johns Hopkins School of Advanced International Studies and her Ph.D. in the International and Comparative Education Program at Stanford University's School of Education. Her dissertation, *Globalization of Knowledge and Its Impact on Higher Education Reform in Transitioning States: The Case of Russia,* focuses on current reform efforts of the higher education system in the Russian Federation. Prior to entering the Ph.D. program, Kuhns was a Fascell Fellow at the American Consulate General in St. Petersburg and director of the Freeman Spogli Institute for International Studies' Initiative on Distance Learning, which offered Stanford courses in international security to a network of Russian regional universities. She has more than fifteen years of experience in international program development and management, particularly in the former Soviet Union.

Jandhyala B. G. Tilak is a professor at the National University of Educational Planning and Administration, New Delhi, India. He obtained his Ph.D. in economics from the Delhi School of Economics and has taught at the University of Delhi, at the Indian Institute of Education, and as a visiting professor at the University of Virginia, Sri Sathya Sai Institute of Higher Learning, and Hiroshima University. He has also worked at the World Bank. Tilak is the recipient of the Swami Pranavananda Saraswati award of the University Grants Commission (India) for outstanding research in education and the Dr. Malcolm Adiseshiah Award for distinguished contributions to development studies. He has authored/edited more than 10 books and 250 research papers on the economics of education and on development studies. He is the editor of the *Journal of Educational Planning and Administration* and is on the editorial board of a number of academic journals.

Rong Wang has a B.S. and M.A. from Peking University and a Ph.D. in education from the University of California, Berkeley. She is currently director and professor of the China Institute for Educational Finance Research (CIEFR), Peking University, and is the founding executive chairwoman of the China National Research Association for Education Financing and a deputy chairwoman of the China National Research Association for the Economics of Education. She is also the youngest member of China's State Education Advisory Committee. Professor Wang is recognized as one of the most important scholars in the field of education finance in China for her role in designing the free rural compulsory education policy and several other important education finance policies since 1999. She is the author of numerous articles on the financing of education and educational reform.

Index

Italic page numbers indicate material in tables or figures.

Lightning Source UK Ltd.
Milton Keynes UK
UKHW011838290820
369023UK00004B/362